# CGI Programming with TCL

# CGI Programming with TCL

David Maggiano

## ADDISON–WESLEY

An imprint of Addison Wesley Longman, Inc.
Reading, Massachusetts • Harlow, England • Menlo Park, California
Berkeley, California • Don Mills, Ontario • Sydney • Bonn
Amsterdam • Tokyo • Mexico City

The publisher offers discounts on this book when ordered in quantity for special sales. For more information, please contact:

AWL Direct Sales
Addison Wesley Longman, Inc.
One Jacob Way
Reading, Massachusetts 01867
(781) 944-3700

Visit AW on the Web: www.awl.com/cseng/

*Library of Congress Cataloging-in-Publication Data*

Maggiano, David, 1956–
    CGI programming with Tcl / David Maggiano.
        p. cm.
    Includes bibliographical references and index.
    ISBN 0-201-60629-1
    1. Internet programming. 2. CGI (Computer network protocol) 3. Tcl (Computer programming language) I. Title.
    QA76.625 .M318 2000
    005.2´762—dc21                                             99–054109

ISBN 0-201-60629-1

Text printed on recycled paper

1 2 3 4 5 6 7 8 9 10—MA—0302010099

First printing, December 1999

# Contents

**Chapter 2**

## *The Common Gateway Interface  33*

**Chapter 3**

## *Getting Started  59*

**Chapter 7**      *Counting Your Hits    139*

**Chapter 8**      *Server Side Includes    151*

**Chapter 9**      *Image Maps    169*

**Chapter 13**    *Building Gateways to Your Data*   273

**Chapter 14**    *Expect in CGI Scripts*   307

## Appendix B    *Tcl Language Summary    405*

# *Preface*

## Why Learn CGI

In the fast-paced information age that we live in, it is almost a necessity to be well versed in the use of the World Wide Web. For many researchers, engineers, scientists, school teachers, and a host of other professionals it is a day-to-day part of our lives.

As companies embrace this technology, it is becoming more common for them to have one or more public Web sites on the Internet, as well as a host of internal Web sites that are available only to employees on a local intranet. Motorola, the company I work for, has many such public and private Web sites. Public Web sites portray a desired image of the company to the outside world; private Web sites allow for internal communication on a level that has never been achieved prior to the invention of the World Wide Web.

As the need for both public and private Web sites increases, so does the need for qualified programmers who can create and maintain them. Many people can write simple HTML files, but the number of people who can write and maintain the code that provides the dynamic content to these pages is in short supply.

The code that provides the dynamic content in most Web sites today is known as Common Gateway Interface (CGI) programming. CGI is a programming specification that defines a standard way for a *Web server* to communicate with a gateway program, typically just called a CGI program. Because Web servers are not designed to access databases, control hardware, or a host of other tasks that are available on most common Web sites today, they rely on these external CGI programs to do this work for them.

As an example, when you connect to a site on the Internet and request some information about your favorite sports team, the Web server passes the request over to a CGI program that interrogates an on-line database. This CGI program will retrieve the information you requested from the database, dynamically build an HTML page containing the results, and return it to your Web browser. In this manner the CGI program acts as a gateway to external resources, like a database or maybe even a camera mounted on the freeway providing traffic information.

A common misconception about CGI programs is that they must be written in Perl. Although Perl is perhaps the most common language for writing CGI programs, at least today, any number of other languages can be used. A CGI program is, after all, just a program and as such can be written in C, C++, Visual Basic, Tcl, Perl, or a host of other languages. Of all these languages, I believe Tcl to be the best match for the job. CGI programs by nature spend a lot of time manipulating text-based HTML documents and files. Tcl's rich set of string manipulation commands makes this type of work a breeze.

## Why I Wrote This Book

It's not that I wasn't busy enough in my current job! As a section manager for a software test team in the Motorola Computer Group, I was looking for ways to be more productive. I liked what I saw with the Tcl/Tk environment. As a hard-core C programmer, I was skeptical about using a scripting language for any type of mission-critical application. I was delightfully surprised with Tcl and became hooked on the language almost immediately. From the moment I executed my first command from the Tcl shell to the first-time execution of a Tcl script without the need for compiling, I started to feel a passion that had long been lost to the day-to-day grind of cranking out code. My enthusiasm became contagious and the number of Tcl users in my area continues to grow.

Because much of Tcl's syntax resembles C, it was possible to slide right into developing reasonably complex applications without feeling all the pain associated with learning a new language. Tcl's feature set is powerful enough to make implementation of reasonably complex algorithms enjoyable!

Our group initially embraced Tcl for its Expect extension. Expect is a powerful tool for dealing with interactive processes that fit the bill perfectly for building a complete, automated regression test environment. This same tool set is in use today validating firmware written for nearly all of the embedded computer products manufactured at the Motorola Computer Group in Tempe, Arizona. The development effort was not only shorter but much more enjoyable than it would have been in other languages I have worked with.

As the test effort expanded, we decided to begin publishing our results on our intranet. I agonized over the prospect of having to support yet another language, such as Perl, to write the CGI code, so I decided to try Tcl. I started with a few routines I had seen in Brent Welch's book *Practical Programming in Tcl and Tk* and was impressed at how easy it was to get interactive Web pages up and running. My library grew quickly and now contains nearly all the procedures required to make CGI programming fun!

Until recently, the majority of CGI programming has been targeted at application development for the Internet, meaning external to the company that developed it. Due to security considerations, these applications are placed in the hands of a very small number of programmers, or Web masters, as they are commonly referred to. An entire company's Web site may be handled by one or two people in this scenario.

As the need to disseminate information grows inside many companies, more and more businesses are looking at the intranet for solutions to their specialized communication needs. Intranets are generally protected networks, isolated from the outside world, used for a company's internal communications. Being more secure, it is becoming customary to let a larger number of CGI developers build applications for intranets. The skill sets of these individuals do not need to be as high as the traditional Web master because they are more isolated from the security risks associated with publishing on the Internet. Therefore, the numbers of individuals available to do this type of work is growing at a rapid rate.

I believe intranet development is exploding across the country, which is why I decided to write this book. As companies learn the advantages of publishing to an internal network, the need for CGI developers will grow exponentially as every group in a given company will begin to develop applications specific to their immediate needs. These may include internal access to localized databases, project-based FAQ lists, or remote control and status monitoring of development hardware or manufacturing systems. The possibilities are limitless! I feel that Tcl is the perfect language for this environment.

Because most of my CGI development for Motorola has been in an engineering environment, I have had to solve some problems outside the realm of traditional CGI programming. Some of these projects have included

- Allowing password-protected Web access to our internal source code repository.
- Web control of power control modules and X10-based switching modules for remote access to lab hardware.
- Web-based data analysis tools for analyzing the results of our automated regression test suites. These test suites validate the firmware shipped with our embedded computer products. The whole automated environment was also written in Tcl and Expect.
- Web interfaces to custom-built and off-the-shelf databases like Oracle. (You don't have to look far inside any company to find a practical use for a good database.)

## Who Should Read This Book

This book is aimed at programmers and technical professionals interested in writing interactive applications for the World Wide Web using the Tcl language. These individuals may include, but are not limited to, application programmers, research assistants, test engineers, system administrators, or Web masters who are not yet familiar with Tcl.

There are large numbers of people who are already using Tcl who may not be aware of its capabilities as a CGI programming language, for example test engineers who are already using the Expect extension to Tcl. These individuals are frequently requested to make their test data available on their local intranet. Learning how to write CGI programs with Tcl allows these individuals to obtain all the benefits of publishing to their internal intranet without having to learn a new language.

C programmers will also love this environment for the logical syntax and its similarity to other procedural programming environments.

### What You Should Know to Read This Book

Because this book is about writing programs that use the Common Gateway Interface (CGI), it assumes the reader is an experienced programmer. Most chapters in this book also assume that the reader is already familiar with Tcl, though this is not a prerequisite. The book has been laid out in such a manner that the material progresses in a steady fashion from simple examples to complex applications.

Experienced programmers not familiar with Tcl should be able to learn Tcl as they read this book. Tcl's delightfully straightforward syntax makes this possible. While reading this book without prior Tcl coding experience would prove quite challenging to an individual who has never programmed before, it should not be difficult for an experienced C or C++ programmer to sit down and work through the examples. Appendix B provides a sufficient reference to learn Tcl as you read the book.

Another important prerequisite is a strong knowledge of HTML. Because a major requirement of most CGI programs is to dynamically produce HTML documents, it is imperative that the CGI programmer be well versed in HTML. An HTML reference is provided in Appendix A, but you should seek out a tutorial-style book on HTML if you have never used the language before.

## What's in This Book

Rather than just illustrating tidbits of CGI programming, this book contains complete Web-based applications. The examples range from a simple Hello World application to interfacing with an Oracle database and a chat room that uses the Tcl Web browser plug-in and Tcl's excellent support for network socket programming. I felt that complete applications were the easiest way to master the principles of CGI programming, so I have done my best to encapsulate all the principles necessary to become a successful CGI programmer inside fully explained, completely functional Web-based programs. The enclosed CD contains the code for all the examples in this book and even provides a point-and-click Web page interface to all the examples. To run the examples in this fashion you will need to have access to a Web server and install the contents of the CD into an executable directory on that Web server. A short synopsis of each chapter's contents follows.

**Chapter 1**, The Internet, provides the necessary background information required to understand the rest of the chapters in this book. CGI programming is just one aspect of a single service available on the Internet. It is important for the reader to understand where CGI fits in, as well as some of the terminology associated with it and the Internet in general.

**Chapter 2**, The Common Gateway Interface, introduces the reader to CGI and explains the rules by which a CGI program operates. An in-depth discussion of HTTP (HyperText Transfer Protocol) is also provided. HTTP is the underlying method of communication between a Web browser and a Web server.

**Chapter 3**, Getting Started, will guide you through the installation of the cgi.tcl library contained on the enclosed CD. It will also show you how to install all the example code so you can run the enclosed examples on your own Web browser.

**Chapter 4**, Hello World, provides the prerequisite Hello World program that is the cornerstone of every comprehensive programming book. This chapter contrasts the difference between a static Web page version and the CGI programming equivalent for producing "Hello World" on the client's Web browser.

**Chapter 5**, A Web-Based Directory Browser, develops a useful tool for browsing source files on the Web server. The "File Viewer" uses information available from the Web server to restrict access to a user-defined list of IP addresses without relying on the operating system. This file viewer can be used to browse the source code contained on the enclosed CD, once the examples are made available through your own Web server.

**Chapter 6**, The Mortgage Calculator, is a Web-based mortgage calculator that can be used to calculate monthly payments on a home loan or a complete amortization schedule. Key concepts in this chapter include the use of HTML form fields, how the CGI program extracts the form data from the Web server, validation of the form data, and dynamic generation of the resulting display.

**Chapter 7**, Counting Your Hits, shows you how to add a page hit counter to the mortgage calculator example of Chapter 6. This chapter deals with using a file in the local file system to maintain state information between invocations of the CGI program.

**Chapter 8**, Server Side Includes, demonstrates a useful feature available inside most Web server applications that allows for dynamic substitution of directives that can be embedded inside your HTML documents. Server Side Includes are not considered CGI programming by themselves but can be used effectively to augment your CGI applications, possibly reducing the amount of code you need to generate to get your job done.

**Chapter 9**, Image Maps, describes how to build *clickable* images on the client's Web browser. These types of images allow users to navigate using graphical links rather than textual ones. A simple conference room example shows how to display a building floor plan and return information about a selected conference room when the user clicks on it.

**Chapter 10**, Putting Data Behind Your Forms, deals with one of the fastest-growing aspects of the World Wide Web today—accessing databases. The first example uses a simple text file to contain a database of Super Bowl statistics for every Super Bowl played. The second introduces a database written entirely in Tcl to store statistics about various NFL players. The source code for the database, which was developed just for this book, is included on the enclosed CD.

**Chapter 11**, Cookies Anyone?, explains what *magic cookies* are and why they are important to the CGI programmer. A cookie viewer is built that can create and destroy cookies on your own Web browser. Also provided is a discussion of the controversy surrounding cookies as it relates to privacy issues.

**Chapter 12**, The Bug Tracker, builds on the information supplied in Chapters 10 and 11 with an interactive database application. The application allows for password-protected, read-write access to the Tcl database described in Chapter 10. A bug tracking program is developed to track problems during new product development. The code can easily be adapted to any type of problem reporting system.

**Chapter 13**, Building Gateways to Your Data, uses an off-the-shelf package named OraTcl to provide an interface to an Oracle database. The example application builds a small database containing information about a few hard drive manufacturers. The database includes specifications on some of the specific hard drives built by these manufacturers. This chapter highlights the advantages of using a powerful, off-the-shelf, relational database program like Oracle and contrasts it to the earlier examples of Chapter 12.

**Chapter 14**, Expect in CGI Scripts, familiarizes the reader with the Expect extension to Tcl and shows how it can be used in CGI programs. The example in this chapter assumes that the user has a login account on the Web server. A login screen is provided and the CGI program uses Expect to create a new shell, log in with the supplied user name and password, and execute shell commands as the new user.

**Chapter 15**, The Tcl Browser Plug-In, reveals a powerful plug-in for Netscape and Internet Explorer that allows Tcl programs, referred to as Tclets, to be executed directly on the client's Web browser! This is analogous to Java applets that execute under the Java Virtual Machine built into these same Web browsers. An in-depth discussion of the plug-in's security model is provided along with an explanation of the Tcl commands that directly support this model.

**Chapter 16**, A Tcl Chat Room, uses Tcl's excellent support for network sockets to build a client-server-based chat room. The browser plug-in is used to build the client-side interface, which communicates with a chat room server running on the Web server's computer. Once the chat room client is loaded from the Web server, network sockets are used for the underlying communication.

**Appendix A**, HTML Reference Guide, provides a quick reference for the HTML tags used most frequently in this book. The information is provided in tabular format containing a short description of the HTML tag and a concise example of its usage.

**Appendix B**, Tcl Language Summary, provides a comprehensive summary of the Tcl command set. Each command is summarized along with short, practical examples that can be executed right from the Tcl shell.

**Appendix C**, cgi.tcl Reference, provides a reference to the cgi.tcl library used throughout this book. A command reference section, in alphabetical order, provides the calling sequence, a description of the command, and a short example of its usage.

**Appendix D**, The Web Browser Plug-In, provides reference material for the Tcl Web browser plug-in. This appendix covers security policies and the configuration files that may be modified to change the default behavior of the plug-in.

### About the cgi.tcl Library

This book includes a library of routines that I named cgi.tcl. The main thrust of this library is to make it easy to obtain the data submitted by the Web browser and dynamically produce HTML-based Web pages. This library was developed for internal use inside Motorola and is now being made available in this book. There is another library of the same name in the public domain that was written by Don Libes, who also wrote the Expect extension to Tcl. Libes's library is very complete, and if you are considering writing CGI programs for a living, you might want to check into it.

## Acknowledgments

I need to thank a number of people who have contributed to the development of this book. First thanks to Mary O'Brien, Lorraine Ferrier, Simone Payment, Chanda Leary, and all the other fine people at Addison-Wesley for their assistance throughout the entire publishing cycle.

There are a number of people at Motorola who deserve mention. First there is Glen McCarty who provided a much-needed user's perspective by reading many of the chapters as they were being written. There's my boss, Dave Nolte, who overlooked my occasional distractions as I was writing the material and supported my decision to write it. And finally, thanks to Joe Sterbenz, who taught me the true meaning of terms like software reuse, encapsulation, and data hiding.

In addition to my coworkers and the staff at Addison-Wesley, numerous reviewers provided constructive criticism, which has hopefully fined-tuned this book into a valuable asset for any CGI programmer.

A special thanks to John Ousterhout for inventing the language in the first place and being available to support it. The accessibility of both John Ousterhout for Tcl and Don Libes for Expect has provided a friendly face to what can sometimes be a faceless industry. These gentlemen provided answers to e-mail questions, often in the same day they were sent. It can be hard to get that kind of response inside your own company!

Two other individuals who were always responsive to my many questions were Brent Welch, author of *Practical Programming in Tcl and Tk*, and Tom Poindexter, who created the OraTcl package that I use in this book to connect with Oracle database systems.

Last, but certainly not least, I would like to thank my wife, Evelyn, her mother, Ilene, and my two wonderful boys, Dillon and Brandon, for their understanding and support over the many long nights and weekends it took to complete this book during an already hectic period in our lives!

*David Maggiano*
*December 1999*

# Chapter 1

## The Internet

In order to fully understand the remainder of this book, it is important to have a reasonable understanding of the Internet and the World Wide Web. The terms are used almost interchangeably these days; however, they refer to two different things. The Internet refers to a vast structure of interconnected networks linking a large number of computers together throughout the world. Each computer connected to the Internet is generally capable of providing multiple services such as e-mail, text retrieval systems, and the World Wide Web.

The World Wide Web is a hypermedia system that uses a text markup language known as the Hypertext Markup Language (HTML) to display interactive documents. It is this hypertext system that allows you to click on a link in one Web page and retrieve another document from the other side of the globe. The World Wide Web also uses its own unique method of formatting messages, which is layered on top of the underlying techniques used on the Internet itself. So, in summary, the World Wide Web is just one of the services available on the Internet.

CGI programs, the topic of this book, are unique to the World Wide Web. They are the cornerstone of many interactive Web sites and allow the otherwise static hypertext system to process complex user requests and return them in a form that is understandable by tools such as Netscape and Microsoft's Internet Explorer. In order to be a successful CGI programmer, it is important to have a good understanding of some of the basic concepts that drive the Internet today as well as a thorough understanding of how the World Wide Web and, more specifically, CGI programs work.

This chapter provides a brief overview of what the Internet is and how it came to be. It then examines two of the most famous protocols in the world today. They are the Internet Protocol (IP) and Transmission Control Protocol (TCP). IP determines how messages are routed from one computer to another on the Internet, and TCP provides a robust applications level interface to the IP layer for ensuring delivery and reconstruction of messages over the Internet.

This chapter also discusses how Internet standards are created and made public through a series of documents known as Request for Comments (RFCs).

> A *protocol*, in data communication terms, is a standardized method by which two different machines exchange information. It is typically a complete set of rules that dictates how messages are initiated, transmitted, and received and what happens when errors occur.

## A Brief History

In the 1960s the world was a vastly different place in terms of computing technology. There were only a small number of computers in existence, and they were large and expensive machines known as mainframes. Typically, the only institutions that could afford these mainframe computers were the government, universities, and large corporations.

In the late 1960s the U.S. government began to realize the benefit that could be derived from connecting these computers. It also realized that not a great deal was known about networking, so through the Advanced Research Projects Agency (ARPA), a branch of the U.S. federal government, it funded a project whose goal was to develop a method of *networking* these computers together. The project became known as the ARPANET. Rather than simply researching the topic, ARPA provided funding to develop a prototype network and encourage researchers to develop the necessary hardware and software to bring the project to life.

The ARPANET experiment served a twofold purpose. It would develop a sound basis for connecting machines together while providing more distributed access to these rare and expensive machines. ARPA helped establish a new precedent of open software by encouraging its researchers to publish their discoveries, making the technology available to anyone that was interested. This single decision has indeed changed the face of technology on a global scale.

The ARPANET project had very humble beginnings. By the end of 1969 there were four computers connected to the ARPANET. By 1971 the network had 15 nodes, and by 1972 it had grown to an astounding 37 nodes! The network was initially used by a small number of scientists, researchers, students, and administrative personnel. Little did anyone expect that it would mature into the largest network on the face of the planet!

## Wide Area Networks

In the early days of the ARPANET, there was typically just one computer at a given site. The computers were connected to a modem that would translate the digital signals into analog voltages. These analog signals were then sent to the target computer through either a standard dial-up phone line or dedicated, leased phone lines, as shown in Figure 1-1. This became known as a wide area network, or WAN, because it usually spanned large geographic distances.

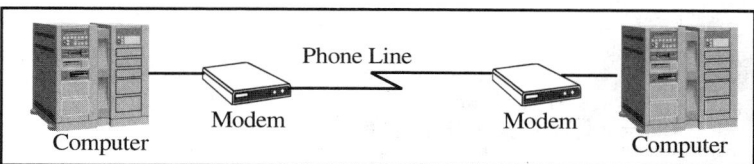

**Figure 1-1** Simple Wide Area Networks

This type of connection is also known as *circuit switching*. In circuit switching an actual connection is made and maintained in the phone company's switching station for the duration of the contact. In order to contact another system, a different connection is made that also lasts for the duration of the contact. Circuit switching has limitations when it comes to connecting multiple computers. The speeds at which data is sent across these lines is slower than the speeds that the computers were able to run because the signal must travel through long transmission cables. A general rule of thumb is the longer the cable, the slower the transmission speed. In spite of these limitations, WANs are still employed today to span large distances.

4

With the advent of the microprocessor in 1974, the price and size of computers began to decline at a very sharp rate. Minicomputers were becoming available, and they cost a fraction of what their mainframe counterparts cost. It now became feasible for smaller organizations or even different departments in the same organization to have a computer specifically tailored to its needs.

At the same time, desktop computers were also becoming available. These microprocessor-based personal computers allowed for localized intelligence that was able to perform complex tasks on its own, off-loading much of the work that was performed by the mainframe or minicomputers. The combination of these two technologies would revolutionize the way most of us work and live.

As the numbers of computers grew, so did the desire to connect local computer systems together into what is now known as a local area network, or LAN. Figure 1-2 is a simplified depiction of a LAN with two machines connected. In a local area network, two or more computers are connected by some physical medium, such as a transmission cable. There is a defined protocol associated with this lowest of layers that dictates physical characteristics such as electrical signal levels, cable length, and transmission speeds. It also dictates how data transmitted across the physical medium is formatted.

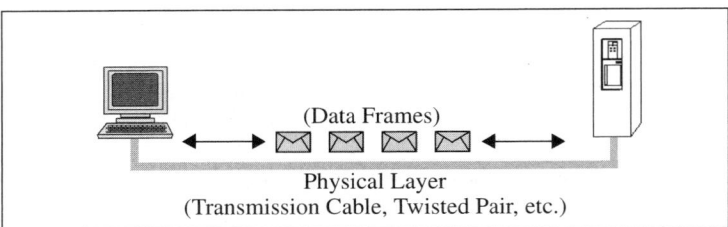

**Figure 1-2** Layered Protocols

Because there are several different networking protocols now available for local area networks, we will use *Ethernet* for the purposes of this discussion. This is a good protocol to pick because it is the most widely used networking protocol in computer-based local area networks. In the case of Ethernet, data is transmitted across the physical medium in small packets of information referred to as *data frames*.

Having some understanding of the relationship between these data frames and the upper-level data packets that flow across the Internet today will make it easier to understand how messages are addressed and delivered in a global network like the Internet.

## Ethernet

In 1976 Robert M. Metcalfe and David R. Boggs, who worked for the Xerox Palo Alto Research Center, published a paper describing a networking technology that they named Ethernet. To put this invention into perspective, Intel, in the same year, had just released their first 8080 microprocessor that ran at 4.77MHz! This is several orders of magnitude slower than the microprocessors of today.

Work continued on Ethernet over the next few years and became a joint venture among Digital, Intel, and Xerox. In September 1980 these three companies published the first commercial Ethernet standard. The standard was easy to understand, implement, and maintain. Ethernet rapidly gained acceptance and today is the most predominant LAN technology in the industry.

Figure 1-3 shows a simplified diagram of an early Ethernet network. It consists of a single transmission cable with multiple *stations* connected to it through a special *tap*. Each station (workstation, PC, printer, etc.) that connects to the LAN has a special network interface card (NIC), which provides the electrical connection to the Ethernet.

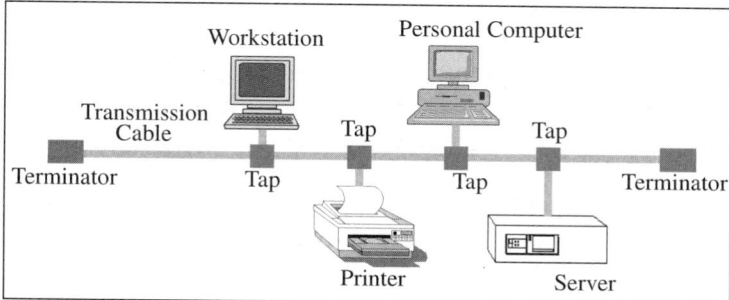

**Figure 1-3** Early Ethernet Configuration

Because the Ethernet standard is an open standard, many vendors began to produce Ethernet interface cards for a variety of different equipment available on the market. This was the first time that equipment manufactured by different vendors could easily be connected together. Local area networks began to spring up overnight.

The reason that a network like Ethernet is called a local area network is that the length of the transmission cable is strictly limited. This is due to the higher transmission rates over the medium. Exceeding the maximum cable length results in degradation of the electrical signal and a resulting failure in communication.

## Ethernet Data Frames

The Ethernet protocol specifies how the electrical signals should behave as well as how the data transmitted across the wire is arranged. The data is transmitted in what is called *data frames*. For the Ethernet Protocol the data frames are structured according to Figure 1-4.

| Preamble 7 Octets | S F D | Destination Address 6 octets | Source Address 6 octets | Length or Type 2 octets | Data 46 to 1,500 octets | FCS 4 octets |
|---|---|---|---|---|---|---|

**Figure 1-4** Ethernet Data Frame

You can see that the frame contains a 6 octet source address and a 6 octet destination address. These addresses are typically known as MAC addresses. The abbreviation stems from the term Media Access Control, which is one of the protocols in the OSI 7 layer model of networking. But that's a little outside the scope of this chapter, so we'll just call it a MAC address. Each MAC address on a given network must be unique, so every manufacturer of Ethernet cards assigns the card a unique address before it is shipped to the customer.

The data field is variable in length and can contain from 46 to 1,500 octets of information. The minimum and maximum lengths of data fields were calculated for optimal transmission rates at the time that Ethernet was designed.

Because the data field in the Ethernet data frame was designed to transport various forms of data under differing protocols, a 2 octet field is reserved for specifying the type of data that is being transferred. Some of the more common types are shown in Table 1-1.

**Table 1-1** A Few Common Frame Types

| Frame Type | Protocol |
|---|---|
| 0800 | IP |
| 0806 | ARP |

**Table 1-1** A Few Common Frame Types

| Frame Type | Protocol |
|------------|----------|
| 8035       | RARP     |
| 8137       | IPX      |

Many companies and organizations embraced Ethernet; many went with competing technologies by other vendors. Soon there were many localized islands of computers that had a difficult time talking to each other, partly because of the use of different LAN technologies and partly because of the distances between them. Wide area networks were still employed to connect these local area networks together, and special devices began to emerge that would translate one networking protocol to another at each end. These special devices, now known as *routers*, are the underlying reason that the Internet works.

## Internetworking and the Internet

In order to connect two dissimilar computers, they must be able to speak the same language. The ARPANET researchers realized this early on and developed a standard method for these machines to communicate, which they called Network Control Protocol (NCP). NCP provided a standardized format for how two different machines would exchange information. The early NCP was adequate to support further research activities performed by various researchers connected to the ARPANET, but it soon become apparent that NCP itself was in need of further research and development.

At about the same time that Ethernet was being developed in the labs of Palo Alto, ARPA had begun funding additional research activities on computer networks using various underlying methods of transmitting data, including radio and satellite communication. In 1973, to keep pace with the development of these new networking strategies, ARPA encouraged research into a new protocol that would supersede the Network Control Protocol and allow for host-to-host communication across any of these disparate networks.

As a result of this effort, a new suite of protocols was developed. This suite is referred to as the Internet Protocol Suite; however, this name is typically overshadowed by two of the more famous protocols produced as a result of this new research: *Internet Protocol* and *Transmission Control Protocol.* You will commonly hear these two protocols referred to as TCP/IP, with each letter said individually. ARPA once again made public the discoveries and the design of their new TCP/IP protocols.

This new protocol suite was intended from the beginning to be a network of networks. This concept was labeled Internetworking, and the actual project became known as the Internet project. Therefore, the Internet is not just a single network but a network of networks that now spans the globe!

One of the principal goals of the Internet was to provide connectivity between dissimilar networks and make it appear as though you are connected to one giant network. The concept, sometimes referred to as a *virtual network*, is illustrated in Figure 1-5.

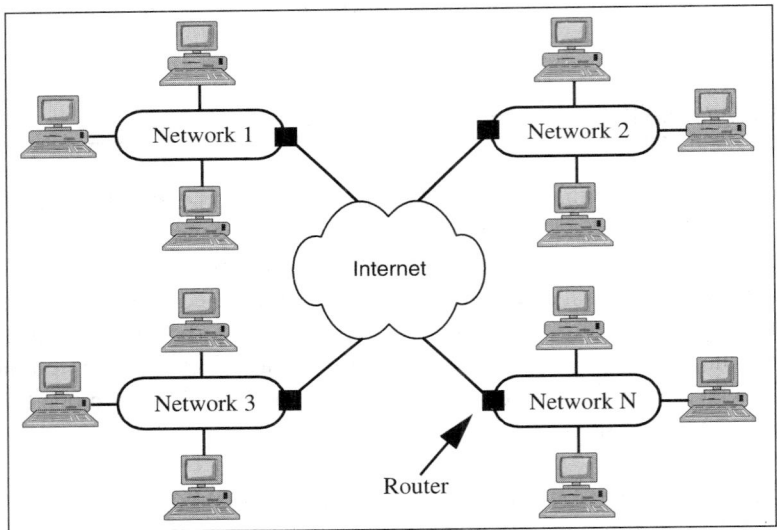

**Figure 1-5** The Internet Appears as One Virtual Network

Of course, the networks are not actually connected to each other for the same reasons that were previously stated: Different LAN technologies are generally incompatible and the distance between the physical networks precludes the use of LAN technology from one network to another.

So, if a LAN can't connect directly to the Internet, how are these networks connected to the Internet? The answer is through a special device called a *router*.

A router is a piece of hardware that sits between the LAN and the Internet and is capable of translating one message format into another.

Initially, routers were just computers with two network interface cards. One card connected to the LAN and the other card connected to the Internet. Software running on the computer would analyze each message on the LAN and decide if the message was intended to be sent to the Internet. In this case the message would be propagated from the LAN to the Internet by the router. If the message was not intended to travel out onto the Internet, the router simply ignored the message and began waiting for the next one to arrive.

## Internet Protocol Layers

The Internet protocol suite is based on four distinct and separate protocol layers. These layers are defined to work synergistically, allowing messages to flow cleanly across any number of dissimilar networks.

In early networks and, indeed, the networks of today, protocols exist for both the physical layer that connects machines together as well as for the logical layer that is used to transmit data across the physical layer. Figure 1-2 illustrated this concept.

In the Internet the IP serves as the delivery mechanism that moves these packets from source to destination. The IP layer routes each packet submitted to it by the TCP to its final destination. Each packet can be routed through a different path to reach its destination.

When discussing Internet communications, it is common to see these two protocols referred to as TCP/IP because TCP is generally layered on top of the lower level IP protocol, as shown in Figure 1-6. These two protocols exist on top of some physical layer comprising the actual network hardware, such as Ethernet. At the highest level is some application layer such as HTTP, ftp, or telnet. HTTP is the application layer that we are most interested in here and will be covered in detail in the next chapter.

## The Internet Protocol (IP)

In order for the various networks connected to the Internet to share data, they must use a common data format once their messages leave their native network and travel out onto the Internet. This common format is IP, and any computer connected to the Internet must format its messages according to the IP. In this section we will take a close look at the IP protocol.

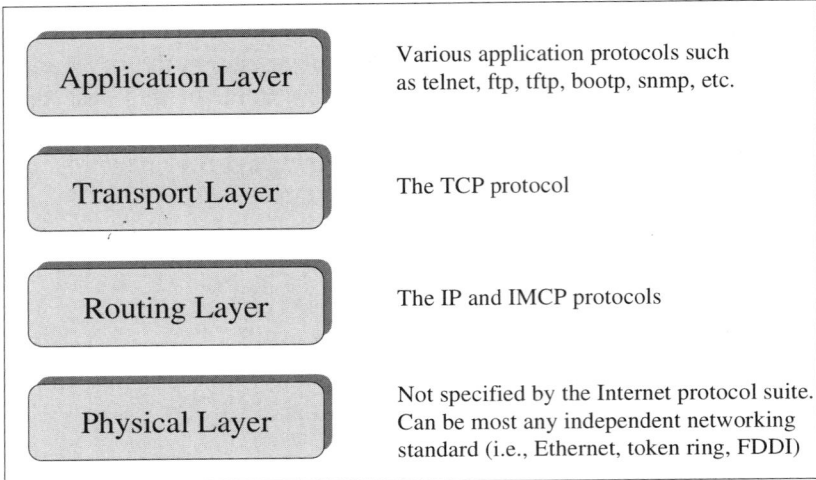

**Figure 1-6** The Four Layer Internet Model

The Internet Protocol exists at the routing layer, as shown in Figure 1-6. This layer rides on top of the physical layer and provides for a method of transporting messages between source and destination machines on the Internet.

IP uses what are known as *datagrams* to transmit data from one machine to another. A datagram is just a defined way of organizing the information before it is sent. Figure 1-7 shows the layout of an IP datagram. Each datagram contains a source and destination IP address comprising 4 octets each, various fields that contain information about the message contents, and a data field that actually contains the data being transmitted.

When a computer on a particular network wishes to send a message to another machine, it packages an IP datagram and sends it out onto its local network. The datagram is actually contained in the data field of the lower-level data frame employed by the particular LAN technology being used. For example, in the case of Ethernet the IP datagram is contained in the data field of the Ethernet data frame field. Refer to Figure 1-4 for the structure of an Ethernet data frame.

IP is known as a connectionless, best-attempt delivery system. Connectionless means that there is no attempt made to verify that the destination machine exists before sending the message. Best-attempt delivery means that although successful delivery of the datagram is important, no guarantee is provided that the message will be delivered. If the message is not successfully delivered, no error status is returned to the sender. The details of establishing a connection with the destination machine and verifying delivery are left up to higher-level protocols that ride on top of the IP delivery system.

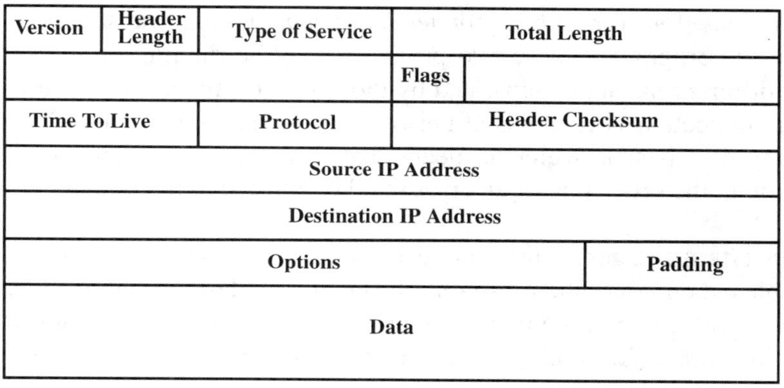

| Version | Header Length | Type of Service | | Total Length | |
|---------|---------------|-----------------|------|--------------|---|
| | | | Flags | | |
| Time To Live | | Protocol | | Header Checksum | |
| Source IP Address | | | | | |
| Destination IP Address | | | | | |
| Options | | | | Padding | |
| Data | | | | | |

**Figure 1-7** IP Datagram

## Packet Switching

One of the visions of the early designers of the Internet was to make it as resilient as possible. They wanted no central authority controlling the flow of information on the Internet, which meant that there would be no single point of failure. Because there would be no central authority, messages had to be free to find their own way through the tangled Web of network connections, finally ending up at their specified destination. The messages are sent out onto the network with both the source and destination address and each network along the way is responsible for routing the message a little closer to its destination. This concept is known as *packet switching*. This system is quite different from the circuit switching concept employed in wide area networks.

IP uses this packet switching concept to deliver messages on the Internet. If the destination address does not exist on the local network, it is the responsibility of that network's router to route the message one step closer to its destination. This process continues until the destination machine claims the message packet.

# The Transmission Control Protocol (TCP)

Riding on top of the routing layer is the transport layer. This layer is responsible for providing more robust delivery than can be provided for by the connectionless, best-attempt delivery Internet Protocol. This layer is where Transmission Control Protocol comes in. TCP is the layer that applications typically interface with to send and receive messages across the Internet.

TCP provides for a *reliable, connection-oriented* data transmission channel between two programs. These two programs may be running on the same computer or different machines separated by thousands of miles. Connection-oriented means a connection is established between the source and destination machines before any data is sent. Reliable means that data sent is guaranteed to reach its destination in the order sent or an error will be returned to the sender.

TCP converts messages at the source machine into *packets* of information and reassembles them into their original form at the destination machine. These packets of information contain a *packet header*, which contains additional information used for both the connection process and to ensure reliable transmission of each packet.

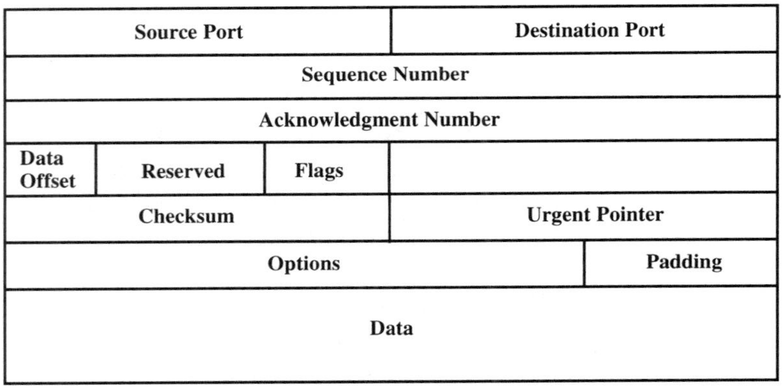

| Source Port | | | Destination Port | | |
|---|---|---|---|---|---|
| Sequence Number | | | | | |
| Acknowledgment Number | | | | | |
| Data Offset | Reserved | Flags | | | |
| Checksum | | | Urgent Pointer | | |
| Options | | | | Padding | |
| Data | | | | | |

**Figure 1-8** TCP Data Packet

Figure 1-8 illustrates the layout of the TCP data packet. Whereas the IP addresses in an IP datagram specify a particular machine on the Internet, the Source Port and Destination Port fields specify a particular process on that machine. This allows messages to be sent to specific applications running on a specific machine.

## Fragmentation

Another important point to understand about TCP is that messages may be fragmented into smaller messages. Part of the reason for this is the limitation on data size for the various local area networks. For example, the data field in an Ethernet data frame can contain a maximum of 1,500 octets of data. If the message to be sent is larger than this limit, the message is fragmented into smaller messages that are compatible with the network technology being employed.

These smaller messages are assigned unique sequence numbers that make it possible to reconstruct the message at the receiving end. The Sequence Number and Acknowledgment Number fields in the TCP header are used for this purpose. Each fragment is assigned a unique sequence number by the source. Likewise, each message package received by the destination must be acknowledged using the Acknowledgment field. In this way all the segments of a given message are guaranteed to arrive at the destination or an error will be returned to the source.

Due to the packet switching nature of the IP protocol, various message segments could conceivably take a different route to their destination address. Due to differing delays in these different network segments, it is also possible that the message segments might show up out of order. Here again, the sequence numbers are used to rearrange the message fragments back into their proper order.

This is analogous to mailing each page of this book in a separate envelope to a reader on the other side of the world. Each letter could be delivered via a different route, utilizing both air and ground transportation. The entire book is then reassembled at the destination location before the reader sits down to read it.

## The Three-Way Handshake

As mentioned earlier, TCP is a connection-oriented protocol, which means that a connection is established between the source and destination machines before any data is actually transmitted. TCP uses two flags in the packet header, known as SYN and ACK, to establish the communication channel before sending any data. The process is known as a three-way handshake and works as follows.

1. The requesting machine sends a packet of information with SYN set and ACK cleared.
2. The receiving host returns a packet that has both SYN and ACK set.

3. The requesting host sends a packet with the SYN flag set and the ACK flag cleared.

This handshake ensures a valid connection between the source and destination machines before the actual data transmission begins. Once the handshake is complete, the process of sending the actual data packets can begin. Each packet contains a unique sequence number that allows the message to be reassembled at the destination.

On the surface, TCP sounds like a perfect method for transmitting information. It not only guarantees delivery but ensures that the messages sent can be reconstructed at their destination. So why would you want to send data any other way? The reason is generally performance. Along with this robust guaranteed transmission from source to destination comes a certain amount of overhead, which slows down the overall throughput. In fact the throughput of TCP can be as much as ten times slower than other protocols such as User Datagram Protocol (UDP).

## User Datagram Protocol (UDP)

UDP is a connectionless protocol that makes a best-effort approach at delivery but does not guarantee successful transmission. There is no guarantee that messages sent will be delivered or delivered in order. UDP is typically used in services that receive periodic updates, so they will not be negatively effected if they miss an occasional message. Many services on networks choose to use this simpler protocol for performance reasons.

A hypothetical example might be a clock synchronization program running on a network with a large number of computers connected. One computer sends out the current time to synchronize the time clock on every other computer on the network. If one of these messages is missed, synchronization will occur on the next one. UDP is typically used by many of the background services, such as naming servers, that run on the Internet where performance is essential and periodic updates are common, reducing the impact of an occasional message being missed.

TCP and UDP are in common use on the Internet today. TCP is typically used for higher-level services where a connection-based, reliable communication stream is required at the application level. UDP is predominantly used for lower-level background services where no serious consequences will occur if an occasional message does not make it to its destination.

## UNIX and the Internet

A large number of the computers that provide services on the Internet today use the UNIX operating system. This is not surprising because UNIX and the Internet grew up together. In fact, the first version of UNIX, initially termed UNICS for (UNIplexed operating and Computing System), was drafted in 1969 by Ken Thompson and Dennis Ritchie of Bell Labs, the same year that the ARPANET was beginning. UNIX was designed to be a time-sharing system. That is, multiple applications could run seemingly in parallel. This is done by providing each application a time-slice to run for a short period of time. When the time is up, the operating system suspends the application's execution and begins running another application for a slice of time. This is also known as multitasking and is the key component of UNIX that allows computers connected to the Internet to provide many different services in parallel.

Because Bell Labs used a number of different types of computer systems, they built UNIX to be general enough that it could be easily moved to other computer systems. Almost more significant than the invention of UNIX was their choice to keep the system proprietary. They allowed universities to obtain copies for research as well as teaching, which proved to be a very beneficial gesture to the rest of the world.

Early on a group of students and faculty from the University of California at Berkeley became interested in UNIX. They developed a series of applications and made improvements to the operating system itself. They shared their work by establishing a distribution system where they would mail tapes with their latest releases to other universities. This variant of UNIX became known as BSD, which stood for Berkeley Software Distribution.

At the same time, ARPA was looking for a way to distribute its Internet software, known as TCP/IP. It felt that the Berkeley distribution was a good medium for this distribution and provided a copy of TCP/IP to Berkeley. Berkeley included TCP/IP software in its UNIX distribution, which allowed other universities to begin studying this system and putting it to use. As a result, UNIX quickly became the operating system of choice for the Internet and continues to be popular among machines connected to the Internet today.

Of course, UNIX is not the only operating system available for machines connected to the Internet. One of the main requirements for an operating system running on an Internet server is the ability to be multitasking, that is, the ability to run multiple applications at the same time. In reality the applications don't actually run at the same time. Instead, the operating system runs one application for a brief period of time, suspends its operation and runs the next application in the list. This makes it appear that the applications are running simultaneously.

UNIX was among the first operating systems to provide this ability, and so it became the natural choice for Internet servers. With the proliferation of other multitasking operating systems, such as Windows NT, over the last ten years, it is now more common to find non-UNIX operating systems running many of the computers connected to the Internet today.

## Internet Addresses

So how do we address messages sent across the Internet? With an Internet address. Every computer connected to the Internet has a unique address in the same way that every family in a given city can have a unique telephone number. If you know a computer's Internet address, you can communicate with it.

An Internet address is a unique 32-bit number that is typically expressed as four 8-bit octets, with each octet separated by a period. Each of the octets can take on any number from 0 through 255. As of the printing of this book, some examples of Internet IP addresses are

```
198.116.142.34      NASA
140.147.248.7       Library of Congress
129.188.137.156     Motorola
```

Each computer connected to the Internet is capable of delivering a number of services. A service is nothing more than an application program intended to perform a specific function. These applications typically wait for requests to come in from the Internet and then process the request. Many of these services have a history much older than that of the World Wide Web. As an example, *telnet* provides a method of logging on to another machine and executing applications remotely, and *ftp* provides a way to interactively transfer files between computers on the Internet. These services and others have been in use since the earliest days of the ARPANET and allow individuals to transfer files from one computer to another, regardless of the distance between them.

## Address Space

Until recently, Internet addresses were divided into five different types or classes. The classes were designated A through E. Class A address space allows a small number of networks but a large number of machines, while class C allows for a large number of networks but a relatively small number of machines per network.

Class A addresses, for example, have the form N.a.b.c, where N is the network number and a.b.c resolves to a specific host on the network. The most significant bit in a class A network must be a 0, so there can only be 128 class A networks on the Internet. Because N occupies only 8 of the available 32-bit address spaces, the remaining a.b.c portion allows for $2^{24}$ or 16,777,216 individual computers on the network. As you can see, class A networks are extremely wasteful. Still, there were several class A networks assigned to some of the early pioneers of the Internet.

Class C addresses are common in most organizations and allow up to 254 hosts per network. The theoretical number would be 256, but the numbers 0 and 255 are typically not used for host addresses. Figure 1-9 lists the five address classes used in classical network addresses.

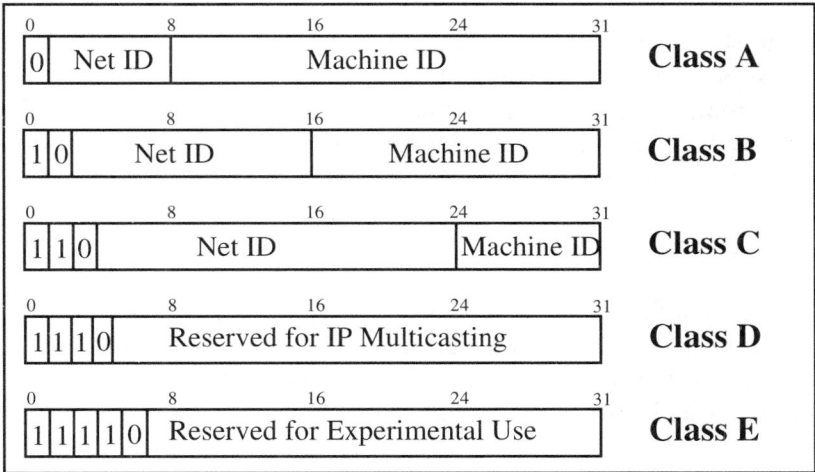

**Figure 1-9** The Five Address Classes

With the potential number of available addresses equaling $2^{32}$ or 4,294,967,296 unique addresses, you would think that we would never run out. In practice, however, the number of available addresses is actually much smaller due to the way addresses were initially assigned.

Regardless of the class of address space assigned, it is almost a certainty that organizations assigned a particular class of address will not utilize the entire address space provided. This is especially true of class A and B address allocation schemes. This type of fragmentation of the available Internet address space has resulted in holes scattered throughout the address domain. Couple this with the explosive growth of the Internet, and it's easy to see why the Internet is running out of available addresses. To combat the dwindling address space, a new form of allocation known as Classless Internet Domain Routing (CIDR) was adopted a few years ago.

## CIDR Addresses

In the Classless Internet Domain Routing model, Internet service providers are assigned a block of addresses with the most significant bits fixed. They are then free to assign individual IP addresses to their subscribers. So a service provider may be given a range of addresses where the first 12 bits are fixed, leaving $2^{20}$ addresses that may be assigned to customers. It is up to the service provider to decide how big a block to allocate to given customers.

CIDR has slowed the erosion of the available address space provided by the 32-bit IP address but certainly has not stopped it. As the number of computers connected to the Internet continues to increase at an explosive rate, the scarcity of available IP addresses is becoming quite a problem for the Internet community. Several schemes are being adopted to relieve this problem. The first solution is virtual hosting, which allows multiple host names to share a single IP address. Most of the major Internet service providers offer this service today.

The second solution being looked at is to expand the number of bits in an IP address from 32 to 128. A new version of the IP protocol, IPv6 (version 6), is being proposed that will do just that. In this new version IP addresses will have 128 bits and should provide sufficient address space for the foreseeable future.

Because every computer on the Internet may offer numerous services, it is not enough to identify the computer we wish to communicate with. We must also be able to specify the particular service that we are interested in using. This is done through the use of *port* numbers.

## Ports

A port is an additional 16-bit number that uniquely identifies a particular service on any given machine on the Internet. Because port numbers are 16 bits wide, each computer on the Internet has a maximum number of $2^{16}$ or 65,536 ports.

Figure 1-10 illustrates this use of ports. Here, three machines are shown connecting to three different ports (applications) running on a single Internet server. The particular application is identified by its unique port number in the same way that a specific television station has a unique channel number.

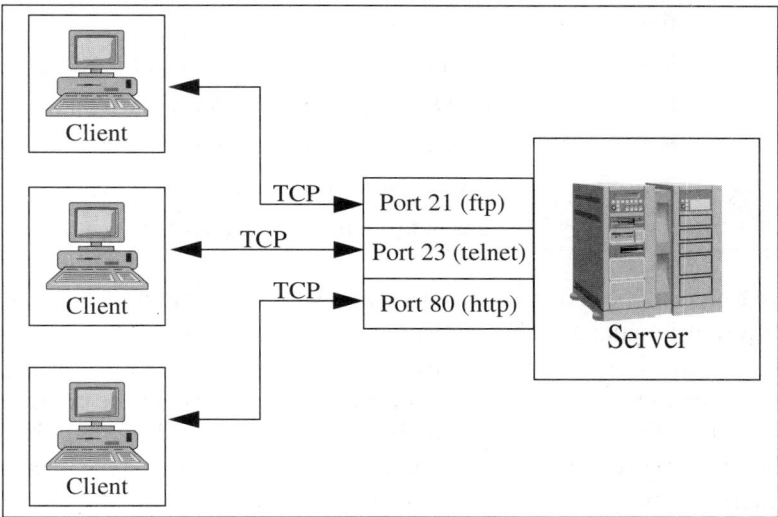

**Figure 1-10** Server Ports

Port numbers are divided into three ranges.

- Well-known ports are those from 0 through 1,023.
- Registered ports are those from 1,024 through 49,151.
- Dynamic and/or private ports are those from 49,152 through 65,535.

Well-known ports, those ranging from 0 through 1,023, are where most common services on the Internet reside. These ports are controlled and assigned by the

Internet Assigned Numbers Authority (IANA) and on most systems can be used only by system (root) processes or by programs executed by privileged users. Table 1-2 lists some typical services available on many Internet servers and the port number these services reside on.

**Table 1-2** Some Typical Well-Known Port Assignments

| Port Number | Service | Description |
|---|---|---|
| 21 | ftp | File Transfer Protocol |
| 23 | telnet | Remote Terminal Access |
| 25 | smtp | Simple Mail Transfer Protocol (electronic mail) |
| 43 | whois | Network Information Center (NIC) whois service |
| 53 | DNS | Domain Name Service |
| 79 | finger | User Information Service |
| 80 | http | HyperText Transfer Protocol (Web servers) |
| 109 | pop2 | Post Office Protocol (electronic mail) |
| 110 | pop2 | Post Office Protocol (electronic mail) |
| 119 | nntp | Network News Transfer Protocol (Usenet) |
| 513 | login | Logs in to a remote UNIX machine |

So the Internet can be thought of as a vast network of computers that each speaks many different languages. These languages, referred to as protocols, define how particular applications exchange information. In order to talk to an application, you must know the language it uses along with the address of the computer that it is running on. Because the 32-bit IP numbers are a little cumbersome to remember, the ability to associate a name with a unique IP address is provided for in the Internet. This name is known as the Universal Resource Locator, or URL, for short.

## The Universal Resource Locator (URL)

Most people type URLs into their browser without a thought as to how they work. As a CGI programmer, you must understand the layout of the URL, know what each piece means, and be able to create URLs dynamically when necessary.

In general, URLs are written as follows:

<scheme>:<scheme-specific-part>

The *scheme* identifies the type of service you are requesting such as ftp, telnet, or HTTP (World Wide Web). The second part of the URL is specific to the scheme being used. The two parts are separated by a colon. The combination of these two items compose what is known as a URL. For example, as of the writing of this book, you would connect to the Addison-Wesley home page by using the URL

http://www.awl.com/corp

For this address the scheme is HTTP, which stands for HyperText Transfer Protocol, and the scheme-specific part of the URL is *//www.awl.com/corp*. The HTTP scheme, discussed in detail in the next chapter, is used by the World Wide Web and dictates how messages are formatted when using this service on the Internet.

Typically, it is the responsibility of the particular application being used to understand the URL format. Examples of such applications would be Microsoft's Internet Explorer or Netscape Navigator. When you use either of these applications, you type in a URL of the location you want to reach. The browser deciphers the URL, formats the message to be sent according to the scheme selected, and contacts the destination machine specified by the scheme-specific part of the URL. Table 1-3 contains some commonly used schemes understood by most browsers on the market today.

**Table 1-3** Protocols Supported in Most Browsers

| Protocolst | Primary Purpose |
| --- | --- |
| http: | HyperText Transfer Protocol |
| ftp: | File Transfer Protocol |
| gopher: | The Gopher Protocol |
| mailto: | Electronic Mail Address |
| news: | Usenet News |
| telnet: | Telnet Session |

# Defining the World Wide Web

The terms "Internet" and "World Wide Web" are used almost interchangeably these days. In fact, the term "Internet" refers to the physical layer consisting of a network of networks that connects a staggering number of computers throughout the world. The World Wide Web, on the other hand, is one of the many services available on the Internet.

The World Wide Web, often referred to as WWW, was invented by Tim Berners-Lee in late 1990 while he was working at CERN, the European Laboratory for Particle Physics. The WWW is a distributed hypermedia environment consisting of documents from around the world. The documents are linked using a system known as Hypertext, where elements of one document may be linked to specific elements of another document. The documents may be located on any computer connected to the Internet. In this context, the word "document" is not limited to text but may include video, audio, graphics, databases, and a host of other tools that can now be accessed from any Web browser. Traversal of the whole hypermedia system is as simple as clicking on an active link in one document that points to another somewhere in the world.

## The Client-Server Model

The World Wide Web, as with most of the services available today, is based on the long-standing client-server model illustrated in Figure 1-11. In this model there are normally many clients accessing a single server. One of the principal reasons for using the client-server model is the consolidation of resources in a central location. The server usually offers some service that many clients are interested in.

An example of such a shared resource would be a database of stock prices that is updated every hour. The client sends a request to the server for information about a particular stock and the server responds with the appropriate data. The shared resource, in this case the stock database, is typically located on the server's computer but could reside on a separate system and be accessed by the server on behalf of the requesting client. The client and server computers may be located in the same building or separated by huge distances.

The information, represented by the arrows in Figure 1-11, is transmitted across some physical connection such as a network or dial-up connection. The server is typically running the UNIX operating system but may operate under other environments such as Linux, AIX, Windows, or one of a number of other operating systems available that have features similar to UNIX. The server is also typically an unattended computer running a variety of applications that wait for requests from clients. Once a request comes in, an application processes the request and performs the requested service.

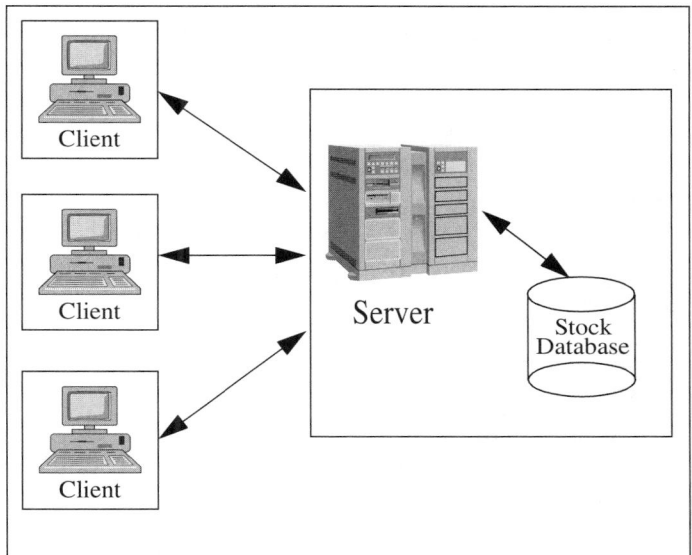

**Figure 1-11** Client-Server Model

The choice of operating systems for the client is broader because the requirements for being a client are typically less stringent than the requirements for being a server.

The client is typically running a Web browser application such as Netscape Navigator. Most of us are familiar with these types of applications because we use them directly in our day-to-day Web browsing activities. The server computer runs another application known as a Web server. Most of us are not as familiar with Web server applications.

## What Is a Web Server?

A Web server is a program that monitors a particular port on the server computer and waits for incoming messages. Web server programs are specifically related to the World Wide Web services that run on the Internet and by default listen to port 80, which has been assigned by the Internet Assigned Numbers Authority. These incoming messages are formatted according to the HyperText Transfer Protocol (HTTP), which is defined in more detail in the next chapter. These HTTP messages request information residing on the Web server's computer.

A Web server will perform one of several activities based on the type of request it receives. If the request is for a simple static document that resides on the Web server's computer, the Web server will retrieve the document and return it to the client that requested it. The request may be for a static document that contains some embedded directives that must first be translated by the Web server before returning the document. Lastly, the request may be to execute a CGI program. The Web server will execute the specified CGI program and make the data passed from the Web client available to the CGI program. When the CGI program completes, the Web server will pass back to the client any information that was returned by the CGI program.

There are a number of Web server programs available on the market today. This author used the NCSA Web server to generate all the examples in this book. The NCSA Web server was one of the first Web server applications available for the World Wide Web. Perhaps the most common one now is the Apache Web server, which is freely available for both Windows and UNIX from the following site:

www.apache.org

> The term "Web server" is often used to refer to either the Web server program or the computer that runs it. This book will use the term "Web server" when referring to the program and "Web server's computer" when referring to the computer to avoid confusion.

The NCSA Web server was the predecessor of the Apache Web server, and unless otherwise noted you can assume that the examples should run on either Web server.

## Documenting the Development

So how do you advance a technology that no one really owns? Through cooperation. The protocols and procedures that form the backbone of the Internet infrastructure are decided on by committee and virtually anyone can participate. In short, the Internet is managed by a large body of loosely organized professionals who donate their time and energy to the further development of the Internet.

In the early days of the ARPANET, the technical infrastructure was researched and embellished by the small number of scientists and businesses that created it. Communication and collaboration on pertinent technical issues was performed by publishing simple documents and soliciting comments. These documents were referred to as Request for Comments.

## The RFC Series

RFC (Request for Comment) documents represent the official publication channel for Internet standards and other related publications of interest to the Internet community. The series of RFC documents began in 1969 as part of the original ARPANET project and continue today as the principal steering mechanism for defining and improving the Internet.

RFCs address a wide range of topics. You will find research papers about early protocols and procedures as discussed by the founders of the Internet and the actual standards that have defined and shaped the Internet throughout the years. Each document in the RFC series is assigned a unique document number that increments sequentially. As of the writing of this book, over 2,700 RFC documents have been published since the first one, RFC 0001, dated April 7, 1969. These documents not only serve to define the Internet as it exists today but can give a historical perspective of its evolution.

RFC documents are maintained in the public record and available from a number of repositories on the Internet. You may retrieve RFCs using a variety of document retrieval systems such as ftp, gopher, or the World Wide Web. One such location for viewing the RFC repository with your Web browser is

   http://www.faqs.org/rfcs/rfc-verbose.html

Several categories have been defined to help delineate an RFC's purpose. Each RFC is clearly labeled with its associated category, and these categories form several subseries of documents that are of particular interest.

Some RFCs document actual Internet standards and form the STD subseries, which defines current Internet standards. When RFCs specify an Internet standard, they are given an additional STD*xxx* number but still retain their RFC number and place in the RFC series.

Other RFCs seek to define the best current practices for the Internet. These documents are assigned an additional BCP*xxx* number and form the BCP subseries of documents, which defines the best current practices for the Internet. Like the STD documents these BCPs also retain their RFC number and place in the original RFC list. RFCs that do not fall into the BCP or STD series are informational in nature and are published within the category of "Informational or Experimental."

### The Internet Standards Track

Those RFCs that are intended to document Internet standards now follow a rigorous standards process. This process is known as the Internet Standards Track and is currently documented by RFC 2026. This process attempts to ensure technical accuracy; prior implementation and testing; and clear, concise documentation while being as timely as possible. There are four levels of maturity that a document must progress through in order to be elevated to the level of an Internet standard.

**Internet Draft**—During the development of a specification, draft versions of the document are made available to the Internet community for informal review and comment. A specific action by the Internet Engineering Steering Group is required to move the document to the next stage in the process.

**Proposed Standard**—A draft elevated to the level of proposed standard is generally stable, well-understood, and has received significant community review. However, during the proposed standard stage, further experience may result in modification of the specification or possibly even retraction before it advances to the next level.

**Draft Standard**—In order for a proposed standard to be elevated to a draft standard, it must be reduced to practice. Two independent and interoperable implementations from different code bases must be developed demonstrating successful operational experience. Elevation to draft standard level is a major advance in status and indicates a strong belief that the specification will be useful.

**Internet Standard**—Standards are only elevated to this level after significant implementation and operational experience have been obtained. Internet standards are characterized by a high degree of maturity and a generally held belief that they provide significant benefit to the Internet community.

An Internet standard is assigned an RFC number along with a STD*xxx* subseries number that defines it as part of the Internet standards. Modifying RFC documents is not permitted once they are published. In order to change an existing Internet standard, or any RFC for that matter, subsequent RFCs that supersede or elaborate on the previous RFCs are submitted. If adopted, the new RFC will make the old RFC obsolete. The obsolete RFCs are never removed from the system, so the lineage of the current documents is always preserved.

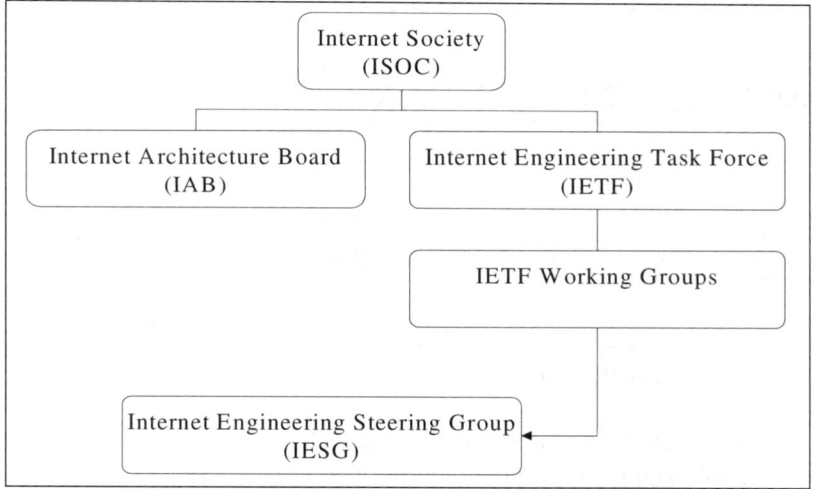

**Figure 1-12** Groups Responsible for Promoting Internet Technology

When the original ARPANET contained just a few nodes and the number of principals involved could be counted on your fingers, it was relatively simple to keep up with the proposals. As of the writing of this book, several organizations exist to facilitate the further advancement of the Internet. Figure 1-12 depicts the hierarchy of these organizations. At the top of the tree is the Internet Society.

The Internet Society (ISOC) is a professional membership society dedicated to maintaining the viability and global scaling of the Internet. Its membership consists of more than 150 organizations and 6,000 individual members from more than 100 countries. Many of these members have been instrumental in the creation of the Internet while others represent entrepreneurial blood looking for new and exciting ways to profit from the technology.

The ISOC provides leadership in addressing issues that confront the future of the Internet. It is also the organizational home for several other groups responsible for establishing Internet standards. These groups include the Internet Engineering Task Force (IETF), the Internet Architecture Board (IAB), and the Internet Engineering Steering Group (IESG).

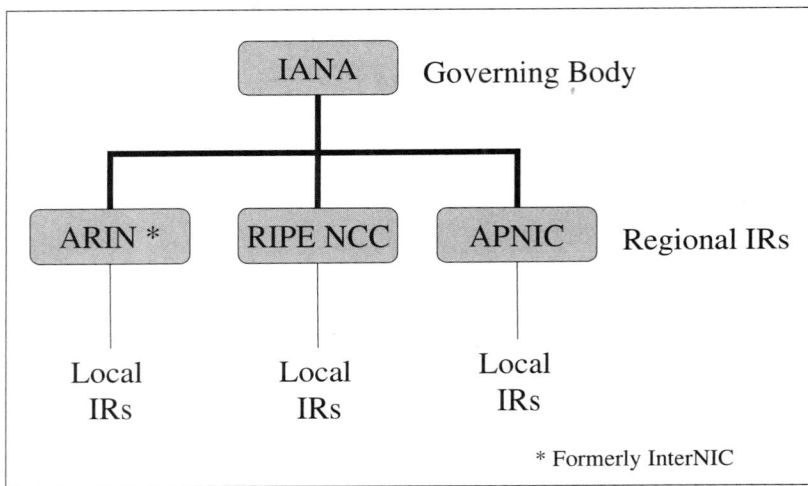

**Figure 1-13** Hierarchy of Internet Naming Authorities

The Internet Architecture Board acts as the technical advisory group to the ISOC. It provides oversight for the architecture of protocols and procedures used by the Internet. The IAB is responsible for editorial management of the RFC document series.

The Internet Engineering Task Force provides a forum for working groups to coordinate their work associated with the development of new standards and protocols. The IETF was established in 1986 to facilitate coordination and communication among contractors for DARPA (Defense Advanced Research Projects Agency) working on the ARPANET. Since that time, it has grown into a large international body concerned with the smooth operation of the Internet today and the future enhancements of tomorrow.

The bulk of the work done by the IETF is performed in working groups aligned more or less along functional boundaries or areas. Each area is led by one or more area directors. Together, along with the chair of the IETF, these area directors form the Internet Engineering Steering Group (IESG). Most of these working groups have a finite lifetime. Once they achieve their objective, they disband. As the technology changes, so will the areas defined in the IESG. The current areas are shown in Table 1-4.

**Table 1-4** Current Areas of the IESG

| Applications | Routing |
| --- | --- |
| Internet | Security |
| IP: Next Generation | Transport |
| Network Management | User Services |
| Operational Requirements | |

## Anyone Can Join

There is no official membership to a working group. The closest thing to a membership list is the mailing list established for each working group. In order to participate in a working group, you simply subscribe to the mailing list. In addition, anyone may attend a working group meeting so long as they cover their own expenses. For additional information you can check out each of these organizations further at the Web sites listed in Table 1-5.

**Table 1-5** Links to Internet Steering Organizations

| Organization | Web Site Address |
| --- | --- |
| Internet Society | www.isoc.org |
| Internet Engineering Task Force | www.ietf.org |
| Internet Architecture Board | www.iab.org |
| Internet Engineering Steering Group | see IETF Web site |

In addition to these Web sites, Table 1-6 contains some of the current RFC numbers that deal with the organizations discussed in this chapter. If you are interested in attending one of the IETF meetings, you should definitely read RFC 1701. This document presents a somewhat humorous account of what first-time attendees should expect.

## Address Management

An obvious question at this point is, "Who assigns Internet addresses?" Needless to say, if multiple computers on the Internet used the same IP address, the results would be just as disconcerting as if someone had your same home mailing address. It would be difficult to get messages to their proper destination.

**Table 1-6** Related RFCs

| | |
|---|---|
| 1601 | Charter of the Internet Architecture Board (IAB) |
| 1701 | The Tao of the IETF |
| 2026 | The Internet Standards Process |

Fortunately, there are governing bodies in place to take care of assigning unique addresses to every computer on the Internet. Until late 1998, the Internet's technical administration was performed by or on behalf of the United States government. As of the writing of this book, these governing bodies had been arranged in a hierarchical fashion as shown in Figure 1-13.

At the top of the tree is IANA (Internet Assigned Numbers Authority), which has authority over all number spaces used in the Internet. IANA allocates portions of the Internet address space to regional IRs (Internet Registries), which are assigned large geopolitical areas such as continents. These regional IRs are responsible for the allocation of Internet address space in their specific regions. The regional IRs, in cooperation with IANA, may create local IRs. These local IRs are usually at the national level and have the same roles and responsibilities as the regional IRs for their specific geographic regions.

The three regional Internet Registries shown in Figure 1-13 are the American Registry for Internet Numbers (ARIN, formerly known as InterNIC), responsible for the assignment of Internet numbers in North America; Réseaux IP Européens Network Coordination Centre (RIPE NCC), the Internet Registry organization for Europe; and the Asia Pacific Network Information Centre (APNIC), the Internet Registry organization responsible for the Asia Pacific region.

As this book goes to press, a new movement is afoot to privatize the technical administration of the Internet. A new nonprofit organization known as the Internet Corporation for Assigned Names and Numbers (ICANN) has been created to take over the activities previously performed by IANA. For more information about the privatization of the Internet, contact the Web sites listed in Table 1-7.

**Table 1-7** Links to Internet Governing Bodies

| Organization | Web Site Address |
| --- | --- |
| Internet Assigned Numbers Authority (IANA) | www.iana.net |
| Internet Corporation for Assigned Names and Numbers (ICANN) | www.icann.net |
| American Registry for Internet Numbers (ARIN) | www.iab.net |
| Réseaux IP Européens Network Coordination Centre | www.ripe.net |
| Asia Pacific Network Information Centre | www.apnic.net |

## Who Uses the Web?

One of the issues facing many application programmers on the Web today is identifying with their audiences. The Internet is growing at such a rapid pace that it is impossible to determine the number of computers that are actually connected to it at any given time. What is rather obvious is that the World Wide Web is one of the largest uses of the Internet today.

Every day new users are trying their hand at surfing the Web. Many of these new users have no knowledge of the other, more complex services that the Internet has to offer. They simply bring up their browser and start clicking on links as they navigate the world of information that is available. This is the true beauty of the World Wide Web. It brings information to you at the click of a button.

So who is using the World Wide Web? According to the tenth WWW user survey conducted by GVU (Georgia Tech's Graphic, Visualization, and Usability Center) in 1998, 33.6% of the respondents were female. The average age of those responding to the survey was 37.6. The largest category of respondents (47.6%) was married, and the average income of those who responded to this question was $57,300.

You can view the results of previous (and check for future) surveys at

http://www.cc.gatech.edu/gvu/user_surveys/User_Survey_Home.html

## Chapter Summary

- No one owns the Internet. It consists of a large number of interconnected, autonomous networks that connect millions of computers across the world.
- These networks support host-to-host communication through voluntary adherence to open protocols and procedures. The underlying premise of the Internet is that connection is its own reward.
- The Internet was begun in 1969 as the ARPANET and was initially funded by the Advanced Research Projects Agency (ARPA) of the U.S. government.
- Internet standards and best practices are documented in the Request for Comments series of documents that also began in 1969. These documents may be found at any number of sites around the world.
- The principal organizations responsible for the further advancement of the Internet are the ISOC (Internet Society), which is the organization home of the Internet Engineering Task Force (IETF) and the Internet Architecture Board (IAB).
- There are many services available on the Internet for document retrieval. The World Wide Web is just one of these services.
- The World Wide Web is based on the long-standing client-server model, where one server handles requests from numerous clients. The principal advantage to this model is the consolidation of resources into a single location for use by multiple users.

# Chapter 2

## The Common Gateway Interface

The last chapter made a clear distinction between the Internet and the World Wide Web. The Internet is a network of networks that connects an ever increasing number of computers together across the world. These computers provide a number of services with one of them being the World Wide Web.

Most readers of this book, regardless of their background, have probably used the World Wide Web for a variety of reasons. You have no doubt accessed Web pages that return dynamic content such as stock reports, weather services, Internet shopping carts, or statistics on your favorite sports team.

One thing all these sites have in common is that the information being requested can change over a given period of time. In the case of a stock report, the information can change from minute to minute. So how does this information get translated into those dazzling Web pages you see when you visit your favorite spot on the Internet? The answer is CGI programming.

*Common Gateway Interface* (CGI) refers to a particular type of program, known as a gateway program. These gateway programs are the backbone of many Web sites running on the World Wide Web today. There is nothing magical about CGI programs. They are just programs with a few special rules about where they get their input and how they deliver their output. Writing CGI applications is easy, can be fun, and adds impressive dynamic content to your Web site. Once you understand the simple rules that a CGI program must follow, you will be generating your own dynamic Web pages in no time at all.

This chapter will review two types of Web transactions: static transactions that do not require a CGI program and dynamic transactions that do. You will learn the rules by which a CGI program obtains information from and passes information to the Web server.

In addition to this you will learn about the underlying communication protocol of the World Wide Web, HTTP, which stands for HyperText Transfer Protocol. Just as TCP is a method of formatting messages that travel across the Internet, HTTP is an application layer protocol that is used to format messages on the World Wide Web. The CGI program is responsible for producing an HTTP-formatted message to return to the Web browser that made the request.

## What's in a Name?

Before getting started it's important to clear up a little confusion about what you call CGI code once it's written. You might notice that throughout this book the terms "CGI program" and "CGI script" are used interchangeably. CGI code can be written in a multitude of languages. You can use high-level languages that must be compiled or simple shell scripting languages such as *cshell* or *korn shell*. This makes it more obvious to call the compiled versions "programs" and the latter "scripts."

With sophisticated scripting languages, such as Tcl, you will often hear the two phrases used interchangeably for the same CGI code. The new generation of scripting languages has many of the programming constructs of compiled languages but does not require compiling. This simplifies and speeds up the development process but also makes it more difficult to draw the line as to what to call them.

So basically this author is not critical about what to call the code and will use the terms "script" and "program" interchangeably in this book. After all, what's in a name? Having said that, now we can get down to the business of learning what CGI programs are all about. But where should we start? One of the best ways to understand what a CGI program is, is to understand what it is not.

# Analyzing Web Transactions

Not all transactions on the World Wide Web require CGI programs. In fact in its infancy most of the information available on the World Wide Web was contained in static documents that required no CGI program at all. The user would click on a link pointing to a static document, and the Web server would retrieve the document and return it to the Web browser.

## Static Web Transactions

Figure 2-1 illustrates a static Web transaction that does not require a CGI program. The user selects a document to be retrieved, and the Web server retrieves the document and returns it to the requesting Web browser.

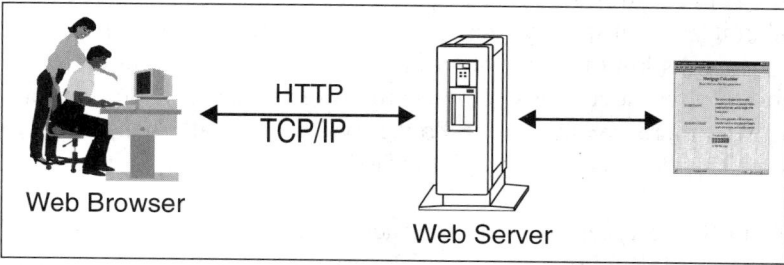

HTTP
TCP/IP

Web Browser

Web Server

**Figure 2-1** Static Web Transaction

Just as people must speak the same language in order to understand each other, the Web browser and Web server must speak the same language in order to send messages back and forth. The language that computers speak on the World Wide Web is known as *HTTP*, or HyperText Transfer Protocol. HTTP defines how messages sent between Web browsers and Web servers are formatted. An HTTP message comprises simple ASCII text and will be discussed in more detail later in this chapter.

When we talk about Web transactions, we usually speak in terms of requests and responses. It is assumed that both the request and response consist of an HTTP-formatted message.

In the World Wide Web, the Web browser will typically generate a request, and the Web server will provide a response. The request generated by the Web browser contains information such as the address of the computer that originated the request, the type of browser used, and, ultimately, the name of the document being requested. The Web server's response will be any message contents returned by the Web server, such as the formatted page to be displayed by the browser, along with a status indicator that indicates if the request was processed successfully.

The browser's request is sent to a Web server that resides at a specific IP address. The Web server is typically running on another computer on the Internet but could be located on the same machine as the Web server. It is the job of the Web server to wait for these requests and, once received, process the requests and return the requested information. In the case of a static document, the Web server need only read the file and return it to the Web browser.

Static documents are typically written using Hypertext Markup Language (HTML). HTML allows you to define how text and graphics will appear on a page. With it you can specify font size and color; create tables of data; build form elements such as buttons, text input areas, and list boxes; and create *hyperlinks* that point to other documents somewhere on the Internet. If you are not familiar with HTML, there are numerous books available on the subject at your local bookstore. This book contains a brief HTML reference in Appendix A.

Once again, these types of static transactions require no additional code at the Web server's end. But how does the Web server know it has received a request for a static document? By the file extension. The Web server will look at the file extension to see if the file requested is a static document or a program. Typically, static documents are saved with .html file extensions, and CGI programs are either saved in a special directory or with a .cgi extension. You configure your Web server for the specific file extension rules that you want it to follow. Configuring you Web server to recognize these file types is defined in more detail in Chapter 3.

## Dynamic Web Transactions

As the World Wide Web matured, users became more sophisticated and began demanding a wider range of services, such as the ability to query databases or order products on line using secured communication to process their credit cards.

Because it would be nearly impossible to design a Web server capable of handling any request a user could imagine, the Web server is kept fairly simple, and the burden of accessing these external resources is left to CGI programs.

As an example, let's say the user wants to access an on-line database that keeps historical information about stock market values. In this case the link selected by the user would point to a CGI program rather than a static HTML document. The Web server would then execute the CGI program and make whatever data was passed to it by the client available to the CGI program.

The purpose of the CGI program would be to interrogate a database of stock prices and return specific information requested by the user. Because this data can change as frequently as the stock market changes, the program must be able to access the database whenever the client requests the information in order to return the most up-to-date information.

Figure 2-2 illustrates a typical dynamic Web transaction involving a gateway (CGI) program. Here the Web server turns over the request to the gateway program, which then accesses the database for the requested information. Once the information is retrieved from the database, the gateway program formats it on the fly, typically into an HTML-style document, and returns it to the Web server. The Web server then passes the information back to the Web browser that requested it.

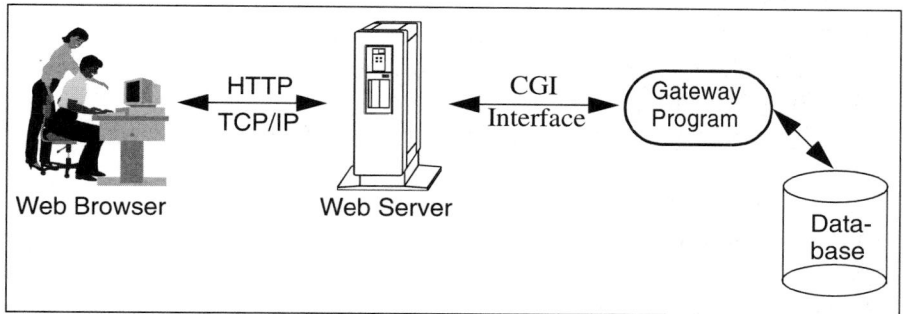

**Figure 2-2** Dynamic Web Transaction

In most cases the user of the Web browser does not notice a difference between a link to a static HTML page or a link to a CGI program that executes on the Web server's end. He or she simply clicks on a link or hits the submit button after filling in an HTML form and expects to get the requested information.

The information returned by the CGI program must be formatted as an HTTP-type message because this is the protocol used to carry messages over the World Wide Web. The CGI program can also return document types other than HTML. For instance, it can return a *gif* or *jpeg* image file or perhaps sound bites or movie clips. Typically, these file types are enclosed inside an HTML-formatted document, but this is not necessary.

There is normally some data associated with the request from the Web browser. In our stock price example, the name of the stock in question would be required. The data may be associated with a form that the user was required to fill out or may be contained in the link itself, placed there by the Web page designer. In either case the Web browser takes this information, packs it up into an HTTP-compliant message, and ships it off to the Web server.

The CGI program must have access to this information before it can process the request. This is where the CGI specification comes in. In order for two programs to communicate, there must be some ground rules about how the communication will take place. This is exactly what the CGI specification provides for CGI programs.

So now we understand two of the three words in Common Gateway Interface, because it is a defined interface for gateway programs to communicate with Web servers. So what's "common" about it? These gateway programs often encompass a tremendous amount of work. As is the case with most computer applications these days, there are several varieties of Web servers that run on a variety of computer platforms running a variety of operating systems, such as UNIX, Linux, Windows NT, and so on. The programmers writing the gateway programs want these gateway programs to be portable among different platforms and Web servers. In order for this to occur, the interface that the Web server uses to communicate with the gateway programs would have to be the same across these different platforms. This prompted the Common Gateway Interface standard to be proposed and adopted. The specification dictates how a Web server, regardless of make or model, can communicate with gateway programs.

The most important aspect of the CGI specification is that it allows you, as the CGI programmer, to write CGI programs that will work with different Web servers on different platforms running different operating systems. Additionally, because the CGI specification does not dictate the language to be used, programmers are free to choose languages that fit their needs.

# The CGI Interface

Once again, CGI stands for Common Gateway Interface and defines how a Web server communicates with CGI programs. An important point to remember is that the CGI standard is an interface specification only. It describes an interface between a Web server and an external application allowing information to be exchanged between the two programs. The CGI standard does not specify how a Web server operates or dictate the language that CGI programs will be written in.

Furthermore, the CGI standard does not describe how information is communicated between a Web browser and a Web server. This is dictated by HyperText Transfer Protocol, discussed later in this chapter. The CGI specification defines how the Web server and the CGI program communicate with each other. The HTTP specification describes how the Web server and the Web browser communicate with each other. It is important to understand the role of each of these specifications when writing CGI programs.

As just stated, the CGI standard does not dictate the programming language to be used when writing CGI applications. CGI programs can be written in a variety of languages including C, C++, Perl, and Tcl. Many people immediately think Perl when they hear the term "CGI," and even those familiar with coding in Web environments may not be aware that other languages are available for the same task. Not only is Tcl well suited for CGI coding, but in some ways it can be superior. Some of the strengths of the Tcl language are summarized here.

- Tcl has a rich set of file handling and string manipulation functions that make it ideal for writing gateway programs.
- Tcl contains most of the standard constructs of higher-level languages like C. In fact Tcl looks a lot like C so it's easy to transition C programmers to Tcl.
- Tcl has an extension known as Tk, which is a very powerful widget library for creating graphical interfaces. This is not directly related to CGI programming but is used by the Tcl Web browser plug-in, which allows the same functionality of Java applets to be created with the Tcl language.
- Tcl has a Web browser plug-in that allows Tcl/Tk code to be embedded directly inside HTML documents. This is just like Java in that you have a full interpreter running inside the browser.
- The Expect extension to Tcl was designed for automating communication with interactive processes. This feature makes it easier to write CGI pro-

grams that can invoke interactive shell commands such as *su* or *rlogin* to remotely log in as a different user.

- Tcl is free, well supported, and cross-platform compatible on Macs, PCs, and UNIX-based machines.
- Tcl is a very readable language and is easy to learn. It is well documented with printed material available at most local bookstores to help you learn the Tcl language. Information on writing CGI code in Tcl is less common, which is the primary reason for writing this book.

> The CGI specification describes how a CGI program can communicate with a Web server; it does not specify the type of language to be used in writing the program.

Under the HTTP specification, there are several prescribed methods for a client to pass information to a server. The two most common methods are GET and POST. The client determines the type of method to be used when generating a request. It turns out that CGI programs receive their information from the Web server in different ways for a GET or POST message.

### The GET Method

The GET method is short and there is little overhead involved. The actual intention of the GET method is to request information from the server, not to alter the server's state. However, there is no enforcement of this concept because the HTTP specification has no way to prohibit a CGI program that receives a GET request from altering the state of the server. It is therefore left up to the CGI programmer to adhere to this suggestion.

When the GET method is specified, the information from the Web browser is passed to the Web server in the query string portion of the URL. This is the portion of the URL that follows the address of the destination Web server. It is separated from the address by a question mark character as shown here:

http://DBinTheSky.com/search.cgi?query_string

This URL would access the fictitious Web site DBinTheSky.com and execute the search.cgi program. The form information, referred to as the query string, would be appended to the URL, following the ? character. In our earlier example of the stock price database, the query_string variable would contain the name of the stock being queried.

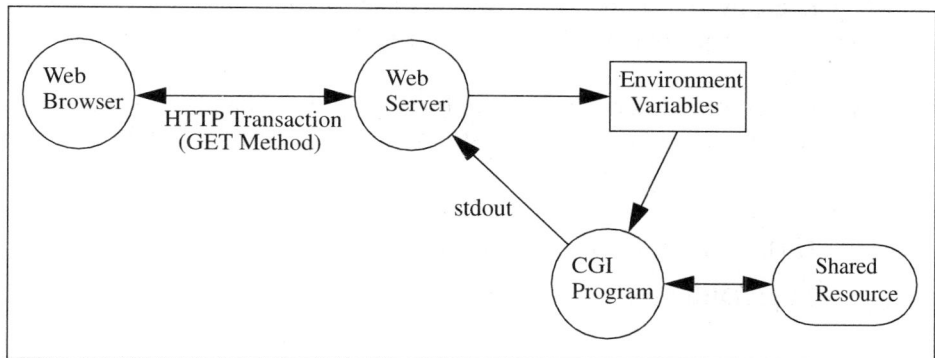

**Figure 2-3** The GET Method

Because the CGI program needs this information, the Web server must have a way to pass the contents of the query string to the CGI program. In the case of a GET method, the server takes this information and places it into an environment variable.

Environment variables are global variables that are accessible to any process (programs) running inside a defined process space. It is the job of the Web server to decide what process space the CGI program will run in and create the necessary environment variables in that space before executing the CGI program. Coincidently, the environment variable that holds the data contained in the query_string section of the URL is called QUERY_STRING.

 Some operating systems place limitations on the length of environment variables so caution should be exercised when using this method to send large amounts of data from your Web browser's page. If you need to send large amounts of data, use the POST method described in the next section.

The QUERY_STRING environment variable holds a series of name/value pairs. When you enter information into an HTML form, you normally type some text into a field on the form or click on a radio-style button to select one of several possible options. Each field in the form has a name assigned by the form designer. This becomes the name attribute of the name/value pair. The value you enter into the form becomes the value portion of the name/value pair.

The query string portion of an URL follows a prescribed format where white space is prohibited. What follows this is a series of name=value statements separated by the ampersand (&) character. White spaces are replaced with + characters. The content of the query_string is case sensitive.

As an example, if our hypothetical form had a field named *stock* and you entered the value *sure winner*, the query string would contain the following string:

```
stock=sure+winner
```

The URL submitted to the server would appear as follows:

http://DBinTheSky.com/search.cgi?stock=sure+winner

When this request is sent, the Web server will extract the query string portion of the URL and place the contents into an environment variable called QUERY_STRING. The Web server then invokes the specified CGI program, which must then parse the QUERY_STRING variable, separate the name/value pairs at each & character, and replace + characters with spaces. The CGI program then has all the form data passed from the Web browser and may do whatever is required to fulfill its purpose for being there in the first place. Figure 2-3 illustrates how data flows to and from a CGI program during a GET request.

First the Web server receives an HTTP message. This message contains all the form data entered by the user, formatted according to the HTTP specification. The Web server analyzes the data and determines that it needs to execute a CGI program. Prior to executing the CGI program, the Web server creates the QUERY_STRING environment variable and places all the name/value pairs received from the Web browser into this variable.

The Web server may also create additional environment variables to pass extra information to the CGI program that may have been communicated in the GET request. We will discuss some of these additional environment variables later in this section.

Once the Web server has created the necessary environment variables, it invokes the CGI program. One of the first things that the CGI program must do is access the proper environment variables. The QUERY_STRING environment variable is oftentimes the only one the CGI program needs to access because it contains all of the form data that was submitted by the Web browser in a GET transaction.

Tcl provides easy access to these environment variables through an array named env. Accessing an environment variable is as simple as reading an element from this array. For example, the QUERY_STRING environment variable can be accessed by simply reading $env(QUERY_STRING). As an example, you can set a variable called form_data to contain the information in the QUERY_STRING environment variable with the following command:

```
set form_data $env(QUERY_STRING)
```

Because the data in QUERY_STRING is encoded, it is necessary to decode the information to break it up into its various field names and values. Tcl provides the regexp command for just this purpose. The regexp command allows regular expression substitution to be performed on any string. Appendix B describes many of the Tcl commands in detail including the use of the regexp command. Fortunately, the included cgi.tcl library allows for decoding of the QUERY_STRING variable with a single call to the cgi_parse routine. Please refer to Appendix C for information on the cgi_parse routine.

> QUERY_STRING name/value pairs are case sensitive. The purpose and case of each pair should be specified up front in some form of documentation that is easily understood by the CGI programmer and the Web page designer.

Once the CGI program extracts the information it needs from the QUERY_STRING environment variable, it may have the full resources of the Web server's computer at its disposal, as well as any peripheral hardware that might be connected to it. The services it can provide are almost unlimited and may range from accessing a database to perhaps retrieving a video frame from a camera mounted on the local interstate highway.

Ultimately, the CGI program will want to communicate some information back to the client (Web browser) that made the request. Because the Web browser expects an HTTP-formatted document back from the Web server, the CGI program must dynamically create the appropriate message and return it to the browser. This message typically contains HTML-formatted text but may include other types of data as well. Once again, dynamically formatting an HTML document is easily done through some simple calls provided in the cgi.tcl library. To return its response to the requesting Web browser, the CGI program writes to standard out, or stdout as it is referred to in Tcl and other programming languages.

Standard out is a communication path from the program to the outside world. When a program is invoked, the operating system normally assigns three communication channels to it. These are standard in, standard out, and standard error, or as they are typically abbreviated stdin, stdout, and stderr. Standard in is the typical communication path for a program to receive input from the outside world and is normally associated with the keyboard. Standard out is the typical communication path for a program to send information to the outside world and is normally associated with the video display. Standard error is the typical communication path for a program to communicate errors and is also normally associated with the video display.

These communications channels can be redirected, which is exactly what the operating system does to stdout before invoking the CGI program. As a result, anything written to stdout by the CGI program will be sent to the Web server, which in turn forwards it to the Web browser that made the request.

## The POST Method

In the case of the POST method, the Web server communicates the data received from the Web browser to the CGI program through its standard input stream, known as stdin, rather than through the QUERY_STRING environment variable. When the POST method is employed, the Web server will create an environment variable named CONTENT_LENGTH that specifies the number of bytes the CGI program must read from standard input.

So, the main difference with POST methods is that the CGI program reads the form data from standard in (stdin) rather than from the QUERY_STRING environment variable. This allows much longer data streams to be passed with the POST method than the GET method. Figure 2-4 illustrates how data flows for a POST transaction.

The POST method still requires the CGI program to access certain environment variables, such as CONTENT_LENGTH, set up by the Web server. Also, the CGI program still returns the dynamically created HTTP-formatted response by writing to its standard out stream. The real difference is that the principal information passed by the Web browser is now read from stdin rather than from the QUERY_STRING environment variable.

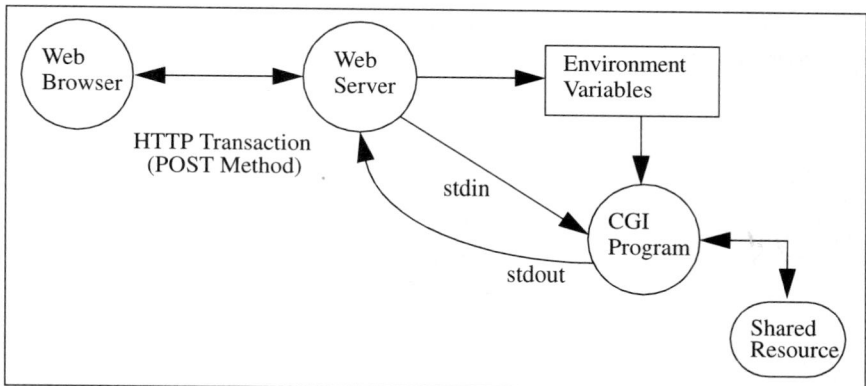

**Figure 2-4** The POST Method

The POST method is meant to change the state of the server and was intended to do things such as update bulletin boards, news groups, or databases. In addition the POST method is also intended to transmit longer messages, which is why the main message is attached as a message body rather than appended to the URL, because the latter scheme often has length restrictions imposed by the Web browser or the operating system running the Web server.

## Environment Variables

So let's summarize some of the key things we know so far about how data is communicated from the Web server to the gateway program.

- For the GET method the Web server places form data from the Web browser into the QUERY_STRING environment variable.
- For the POST method, the CGI program reads the number of bytes to be read from the CONTENT_LENGTH environment variable and then reads this number of bytes from standard input.

For most CGI programming tasks, this is all the information necessary to build effective, useful gateway programs. Oftentimes there will be additional information available to CGI programs. This information is provided to the CGI program through other environment variables initialized by the Web server. The CGI coding examples in this book will not deal with all of the environment variables listed here, but it will present sufficient examples so that the reader should feel confident exploring any of the others on his or her own.

Table 2-1 presents a list of these various environment variables and the information they contain.

**Table 2-1** CGI Environment Variables

| Variable | Description |
|---|---|
| AUTH_TYPE | Contains the authentication method used to validate the user. This variable is only set if the server supports user authentication and the program to be run is protected. |
| CONTENT_LENGTH | (POST method only) Contains the number of bytes to be read from standard input (stdin).<br>    If no data is being transferred through standard in, then this variable will be NULL. |
| CONTENT_TYPE | (POST method only) Contains the media type of the data to be read from standard input.<br>    There is no default value for this variable. If it is unset, then the program may attempt to determine the media type from the data received. If the type remains unknown, then application/octet-stream should be assumed. |
| GATEWAY_INTERFACE | This is the version of the CGI specification that the server is currently in compliance with. The value of this variable will take the form **CGI/revision**, where *revision* contains separate major and minor version numbers separated by a period. Leading zeros are to be ignored by programs and should not be generated by servers. |
| HTTP_* | Used to pass along additional information contained in HTTP header lines not covered by this defined set of environment variables. The resulting variable name will be prefaced HTTP_ followed by the header name. All dashes will be changed to underscores and all other characters are converted to upper case.<br>    The server is not required to create environment variables for all header lines that it receives. |

**Table 2-1** CGI Environment Variables (Continued)

| Variable | Description |
|----------|-------------|
| PATH_INFO | This variable contains any extra information that might have been appended to the URL by the client trying to access the program. This variable is rarely used because the use of form elements is much more efficient for transferring data. |
| PATH_TRANSLATED | The absolute pathname to the location of the program in the server's file system. This allows the Web server to map its files anywhere in the local file system. The CGI program can read this variable to determine where it currently lives in the server's file system and use this information to access local files it needs. |
| QUERY_STRING | The QUERY_STRING variable contains any information that was appended to the URL after a question mark character. This variable is set for requests submitted using the GET method. |
| REMOTE_ADDR | The IP address of the client machine sending the request to the server. |
| REMOTE_HOST | The fully qualified domain name of the client sending the request, if available. If it's not available, then this environment variable is not set and the REMOTE_ADDR variable can be used to obtain the requesting client's IP address. |
| REMOTE_IDENT | If the server supports remote user identification, then this variable will be set to the remote user name retrieved from the server. The contents of this variable should be used for logging only. |
| REMOTE_USER | Used to authenticate the user to the CGI program. Only present if an authentication method is used. In this case the authentication method will be specified by the AUTH_TYPE environment variable. |
| REQUEST_METHOD | Specifies the HTTP request method used in the message and contains GET, HEAD, or POST. Allows the CGI program to determine how the information is being passed from the server to the program. |

**Table 2-1** CGI Environment Variables  (Continued)

| Variable | Description |
| --- | --- |
| SCRIPT_NAME | A virtual path to the CGI program being executed in URL format. This information can be used by programs that contain references to themselves, known as self-referencing programs. |
| SERVER_NAME | This variable contains the host name, DNS alias, or IP address of the server that's responding to the request. |
| SERVER_PORT | This is the server's port number to which the request was sent. Servers can be assigned port numbers just as homes on a street have house addresses. The default port for Web servers is 80. |
| SERVER_PROTOCOL | The name and revision number of the protocol this request came in with. This takes the form protocol/revision. By convention, "protocol" is in uppercase. |
| SERVER_SOFTWARE | This variable contains the name and version number of the software running on the server that is answering the request from the client. |

Before you let this rather lengthy list of environment variables intimidate you, remember that you generally need only concern yourself with the few mentioned here. The cgi.tcl library contained in this book does all the work of determining if the transaction is a GET or a POST and presenting the form data in an easily accessible format.


## The HTTP Specification

The HyperText Transfer Protocol is the basis for communication on the World Wide Web today. This specification defines how transactions occur between a client and a server and how the messages are formatted. A transaction in this book is considered to be a request from a Web browser and a response from a Web server. Because the CGI program must deliver its contents wrapped in an HTTP message, it is important to understand the format of an HTTP response.

HTTP has been in use since 1990, and the HTTP 1.0 specification is defined in RFC 1945, dated May 1996. This RFC was actually just informational in nature and was never on the Internet Standards Track. Still, most browsers implement the 1.0 version of this protocol. As of June 1999, HTTP 1.1 has become the new Internet standard as described in RFC 2616. This version provides a more rigorous description of the HTTP specification.

This book is not intended to provide a rigorous study of the HTTP specification. It is intended to convey the necessary information about the specification that is pertinent to the generation of CGI programs in a dynamic Web environment. Unless otherwise stated, all the topics in this section will apply to either the 1.0 or the 1.1 specification. For those interested in reading the actual specification itself, you can refer to the following link:

> http://www.w3.org/Protocols/Specs.html#HTTP1.1

An important observation to make here is that the HTTP specification does not define how the information is physically transmitted between computers. It defines how the messages are formatted. HTTP could be used in other application environments as well because it is a generic application layer protocol. As you might remember from our discussion in Chapter 1, the application layer is the highest layer in the Internet protocol layers as shown in Figure 2-5.

In this case the applications in question are the Web browser at one end of the connection and the Web server at the other end. It is the Web server's job to interpret HTTP-formatted messages and provide the information to the CGI program as discussed in the previous sections. This means that we don't have to concern ourselves with all the intricacies of the HTTP specification as long as we understand the relationship between it and the CGI program.

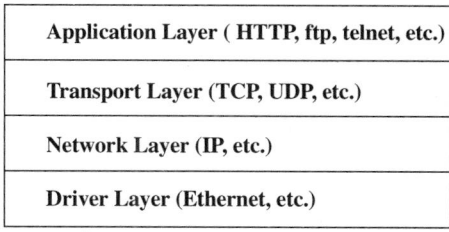

| Application Layer ( HTTP, ftp, telnet, etc.) |
| Transport Layer (TCP, UDP, etc.) |
| Network Layer (IP, etc.) |
| Driver Layer (Ethernet, etc.) |

**Figure 2-5** Protocol Layers

## A Stateless Protocol

The HTTP protocol is a generic, stateless application level protocol that can actually be used for a variety of purposes. Its most famous application, of course, is in the Web browsers and Web servers that many of us use daily. Understanding that HTTP is a stateless protocol is a key aspect of understanding some of the issues that CGI programmers are currently faced with. What this means is that HTTP does not provide any means for remembering what happened during the previous transaction. The burden of remembering what happened with a particular client in a previous transaction is left to the CGI program.

This is complicated by the fact that the CGI program is executed by the Web server and typically terminates once it has processed the current request. In order to remember what happened during this transaction, it must typically embed some information in its response to the Web browser that may be used the next time it is executed. This is typically done through the use of hidden fields in HTML pages or through a mechanism known as *cookies*. Both these methods will be discussed in more detail throughout this book.

It is not necessary in all CGI applications to remember a client's previous state. Our stock market database example earlier in the chapter only required a single transaction to fulfill the needs of the client. In this type of application, the CGI program comes to life, processes the request, and then exits. There is no need to remember any information because the request is handled completely with a single invocation of the CGI program.

In other applications this can be a considerable problem. Consider a shopping cart application, where users can browse in an Internet shopping mall and place items in their electronic shopping cart. Because each transaction is separate from the transaction that transpired before it, there must be some way to communicate this information back and forth. Once again, several methods for maintaining this type of information will be shown in this book.

As was mentioned at the beginning of this section, there are two parts to an HTTP transaction: a request and a response. In the typical World Wide Web scenario, the Web browser generates the request and the Web server generates the response. Let's first look at the HTTP request and then examine the HTTP response.

## The HTTP Request

In general it is not necessary to understand what an HTTP request looks like because the request is typically handled by the Web server and the resulting information is conveyed to the CGI program in the manner described by the CGI specification. However, because most of us like to know where things begin, it is useful to discuss the HTTP request before moving on to the HTTP response.

An HTTP request is simply an ASCII text message sent from a client to a server. The message has a well-defined format where the first line specifies the type of request being made, such as a GET or POST transaction. This line is followed by any number of header lines that may include additional information about the client making the request and the content of the request. These header lines are followed by a mandatory blank line, which may optionally be followed by a message body. The message body may be encoded, in which case the type of encoding will be specified in one of the header lines that precedes it.

The format of an HTTP message as described in HTTP 1.0 is MIME-like. MIME stands for Multipurpose Internet Mail Extensions and forms the rules by which Internet mail messages are sent. The MIME specification is currently defined in five different RFCs numbered 2045 through 2049. Much of the syntax of HTTP messages follows the MIME specification. In general an HTTP message follows the same rules as a MIME-compliant e-mail message but does not enforce all the rules required to be considered a truly MIME-compliant message.

The following example illustrates how a typical HTTP request might appear:

```
GET /johndoe/home.html HTTP/1.0
Referer: http://www.finduser.com/index/index.html
User-Agent: Netscape/4.0
Accept: image/gif
Accept: image/jpeg

.... if a message body is part of the message it would go here ....
```

The first line indicates the type of request, which in this case is the GET method. This method type is intended to retrieve information from the Web server without altering the server's state. The next item in this line is the address of the information to be retrieved, in URL format. In this request the URL is /johndoe/ home.html. Notice this is not a complete URL. The machine name has been omitted because the connection with the server has already been established before the message is sent. The last field of the request line specifies the revision of the HTTP specification used by the client making the request, which in this case is version 1.0.

Any number of header lines may follow this first line. These header lines contain additional information about the client and/or the message contents of the request. The *Referer* header contains the URL of the page that initiated the request. The *User-Agent* header line contains the name and version number of the client software that initiated the request. The next two *Accept* headers tell the server about the *media types* that can be handled by the client. The two headers are straightforward and tell the server that the client can handle *gif* and *jpeg* images.

An optional message body may be included in a GET transaction. This would most likely be the query string portion of the URL if any form data was appended to it. However, it is not necessary for a GET message to have a message body.

Table 2-2 summarizes the header types that may optionally appear after the required request line. This table should give the reader some insight as to the types of information that can be conveyed in an HTTP message as well as an appreciation for the complexities involved in writing an HTTP-compliant Web browser or Web server application.

**Table 2-2** HTTP Header Types

| Header | Description |
| --- | --- |
| Accept | Used to indicate what media type the client making the request can handle. This header is not actually part of the HTTP 1.0 specification but is in common use anyway. |
| Authorization | This header provides information that can be used by the server to determine if the client has the necessary access privileges to access secure areas. |
| Content-encoding | Tells the server that the message body is encoded in some way such as encryption or compression. |
| Content-type | Specifies the media type of the information contained in the message body. |
| Content-length | If the request contains a message body, this header type specifies the length, in number of bytes, contained in the message body. |
| Date | Indicates the date and time that the request was generated. |

**Table 2-2** HTTP Header Types  (Continued)

| Header | Description |
|--------|-------------|
| From | If the e-mail address of the user associated with the client is available, it will be provided with a From header. This information is not always available. |
| If-modified-since | Makes the request conditional to limit traffic over the Internet. This header contains time/date information and instructs the server to only return the requested information if it is newer than the date specified.<br><br>Because most static HTML pages don't change frequently and most browsers cache Web pages, this eliminates the need for the server to resend pages that have not changed. |
| MIME-version | Provides the version of the MIME specification used to generate the message body. |
| Pragma | Contains any additional information that the client wishes to provide to the server. |
| Referer | This header contains the URL of the page that initiated the request to the server in the first place. This word is intentionally misspelled as this is the way it is specified in the HTTP specification. |
| User-Agent | Contains the name and version of the client software being used to generate the request, which is generally some off-the-shelf Web browser application such as Microsoft's Internet Explorer. |

## The HTTP Response

Once an HTTP request has been received by the Web server, the server analyzes the message and determines what action needs to be performed. In the case of a request to execute a CGI program, the Web server is not responsible for generating the HTTP response, the CGI program is.

The HTTP response, like the request, is a simple ASCII text message. As with the HTTP request, the response has three sections. The first line is a status line that indicates the success or failure of the request. This line is followed by any number of header lines containing information about the message and the Web server that responded to the request. The header lines are optionally followed by a message body that is separated from the last header line by a mandatory blank line.

The following text shows how a typical response from an HTTP server might appear when accessing John Doe's Hello World page.

```
HTTP/1.0 200 OK
Date: Mon, 20 Jul 1998 13:35:21 GMT
Server: NCSA/1.4.2
Content-type: text/html
Last-Modified: Sat, 18 Jul 1998 11:21:00 GMT
Content-length: 111

<HTML>
<HEAD>
<TITLE>John Doe's Home Page</TITLE>
</HEAD>
<BODY>
<P></P>
<H1>Hello World</H1>
</BODY>
</HTML>
```

The first line indicates that the server generating the response conforms to the HTTP 1.0 specification. This is followed by a status of 200 and the brief textual description of its meaning: **OK**.

The remaining five header lines contain additional information about the Web server generating the response and the message contents. Most of this information is self-explanatory. The *Date* header indicates the time and date, in Greenwich mean time, as to when the response was generated. The *Server* header line contains the name and version number of the Web server software that generated the response. The *Content-type* header tells the receiving Web browser two things. The first is that a message body is included in the response, because this is the only case where the *Content-type* header will be present. The second is that the message body is in text/html format, which is what the browser likes to see. The *Last-Modified* header gives the date and time that the returned file was last modified, again in Greenwich mean time, and the *Content-length* header indicates how long the message body is.

In this case the HTTP response contains a message body that is the actual text of the HTML page required to display the Hello World message on the client's Web browser.

## Status Codes

There are a variety of published status codes that may be returned as part of the HTTP response depending on the success or failure of the request. The status codes are always three-digit numbers, where the most significant digit indicates the class of the status code and the remaining two digits refer to the actual status message.

There are currently five defined categories in the HTTP/1.1 specification, which take the form of 1*xx*, 2*xx*, 3*xx*, 4*xx*, and 5*xx*. Table 2-3 contains a brief description of the various classes.

**Table 2-3** HTTP Error Classes

| Class | Description |
|-------|-------------|
| 1*xx* | **Informational**—Indicates a provisional response from the server consisting of only the status line and optional headers. The HTTP/1.1 specification did not define this class so servers should never return this class of status code to an HTTP/1.0 client. |
| 2*xx* | **Successful**—This class indicates that the operation request was successfully received, understood, and accepted by the server. |
| 3*xx* | **Redirection**—Indicates that further action needs to be taken by the client in order for the request to be completed. |
| 4*xx* | **Client Failure**—Indicates the client appears to have made a mistake such as sending a malformed request or trying to access a nonexistent resource. |
| 5*xx* | **Server Failure**—This class of status code indicates that the server has encountered an error during its operation. The server should return an indication of what its error was and if it is temporary or permanent. |

Table 2-4 contains the actual status codes in numerical order along with the defined textual description that will accompany the response. This is the published list of the HTTP/1.1 specification.

As you can see from this overview of the HTTP protocol, there is a lot of underlying complexity to sending and receiving HTTP messages over the World Wide Web. Fortunately, the job of generating static or dynamic Web pages is considerably simpler than writing an HTTP-compliant Web browser or Web server. As a CGI programmer, you must have a working knowledge of the underlying format of an HTTP transaction because the output of your CGI programs must be an HTTP-compliant message.

**Table 2-4** HTTP Status Codes

| Status Code | Textual Description |
| --- | --- |
| 200 | OK |
| 201 | Created |
| 202 | Accepted |
| 203 | Non-Authoritative Information |
| 204 | No Content |
| 205 | Reset Content |
| 206 | Partial Content |
| 300 | Multiple Choices |
| 301 | Moved Permanently |
| 302 | Found |
| 303 | See Other |
| 304 | Not Modified |
| 305 | Use Proxy |
| 307 | Temporary Redirect |
| 400 | Bad Request |
| 401 | Unauthorized |
| 402 | Payment Required |
| 403 | Forbidden |
| 404 | Not Found |
| 405 | Method Not Allowed |
| 406 | Not Acceptable |
| 407 | Proxy Authentication Required |
| 408 | Request Time-out |
| 409 | Conflict |
| 410 | Gone |
| 411 | Length Required |
| 412 | Precondition Failed |

**Table 2-4** HTTP Status Codes  (Continued)

| Status Code | Textual Description |
| --- | --- |
| 413 | Request Entity Too Large |
| 414 | Request-URI Too Large |
| 415 | Unsupported Media Type |
| 416 | Requested Range Not Satisfiable |
| 417 | Expectation Failed |
| 500 | Internal Server Error |
| 501 | Not Implemented |
| 502 | Bad Gateway |
| 503 | Service Unavailable |
| 504 | Gateway Time-out |
| 505 | HTTP Version Not Supported |

## Chapter Summary

- CGI stands for Common Gateway Interface and dictates how a CGI program can exchange information with the Web server.
- No CGI program is required when a client is simply requesting an existing static HTML-type document from the Web server.
- The CGI specification does not dictate the language to be used. There are many languages appropriate for the generation of CGI programs, including C, C++, Perl, and Tcl.
- The CGI specification does not dictate the type of Web server software to be used.
- Following the CGI specification should allow your CGI programs to be transported easily from one environment to another regardless of the operating system or the Web server software being used.
- Because the output of a typical CGI program is normally formatted in HTML, the CGI programmer must be well versed in HTML and how to generate HTML documents dynamically.
- HTTP stands for HyperText Transfer Protocol and specifies how message packets are formatted in the World Wide Web.

- The HTTP specification does not define how messages are physically transmitted from the client to the server, or vise versa.
- When a Web server receives an HTTP GET message, it will place any form data into the QUERY_STRING environment variable.
- When a Web server receives an HTTP POST message, it will place the form data into the CGI program's standard input channel and indicate the number of bytes to be read with the CONTENT_LENGTH environment variable.

# Chapter 3

## Getting Started

This book contains numerous examples containing both HTML and CGI code. All of the examples are included on the enclosed CD. This chapter details the installation of the code provided on the CD. There are several requirements that must be met in order to run the examples, but they can be summarized in a few basic steps.

First, you must have access to a computer running a Web server, either NCSA or Apache. All of the code in this book was developed under AIX, a UNIX derivative, using an NCSA Web server but should run equally well on other flavors of UNIX running either NCSA or Apache.

Second, you must have the appropriate privileges to install software on the computer that contains the Web server. If you do not have permission to perform the installation, then you must recruit the help of your local system administrator or Web master.

Third, you must have a current version of Tcl installed on your machine. As of the writing of this book, the latest version of Tcl is 8.1, but new updates have been released about every three months. There are numerous sites where Tcl is available, but you might want to retrieve it from Scriptics at

http://www.scriptics.com

Tcl is available for a variety of platforms, but this book deals exclusively with the UNIX operating system, or any of its derivatives. Actually, the examples in this book were developed using IBM's AIX operating system, but any standard UNIX derivative should work. Because there are typically no binary distributions of Tcl readily available for most UNIX systems, you must download the source and compile it directly on the target platform. This is one disadvantage of dealing with the UNIX world, but it is made up for by the robust performance under these systems. So the first thing that we should tackle is installing Tcl.

## Obtaining and Installing Tcl

This section contains a summary of the installation steps necessary to obtain the Tcl source code and compile it into an executable program on your UNIX platform. The Web site at www.scriptics.com contains numerous informative pages about the organization of the package and how to obtain and install it. The following steps should get you up and running quickly, but if you experience problems, check out the helpful pages at Scriptics.

Download the UNIX version source code from www.scriptics.com or any of the many other sites available on the Internet. You will be downloading a single compressed file that contains all the source code necessary to build the executable version of Tcl. You should typically download this file directly to the directory where you want to do your build.

Because the file you will download is in a compressed format, you will have to decompress it with one of the commands listed in Table 3-1. This author normally chooses the tar.gz file type on UNIX platforms.

You should now have a subdirectory named with the version of the release in the directory where you downloaded the compressed file. Now change to the UNIX subdirectory, which is where you will do the actual compiling. For example, if you downloaded the tcl8.0.3 release into a directory named tclsource, you would change directories to /tclsource/tcl8.0.3/unix.

In this directory you will find a README file that contains more detailed instructions on compiling Tcl, including various options that are available. The installation described here is the easiest, most generic installation and should be sufficient to get you up and running quickly.

**Table 3-1** Commands to Decompress Files

| File Type | Command |
|-----------|---------|
| tar.gz | gunzip -c tcl8.1.1.tar.gz \| tar xf - |
| tar.Z | zcat tcl8.1.1.tar.Z \| tar xf - |
| .zip | unzip tcl811.zip |

From the UNIX subdirectory type **./configure**, which will generate all the necessary *make* files for the build. For those of you not familiar with make files, they contain the rules for how to compile a program. The configure command will evaluate your current system environment and create the appropriate make file for your system's configuration.

By default, the configure command will create a make file option that will install the compiled executables in the /usr/local directory. If you wish the installation to be performed to anywhere but the /usr/local default directory, you must use the --prefix option to the configure command to change the default installation directory. For example, if you want to have the code compiled in /tclstuff, you would execute ./configure --prefix=/tclstuff.

Depending on the speed of your system, the configure command might take anywhere from 30 seconds to several minutes to complete. Once the command completes, simply type make, which will compile the downloaded source files.

The configure command does not default to the GCC compiler. If you wish to compile Tcl under the GNU tool chain compiler, see the included README file in the UNIX subdirectory.

Type **make install** to distribute the Tcl binaries and support script files to the locations you specified to the configure command. The defaults for the installation directories are listed in Table 3-2.

**Table 3-2** Standard Distribution Directories

| | |
|---|---|
| Binary | /usr/local/bin |
| Support scripts | /usr/local/lib |
| Header files | /usr/local/include |

Of course in order to install Tcl to these directories you need to have write permissions on the installation directories or you will need to get your system administration people to help you.

If the build and the installation are successful, you should be able to go to the bin directory where the installation was performed and type **tclsh**. So, if you installed it to the default location of /usr/local, change directories to /usr/local/bin and type **tclsh**.

## Understanding Your Web Server's Configuration

Your Web server configuration will depend on which Web server program you have (that is, Apache or NCSA), as well as the particular version you may be running. For example, the NCSA Web server uses three configuration files, which should be located in the conf subdirectory of your NCSA installation directory. These files are access.conf, httpd.conf, and srm.conf. Earlier versions of the Apache Web server also had these same three files. The newer versions of Apache still have three files, but everything can be controlled from the httpd.conf file while leaving the other two files empty. The similarity stems from the fact that the Apache Web server was a spin-off of the NCSA Web server.

So, before you install the example code that comes with this book, you must first decide on the appropriate location for the code to reside. There are a couple ways to configure either Web server. The first way, which is preferred by many Web masters and system administrators, is to place all CGI programs underneath a single directory. You specify this special directory with the ScriptAlias directive in the server resource map file (srm.conf) on the NCSA server. On the Apache Web server this will be specified in the same file, if it exists, or may be specified in the httpd.conf file if you have elected to set it up this way.

```
ScriptAlias/cgi-bin/ /home/httpd/cgi-bin/
```

With the server configured in this manner and a user accessing the following URL (your-computer.com is the path to the machine running your Web server):

```
http://your-computer.com/cgi-bin/hello_world
```

the following program would be executed by the Web server:

```
/home/httpd/cgi-bin/hello_world
```

You are not limited to a single directory for your CGI programs. By specifying multiple ScriptAlias directories, you can place your CGI programs into more than one directory on the system.

```
ScriptAlias/cgi-bin//home/httpd/cgi-bin/
ScriptAlias/test-cgi-bin//home/httpd/test-cgi-bin/
```

The principal reason for placing all CGI programs under a few special directories is enhanced security. By placing all CGI programs in a few common directories, the system administrator has complete control over who can generate CGI programs and what CGI programs may be accessible to the outside world. A poorly written CGI program can allow malicious users to destroy data on your machine or corrupt control over all the CGI programs that are placed onto the system. This is generally the desired approach when publishing documents to the Internet.

The NCSA Web server also provides a way to execute CGI scripts based on their file extension rather than their physical location in the file system. The **AddType** also in the same srm.conf file allows you to set up execution of CGI programs based on the file extension. The most common file extension is .cgi, but the **AddType** directive could be set up to allow numerous file extensions to be executed as CGI programs. The following line would configure the Web server to execute files with .cgi, .sh, or .tcl to execute as CGI programs:

```
AddType application/x-httpd-cgi .cgi .sh .tcl
```

In most instances you will most likely need the assistance of your network administrator to ensure that the software is installed correctly and the Web server is configured appropriately.

## Installing the CD

Now that you have Tcl installed and the Web server configured appropriately, it is time to copy the contents of the enclosed CD to your Web server. The CD is divided into two directories. The first directory, named examples, contains all the HTML files and CGI scripts necessary to recreate the examples in the book.

The examples were built on a system where the Web server was configured to allow any file with a .cgi extension to be executed as a CGI program. In this type of environment, you can locate the examples directory anywhere that the UNIX permissions allow access from the Web server.

If your Web server is configured for a special cgi-bin type directory, then it will be necessary to install the examples directory in a subdirectory of this special directory.

The second directory on the enclosed CD is named packages and contains the various packages used by the CGI program examples. The cgi.tcl package, among others, is located in this directory. For the complete reference on the cgi.tcl package, please refer to Appendix C.

These packages are written in accordance with the Tcl package facility available in the 8.*x* versions of Tcl. This facility is a generic way to add modularity to your code and add version control to your packages. It also makes it easier for programs that want to use these packages to load them without having to know the location of the packages.

The packages directory should be installed on the computer where your Web server program is running. You must place the packages directory in a directory that is defined by the Tcl auto_path variable. This is due to the fact that the Tcl package require command will follow these paths to find the requested packages. The default paths are set relative to the installation directory specified when you built Tcl. Tcl normally expects to find packages in the *lib* subdirectory of the Tcl installation. To verify what the default paths are set to on your computer, simply execute the tclsh command and examine the auto_path variable as shown:

```
% set auto_path
/usr/local/lib/tcl8.1 /usr/local/lib
```

The auto_path variable is actually a list of pathnames to be searched for packages that are specified by the package require command. As you can see in this example, there are two paths defined from the installation, /usr/local/lib/tcl8.1 and the more generic /usr/local/lib.

If you need to locate packages in some other directory, you have a couple different options available: some better than others. The easiest option is to change the auto_path variable to contain your new directory path. To do this you would have to place a statement inside of your CGI program that updates the auto_path variable. The perferred method for doing this is to append the new path to the auto_path variable using the lappend command. Modifying the auto_path variable in this fashion does not overwrite the existing paths already defined, allowing other packages that may be located in these preexisting paths to still load properly. The disadvantage of this approach is that the CGI program must know where the packages live, which is not the intention of the package facility.

A second approach is to define an environment variable named TCLLIBPATH and set it equal to the new path that you want to append to the auto_path variable. When Tcl initializes, it will check this variable and append its contents to the auto_path variable for you. One trap here is that it is easy for you as a user to modify your own user profile, but typically CGI programs execute as another user. Therefore, for this approach to work, you must be able to modify the profile of the user that the CGI scripts will be executed under. More than likely you will have to get your system administrator to help you with this one; unless, of course, you are the system administrator, in which case this chapter is most likely a repeat of information that you are already well aware of.

## Using the cgi.tcl Library

One of the packages in the packages directory is the author's *cgi.tcl* package, which contains many procedures to help you parse the form data passed to you by the Web server, generate static HTML files, or dynamically return HTML documents back to the Web server making the request.

In order to use the cgi.tcl library package, you need only use the Tcl package require command to include it in your CGI script as shown:

```
package require cgi.tcl
```

If you do not specify a version number at the end of the command, Tcl will automatically load the most current version of the package. You may optionally specify a version number at the end of the command, and Tcl will use the version you specify, assuming it is available. If you choose not to specify a version as we have done in the preceding example, Tcl will use the latest version of the package available. Version 1.1 of the cgi.tcl package is provided in this book.

You can test the installation by manually bringing up the tclsh program and executing the package require command as shown:

```
% package require cgi.tcl
```

```
1.1
```

The version number returned from the command indicates that Tcl found the package successfully. To doublecheck you can execute the package names command to check what packages are currently available to the Tcl interpreter:

```
% package names
Tcl cgi.tcl
```

Tcl returns a list of the packages available to you. Notice that Tcl itself appears as a package named Tcl. With the package successfully installed, you are ready to start writing CGI scripts. As mentioned in the previous chapter, a CGI script is nothing more than a Tcl program that relies on the CGI standard to communicate with the Web server that invokes the script. If you are using the standard Tcl interpreter, you may use any Tcl command available to get your job done.

## Modularity and the Tcl Package Facility

As you begin to experiment with the cgi.tcl package provided, you will no doubt be tempted to sit down at the keyboard and begin coding immediately. A natural temptation is to start writing programs that include the cgi.tcl package and then just begin coding solutions to the problem at hand. This brings up the old proverb that the sooner you start coding, the longer the program will take to complete. This may sound contradictory at first but with a little analysis it makes sense.

A CGI program is just a program with some predefined rules about how it receives input and how it generates output. As such, the same goals of software engineering should apply. One of these principles is the use of reusable packages.

The cgi.tcl code provided in this book is written as a reusable package so it can be easily used by any CGI program you write. This improves your efficiency and dramatically reduces the time it takes to generate solutions to CGI coding problems. The cgi.tcl package should not be the only reusable package in your repertoire. It is a good idea to strive for the same level of reuse in the rest of the code you generate. When you sit down to analyze the requirements for a CGI program, look for modules of code that can be reused and then use the Tcl package facility to build these packages. In general, your program should be thought of as a collection of reusable packages with a little nonreusable code to hold the packages together. Figure 3-1 shows how this concept works.

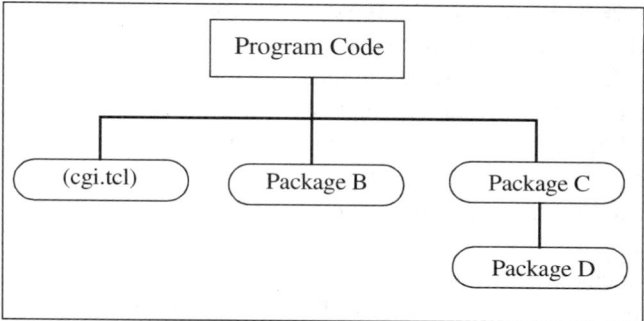

**Figure 3-1** Logical Layout for a CGI Program

The program code is the Tcl script file that contains a small amount of nonreusable code that is unique to the program. This program code will include any packages to be used by the program with the **package require** command. As Figure 3-1 shows, a CGI program would include the cgi.tcl package (Package A). The remaining packages would implement other logical functionality required by the CGI program. As an example, if the CGI program needed to access a database program, one of the packages might be a database interface package that allows a program to create, open, edit, and delete databases. In the mortgage calculator example a little later in this book, one of the packages provides the amortization routines. The goal should always be to maximize the reusable code and minimize the nonreusable code.

Packages may include other packages as shown in Figure 3-1. A little word of caution here: Nesting packages does not work well in earlier versions. So if you want to write packages that require other packages be sure you have the latest version of Tcl.

## Naming Conventions

Another good practice is the use of naming conventions. Because packages can be combined with any number of other packages to form a program, a serious potential for naming collisions exists when mixing and matching packages. A naming collision is when two globally available variables or procedures have the same name.

As an example, let's say you have a program that includes two packages. One package provides a small database written in Tcl and the other package provides a collection of telnet functions. Each of these packages might want to contain a procedure named open, which would have completely different functionality depending on which package you invoke it from. In the database package, the open command would open an existing database. In the telnet package, the open command would establish a telnet connection with some telnet server. These packages may have been developed by different engineers, and in both cases the open procedure made a lot of sense at the time. It's not until you mix the packages together that you have a serious naming collision problem.

This type of problem can be difficult to track down. Tcl is an interpreted language, which is neither compiled nor linked like C. This means that there is no linker to warn you about duplicate procedure names when you build your program. In fact Tcl will simply overwrite the current procedure definition with a newer one in the case where two files are loaded that contain duplicate function names. You will not receive any error until you attempt to call the procedure with improper arguments.

To avoid this problem you should assign your package a unique name and preface any global variable or procedure with this package name followed by an underscore character. As you review the code in the cgi.tcl library, you will see that each procedure begins with the characters cgi_. This naming convention helps eliminate problems. In the preceding discussion we could have prefaced each procedure in the database package with db_ and each procedure in the telnet package with telnet_. This would eliminate naming collision problems when the packages were combined at a later time. It is also much clearer when reading the code to see the names db_open and telnet_open. This can eliminate a lot of confusion when debugging programs at a later date.

This is the naming convention that the author has used successfully with various programming languages. Because Tcl 8.x also contains a way to group functions and variables together under a common namespace, it is worth talking about this for a moment. The namespace command allows you to create a separate namespace for a group of procedures and functions.

The development of proper coding styles and naming conventions early on will help reduce code maintenance down the road. There are several documents that deal with Tcl writing styles available on the World Wide Web. One of the best written and most complete is a document by Ray Johnson and can be found at the following link:

http://www.sco.com/Technology/tcl/README/styleGuide.pdf

## Namespaces

Tcl also provides a namespace command, which provides the ability to encapsulate multiple procedures and variables inside a common namespace. This is somewhat analogous to the way languages such as C++ provide for encapsulation of many function calls into a single object and allows for hiding local variables and functions.

Many new programs being developed today utilize the namespace feature in Tcl. At this point in time it is quite common to see the use of naming conventions as well as the use of the namespace concept combined inside the same program. Whatever your style, paying attention to naming issues up front will make it easier to combine your packages later on.

This brings up an interesting issue. Many people believe that when you wrap procedure calls inside a namespace, there is no need to use naming conventions because you can reference the command by its fully qualified name. This is fine as long as you always use the fully qualified name when referring to the procedure in question and do not import it into your current namespace. If you like to import procedures from a package into your current namespace, then you should continue to use naming conventions because it makes it easier to identify which packages the procedure calls you're using came from. If you don't use a naming convention and you import procedures from different packages, then you may get errors if you try to import commands that already exist in your current namespace. Of course you can use the -force option to force the namespace to overwrite existing commands, but this is a bad idea as well because you don't know which commands you may be overwriting. So, my recommendation is to always use the fully qualified name and do not use the import option to the namespace command, or use the import option and stick with the naming convention inside the namespace.

# Chapter Summary

- When installing Tcl on a UNIX environment, you will have to obtain the source code and compile on the platform where you wish to run it.
- Tcl releases are available from many sites around the world but Scriptics, run by the man that invented Tcl, is a good source for both Windows binary releases and UNIX source distributions.

- Compiling the source distribution is straightforward and only requires you to execute a few commands.
- The code in this book was designed under the NCSA Web server but should work equally well on an Apache Web server.
- You can configure your Web server to execute any file with a .cgi extension as a CGI program or restrict files to special directories that normally have a name like cgi-bin.
- The cgi.tcl library is written as a reusable package and allows for easy dynamic generation of HTML documents. It also provides commands to parse the form data passed to the Web server from the Web browser.
- The Tcl **auto_path** variable must be configured properly to be able to load packages without having to know their location.
- It is good to adopt some naming conventions early if your packages do not use the Tcl **namespace** command. If they do employ this command and you always use the fully qualified domain name, then the need for a naming convention is lessened.
- The use of the relatively new namespace facility in Tcl can alleviate name conflicts that can arise when you mix multiple packages in the same program.

# Chapter 4

## Hello World

This chapter will review several variations of the typical Hello World program, which is the cornerstone of every good programming book! Before proceeding you should ensure that the software on the enclosed CD has been installed according to Chapter 3, Getting Started, on page 59.

In the first version of our Hello World program, we will examine a static HTML page that simply displays the words "Hello World" on your Web browser. This example will be used to study the structure of a simple HTML document.

The next example will show how to dynamically generate the same HTML code using a simple CGI script that requires no form data. This program creates a dynamic HTML page that will cause the client browser to display Hello World. You simply point your browser to a page containing a link to the CGI program and it returns the "Hello World" message. This example will introduce you to a real working CGI program that is complete, although simple.

The last program covered in this chapter is a form-based version of the Hello World CGI program. The program will be generalized to accept any string input and a size specification. It will then return the HTML document that displays the specified text in the specified size. This example, though still simple, illustrates most of the aspects of a typical interactive CGI program that must obtain the required form data from the Web server according to the CGI specification, process the data, and then dynamically generate an HTML document to return to the client's Web browser.

## A Word about Tools

When faced with generating simple HTML documents, I prefer to use one of the available tools for constructing HTML documents that are available from your local software retailer. My preference is Visual Page by Symantec. This tool lets you construct rather complicated HTML documents with point-and-click ease. Most of the static HTML documents and code that will be illustrated in this book have been built using this tool.

Another invaluable aspect of a tool like this is that it lets you build rapid prototype pages that ultimately need to be constructed dynamically by your CGI program. This significantly reduces the brain power required during the implementation phase when you are trying to get your CGI program to spit out the necessary HTML code because you already have some example code to work with. With a few simple modifications to this static HTML code produced by your point-and-click Web tool, you can construct a Web template by capturing the whole text as a string and then inserting some Tcl variables into the code that will be replaced at runtime by the Tcl interpreter. Examples of all these techniques will be shown throughout the remainder of this book.

## Example 1: The HTML Version

No rocket science here. Using Visual Page, type **Hello World** in the main window. With a few more button clicks, you can specify the page title and the color of the text and background. Click the save button, and the tool creates the following code:

```
<!DOCTYPE HTML PUBLIC "-//W3C//DTD HTML 3.2//EN">
<HTML>
<HEAD>
<META HTTP-EQUIV="Content-Type" CONTENT="text/html;CHARSET=iso-8859-
1">
<TITLE>Hello World</TITLE>
</HEAD>
<BODY BGCOLOR="#FFFFFF">
```

```
<P></P>
<P>Hello World
</BODY>
</HTML>
```

What you see here is a complete static HTML document that displays Hello World on any browser that happens to receive it. The file would be saved in a directory on some Web server located somewhere on the World Wide Web. This file would typically have an .htm or .html extension that lets the Web server know that it is a static HTML document. When you click on a link that points to this document, the Web server checks the file extension, determines that it is a static HTML document, and then simply retrieves the HTML text contained in the document and returns it to you. Absolutely no CGI programming is required. So why show you? Just to have a baseline document to compare against the dynamically created version that we will do in the next example.

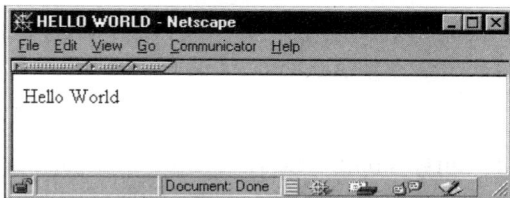

**Figure 4-1** Static HTML Hello World Page

Figure 4-1 shows the static HTML text displayed on Netscape's browser. Our challenge now is to duplicate this code, more or less, with a CGI program that dynamically produces the same kind of output using the included cgi.tcl library. The output of our CGI program should be identical to that of the static HTML version if we do everything correctly.

## The CGI Approach

There are a couple of things you must first decide when sitting down to write a CGI program. The first is where will it live on your Web server. Does it need to exist in the special cgi-bin directory, or has the Web server been configured to execute programs with .cgi extensions? These are issues that you must resolve with your Web administrator. See Chapter 3, Getting Started, on page 59 for more information on configuring your Web server.

Once you have your environment configured, the next thing you need to establish is what form data, if any, you will be processing. Remember from Chapter 3 that form data is a series of name/value pairs that contain the information the user entered into the fields on his or her Web browser form prior to submitting it. Because this example will not require any input, we will postpone the remainder of this discussion until the next example in which we will process some form data.

The goal here is reasonably straightforward: create a small CGI program that requires no input and generates the HTML code necessary to display Hello World.

```
#!/usr/local/bin/tclsh

# This script will create an HTML document that displays
# Hello World on the requesting browser.
package require cgi.tcl

cgi_header "Hello World" {BGCOLOR=white TEXT=black}
cgi_puts "Hello World"
cgi_end
return 0
```

As you can see, the program is fairly small. The first three lines of the program invoke the Tcl shell (tclsh) utilizing the existing paths defined in the current process environment. The next line loads the **cgi.tcl** package using the **package require** command. Because no version is specified, Tcl will load the most current version of the package. In this particular case the **cgi.tcl** package was located in the /usr/local/lib directory, which is one of the directories contained in the default **auto_path** variable shipped with Tcl. For example, if you accept the default options for building Tcl on a UNIX machine, you will set the following variables in the **auto_path** variable.

```
% set auto_path
/usr/local/lib /pt/usr/local/lib/tcl8.0
```

If you decide that you would like to locate the cgi.tcl directory in some other directory rather than the standard defaults in the **auto_path** variable, you just need to append the new pathname to the **auto_path** variable using the **lappend** command prior to issuing the **package require** command. The following two commands would set the **auto_path** variable to /tclstuff and then load the cgi.tcl library from this directory. A note of caution here: If a package by the same name exists in one of the other directories listed in the **auto_path** variable, you may pick this package up by mistake and get confusing results and errors.

```
lappend auto_path /tclstuff
```

```
package require cgi.tcl
```

The contents of the **auto_path** variable should now appear as shown:

```
/usr/local/lib /pt/usr/local/lib/tcl8.0 /tclstuff
```

You may be wondering why we did not simply change the **auto_path** variable with the **set** command. The answer is that the **set** command would overwrite the existing **auto_path** variable, and any existing packages that may have existed in the directories previously defined by the **auto_path** variable would not exist anymore. Therefore, the packages that exist in those directories could not be found by the Tcl interpreter. If this is acceptable behavior to you, then go ahead and overwrite the **auto_path** variable with the **set** command.

The actual code that generates the HTML code is only three lines, which are the three consecutive calls to the cgi.tcl library. Most CGI scripts that you will write using the cgi.tcl library will most likely follow this format.

```
call to the cgi_header routine
code that generates the body of the HTML document
call to cgi_end
```

The following code was generated by our simple CGI program and returned to the browser:

```
<HTML>
<HEAD>
<TITLE>Hello World</TITLE>
</HEAD>
<BODY BGCOLOR=white TEXT=black>
Hello World
</BODY>
</HTML>
```

The first procedure call, **cgi_header**, generates the first five lines of code that contain all the correct header lines for an HTML document. The **cgi_puts** simply writes Hello World to stdout and the **cgi_end** procedure call completes the document with the closing BODY and HTML tags.

This is about as simple as a CGI program can get, but it's not very practical. Most CGI programs will be invoked as the result of users submitting a form that they have filled out on their local browser. The form will contain various fields that hold important information the CGI program needs to access in order to get its job done. This data is typically called *form data*, and this is how we will refer to it throughout this book.

As was shown in Chapter 2, The Common Gateway Interface, this form data consists of any number of name/value pairs. Remember that the name is case sensitive. The CGI program must determine where to get this information from. For the GET method, the data needs to be extracted from the QUERY_STRING environment variable. In the case of the POST method, the CGI program must obtain the size of the data from the CONTENT_LENGTH environment variable and then read this amount of data from standard in. This will be discussed in more detail next.

There is no type checking available in the CGI world, so there must be close coordination between the designer of the HTML form and the CGI program that processes the form data. It is considered good practice to document the form data that is expected by the CGI program as a comment in the beginning of the file. It is also good practice to do some error checking on the form data that is received to ensure the form names received match what the CGI program expects.

Fortunately, the cgi.tcl library provides a simple call, **cgi_parse**, to get the name/value pairs regardless of how the data was passed to the Web server and place it into an array named CGI for use by the program. In this array the element name corresponds to the form name, and the value contained in this array element corresponds to the value entered by the user submitting the form. As an example, if the form contained an element named USER_NAME, which was meant to contain the name of the individual submitting the HTML form, the element cgi(USER_NAME) would contain the value of the USER_NAME field as it was filled out by the person submitting the request.

Another simple call, **cgi_validate_fields**, may be called to ensure that the form data fields that were expected by the CGI program actually exist in the CGI array after the call to **cgi_parse**. If the proper fields were not received, a single call to **cgi_print_error** will return the appropriate error to the browser that submitted the request.

## The Hello World Form

This section will illustrate how to process form data from the Hello World HTML form shown in Figure 4-2. This form provides a text field where the user may enter any text string he or she desires. For the purposes of this example, we will enter "Hello World."

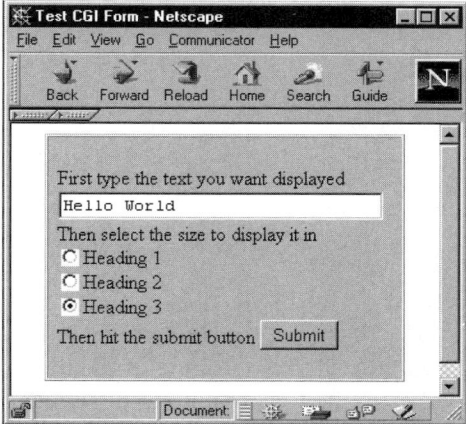

**Figure 4-2** The Hello World Control Panel

The form also allows the user to select the size in which to display the text by selecting one of three radio buttons labeled "Heading 1" through "Heading 3." The radio buttons are mutually exclusive, allowing the user to only select one of them. For appearance's sake, these input fields are located inside a table, which makes it easier to align the fields and center the whole input screen. Once again, this is all accomplished with a few simple point-and-click operations using Visual Page.

The code listing for the form element is as follows:

```
<!DOCTYPE HTML PUBLIC "-//W3C//DTD HTML 3.2//EN">
<HTML>
<HEAD>
<META HTTP-EQUIV="Content-Type" CONTENT="text/html;CHARSET=iso-8859-
1">
<TITLE>Test CGI Form</TITLE>
</HEAD>
<BODY BGCOLOR="#FFFFFF">
<FORM ACTION="helloform.cgi" METHOD="POST" ENCTYPE="application/x-www-
form-urlencoded">
<CENTER>
<P>
<TABLE BORDER="1" CELLPADDING="7" CELLSPACING="1" WIDTH="282"
HEIGHT="201" BGCOLOR="#C0C0C0">
<TR>
<TD WIDTH="100%">First type the text you want displayed<BR>
<INPUT TYPE="TEXT" NAME="TEXT" SIZE="30" VALUE="Hello World"><BR>
```

```
Then select the size to display it in<BR>
<INPUT TYPE="RADIO" NAME="SIZE" VALUE="1" CHECKED>Heading 1<BR>
<INPUT TYPE="RADIO" NAME="SIZE" VALUE="2">Heading 2<BR>
<INPUT TYPE="RADIO" NAME="SIZE" VALUE="3">Heading 3<BR>
Then hit the submit button <INPUT TYPE="SUBMIT" NAME="Submit"
VALUE="Submit"></TD>
</TR>
</TABLE>
</CENTER>
<P>
</FORM>
</BODY>
</HTML>
```

What distinguishes an HTML form from static HTML documents is the presence of the FORM tag. This tag is the browser's cue that form data must be packaged and sent to the CGI script specified by the ACTION attribute of the FORM tag. In this case it tells the browser to invoke the helloform.cgi script, which must be located in the same directory as the helloform.html document because the URL specified is relative to the current directory. Between the <FORM> and the </FORM> tag are the field definitions to be displayed on the Web browser.

Most forms contain a submit button that causes the browser to send the contents of the input fields to the resource specified by the ACTION attribute of the HTML FORM element. In our example the browser will set the value of TEXT equal to Hello World and the value of SIZE equal to 3 and then send the request to the helloform.cgi script once the user hits the submit button. It is then the job of the helloform.cgi script to read the name/value pairs from the standard in (because this is a POST operation) and generate an HTML document dynamically that displays the supplied text in the appropriate header size.

The code listing for the helloform.cgi program follows. Once again, this program uses the **package require** command to pull in the **cgi.tcl** package before executing any calls to the cgi.tcl library. Notice that the expected fields are documented at the top of the CGI program.

```
#!/usr/local/sh/tclsh

# CGI program name: helloform.cgi
# Language: Tcl
#
# Description
#   This CGI script will generate the HTML code to display
#   a given text string in a specific header size.
#
```

```
# Expected Fields
#
# TEXT
#  This is the string to print.
# SIZE
#  This parameter specifies what header size to use
#  for the displayed text.
#

# Load the tcl cgi library.
package require cgi.tcl

# Parse the cgi parameters and validate the fields.
cgi_parse
if { [cgi_validate_fields [list TEXT SIZE]  err_msg] } {
   cgi_print_error $err_msg
   return
} else {
   set size $cgi(SIZE)
   set text $cgi(TEXT)
}

# Return the string in the appropriate header size.
cgi_header "TEST CGI" {BGCOLOR=white TEXT=black}
cgi_br
cgi_h$size $text
cgi_br
cgi_end
```

## Obtaining the Form Data

The cgi_parse procedure does all the work of figuring out whether the request from the client Web browser was submitted with a GET or a POST operation and reads the CGI data from the Web server appropriately. It creates a tcl array named CGI and places all the name/value pairs sent from the Web browser into that array. The code for the cgi_parse follows for the sake of this discussion. If the code in this routine looks a little challenging, you might want to refresh your Tcl knowledge a bit with some of the reference material listed in the book's introduction.

```
proc cgi_parse {} {

   global cgi_out_stream env cgi cgi_query

   if {[info exists env(CONTENT_LENGTH)]} {
      set cgi_query [read stdin $env(CONTENT_LENGTH)]
   } elseif {[info exists env(QUERY_STRING)] &&\
            [string length $env(QUERY_STRING)] > 0 } {
```

```
        set cgi_query $env(QUERY_STRING)
} else { return 1 }

regsub -all {\+} $cgi_query { } cgi_query
foreach {name value} [split $cgi_query &=] {
    if [info exists list($name)] {
        set cgi($name) [list $cgi($name) [cgi_decode $value]]
        unset list($name)
    } elseif [info exists cgi($name)] {
        lappend cgi($name) [cgi_decode $value]
    } else {
        set cgi($name) [cgi_decode $value]
        set list($name) 1
    }
}
return 0
}
```

This routine gets the message contents sent from the Web browser from one of two places depending on the method of the request. If the method was a GET operation, the QUERY_STRING environment variable will be defined and have a positive length. In this case the message contents are contained in the QUERY_STRING variable. If the request was made with the POST method, then the CONTENT_LENGTH variable will be defined, identifying how many bytes should be read from standard in. The QUERY_STRING environment variable will not be defined or will have a zero length in this case.

The cgi_parse routine will read the data from the appropriate place and store it in a global variable named cgi_query. Remember from Chapter 2, The Common Gateway Interface, that the name/value pairs are encoded to eliminate white space. This means that the cgi_parse routine must decode this information to extract the name/value pairs. It does this with the help of the regsub command. The cgi_parse routine then builds an array named CGI, where each element name of the array corresponds to the names of the name/value pairs and the contents of each element of the array equal the value portion of the name/value pair. In our current example, the CGI array will look as follows:

```
cgi(TEXT) - will contain the contents of the TEXT field from the Web
browser's form.
cgi(SIZE) - will contain the contents of the SIZE field from the Web
browser's form.
```

Armed with this information the cgi.script is now ready to perform the next standard step required by a CGI program. It needs to validate that the correct field names were received from the Web browser. The program does this with a simple call to **cgi_validate_fields**. This procedure accepts a list of field names and a buffer where error messages may be stored and returned to the caller. The code for the **cgi_validate_fields** procedure follows for reference. The procedure resolves the address of the *cgi_array_name* and *error_buffer* arguments in the caller's address space using the **upvar** command. This is the equivalent of pass by reference in C where a pointer to the caller's variable is used to access the caller's variable directly.

The **cgi_validate_fields** routine is fairly straightforward. It first ensures that a CGI array actually exists and then loops through the list of field names supplied by the caller in the *field_list* argument and checks to make sure that a corresponding named element exists in the CGI array built by the **cgi_parse** routine. If any discrepancies are found, an appropriate error message is generated and returned to the caller in the *error_buffer* argument. The procedure returns a 0 if successful and a 1 if a failure occurs.

```
proc cgi_validate_fields { field_list error_buffer } {

    global cgi
    upvar $error_buffer err_buff
    if { ![info exists cgi] } {
        set err_buff "no cgi_array defined"
        return 0
    } else {
        foreach field $field_list {
            if { ![info exists cgi($field)] } {
                set err_buff "field name '$field' required but not defined"
                return 0
            }
        }
    }
    set err_buff ""
    return 1
}
```

If the data received from the Web browser is indeed valid, the CGI program will process the data and build an HTML document to return to the requesting browser. In this case the HTML document will simply print the text specified in the size specified. The output of this CGI script looks virtually the same as the output from the previous two examples so it won't be shown here, but you can try any of these examples using the included source on the enclosed CD.

# Debugging CGI Programs

In the real world this all looks pretty simple, but what happens when something goes wrong? One of the unfortunate aspects of Web servers is that they are not tremendously friendly when it comes to receiving errors from one of their CGI programs.

Let's say that in the course of writing your CGI program you forgot to put a closing brace somewhere in the code, causing the CGI program to die horribly when the Web server tries to execute it. The poor user, which is usually you while you are debugging the script, will see a message similar to this on the Web browser:

```
500 Server Error

The server encountered an internal error and was unable to complete
your request.
Please contact your system administrator and inform him/her of the time
the error occurred, and anything you might have done that may have
caused the error.
Error: httpd: malformed header from script
```

This can be quite frustrating. Tcl is generally very good at giving appropriate error dumps when a program blows up, but in this case you don't get to see the dump. So how can you fix the program?

## Command Line Execution

An easy way to detect some fatal errors is to go to the directory on the server where the program exists and simply execute the CGI program. If the program terminates abnormally, Tcl will give a useful dump of what went wrong. This is usually sufficient to track the problem down fairly quickly.

In some cases, however, the program may not exhibit a fatal error but may be generating invalid HTML code that is causing the server to generate the same message. In this case your debugging attempts will most likely be thwarted by some output similar to this:

```
> helloform.cgi
Content-Type: text/html

<HTML>
<HEAD>
```

```
<TITLE>CGI FIELD DUMP</TITLE>
</HEAD>
<BODY BGCOLOR=white TEXT=black>
<H3>No query data found</H3>
</BODY>
</HTML>
```

This is the normal response from the helloform.cgi program if it does not find any query data when **cgi_parse** is called. The CGI program expects input from the Web server in the form of environment variables, which it won't find if you execute it from the command line. Because the error checking that looks for valid input is usually at the beginning of the CGI script, you may see the results from the error checking code before you get to the code that is actually causing the problem.

## Set Up the Environment Variables

Most CGI programs require input from the browser that calls them. A properly written CGI program will first validate the data received and terminate with an appropriate message if the proper data has not been received. The trick here is to get the CGI program to execute along the same path as it would when executed by the Web server. To do this you must set up certain environment variables yourself. The following two lines set up the QUERY_STRING environment variable, which will allow you to check the output of the helloform.cgi program.

```
> QUERY_STRING="TEXT=hello world&SIZE=2"
> export QUERY_STRING
```

This is the common way to set an environment variable on UNIX systems and make it available to programs that run in that process space. After setting this variable, executing the helloform.cgi program will yield the expected results as shown:

```
> helloform.cgi
Content-Type: text/html

<HTML>
<HEAD>
<TITLE>TEST CGI</TITLE>
</HEAD>
<BODY BGCOLOR=white TEXT=black>
<BR>
<H2>hello world</H2>
<BR>
</BODY>
```

```
</HTML>
>
```

One of the typical errors you will run into is improperly formatted HTML code generated by your CGI script. This may result in either a blank screen or a 500 error as shown earlier. Your job then is to review the HTML output of the CGI script for a given set of input conditions and find any syntax errors. Of course, if the error is a Tcl coding error, you will most likely receive a meaningful message from the Tcl interpreter that will lead you quickly to the problem.

Also remember the principal function of most CGI programs is to dynamically generate HTML code that can be returned to the requesting browser. According to the CGI standard, the way the CGI program sends this information to the Web server is by writing to standard out. This means that any extraneous information that your program may inadvertently send to standard out may confuse the Web server or Web browser. Therefore, it is important that you structure your programs carefully to avoid writing improper information to standard out.

## Displaying User Input

While developing your CGI programs, it is often useful to know for sure what information has been received by the CGI program. The **cgi_dump_fields** routine is provided for just this reason.

Notice in the following code that a call to **cgi_dump_fields** is made immediately after the package require statement. The **cgi_dump_fields** procedure takes no arguments, calls the **cgi_parse** routine itself, and then builds the appropriate HTML code to display the CGI arguments received by the CGI program. You then return immediately from the CGI script.

```
# Load the tcl cgi library
package require cgi.tcl
 cgi_dump_fields
 return 0
```

The screen capture in Figure 4-3 shows the resulting Web page that is generated with a call to this procedure. You can include these couple of lines of code in your CGI programs and comment them out until you need them and then just return the comment characters and call the script.

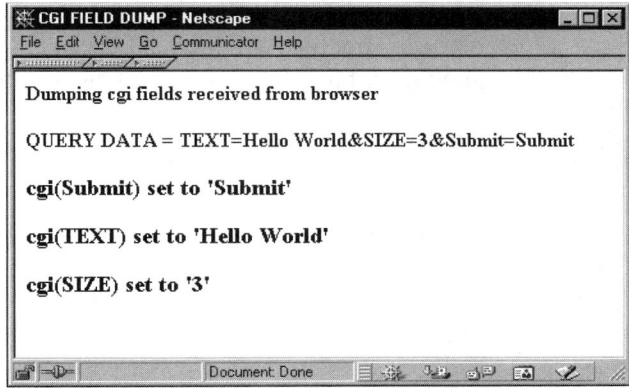

**Figure 4-3** Displaying CGI Field Data with `cgi_dump_fields`

## Using Embedded puts Commands

Oftentimes you may have subtle problems in some of the more complex code inside a CGI program. The program may be executing properly but giving unexpected results. For these types of logic errors you might consider placing embedded puts commands inside your code at strategic locations. Then, when you access the CGI program through your Web browser, you will see periodic debug statements that tell you where you are. For example, you might display the value of certain variables or display entry and exit points in certain procedure calls.

## Trapping Errors with catch

Another common practice is to wrap sections of code, or possibly the entire CGI program, inside the Tcl catch command. This is most useful when your program is exiting abnormally but you cannot track the problem down through any of the other methods listed so far. This is easy to add and then remove after the error has been tracked down.

The general format for the catch command, used in this fashion, would be

```
if { [catch {
    .... code to debug
} err ] } {
    cgi_print_error $err
}
```

If an exception occurs during the execution of the code inside the catch command, then the cgi_print_error procedure will be called to display the contents of err. This can lead to quick solutions to even the most elusive bugs.

## Interactive Debugging

Throughout this book, several references will be made to Expect. Expect is a powerful extension to Tcl for dealing with interactive processes/programs. In addition to its primary usage, Expect also provides a powerful debug environment that can be effectively used to debug CGI programs or most other Tcl code.

Expect has two useful commands that allow you to interactively debug programs while they are running and may be inserted anywhere inside an Expect program. The first command is interpreter, which can be used to bring up an interactive interpreter at any point in your program. Once in the interpreter, you can examine/modify variables, execute commands, or even create variables and new procedures, as well as include additional packages that may be useful for debugging. The debug command enters an interactive debug mode with most of the functionality of a symbolic debugger. With it you can do the following:

- step into procedures
- step over procedures
- return from procedure
- set, clear, and show breakpoints
- continue
- show stack
- change scope up
- change scope down
- display a help screen
- repeat last action

By now you are no doubt wondering how this will help you because you have a Tcl script, not an Expect script. Well, for most conditions you can execute the same script under either Tcl or Expect. The only thing you need to change is the first couple of lines of the script that tell the operating system which interpreter to use to execute the program. In the preceding helloform.cgi example, the first few lines appear as follows:

```
#!/bin/sh
# \
```

```
exec tclsh "$0" ${1+"$@"}
```

This is a path-independent way to execute the tclsh interpreter using the current PATH to find the program. You could also just put one line that says:

```
#!/usr/local/bin/tclsh or some such thing.
```

Anyway, no matter how you choose to specify the interpreter to run, you can change the script to run Expect by changing the first line of your script to specify Expect rather than the tclsh, as long as you have Expect installed and running on your system. If you want to stop just after the CGI arguments are processed, you could place the interpreter command as shown here:

```
#!/bin/sh
# \
exec expect "$0" ${1+"$@"}

# CGI program name: helloform.cgi
# Language: Tcl
#
# Description
#  This CGI script will generate the HTML code to display a given text
string in a specific header size.
#
# Expected Fields
#
# TEXT
#  This is the string to print.
# SIZE
#  This parameter specifies what header size to use
#  for the displayed text.
#

# Load the tcl CGI library
package require cgi.tcl

# Parse the CGI parameters and validate the fields
cgi_parse
if { [cgi_validate_fields [list TEXT SIZE] cgi err_msg] } {
   cgi_print_error $err_msg
   return
} else {
   set size $cgi(SIZE)
   set text $cgi(TEXT)
}
interpreter
cgi_header "TEST CGI" {BGCOLOR=white TEXT=black}
cgi_br
cgi_h$size $text
cgi_br
```

```
cgi_end
```

Now when you run the program, execution will be suspended and you will be presented with an interpreter prompt at the line where you placed the **interpreter** command.

```
> QUERY_STRING="TEXT=hello world&SIZE=2"
> export QUERY_STRING
> helloform.cgi
expect2.1>
```

At this point, you can do anything that you could do in the **tclsh** interpreter. For example to examine the contents of the size and text variables, just use the **set** command.

```
expect2.1> set size
2
expect2.2> set text
hello world
expect2.3>
```

## The Debug Command

Expect also provides a **debug** command, which may be used to enter the interactive debugger. There are two ways to enter the debugger. In the preceding example, where you have already inserted an **interpreter** command in the program and stopped at the interpreter prompt, you may type the command **debug 1** to enable the debugger. If you wish to enter the debugger immediately rather than stopping at the interpreter prompt first, you may place the command **debug 1** in the script in place of the **interpreter** command. This will cause execution to halt at that point and present you with the debugger prompt.

Once you are at the debugger prompt, the keystroke·commands listed in Table 4-1 are available.

**Table 4-1**  Debugger Keystrokes

| Keystroke | Function |
| --- | --- |
| s | step into procedure |
| n, N | step over procedure |
| r | return from procedure |
| b | set, clear, show breakpoint |

**Table 4-1** Debugger Keystrokes (Continued)

| Keystroke | Function |
|-----------|----------|
| c | continue |
| w | show stack |
| u | change scope up one level |
| d | change scope down one level |
| h | help |
| return | repeat last action |

## Tcl Debuggers

As Tcl has gained in popularity, several debugging packages have become available. Some of the debuggers have graphical interfaces, some are command line oriented. Many of these packages are freely available in the public domain.

Table 4-2 lists some of the debuggers that have been mentioned during the review process on this book. They are listed here for your convenience. For these tools and others, a good source of public domain code can be found at www.neosoft.com/tcl. At this site, you will find the Contributed Source Archives, which contains many packages of different types written by many different people. If you write Tcl code for a living, you might consider the TclPro environment from Scriptics (www.scriptics.com), which contains a compiler, debugger, and a few other nice tools as well as the complete Tcl/Tk release and associated documentation. The debugger has a graphical front end and is well suited for debugging CGI programs. It is also well worth the price, as the features may pay for themselves quickly on your next few projects.

**Table 4-2** Debuggers Available

| Name | URL | Public Domain |
|------|-----|---------------|
| TclPro | www.scriptics.com | No |
| tcl-debug | www.neosoft.com/tcl | Yes |
| tk-debug | www.neosoft.com/tcl | Yes |

## Chapter Summary

- The cgi.tcl library on the enclosed CD is written as a reusable package that may be loaded in your program using the Tcl **package require** command. The library contains many useful routines that can aid you in the implementation of your CGI programs.

- When designing your CGI programs, you should attempt to isolate the user interface code from your main application code whenever possible. This makes it easier to build a library of reusable modules, which can help shorten application development time.

- Your CGI applications may receive POST or GET type requests from a Web browser client. The type of transaction determines where the CGI program must look for the data. In the case of the GET transaction, the data is located in the QUERY_STRING environment variable. In the case of the POST transaction, the data must be read from standard in and the CONTENT_LENGTH environment variable contains the data length to be read.

- The **cgi_parse** routine in the cgi.tcl library will extract the form data regardless of the method used. The data is then available to the application in a global array named cgi. A corresponding element name exists for each form item sent over from the Web browser.

- The CGI program must know which form elements to expect from the client Web pages. The **cgi_validate_fields** routine may be used to validate that the appropriate field names were received from the HTML form that called it.

- The **cgi_dump_fields** routine is a quick way to verify what data your CGI program received from the client.

- CGI programs can be debugged manually by setting the environment variable QUERY_STRING and executing the CGI program from the command line. This is an effective way to find fatal errors that can be difficult to find when running the application from a Web browser.

- Expect is a powerful extension to Tcl that provides an interactive debugger that can be useful for finding problems in your Tcl scripts. Tcl scripts can easily be executed under the Expect shell if this feature is desired. Expect also provides some powerful commands for dealing with interactive processes.

# Chapter 5

## *A Web-Based Directory Browser*

This chapter will show you how to write a CGI program that acts like a directory browser. The program will allow you to drill down into directories and view files contained in those directories. The program will restrict access to those files by the IP address of the host that is trying to contact it and politely refuse access to anyone that is not originating from a valid subnet. The program also starts from a specified base path and will not allow the user to examine any parent directory of the specified base path.

This chapter actually contains two examples. The first example contains a text-only browser that allows you to select subdirectories and files but does not provide a way to return to upper-level directories other than the browser's Back button.

The second example expands on the first to add graphical icons to display folder and file information. It also provides the standard double dot symbol to return to the parent directory. For security reasons the second example will only display the relative path of the file and hides the actual base path, which might be desirable so users will not know where in the file system the actual files reside.

This is a good example of starting with a simple solution to a proposed problem and then enhancing it once you have met the principal requirements.

## Security Considerations

One consideration when providing directory service over the Web, even on an intranet, is security. You don't want to give all users carte blanche access to view the contents of any directory or file they wish. There are a couple of easy things that can be done that will satisfy most security requirements.

- Restrict access based on the IP address of the requesting Web browser.
- Specify the starting directory and allow access only to subdirectories from that point.

When the HTTP request is sent from the Web browser to the Web server, the IP address of the client making the request is included in the message. The Web server passes this information along to the CGI script by placing the requesting IP address in an environment variable. It is a fairly simple process to read this variable and compare it against a list of valid IP addresses to ensure that the requesting client has the proper access rights to view the requested trees. Before we look at the complete tree browser, let's see how simple it is to obtain this information about the client making the request.

### Obtaining the Client's IP Address

The dumpip.cgi script in the chapter3 examples directory contains the code necessary to obtain both the host name of the client making the request, if available, from the REMOTE_HOST environment variable and the IP address of the client making the request from the REMOTE_ADDR environment variable.

The beginning of the script looks similar to the examples we saw in the last chapter. The script begins with a few lines that tell the Web server to use the tclsh command as the interpreter when running this program. Next we see that familiar package require cgi.tcl line, which tells this script to use the most current version of the cgi.tcl package available in the path currently defined by the auto_path variable.

```
#!/usr/local/bin/tclsh

# This cgi script will display the remote host name of the requesting
# client as well as the IP address of the requesting client.

package require cgi.tcl

cgi_header "dumpip.cgi" {BGCOLOR=white TEXT=black}
```

```
if { [catch { set remote_name $env(REMOTE_HOST) }] } {
   cgi_puts "Remote Host name not available"
} else {
   cgi_puts "Remote Host making request is $remote_name"
}
cgi_br
if { [catch { set remote_ip $env(REMOTE_ADDR) } ] } {
      cgi_puts "Remote Address not available"
} else {
    cgi_puts "Remote Address making request is $remote_ip"
}
cgi_end
```

The first line of code is a call to **cgi_header**, which generates the required HTML header code necessary for a valid HTML document. This call also specifies the title line to be displayed by the Web browser, which in this case is simply the name of the CGI script. This call also sets up the background color and default text color the Web browser will use to display the output.

The next few lines of code attempt to assign the value of the REMOTE_HOST and REMOTE_ADDR environment variable to a couple of local variables. The Tcl **catch** is used to detect any errors in the assignment. Of course the most common error would be that one or both of these environment variables do not exist.

If the environment variable exists, the code generates an HTML header that displays the contents of the variable. If the environment variable does not exist, then a header line of the same size is generated indicating that the environment variable does not exist.

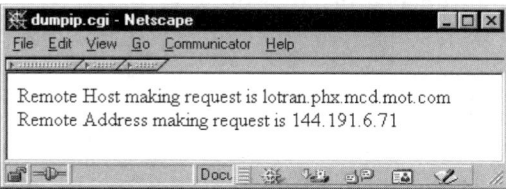

**Figure 5-1** Displaying the Connection Information

Figure 5-1 shows the output as it appeared on the particular workstation where the code was developed. Notice that both variables contain the same information. This is typical among HTTP transactions when the REMOTE_HOST name is not available. In many cases the REMOTE_HOST name will not be made available to the Web server, and the best we can obtain on the server side is the remote IP address of the client.

## Restricting Access Using REMOTE_ADDR

Now that you see how easy it is to obtain the information, let's see how the directory browser program uses this information to restrict access. As you can see from Figure 5-2, the tree.cgi program uses a file named valid_subnets.tcl to contain the valid subnet addresses. When the tree.cgi program is invoked, it checks the contents of the REMOTE_ADDR environment variable and compares it against the list of valid subnets obtained from the valid_subnets.tcl file.

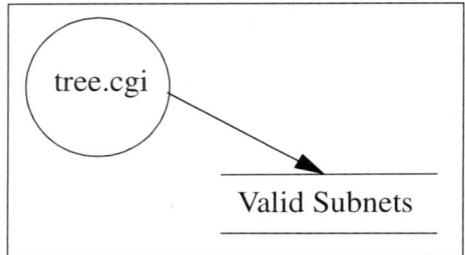

**Figure 5-2** Use of the Valid Subnets File

This file also contains the base path for viewing. The tree.cgi program will let you drill down into the directory specified by the current_path variable defined in the valid_subnets.tcl file but will not let you go higher than the initial current path definition. This is another level of security that prevents users from browsing the entire server. The file also contains the file types that the directory browser will display. The contents of the valid subnets file are as follows:

```
set valid_subnets "144.191.6    144.191.11    144.191.17    144.191.24
144.191.26"
set base_path "/home/dmaggian/public_html/book"
set file_types "*.html *.cgi" *.tcl *.exp
```

Notice the use of the Tcl **set** command in this file. This trick can often be used to save configuration data in a file. By placing data in a file in this manner, you can use the Tcl **source** command to read in the file contents and set the value of some variables, all with a single line of code. This command actually generates a Tcl list that contains five IP addresses. It may look like the **valid_subnets** variable is being initialized with a string, but remember that Tcl lists and Tcl strings are interchangeable.

Also, notice that these are not complete IP addresses because they only specify an address down to the subnet level. It would be an easy modification to the code to limit access to a single IP address, but it is probably more common to limit access to a subnet when working on an intranet.

This may sound secure, but there are a number of holes in our security plan that we will discuss as we progress through the chapter. This type of security is usually adequate for an intranet, but just like our homes, locks are really only there to keep out the honest individuals or the less-motivated crooks. A talented hacker can be very difficult to defeat. On to the code. The complete listing for the tree.cgi program follows.

```tcl
#!/usr/local/bin/tclsh

# This cgi script will display the directory as a series of
# clickable links. If the link is a directory, this program
# will generate another page of links that contains the
# directory entries. If the link is a file, this code will
# return the file in HTML viewable format.
#
# The program will reference the valid_subnets file in the
# same directory that contains a list of valid subnets that
# may access the base path directory. The base path is also
# specified in this file.
#
# The program looks for a field named DIR, which will contain
# the name of the directory or the file to be viewed. If DIR
# is not present, the program will default back to the base path
# specified in the valid_subnets.tcl file.

package require cgi.tcl

# Source in the valid_subnets file and validate the subnet
# address received from the client against the list contained
# in the valid_subnet file .
if { [catch {source valid_subnets} err_msg]} {
   cgi_print_error "Error reading valid subnets was $err_msg"
   return 1
} elseif { [catch { set remote_ip $env(REMOTE_ADDR) } ] } {
     cgi_print_error "REMOTE ADDRESS not available for authentication"
     return 1
} else {
    set subnet_ip [file rootname $remote_ip]
}

if { [lsearch $valid_subnets $subnet_ip] == -1 } {
   cgi_print_error "Requesting IP address '$subnet_ip' is\
                    not authorized for this action"
   return 1
```

```
    }

    # Parse the QUERY_STRING info if any.  If none, then start
    # at the default path specified in the valid_subnets file.
    cgi_parse
    if { [info exists cgi(DIR) ] } {
       set base_path $cgi(DIR)
    }


    # Generate the output page
    if { [file isdirectory $base_path] } {
       # Build a page of links for the contents of a directory.
       cd $base_path
       set file_list "[lsort [glob -nocomplain */]]\
                      [lsort [eval glob -nocomplain $file_types]]"

       cgi_header "Source Browser Tool" {BGCOLOR=white TEXT=black}
       cgi_h4 "Current Directory = $base_path"
       cgi_hr
       foreach item $file_list {
          if { [file isdirectory $item] } {
             cgi_puts [cgi_link "$item" "tree.cgi?DIR=[pwd]/$item"]
          } else {
             cgi_puts "    "
             cgi_puts [cgi_link "$item" "tree.cgi?DIR=[pwd]/$item"]
          }
          cgi_br
       }
    } else {
       if { [catch {set file_ptr [open $base_path r] } err_msg ] } {
          cgi_h4 "Error Opening File Named $base_path was %err_msg"
       } else {

          # read the file and send it to the browser
         cgi_header "Source Browser Tool" {BGCOLOR=white TEXT=black}
          cgi_h4 "Current File  = $base_path"
          cgi_hr
          cgi_pre
          set text [read $file_ptr]
          # Replace < with &lt and > with &gt to keep the browser from
          # trying to interpret these tags
          regsub -all "&" $text "\\&amp;" text
          regsub -all "<" $text "\\&lt" text
          regsub -all ">" $text "\\&gt" text
          foreach line [split $text "\n"] {  puts $line  }
          close $file_ptr
          cgi_pre_end
       }
    }
    cgi_end
```

As you can see, the program is not very long but there are a few tricks worth talking about. First, let's look at the code that does the IP subnet validation at the beginning of the file. This code is there to ensure that the requesting client is coming from a known, valid subnet. The first thing this code does is to source in the valid_subnets.tcl file. This action is performed inside of a **catch** command in case the file does not exist, in which case an error message is generated with the **cgi_print_error** procedure and the program exits.

If the valid_subnets.tcl file does exist, the program attempts to obtain the contents of the REMOTE_ADDR environment variable. This action is also performed inside of a **catch** command in case this variable does not exist, in which case access is denied with an appropriate error message because there is no way to authenticate the client.

If the valid_subnets.tcl file exists and the REMOTE_ADDR variable has been defined by the Web server, then the CGI program searches the valid_subnets list to see if there is a match against REMOTE_ADDR value. If no match is found, the program prints an error using the **cgi_print_error** procedure and returns with a status of 1.

### Guarding the Back Door

The security outlined in the preceding section is not foolproof but should be adequate for most cases. There are, however, some loopholes. It can be tricky to get the CGI script and the files it needs to access, such as the valid_subnets.tcl file, set up with the right permissions. Because the default for CGI script execution is to execute as a user with a limited set of permissions, aka "nobody," it is tempting to open up the access privileges on the files it needs to read to get the whole mess up and running. Just remember, if a CGI script running as nobody can read the file, then so can anyone else. Theoretically, it would be possible for a talented hacker to browse the directory with the normal Web browser's ability, look at the valid_subnets.tcl file, and fake a message that contains the right subnet.

## Using QUERY_STRING for State Information

If all of the access tests pass, the tree.cgi program will then go about its business of reading directories and returning a Web page to the client. The tree browser program dynamically builds pages that contain links for subdirectories and text for files. Figure 5-3 shows how the directory browser should appear on your Web browser.

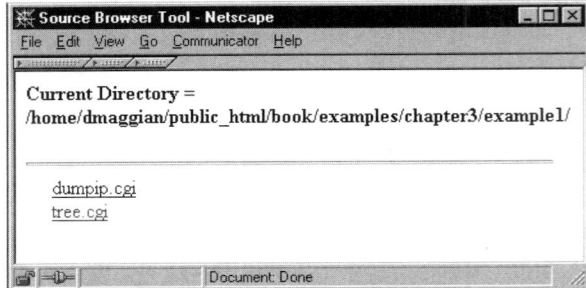

**Figure 5-3** The Tree Browser Display

The screen display is simple. Subdirectories are presented in the left column and files are indented. Subdirectories also show up as blue-colored links and files are presented as black links. This format allows the user to just point and click to navigate the tree. Clicking on a subdirectory link displays the contents of that directory as a new page. Clicking on a file will display the contents of that file.

So how does the CGI program know what information to return to the client when one of the links is selected? The tree.cgi program does this by using the query string portion of the URL. As we discussed in Chapter 1, the URL may contain additional information separated from the address by a question mark as shown in the following example. The letters URL in the address represent any standard domain name that may occur in an Internet address.

```
URL?QUERY_STRING
```

The trick here is when the CGI program created the page of links in the first place, it added this extra query string information to the URL. You will notice that when you place your cursor over the top of one of the links, the directory browser program displays a URL similar to this one:

```
URL?DIR=domain_name/~/home/dmaggian/public_html/book/chapter3
```

where the domain name would be something like http://my_computer.com/ or whatever the particular domain name of the server you are running these examples is. What this extra query string does is communicate a name/value pair to the tree.cgi program each time it is called. This is essentially the same as having a field in a form that is sent to the CGI program when the Submit button is pressed, except this is accomplished through a link.

If you're keeping ahead of me, you may be wondering what happens the first time the tree.cgi program is selected from some other Web page that is simply a link with no additional query string information. As we will see, the tree.cgi program anticipates this and defaults to a base directory that is specified in the valid_subnets.tcl file along with the subnets that are authorized to access the directory.

Now let's look at the code that follows the access validation at the top of the file to see how the browser displays are actually generated.

The first few lines parse the message data, if any, and then check for the existence of a field named DIR. If the field is defined, then the **current_path** variable is set to the contents of the DIR field.

```
# Parse the QUERY_STRING info if any. If none then
# start at the default path specified in the valid_subnets.tcl file.
cgi_parse
if { [info exists cgi(DIR) ] } {
    set current_path $cgi(DIR)
}
```

The remainder of the code generates the dynamic HTML page that either represents the contents of a directory or displays the contents of a file. First the HTML header code is generated with the **cgi_header** procedure call. The current directory path is written out as a level 3 header with the **cgi_h3** procedure, and a horizontal rule is created to separate this from the rest of the page with the **cgi_hr** procedure.

```
# Generate the output page
cgi_header "SOURCE BROWSER TOOL" {BGCOLOR=white TEXT=black}
cgi_h3 "CURRENT DIRECTORY = $current_path"
cgi_hr
```

The remainder of the code will either present a directory structure or actually display a file. The file command is used to determine if the **current_path** variable contains a directory path or points to a real file, resulting in the execution of the appropriate code. The following short pseudo code block shows this decision without the actual code in place for clarity. If the link points to a directory, the code inside the if statement is executed. If the link points to a file, the code inside the else statement is executed.

```
if { [file isdirectory $current_path] } {
    ..... display a directory screen
} else {
    ..... display a file
}
cgi_end
```

## Building the Directory Screen

The following code block appears inside the if portion of the if-else statement and builds the directory page to be returned to the Web browser. The first action taken is to actually change directories to the one specified by the **current_path** variable using the **cd** command.

The **glob** command is then used to get the list of files in the current directory. The list returned by the **glob** command is sorted with the **lsort** command. The goal here was to get a little more structure in the display than the **glob** command returns. Subdirectories are presented first, sorted alphabetically, followed by the files in the directory, also sorted alphabetically. This is the reason that the **glob** command is executed twice. The first time is to obtain the list of directories, which is accomplished by passing glob the pattern */, telling it to return only directories. The second execution reads the files from the current directory. This execution uses the pattern read from the valid_subnets.tcl file, which for the chapter3 examples is "*.html *.cgi *.tcl", which will return all files with a .cgi, .html, or .tcl file extension. This ensures that we only read text type files, because the current tree.cgi program is only designed to handle files of this type. Also notice the **-nocomplain** option passed to the **glob** command. This option prevents the **glob** command from generating an error if no files or directories are found. In this case the **glob** command simply returns an empty string.

```
     # Build a page of links for the contents of a directory.
    cd $current_path
    set file_list "[lsort [glob -nocomplain */]]\
                  [lsort [eval glob -nocomplain $file_types]]"

    cgi_header "SOURCE BROWSER TOOL" {BGCOLOR=white TEXT=black}
    cgi_h3 "CURRENT DIRECTORY = $current_path"
    cgi_hr
    foreach item $file_list {
       if { [file isdirectory $item] } {
          cgi_puts [cgi_link "$item" "tree.cgi?DIR=[pwd]/$item"]
       } else {
          cgi_puts "    "
          cgi_puts [cgi_clink black "$item" "tree.cgi?DIR=[pwd]/$item"]
       }
```

```
       cgi_br
   }
```

Once the sorted list of directories and files has been created, a **foreach** loop is used to iterate through the list and write out the HTML code that contains the links to the individual directories or files. The **file isdirectory** command is used to determine if the file is a directory. The only difference between the way a file and a directory are written out is that files are indented by writing out four &*nbsp;* codes, which are used in HTML to insert nonbreaking spaces. The links themselves are generated with the **cgi_link** procedure call. Once the list is exhausted, the **cgi_end** command (not shown in the preceding example) at the end of the file would be called to place the closing HTML code, and the tree.cgi program would exit normally.

The following HTML code was generated by the tree.cgi program for the selection of the chapter3 subdirectory. The Content-Type header line is generated by the tree.cgi program, but you will not see it if you view the source from your Web browser. This listing was actually generated by going to the chapter3 examples directory and setting the QUERY_STRING environment variable equal to DIR=. to specify the current working directory:

```
> QUERY_STRING="DIR=."
> export QUERY_STRING
```

and then executing the tree.cgi program from the command line.

```
Content-Type: text/html
<HTML>
<HEAD>
<TITLE>SOURCE BROWSER TOOL</TITLE>
</HEAD>
<BODY BGCOLOR=white TEXT=black>
<H3>CURRENT DIRECTORY = /home/dmaggian/public_html/book/chapter3/</H3>
<HR>
<A href=
 "tree.cgi?DIR=/home/dmaggian/public_html/book/chapter3/temp/">
 temp/</A>
<BR>
 
<A href=
 "tree.cgi?DIR=/home/dmaggian/public_html/book/chapter3/dumpip.cgi">
 <FONT COLOR=black>dumpip.cgi</FONT></A>
<BR>
 
<A href=
 "tree.cgi?DIR=/home/dmaggian/public_html/book/chapter3/tree.cgi">
 <FONT COLOR=black>tree.cgi</FONT></A>
```

```
<BR>
</BODY>
</HTML>
```

If the user clicks on a link that is a file, the tree.cgi program opens the file for reading and dynamically builds an HTML page that displays the file on the client's Web browser. There are a couple things to keep in mind when you decide to dump the contents of a file to a Web browser window. The first is that HTML tends to ignore things like paragraph breaks in normal text unless you specifically surround the text with the <PRE> tag to tell the browser to display the text like it is. The second is that HTML tags are still interpreted inside of the <PRE> tag. Therefore, it is a good idea to filter the text before you pass it back to the Web browser. There are several characters that you should substitute with a predefined set of Escape codes provided by HTML before returning the file text back to the requesting Web browser. These codes are shown in Table 5-1.

**Table 5-1** HTML Escape Codes

| Code | Meaning |
| --- | --- |
| &lt; | < |
| &gt; | > |
| &amp; | & |
| &quot; | " |

The first two characters, the greater than (>) and the less than (<) symbols, will be interpreted by the browser as the opening and closing delimiters for HTML tags. The next character is not quite so obvious. It is the ampersand (&) character. This is the character that is used as the escape character and therefore must be substituted as well. The last character is the quote ("), but although it has an escape code provided, I have never seen a browser confused on quote characters. The following code opens the file and performs the substitutions:

```
# read the file and send it to the browser
cgi_header "SOURCE BROWSER TOOL" {BGCOLOR=white TEXT=black}
cgi_h3 "CURRENT FILE  = $current_path"
cgi_hr
cgi_pre
set text [read $file_ptr]
# Replace < with &lt and > with &gt to keep the browser from
# trying to interpret these tags
regsub -all "&" $text "\\&amp;" text
regsub -all "<" $text "\\&lt" text
regsub -all ">" $text "\\&gt" text
```

```
foreach line [split $text "\n"] {  puts $line  }
close $file_ptr
cgi_pre_end
```

Here, the **regsub** command is used to turn all occurrences of the < character into the string &lt and all occurrences of the > character into the string &gt. These two codes, &lt and &gt, are displayed by the Web browser as the literal characters they represent. This allows you to display text that might contain these characters without the browser trying to interpret the information as HTML tags.

Actually, there is a procedure in the cgi.tcl lib called cgi_dump_text_file that does all the work for you. The preceding section can be replaced with a single call to this procedure as follows:

```
cgi_dump_text_file $current_path
```

The results are the same as for the tree.cgi program when viewing a file. Figure 5-4 shows the output of the tree.cgi program when used to view the contents of the dumpip.cgi file in the examples1 directory.

## Enhancing the Browser

Now that we have the program working, lets jazz up the interface a little and add some more functionality. This next example will provide the following improvement.

- Add a double dot symbol to the directory list to allow users to go back a level without using the browser's Back button.
- Provide icons to represent closed folders, open folders, and files.
- Hide the root pathname from users so they will not know where the actual files reside on the file system.

All of these enhancements were done with just a few additional lines of code and a couple of modifications to the original program. The resulting interface change is shown in Figure 5-5. As you can see, the current directory is now represented by an open folder icon at the top of the page that displays the relative path rather than the absolute path. Immediately below this is the traditional double dot that takes you back one level. The contents of the directory are then displayed as either closed folders or files. Clicking on a folder will drill down into the chosen directory, whereas clicking on a file will open the file, just as it did with the previous display.

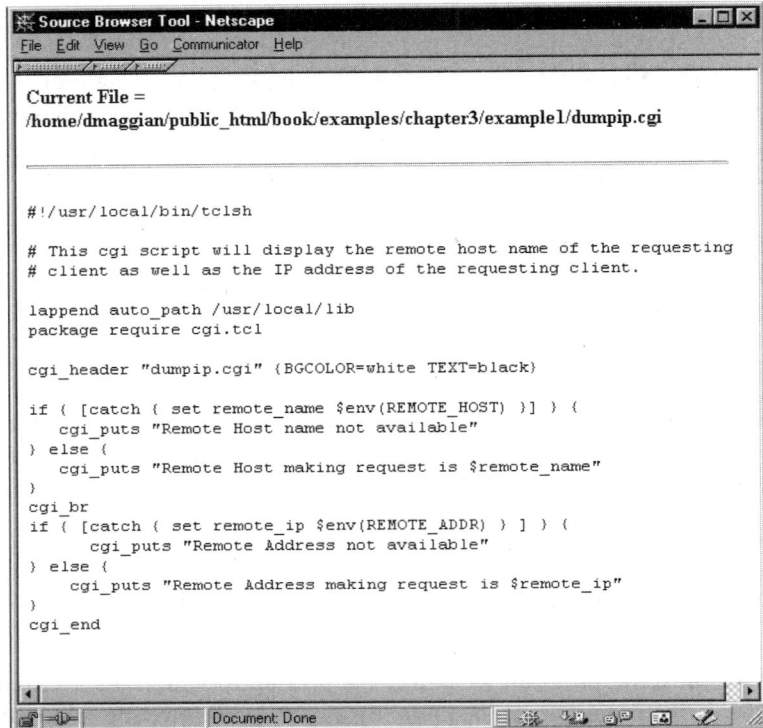

**Figure 5-4** Displaying Selected Files

As you can see from the following code listing, it is about the same size as our previous examples. This is partly because of the use of the cgi_dump_text_file to display files. This eliminated quite a few lines of code. Let's analyze the changes one by one.

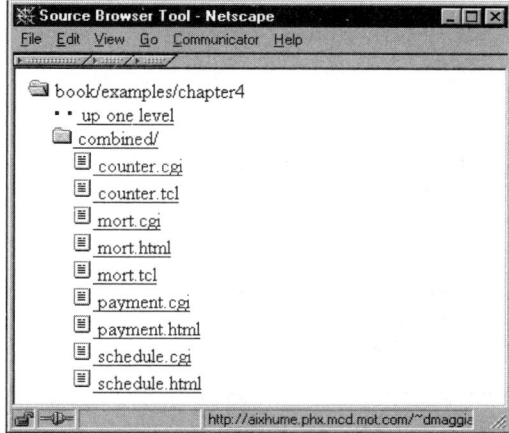

**Figure 5-5** The Enhanced Display

```
# This cgi script will display the directory as a series of
# clickable links. If the link is a directory, this program
# will generate another page of links that contains the
# directory entries. If the link is a file, this code will
# return the file in HTML viewable format.
#
# The program will reference the valid_subnets file in the
# same directory that contains a list of valid subnets that
# may access the base path directory. The base path is also
# specified in this file.
#
# The program looks for a field named DIR, which will contain
# the name of the directory or the file to be viewed. If DIR
# is not present, the program will default back to the base path
# specified in the valid_subnets.tcl file.

lappend auto_path /usr/local/lib
package require cgi.tcl

# Source in the valid_subnets file and validate the subnet
# address received from the client against the list contained
# in the valid_subnet file
if { [catch {source valid_subnets} err_msg]} {
   cgi_print_error "Error reading valid subnets was $err_msg"
   return 1
} elseif { [catch { set remote_ip $env(REMOTE_ADDR) } ] } } {
      cgi_print_error "REMOTE ADDRESS not available for authentication"
      return 1
} else {
    set subnet_ip [file rootname $remote_ip]
}
```

```tcl
if { [lsearch $valid_subnets $subnet_ip] == -1 } {
   cgi_print_error "Requesting IP address '$subnet_ip' is\
                    not authorized for this action"
   return 1
}

# Parse the QUERY_STRING info if any.  If none, then start
# at the default path specified in the valid_subnets file.
cgi_parse

# Determine the root path that we will not go above and
# set up a variable containing the current path.  All
# CGI input will be in the form of a relative path
set root_path [file dirname $base_path]
if { [info exists cgi(DIR) ] } {
   set current_path [string trimright $root_path/$cgi(DIR) /]
} else {
   set current_path $base_path
}

# Mask off the base_path and only send the relative names
regsub [file dirname $base_path]/ $current_path "" display_path

# Generate the output page
if { [file isdirectory $current_path] } {
   # Build a page of links for the contents of a directory.
   cd $current_path
   set file_list "[lsort [glob -nocomplain */]]\
                  [lsort [eval glob -nocomplain $file_types]]"

   cgi_header "Source Browser Tool" {BGCOLOR=white TEXT=black}
   cgi_puts "[cgi_img ../../images/ofolder.gif BOTTOM 0] $display_path"
   cgi_br

   if { ![string match $current_path $base_path] } {
      cgi_puts "    "
      cgi_puts [cgi_link "up one level" \
              "tree.cgi?DIR=[file dirname $display_path]" \
              [cgi_img ../../images/doubledot.gif BOTTOM 0]]
      cgi_br
   }

   foreach item $file_list {
      if { [file isdirectory $item] } {
         cgi_puts "    "
         cgi_puts [cgi_link "$item" "tree.cgi?DIR=$display_path/$item"\
                   [cgi_img ../../images/cfolder.gif BOTTOM 0]]
      } else {
         cgi_puts "        "
         cgi_puts [cgi_link "$item" "tree.cgi?DIR=$display_path/$item"\
                   [cgi_img ../../images/file.gif BOTTOM 0]]
      }
```

```
        cgi_br
   }
} else {
   # read the file and send it to the browser
   cgi_dump_text_file $current_path
}
cgi_end
```

## Hiding the Absolute Path

The new tree.cgi program set the links to be displayed with a relative path rather than an absolute path. The following code calculates a root path from the base path defined in the valid_subnets file by using the **file dirname** command to string off the last directory level.

```
# Determine the root path that we will not go above and
# set up a variable containing the current path. All
# CGI input will be in the form of a relative path
set root_path [file dirname $base_path]
if { [info exists cgi(DIR) ] } {
   set current_path [string trimright $root_path/$cgi(DIR) /]
} else {
   set current_path $base_path
}

# Mask off the base_path and only send the relative names
regsub [file dirname $base_path]/ $current_path "" display_path
```

It also sets up a variable named **current_path**, which holds the absolute pathname to the current selection and is only used internally by the CGI program. If the DIR field name *cgi(DIR)* has been returned, it indicates the user has selected one of the links. In this case the **current_path** variable is set by concatenating the **root_path** and the value of **cgi(DIR)** together. Notice that the **string trimright** command is used to remove the trailing slash "/" character. The earlier **glob** command returned the directory leafs with a trailing slash. The rest of the code works better without it, so we trim it off. If cgi(DIR) does not exist, then the program has been called for the first time, so we default **current_path** to the value of **base_path**.

The last variable that is created is the **display_path** variable, which is the relative pathname obtained by replacing the **root_path** portion of the **current_path** variable with the null string using the **regsub** command.

## Adding the Icons

The code that adds the icons uses a combination of the **cgi_link** command and the **cgi_img** command.

```
cgi_puts [cgi_link "$item" "tree.cgi?DIR=$display_path/$item"\
            [cgi_img ../../images/cfolder.gif BOTTOM 0]]
```

Both of these commands return a string rather than writing to standard out so they can be inserted as attributes of other tags. The **cgi_img** call is used as the optional attribute to the **cgi_link** call. The **cgi_img** call takes three arguments.

cgi_img *image_name alignment border*

The **image_name** is the file name of the graphic to be displayed. The last two arguments are optional as they have defaults of BOTTOM and 0, respectively. An example output line of these two commands combined in this way is

```
<A HREF="tree.cgi?DIR=book/examples/chapter3/example2/dumpip.cgi"><IMG
SRC="../../images/file.gif" ALIGN="BOTTOM" BORDER="0"> dumpip.cgi</A>
```

This has the effect of making both the link text and the graphic selectable as the same link. There are four instances where this graphical link is displayed. The first occurrence displays the top level open folder that shows what directory you are currently in. The second instance is optional and presents the double dot "up one level" icon, but only if we are below the root directory where it is legal to go up a level. The third instance is in the **foreach** loop if the item in question is a directory, and the last instance is in the **foreach** loop if the item is determined to be a file.

## Providing the "Up One Level" Icon

The following code shows how the determination is made whether to display the double dot icon.

```
if { ![string match $current_path $base_path] } {
   cgi_puts "    "
   cgi_puts [cgi_link "up one level" \
       "tree.cgi?DIR=[file dirname $display_path]" \
       [cgi_img ../../images/doubledot.gif BOTTOM 0]]
   ....
```

This code checks for a match between the **current_path** and the **base_path** variables as they are read from the **valid_subnets** file. If they match, we are already at the base path level, so the "up one level" icon should not be displayed. If they don't match, then it is okay to go up one level, and it is displayed in the manner described in the section Adding the Icons on page 108.

## Chapter Summary

This chapter presents another example of how a useful tool can be built quickly using the cgi.tcl library included in the book. Here are some of the key points that you should remember.

- The REMOTE_ADDR environment variables contain the IP address of the client that sent the request and can be used to restrict access to a list of authorized subnets that you maintain.
- The REMOTE_HOST environment variable, when available, contains the host name of the client making the request. This is often not available.
- The second example provides two levels of security. First, it restricts access to valid subnets, and second, it presents only relative pathnames to the browser display so the user does not know the absolute pathname of the file in the server's file system.
- When dumping the contents of text files to a browser, it is necessary to substitute certain characters with their HTML escape code equivalents. This will keep the browser from trying to interpret them as HTML tags.
- The <PRE> and </PRE> tags can be used to maintain a text file's original formatting when displaying it to the browser's screen.

# Chapter 6

## The Mortgage Calculator

By this time you should be getting the hang of structuring a CGI program. Once you understand the CGI protocol, it's easy to leverage your knowledge of Tcl into some useful utilities. This chapter presents an on-line mortgage calculator that illustrates several key CGI programming concepts not discussed so far. Here again, the routines in the cgi.tcl library will help during the implementation, but there are several design issues that must be dealt with up front before sitting down to code the program. For example, the names of the fields in your Web-based forms are case sensitive and must be agreed upon by the CGI programmer and the Web page designer in the beginning.

You must also consider how to structure your program. In this chapter we will place the code that deals with computing the monthly payments and amortization schedule into a separate package that is used by the CGI program. This makes the code easily available for any other programs that might want to reuse it at a later time. This is an important aspect of any programming task and will make your code easier to produce and much easier to maintain.

This chapter shows how to use the Tcl *package* facility as well as the Tcl *namespace* facility to produce these types of reusable packages. A package named mort.tcl is used as the example and provides the following functionality:

- Allows for the calculation of a monthly payment based on the principal, interest, and number of payments
- Produces an amortization schedule derived from the principal amount, monthly payment, and annual interest

As you will see, once you understand the basics of the CGI interface, the hardest work is sometimes in the code that has nothing to do with the Web interface.

# The Formulas

Before getting down to the actual CGI coding, the first order of business is to determine what formulas or algorithms are needed to solve the problem. The monthly payment formula is a simple calculation that can be done with a few lines of Tcl. Calculating an amortization schedule is an iterative process that requires a bit more complicated algorithm.

## Monthly Payment

The following formula assumes a typical conventional loan where the interest is compounded monthly. You can find this formula in books that deal with finance or by searching the Web.

$$M = P \times \frac{J}{1 - (1 + J)^{-N}}$$

In this formula, $M$ = the monthly payment, $P$ = the principal amount of the loan, $J$ = the monthly interest rate represented as a decimal number, and $N$ = the number of monthly payments. Because it is more common to deal with interest rates as an annual percentage and the payoff in years rather than months, a couple of conversions will be required in the code that implements this formula. The first conversion is to divide the annual interest by 1200 to represent it as a monthly interest charge in decimal form. The second is to multiply the payoff in years by 12 to get the number of monthly payments.

### Amortization Schedule

In order to calculate an amortization table, the code will need to do some iteration as shown in Figure 6-1. This algorithm calculates the monthly interest charge on the remaining principal balance and then reduces the principal balance by the payment less the monthly interest charge. The algorithm continues in a loop until the principal balance is reduced to 0 or some amount less than the monthly payment. The number of months is incremented each time through the loop as well as tallying up the total cost of the loan by adding up the monthly interest charges each time through the loop.

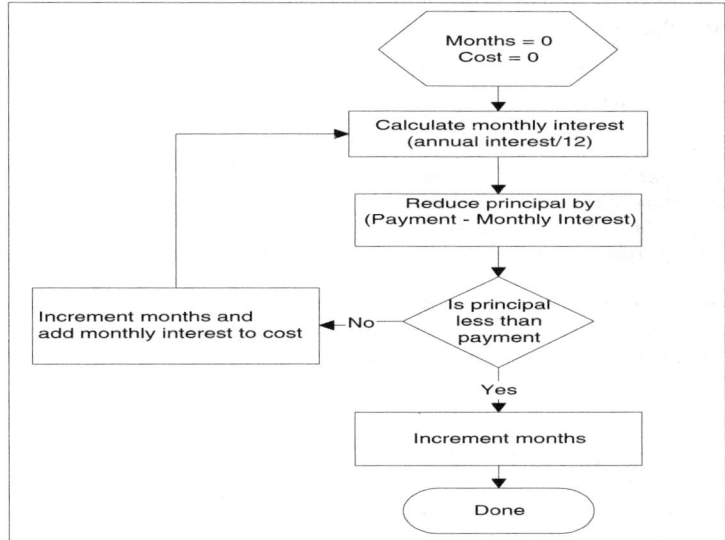

**Figure 6-1** Flowchart of Amortization Calculator

## The mort.tcl Package

One of the first rules in designing any program is to look for common, reusable code blocks and turn them into modular packages. These packages can be combined with other packages to create useful programs. As your collection of reusable packages grows, the amount of time necessary to generate a program will shrink.

The routines for calculating the monthly payment and amortization schedule are an obvious place to use this package concept. The idea is to separate the code that performs the calculations from the code that displays the results of the calculations. This will allow you to easily reuse the code that performs the calculations in other applications that might want to display the results differently, such as a command line application or perhaps a standalone application using Tk as a graphical user interface.

The mort.tcl package contains the following code that performs the calculations for our mortgage calculator example. It contains routines to calculate the monthly payment, generate an amortization schedule, format the amortization schedule, and validate the data passed to these routines.

```
#<:-------------------------------------------------------------------
# PACKAGE mort.tcl
#
#   Description
#       This package provides routines for calculating
#       mortgage-related information. This package will calculate
#       either a monthly payment or generate an amortization schedule.
#       The following procedures are intended to be public.
#
#       mort::payment           Calculate a monthly payment
#       mort::schedule          Generate an amortization schedule
#       mort::format_schedule   Return an ASCII-formatted schedule
#
#:>-------------------------------------------------------------------

package provide mort.tcl 1.1

# Create the mort namespace used to hold all the related variables
# and procedures.
namespace eval mort:: {
   namespace export schedule format_schedule payment
}


#<:-------------------------------------------------------------------
# PROC mort::schedule
#
#   Description
#       This procedure will generate an amortization schedule based on
#       the amount of the loan, the monthly payment, and the yearly
#       interest. The resulting amortization schedule is returned as a
#       Tcl list where each element of the list is itself a list
#       containing the following information:
#           month, principal paid, monthly finance charge, total finance
#           cost,  principal balance
#
```

```
# Arguments
#    amount
#        The original loan amount.
#    payment
#        The monthly payment.
#    interest
#        The annual interest rate.
#    schedule_buff
#        When the procedure completes, this user-defined buffer will
#        contain the amortization schedule.
#    cost_buff
#        When the procedure completes, this user-defined buffer will
#        contain the total interest paid over the life of the loan.
#    months_buff
#        When the procedure completes, this user-defined buffer will
#        contain the number of months required to pay off the loan.
#
# Return Values
#    1  if successful
#
#:>------------------------------------------------------------------
proc mort::schedule {amount payment interest schedule_buff\
                     cost_buff months_buff} {

    upvar $schedule_buff payoff
    upvar $cost_buff cost
    upvar $months_buff months

    # Validate the fields. Only positive, numeric values are allowed
    if { [ regexp {^[0-9.]+$} $amount] == 0 } {
        set payoff "AMOUNT FIELD INVALID:\
                Only positive numeric values allowed"
        return 0
    } elseif { [ regexp {^[0-9.]+$} $payment] == 0 } {
        set payoff "PAYMENT FIELD INVALID:\
                Only positive numeric values allowed"
        return 0
    } elseif { [ regexp {^[0-9.]+$} $interest] == 0 } {
        set payoff "INTEREST FIELD INVALID:\
                Only positive numeric values allowed"
        return 0
    } else { set payoff "" }

    # Make sure the interest charge is not larger than the payment.
    if { [expr $amount * $interest/1200.00] >= $payment } {
        set payoff "Payment is less than monthly interest,\
                    loan will never be paid off"
        return 0
    }

    set cost 0
    set months 0
```

```tcl
    # Iteratively reduce the principal balance by the monthly payment
    # less the monthly finance charge until the principal balance is
    # less than the monthly payment. Keep a running total of the
    # finance charge as we go.
    while {$amount >= $payment} {
        set charge [expr $amount * $interest/1200.00]
        set principal_paid [expr $payment - $charge]
        set amount [expr $amount - $principal_paid]
        set cost [expr $cost + $charge]
        incr months
        # Write values to a list as they are generated.
        lappend payoff [format "%d %.2f %.2f %.2f %.2f"\
                    $months $principal_paid $charge $cost $amount]

    }
    # If any residual amount is left, bump the month by 1 and write
    # out a final record to the payoff schedule
    if {$amount > 0} {
        set principal_paid $amount
        set amount 0
        set charge 0
        incr months
        lappend payoff [format "%d %.2f %.2f %.2f %.2f"\
                    $months $principal_paid $charge $cost $amount]
    }
    set cost [format "%6.2f" $cost]
    return 1
}


#<:------------------------------------------------------------------
# PROC mort::format_schedule
#
#  Description
#     This procedure may be used to format the output from the
#     mort::schedule procedure into an ASCII-printable format.
#     Because spaces are used to align columns, the display should
#     use a monospace font.
#
# Arguments
#     schedule
#        The amortization schedule returned from the
#        mort::schedule procedure.
#     output_buffer
#        When the procedure completes, this user-defined buffer will
#        contain the amortization schedule as an ASCII printable
#        string.
#
#  Return Values
#     1  if successful
#
#:>------------------------------------------------------------------
proc mort::format_schedule { schedule output_buffer } {
```

```
    upvar $output_buffer output
    set output ""
    append output\
        "              To            To          Total      \n"
    append output\
        "Month      Principal      Interest     Interest      Balance\n"
    append output\
        "------------------------------------------------------------\n"

    foreach row $schedule {

        # Write values to a list as they are generated.
        append output [format "%4d %12.2f %12.2f %12.2f %12.2f\n"\
                    [lindex $row 0]   [lindex $row 1]   [lindex $row 2]\
                    [lindex $row 3]   [lindex $row 4]]
    }
    return 1
}


#<:-------------------------------------------------------------------
# PROC mort::payment
#
#   Description
#       This procedure will calculate a monthly payment based on
#       a loan amount, an annual interest rate, and the number of
#       years desired for the payoff.
#
#   Arguments
#       amount
#           The amount of the loan.
#       interest
#           The interest rate of the loan.
#       years
#           The number of years desired to pay off the loan.
#       err_buff
#           A user-defined buffer to hold an error message if the
#           supplied fields are not valid.
#
#   Return Values
#       1   if the payment is successfully calculated.
#       0   if the payment could not be calculated. In this case the
#           payment_buff argument will contain an appropriate error
#           message.
#
#:>-------------------------------------------------------------------
proc mort::payment { amount interest years payment_buff} {

    upvar $payment_buff payment

    # Validate the fields. Only positive, numeric values are allowed
    if { [ regexp {^[0-9.]+$} $amount] == 0 } {
```

```
        set payment "AMOUNT FIELD INVALID:\
              Only positive numeric values allowed"
        return 0
} elseif { [ regexp {^[1-9][0-9.]*$} $years] == 0 } {
        set payment "YEARS FIELD INVALID:\
              Only positive numeric values allowed"
        return 0
} elseif { [ regexp {^[0-9.]+$} $interest] == 0 } {
        set payment "INTEREST FIELD INVALID:\
              Only positive numeric values allowed"
        return 0
} else { set payment "" }

# Calculate monthly interest in decimal form
set J [expr ($interest/1200.00)]
set K [expr $J+1]
set N [expr $years * 12]

set payment [format "%.2f" [expr $amount * ( $J/(1-pow($K,-$N)))]]
return 1
}
```

## Package Structure

Because this is the first time that a package including a namespace has been used in this book, it is worthwhile to spend a moment and analyze the structure of the package. There are two concepts you need to be familiar with when creating these types of reusable packages. The first is the Tcl package facility. This facility allows you to build versioned packages that may be easily loaded by any program with the Tcl **package** command. Inside the package you provide a name and a version with the **package provide** statement. For example the mort.tcl package contains the following line of code:

```
package provide mort 1.1
```

This line names the package mort.tcl and assigns it a 1.1 version number. The numbering scheme is intended to follow the typical major.minor revision change used by most programmers today. The major digit indicates a major change that is guaranteed to impact existing code if you switch to a new version. Examples of this would include changing the number, or meaning, of arguments in an existing procedure or the elimination of an existing procedure that may be currently used by programs that included earlier versions of the package. Updating a program with this newer version without changing the program code would cause the program to behave incorrectly or even crash.

Programs that wish to use a predefined package obtain it with the **package require** command. As an example, this chapter's payment.cgi program, discussed next, pulls in the **mort.tcl** package with the following command:

```
package require mort.tcl
```

This command causes the Tcl interpreter to search the paths defined by the **auto_path** variable and find the package named **mort.tcl**. Because a version number is not specified, the latest version of the package available will be loaded. If the version number was specified as the last argument, then the specified version would be returned.

The second concept that now commonly goes hand in hand with the Tcl package facility is the Tcl namespace facility. The namespace facility lets you group variables and procedures into their own context. Tcl has always had one such namespace, which is the *global* namespace. By default any procedures declared in Tcl, outside of a procedure, exist in the global namespace. The **namespace** command, new to Tcl 8.*x*, allows you to create user-defined namespaces containing user-defined variables and procedures. This is similar to the way the C++ *class* command groups variables and functions together.

The **mort.tcl** package exists under the examples directory of the enclosed CD. Its structure is similar to the other packages in this directory. The file mort.tcl contains the code, and the file pkgIndex.tcl is the index file necessary for the Tcl package facility to work. This pkgIndex.tcl file is created by executing the Tcl **pkg_mkIndex** command.

The first few lines of code inside the mort.tcl file use the **namespace eval** command to create a namespace named mort.

```
# Create the mort namespace used to hold all the related variables
# and procedures.
namespace eval mort:: {
    namespace export schedule format_schedule calculate_payment
}
```

The **namespace eval** command creates the specified namespace, if it doesn't already exist, and then executes the script provided inside that namespace. In this case there is only a single command executed, the **namespace export** command, which specifies the procedures that will be imported by other namespaces. This is also one of the few cases in Tcl that you can reference a procedure name before it has actually been defined.

Unlike the C++ *class* command, the Tcl namespace facility doesn't allow you to mark procedures public or private. All procedures contained in a Tcl namespace are public. Any user of the namespace may access any function declared in that namespace by using the fully qualified name of the procedure. The only control you have is whether the commands from a namespace can be imported into a different namespace with the namespace import command. As an example, this code uses the namespace export command to allow the schedule, format_schedule, and calculate_payment procedures to be imported into some other namespace. If additional procedures existed in this package that you did not wish to be imported to other namespaces, you could exclude them from the list of procedures provided to the namespace export command. This does not preclude other namespaces from accessing them. The procedures can always be accessed using the fully qualified procedure name. This does not provide the same level of encapsulation as C++, where you can make functions private. This would indeed be a nice enhancement to Tcl. If you prefer not to use the namespace facility, you can achieve the same results by sticking with a good naming convention for your package procedures and variables.

> The Tcl namespace command allows you to group procedures and variables inside their own namespace, but it does not allow you to hide procedures from the outside world. Any procedure inside a namespace can always be accessed using the fully qualified name.

The rest of the mort.tcl file contains the actual procedures. Each procedure is defined using the fully qualified name, such as mort::payment, which calculates the monthly payment given the amount of the loan, the term in years, and the annual interest rate. Following this type of convention allows you to more easily break the code up into multiple files. It also eliminates the need for indenting each procedure, which would be necessary if you included each procedure declaration inside the original namespace eval command, as is the case with many current examples on the market today.

For more information on the package command or the namespace command, please refer to Appendix B or consult the documentation shipped with the Tcl release. Now let's analyze each of the procedures in a little more detail.

## The mort::payment Procedure

This procedure requires three arguments: the amount of the loan, the annual interest, and the term of the loan in number of years.

```
proc mort::payment { amount interest years payment_buff} {

upvar $payment_buff payment

    # Validate the fields. Only positive, numeric values are allowed
    if { [ regexp {^[0-9.]+$} $amount] == 0 } {
        set payment "AMOUNT FIELD INVALID:\
                Only positive numeric values allowed"
        return 0
    } elseif { [ regexp {^[1-9][0-9.]*$} $years] == 0 } {
        set payment "YEARS FIELD INVALID:\
                Only positive numeric values allowed"
        return 0
    } elseif { [ regexp {^[0-9.]+$} $interest] == 0 } {
        set payment "INTEREST FIELD INVALID:\
                Only positive numeric values allowed"
        return 0
    } else { set payment "" }

    # Calculate monthly interest in decimal form
    set J [expr ($interest/1200.00)]
    set K [expr $J+1]
    set N [expr $years * 12]

    set payment [format "%.2f" [expr $amount * ( $J/(1-pow($K,-$N)))]]
    return 1
}
```

The first thing this procedure does is to validate the arguments to ensure that they are positive values. This is one of the many handy uses of the Tcl **regexp** command. The annual interest and term are then converted to the monthly interest and number of months as required by the formula being used. This could have been done as one line, but I like to keep the code more readable. The variables are then plugged into the formula, discussed at the beginning of this chapter, and returned through the original *payment_buff* argument.

## The mort::schedule Procedure

You pass this procedure the amount to be amortized, the monthly payment, and the annual interest along with two buffers that will contain the amortization schedule and the total finance charge when the procedure returns. The amortization schedule is a list of lists containing the following fields for each month of the payoff schedule:

```
month, principal paid, monthly finance charge, total finance cost,
principal balance
```

The total finance charge returned is the total cost of the loan and is there for convenience so you don't have to build it from the amortization schedule. The code for the **mort::schedule** procedure is as follows:

```
proc mort::schedule {amount payment interest schedule_buff\
                     cost_buff months_buff} {

    upvar $schedule_buff payoff
    upvar $cost_buff cost
    upvar $months_buff months

    # Validate the fields. Only positive, numeric values are allowed
    if { [ regexp {^[0-9.]+$} $amount] == 0 } {
        set payoff "AMOUNT FIELD INVALID:\
                Only positive numeric values allowed"
        return 0
    } elseif { [ regexp {^[0-9.]+$} $payment] == 0 } {
        set payoff "PAYMENT FIELD INVALID:\
                Only positive numeric values allowed"
        return 0
    } elseif { [ regexp {^[0-9.]+$} $interest] == 0 } {
        set payoff "INTEREST FIELD INVALID:\
                Only positive numeric values allowed"
        return 0
    } else { set payoff "" }

    # Make sure the interest charge is not larger than the payment.
    if { [expr $amount * $interest/1200.00] >= $payment } {
        set payoff "Payment is less than monthly interest,\
                    loan will never be paid off"
        return 0
    }

    set cost 0
    set months 0
    # Iteratively reduce the principal balance by the monthly payment
    # less the monthly finance charge until the principal balance is
    # less than the monthly payment. Keep a running total of the
    # finance charge as we go.
    while {$amount >= $payment} {
        set charge [expr $amount * $interest/1200.00]
        set principal_paid [expr $payment - $charge]
        set amount [expr $amount - $principal_paid]
        set cost [expr $cost + $charge]
        incr months
```

```
      # Write values to a list as they are generated.
      lappend payoff [format "%d %.2f %.2f %.2f %.2f"\
                  $months $principal_paid $charge $cost $amount]

   }
   # If any residual amount is left, bump the month by 1 and write
   # out a final record to the payoff schedule.
   if {$amount > 0} {
      set principal_paid $amount
      set amount 0
      set charge 0
      incr months
      lappend payoff [format "%d %.2f %.2f %.2f %.2f"\
                  $months $principal_paid $charge $cost $amount]
   }
   set cost [format "%6.2f" $cost]
   return 1
}
```

The procedure also validates the arguments by checking to make sure the first three are positive numbers. The next thing the procedure does is ensure that a negative amortization situation does not exist. This is done by verifying the monthly payment is larger than the monthly interest charges. If this is not the case, an appropriate error message is returned. If the validation checks succeed, the code iterates through the algorithm just described until the full amortization schedule is generated.

> Negative amortization occurs when the monthly payment is smaller than the monthly interest charge. In this condition the principal amount will grow and the loan will never be paid off.

The mort::schedule procedure returns a 0 if everything goes smoothly, in which case the *schedule_buff* argument will contain the amortization schedule and the *cost_buffer* argument will contain the total finance charge for the loan. If an error occurs, the procedure returns a 1 and the *schedule_buff* argument will contain a textual description of the error.

As long as you have the Tcl shell (tclsh) program available and have installed the code from the enclosed CD, you can easily test this procedure using the package require mort.tcl command from the tclsh and execute the mort::schedule procedure with the appropriate arguments. The following example shows this transaction for a loan amount of $2,000, a monthly payment of $225, and an annual interest rate of 7.0%.

```
> tclsh
% package require mort
1.1
%  mort::schedule 2000 225 7.0 schedule cost months
0
% set cost
59.58
% foreach row $schedule { puts $row }
1 213.33 11.67 11.67 1786.67
2 214.58 10.42 22.09 1572.09
3 215.83 9.17 31.26 1356.26
4 217.09 7.91 39.17 1139.17
5 218.35 6.65 45.82 920.82
6 219.63 5.37 51.19 701.19
7 220.91 4.09 55.28 480.28
8 222.20 2.80 58.08 258.08
9 223.49 1.51 59.58 34.58
10 34.58 0.00 59.58 0.00
%
```

You can see from the results that the total finance charge for the loan is $59.58 and it will take 10 months to pay off the loan. This type of routine makes it easy to play the what-if scenario with different numbers and see how much your loan is costing you. Notice that the data returned through the schedule buffer argument is a list of lists. This is a convenient way of passing data around in a Tcl program.

By creating a small package out of these mortgage routines, you can now easily build a standalone Windows program using Tk to wrap the mort.tcl package or pull it into other Web applications that may require similar calculations. It is always best to try and separate as much code from the actual CGI program as you can. This makes your code more reusable and your CGI programs smaller and easier to follow.

## Designing Web Pages

Because a normal interactive Web page is usually a collection of both static HTML documents and CGI programs, it can be helpful to sketch a diagram showing what files are necessary and how the files are related. Once you start writing applications that contain multiple files, a picture really is worth a thousand words, or more!

Figure 6-2 shows the layout of the mortgage calculator example. You can see from this diagram that there are a total of five files that comprise the mortgage calculator example. The first observation to make is that the static documents all have .html extensions, whereas the CGI programs all have .cgi extensions. Another convenient piece of information available from the diagram is the fact that payment.html and schedule.html are html forms and send their request to the server using the GET method.

Still another piece of information that is critical in an application like this is the actual name of the arguments for the two CGI programs: payment.cgi and schedule.cgi. These names are case sensitive and the fact that the CGI program expects them implies that the HTML form sends them.

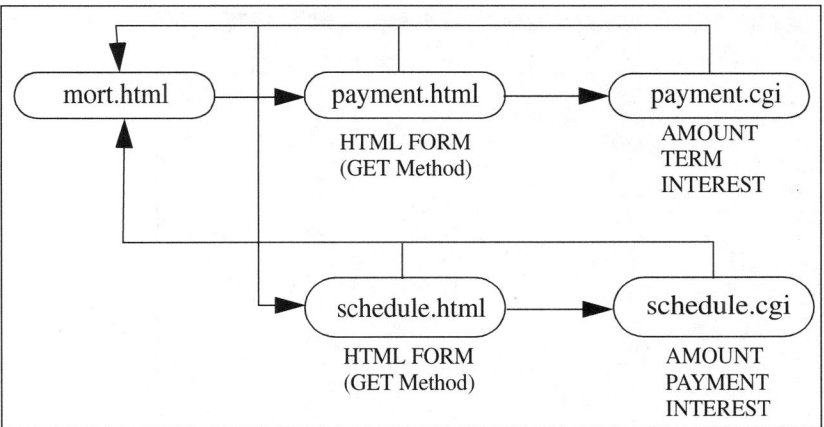

**Figure 6-2** CGI Form Layout

There is a lot of implied information in a diagram like this. One such piece of information is that an HTML form usually contains a submit button, but because it is not specifically called out in the CGI program, it can be ignored. Much of the information must be interpreted in context, which requires a certain level of experience on the part of the reader. Solid arrows from an HTML document indicate a link, whereas solid arrows from an HTML form may indicate a form submission, using either the GET or POST method if the target is a CGI script. Solid arrows from an HTML document indicate a link if the target is another HTML document. However you choose to document the association between your CGI scripts and HTML Web pages, the key is to document them. There are a lot of implied relationships between the CGI programs and HTML Web pages and there is no type checking to protect you as there is in a language like C!

## The Mortgage Calculator Screen

The top level document in our mortgage calculator example is mort.html, shown in Figure 6-3.

This is a static HTML document that contains two links to the payment.html and schedule.html pages. The source code for this page will not be reproduced here, but once again, as you build fancier screens that include backgrounds, tables for centering objects, picture files, and the like, it is much more convenient to work with a Web authoring tool than to attempt writing the HTML code yourself. This screen is not all that complicated in appearance, but the HTML code is already approaching the confusing state!

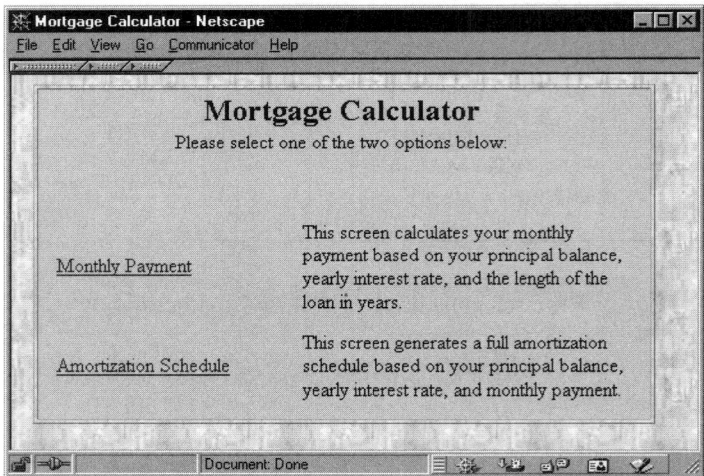

**Figure 6-3** The Mortgage Calculator Top Level Screen

## The Payment Calculator Screen

The monthly payment link points to the payment.html page. The payment.html page is an HTML form with three text elements and a Submit button (see Figure 6-4). The user must fill in the loan amount in dollars, the term in years, and the yearly interest rate. When the form is filled out, the user hits the Submit button to submit the form to the Web server.

The source code for this page is reproduced here to highlight a few important details.

```
<!DOCTYPE HTML PUBLIC "-//W3C//DTD HTML 3.2//EN">
<HTML>
<HEAD>
<META HTTP-EQUIV="Content-Type"
 CONTENT="text/html;CHARSET=iso-8859-1">
<TITLE>Mortgage Calculator</TITLE>
</HEAD>
<BODY BACKGROUND="../images/oakbkgd.jpg" BGCOLOR="#CCFFFF">
<FORM ACTION="payment.cgi" METHOD="GET">
<CENTER>
<P></P>
<P><BR>
<TABLE BORDER="1" WIDTH="425" BGCOLOR="#D8D8D8">
<TR>
<TD WIDTH="100%">
<CENTER>
<P>
<TABLE BORDER="0" WIDTH="100%">
<TR>
<TD WIDTH="100%">
<P ALIGN="CENTER"><B><FONT SIZE="4">Payment Calculator</FONT></B>
</TD>
</TR>
<TR>
<TD WIDTH="100%">
<P ALIGN="CENTER">This tool will calculate a payoff schedule for any
principal balance.<BR>
Simply fill in the required fields below and hit the submit button.
</TD>
</TR>
</TABLE>
<BR>
<TABLE BORDER="1" WIDTH="35%">
<TR>
<TD WIDTH="35%">Loan Amount</TD>
<TD WIDTH="65%"><INPUT TYPE="TEXT" NAME="AMOUNT" SIZE="17"></TD>
</TR>
<TR>
<TD WIDTH="35%">Term (Years)</TD>
<TD WIDTH="65%"><INPUT TYPE="TEXT" NAME="TERM" SIZE="17"></TD>
</TR>
<TR>
<TD WIDTH="35%">Yearly Interest</TD>
<TD WIDTH="65%"><INPUT TYPE="TEXT" NAME="INTEREST" SIZE="17"></TD>
</TR>
</TABLE>
</P>
</CENTER>
<CENTER>
<P><INPUT TYPE="SUBMIT" NAME="Submit" VALUE="Submit"></P>
</CENTER>
<P><A HREF="mort.html">Return to main screen</A>
```

```
</TD>
</TR>
</TABLE>
</CENTER>
<P>
</FORM>
</BODY>
</HTML>
```

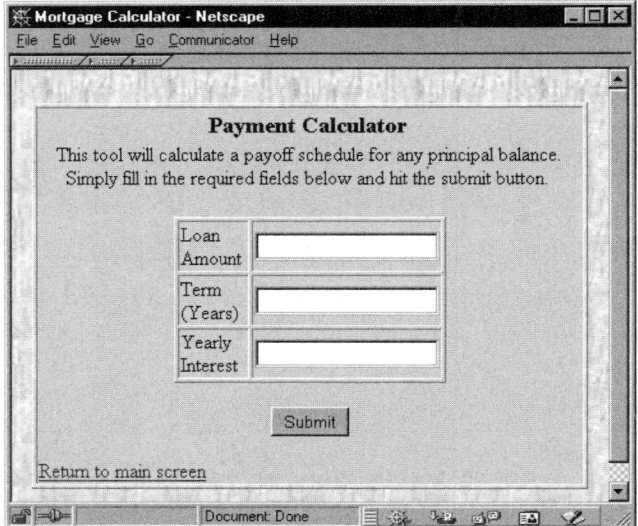

**Figure 6-4** The Payment Calculator Screen

The FORM ACTION statement specifies the type of form submission and the name of the CGI script to call when the Submit button is pressed.

```
<FORM ACTION="payment.cgi" METHOD="GET">
```

This program will call the payment.cgi program and transfer the information using the GET method. Remember that the GET method tells the Web server to transfer the form data to the CGI program via the QUERY_STRING environment variable and not through standard in. You should also notice the three INPUT TYPE declarations that specify the names of the three text boxes to be filled in by the user.

```
<TD WIDTH="65%"><INPUT TYPE="TEXT" NAME="AMOUNT" SIZE="17"></TD>
<TD WIDTH="65%"><INPUT TYPE="TEXT" NAME="TERM" SIZE="17"></TD>
<TD WIDTH="65%"><INPUT TYPE="TEXT" NAME="INTEREST" SIZE="17"></TD>
```

Additionally, the form contains a Submit button. The name of the Submit button is "Submit" and the value of the submit is also "Submit":

```
<P><INPUT TYPE="SUBMIT" NAME="Submit" VALUE="Submit"></P>
```

In this program it is irrelevant what name or value the Submit button has, because the CGI program does not care that a Submit button exists. If the data was delivered to the Web server, the Submit button performed its function! This may be the case in many CGI programs that process data from a single HTML form. In other cases the HTML form may have multiple Submit buttons or may be one in a series of forms that call the same CGI program. In these cases the name and value of the Submit button are important because the CGI program will switch off the value of the Submit button to decide how to process the input.

When the user fills in the form and presses the Submit button, the payment.cgi program is called. Once again, the program includes the cgi.tcl package and the mort.tcl package. The first thing the program does is call the cgi_parse routine to get the form data from the Web server. If an error is returned from this routine, the program calls the cgi_print_message procedure to report the error condition and returns. The source code for this program follows.

```
#!/usr/local/bin/tclsh8.0

# This script will take the form data from the mortgage calculation
# form and calculate a payoff schedule and return it to the user.
# The required field names that this form will look for are shown
# below. These field names are case sensitive.
#
# AMOUNT    This is the amount of the loan to be amortized.
# TERM      This is the length of the loan in years.
# INTEREST  This is the annual interest rate.

package require cgi.tcl
package require mort.tcl

# Parse the cgi arguments to create the cgi() data array and check for
# the required cgi fields

if { [cgi_parse] } {
    cgi_print_message "mort.cgi received no input from form"\
                      "Back to Mortgage Calculator"\
                       mort.cgi

    return 1

}

if { [cgi_validate_fields "AMOUNT TERM INTEREST" err_msg] } {
```

```
      cgi_print_message $err_msg "Back to Mortgage Calculator" mort.cgi
      return
} else {
   set amount $cgi(AMOUNT)
   set term $cgi(TERM)
   set interest $cgi(INTEREST)
}

# Calculate the monthly payment
if {  ![mort::payment $amount $interest $term payment ] } {
   cgi_print_message $payment "Back to Mortgage Calculator" mort.cgi
   return 1
}

# Return the results to the browser.
cgi_header "MONTHLY PAYMENT" {BGCOLOR=white TEXT=black}
puts [cgi_link "Back to Mortgage Calculator" mort.html]

cgi_pre
puts "Loan Amount    \$$amount"
puts "Term           $term"
puts "Interest       $interest%\n"
puts "Payment = \$$payment"
cgi_pre_end
return 0
```

The cgi_validate_fields routine is used to verify that the cgi array produced by the cgi_parse routine contains the proper field names expected by this program. In this case the field names are AMOUNT, TERM, and INTEREST. If these names were not received from the Web browser, the program prints a message indicating which required field was missing and exits.

If the required fields are present, the program sets some local variables equal to the values in the cgi array and then calls the mort::calculate_payment procedure to get the monthly payment. The remainder of the program makes a few simple calls to the cgi.tcl library to generate the HTML output. The actual HTML code produced by the CGI program is small and clean. Can you see the correlation between the payment.cgi code and the resulting HTML code shown here?

```
<HTML>
<HEAD>
<TITLE>MONTHLY PAYMENT</TITLE>
</HEAD>
<BODY BGCOLOR=white TEXT=black>
<A href="mort.html">Back to Mortgage Calculator</A>
<BR> <BR>
<H4>LOAN AMOUNT = 10000; TERM = 30; INTEREST = 7 </H4>
<BR>
```

```
<H3>Monthly payment is 66.5414</H3>
</BODY>
</HTML>
```

The screen in Figure 6-5 results when submitting a loan amount of $10,000 with a term of 20 years and an annual interest rate of 7%.

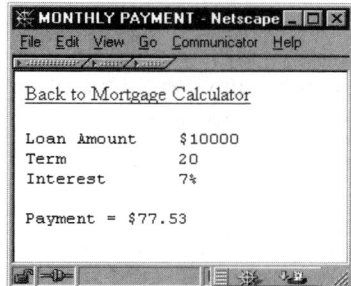

**Figure 6-5** Monthly Payment Results Screen

## The Amortization Schedule

Going back to the main (mort.html) screen and clicking on the Amortization Schedule link brings up the screen shown in Figure 6-6.

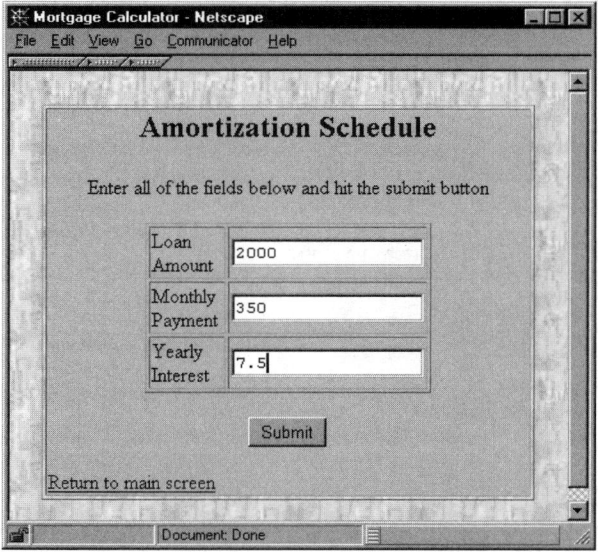

**Figure 6-6** Entry Screen for the Amortization Schedule

In this case we have entered a loan amount of $2,000 with a monthly payment of $350 and an annual interest rate of 7.5%. No need to look at the HTML code for this form because it is nearly identical to the payment.html form from the last section. The only real difference is the monthly payment field (PAYMENT) in place of the term (TERM) field. This form calls the schedule.cgi script upon submission and once again uses the GET method for form submission.

The schedule.cgi code that calculates the amortization schedule is not much longer than the program that calculated the monthly payment. One of the reasons for this is that we elected to build a mortgage package to do the calculations for us and simply include this package in our CGI program.

```
# This script will take the form data from the mortgage calculation
# form and calculate a payoff schedule and return it to the user.
# The required field names that this form will look for are shown
# below. These field names are case sensitive.
#
# AMOUNT     This is the amount of the loan to be amortized.

# PAYMENT    This is the monthly payment to be made.
# INTEREST   This is the annual interest rate.

package require cgi.tcl
package require mort.tcl

# Parse the cgi arguments to create the cgi() data array and check for
# the required cgi fields

if { [cgi_parse] } {
   cgi_print_message "mort.cgi received no input from form"\
                     "Back to Mortgage Calculator"\
                     mort.cgi
   return 1
}

if { [cgi_validate_fields "AMOUNT PAYMENT INTEREST" err_msg] } {
   cgi_print_message $err_msg "Back to Mortgage Calculator" mort.cgi
   return
} else {
   set amount $cgi(AMOUNT)
   set payment $cgi(PAYMENT)
   set interest $cgi(INTEREST)
}

if {  ![mort::schedule $amount $payment $interest payoff cost months ]
} {
   cgi_print_message $payoff "Back to Mortgage Calculator" mort.cgi
   return
}
```

```
mort::format_schedule  $payoff output

cgi_header "PAYOFF SCHEDULE" {BGCOLOR=white TEXT=black}
cgi_h4 "AMORTIZATION SCHEDULE"
cgi_h4 "Loan Amount = \$$amount; Payment = \$$payment; Interest =
$interest%\n"
cgi_pre
cgi_puts $output
cgi_pre_end
cgi_h4 "Total Interest Paid = \$$cost  Total Months = $months\n"
puts [cgi_link "Back to Mortgage Calculator" mort.html]
cgi_end
return 0
```

The CGI program calculates the amortization schedule and dynamically generates an HTML-formatted page as shown in Figure 6-7. This code will produce an amortization schedule for any loan amount. However, large loan amounts may result in a very large table. This requires you to scroll the entire window and can make the design of Web pages difficult if you need to include other information on the page with the returned amortization schedule.

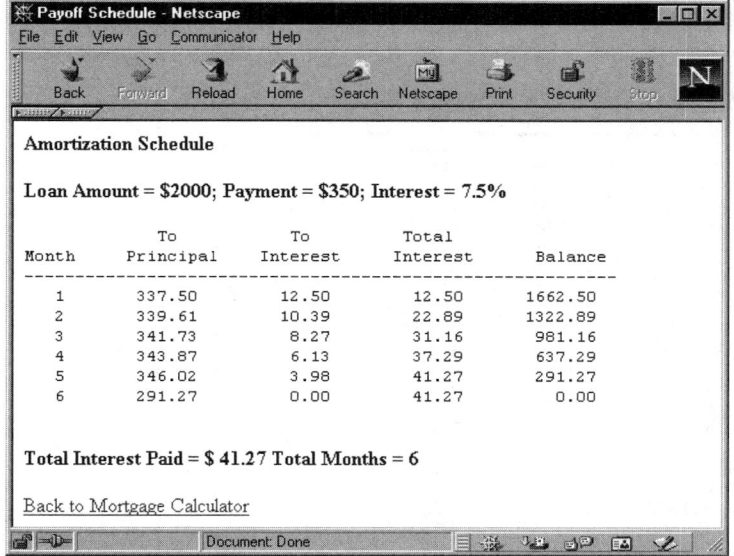

**Figure 6-7** Amortization Schedule Results Screen

The program steps should be starting to look familiar by now.

- Include cgi.tcl and mort.tcl.
- Call **cgi_parse** to get the form data from the Web browser.
- Call **cgi_validate_fields** to ensure that the Web browser sent the proper data.
- Process the data: in this case a call to **mort_schedule** with the amount, payment, interest, and a buffer to place the payoff schedule, the total cost, and the total months. Because **mort_schedule** returns a list for the payoff schedule, it is first converted to a printable form with the **mort_format_schedule** procedure call.
- Dynamically build an HTML form that includes the processed data.

### A Cleaner Display

One solution to this problem is to return the data in a scrolling text window using the **cgi_text_area** command to produce a more user-friendly screen as shown in Figure 6-8.

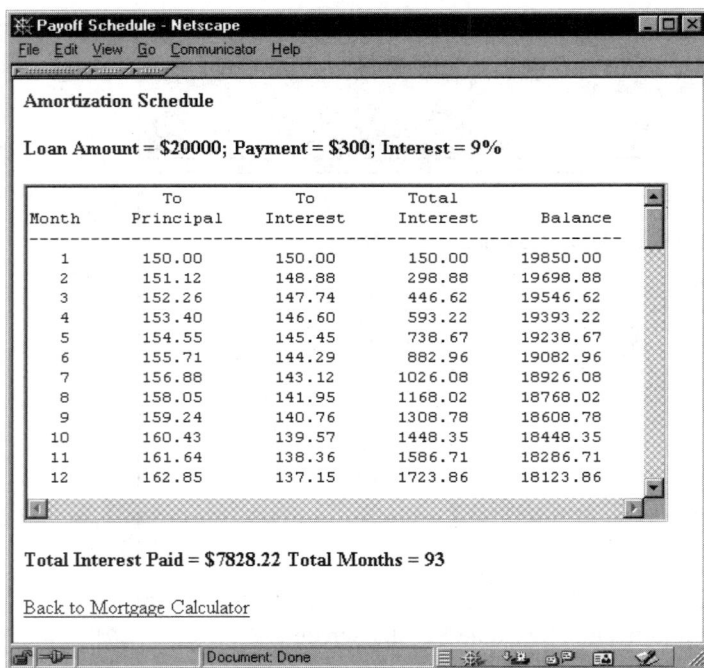

**Figure 6-8** A Better Amortization Schedule Display

One thing to remember when taking this approach is that the text area element is really a form element and therefore needs to be placed inside of the form tags.

Now that the size of the display is more predictable, you can format the screen for easier understanding. Notice that the total interest and months appears at the bottom of the screen along with the link that returns to the main calculator page. This makes it easier for the reader to pull out the information he or she is interested in.

The code modifications were slight but the change in appearance, especially for large amortization tables, is significant:

```
#!/usr/local/bin/tclsh8.0

# This script will take the form data from the mortgage calculation
# form and calculate a payoff schedule and return it to the user.
# The required field names that this form will look for are shown
# below. These field names are case sensitive.
#
# AMOUNT    This is the amount of the loan to be amortized.
# PAYMENT   This is the monthly payment to be made.
# INTEREST  This is the annual interest rate.

package require cgi.tcl
package require mort.tcl

# Parse the cgi arguments to create the cgi() data array and check for
# the required cgi fields

if { [cgi_parse] } {
   cgi_print_message "mort.cgi received no input from form"\
                     "Back to Mortgage Calculator"\
                      mort.cgi
   return 1
}

if { [cgi_validate_fields "AMOUNT PAYMENT INTEREST" err_msg] } {
   cgi_print_message $err_msg "Back to Mortgage Calculator" mort.cgi
   return
} else {
   set amount $cgi(AMOUNT)
   set payment $cgi(PAYMENT)
   set interest $cgi(INTEREST)
}

if {  ![mort::schedule $amount $payment $interest payoff cost months ]
} {
   cgi_print_message $payoff "Back to Mortgage Calculator" mort.cgi
   return 1
```

```
    }

    mort::format_schedule  $payoff output

    cgi_header "PAYOFF SCHEDULE" {BGCOLOR=white TEXT=black}
    cgi_h4 "AMORTIZATION SCHEDULE"
    cgi_h4 "Loan Amount = \$$amount; Payment = \$$payment; Interest =
    $interest%\n"
    cgi_form "default.cgi"
    cgi_text_area 15 60 textbox $output
    cgi_form_end
    cgi_h4 "Total Interest Paid = \$$cost  Total Months = $months\n"
    puts [cgi_link "Back to Mortgage Calculator" mort.html]
    cgi_end
    return 0
```

The only difference in this code are the few lines at the bottom of the file that create a form with an included text box. The text box is used to contain the output from the **mort::format_schedule** procedure. This one call to the cgi_text_area box creates the scrolling text box with the amortization schedule inside.

```
    cgi_form "default.cgi"
    cgi_text_area 15 60 textbox $output
    cgi_form_end
```

## Chapter Summary

As you can see, a CGI program does not have to be very large to provide some useful functionality. This chapter should have demonstrated the following points to you.

- The cgi.tcl library takes care of most of the details of obtaining and validating the form data that is made available by the Web server.
- Creating small, reusable modules that produce HTML code allows you to mix and match building blocks to create meaningful content in your Web documents.
- Creative use of available Web editing tools and variable substitution can reduce the work required to build your forms.
- Hidden fields can be used to convey information to the CGI program that is not displayed to the client's Web browser screen.

You may have even reached some conclusions of your own along the way. For example, you may be thinking that it was a lot of work to add a counter to an otherwise static HTML document. Surely there must be a better way! There is. Some Web servers contain a feature that makes it easier to embed dynamic code inside your static HTML documents. This feature is known as Server Side Includes and will be covered in Chapter 8. We will use this feature to embed the counter inside the static HTML document without having to convert it to a CGI program.

If you are an experienced programmer, you might also have taken some exception to the burden placed on the Web server to validate the form data sent from the client's Web browser before actually processing the data. Unfortunately, one of the inefficiencies of the HTML language is that there is no way to validate form data, at least under the 3.$x$ specification at the client's end. This actually creates quite a bit of excess traffic on the World Wide Web, which could be avoided with just a little more intelligence on the client machine side.

Chapter 15 will show you how to use the Tcl Web browser plug-in to reduce some of this traffic by performing field validation at the client's Web browser. The browser plug-in allows you to embed Tcl code inside the returned HTML document, which is then processed by the Web browser plug-in. This eliminates extraneous messages that simply deal with field validation issues, thus reducing traffic on the Web and increasing the performance of your CGI programs. In fact a simple program like this can be executed entirely at the client's end after the initial transaction to the Web server to retrieve the page with the embedded Tcl code.

# Chapter 7

## Counting Your Hits

Many Web pages on the World Wide Web employ some type of counter to record the number of times a particular Web page has been accessed. You have no doubt encountered these types of *hit counters* at various sites. This chapter will show you how to modify the top level Mortgage Calculator screen from the last chapter to include a counter that will increment each time the server executes the cgi script.

This involves turning the top level screen into a CGI program that dynamically displays a counter with the appropriate count each time the program is executed. Because it's a shame to waste all that HTML code our Web editing tool produced for us in the last chapter, this chapter will show you how to reuse it.

One of the key points addressed by this chapter's example is how a CGI program can remember its state from one execution to the next. In order for the counter to increment, there must be a way for the CGI program to remember the previous value of the counter. The most straightforward way to do this is to save the counter value away in a file. The CGI program then accesses the file each time it is executed to find out what the last count was. This method can be used to hold any type of state information that must be maintained by the CGI program. This chapter uses an external file as a way to maintain this state information.

## The counter.tcl Package

The counter.tcl package included in the package's subdirectory on the enclosed CD is a simple but effective package for generating a counter using standard HTML tags. The package relies on an external file to hold the count value between executions.

Once again, we use the **package require** command to obtain the cgi.tcl package and our new counter.tcl package.

```
package require cgi.tcl
package provide counter.tcl 1.1
```

In contrast to the mort.tcl package, this package will not utilize a namespace. This has been done so you can see an example of naming conventions being employed to achieve the same results. There are only two procedures in the package, counter_display and counter_get_count. The counter_display procedure is used by the CGI program to dynamically build the counter with the appropriate count. The counter_get_count procedure is used to obtain the current count from the user-defined file. We will examine the counter_get_count procedure first.

### The counter_get_count Procedure

This procedure is intended to be a local procedure to the counter.tcl package. It is called by the counter_display procedure to read the count to be displayed from the user-defined file. The procedure accepts a filename argument and attempts to open the file in a loop. The reason for the loop is to solve some concurrency issues that might exist if another client is accessing the file at exactly the same time. Perl contains a useful function called flock, which will get exclusive access to a file and wait if the file is busy. There is no such mechanism in Tcl, but the scheme just presented will work fine for most situations. If the program loops ten times, then an error string is returned through the error argument to the procedure and the procedure returns a -1.

If the file is successfully opened, the first of the file is read into a variable named value. The first line of the file must contain a string representation of the current count. White space is ignored using the **string trim** command. The value that is read is incremented and then immediately written back to the file and the file is closed. This must be an autonomous operation so that any other programs trying to read the number will not read the contents in the middle of it being modified. The value read from the file is then returned as the return parameter of the function.

```
#<:----------------------------------------------------------------
# PROC counter_get_count
#
#  Description
#     Get the current count from the file name passed in from
#     the caller.
#
# Arguments
#     fname
#        The name of the file that holds the count.
#     error
#        A buffer to pass back any error that occurs during the
#        file access.
#
#  Return Values
#     1  if successful
#
#:>----------------------------------------------------------------
proc counter_get_count { filename error } {

    upvar $error err
    # Loop trying to open file in case it is locked
    for { set i 0 } { $i < 10 } { incr i } {
        if { [catch { set fptr [open $filename r+] } err_msg] } {
            if { $i < 10 } {
                after 1000
                continue
            }
        } else { break }
    }

    # Error out if we could not read the file
    if { $i == 10 } {
        set err "Could not access count file: error was $err_msg"
        return -1
    }

    set value [string trim [gets $fptr]]
    seek $fptr 0 start
    puts $fptr [expr $value + 1]
    close $fptr
    return $value
}
```

## The counter_display Procedure

Now we can turn our attention back to the **counter_display** procedure. This procedure is called in line by the CGI program and outputs the HTML code for the counter display. This means that the CGI program must have already output the appropriate header information.

The **counter_display** procedure accepts a number of arguments that specify the file name the count is stored in and the display attributes of the counter. The first thing the procedure does is call the **counter_get_count** to read the count from the file name passed in by the caller. In our example the file name is counter_value. If the **counter_get_count** procedure fails, then the counter procedure simply outputs an error message and returns. It does not output any of the necessary header information; this is the job of the caller.

```
#<:------------------------------------------------------------------
# PROC counter_display
#
#   Description
#       This procedure displays the counter. The count is read
#       from the file name passed in by the caller.
#
# Arguments
#       fname
#           The name of the file that holds the count.
#       bkcolor
#           The background color of the counter.
#       fgcolor
#           The foreground color of the counter.
#       border
#           The width of the table border.
#       width
#           The width of the table. If followed by a % sign,
#           it specifies a width in terms of a percentage of the
#           browser page, otherwise it is the number of pixels.
#    font
#           The font size to be used for digits of the counter.
#
#   Return Values
#       1  if successful
#
#:>------------------------------------------------------------------
proc counter_display { fname bkcolor fgcolor border width font } {

    if { [set counter_value [counter_get_count $fname err]] == -1 } {
        cgi_h4 "could not build counter, err was '$err'"
        return 1
    }
```

```
    set counter_value [format "%06d" $counter_value]
    cgi_puts "<TABLE BORDER=\"$border\">"
    cgi_tr
    for { set x 0 } { $x < [string length $counter_value] } { incr x } {
        cgi_puts "<TD WIDTH=\"12\"BGCOLOR=\"$bkcolor\">
                  <FONT SIZE=\"$font\"COLOR=\"$fgcolor\">
                  [string index $counter_value $x]</FONT></TD>"
    }
    cgi_tr_end
    cgi_table_end
}
```

Assuming no error occurs reading the counter_value file, this procedure takes the value and formats it to be a six-place decimal number, padded with leading zeros. The formatting is accomplished with the Tcl **format** command. The format specifiers are the same as they are in the C programming language. The rest of the code then writes out the HTML code for a table with one row, where each column contains one digit of the counter. You can check the output by using the tclsh. Simply execute the **tclsh** command from the command line in the directory where this code exists and call the procedure to see the code it returns.

```
> tclsh
% package require counter.tcl
% counter red white 1 112 5
<TABLE BORDER="1">
<TR>
<TD WIDTH="12"BGCOLOR="red"><FONT SIZE="5" COLOR="white">0</FONT></TD>
<TD WIDTH="12"BGCOLOR="red"><FONT SIZE="5" COLOR="white">0</FONT></TD>
<TD WIDTH="12"BGCOLOR="red"><FONT SIZE="5" COLOR="white">0</FONT></TD>
<TD WIDTH="12"BGCOLOR="red"><FONT SIZE="5" COLOR="white">0</FONT></TD>
<TD WIDTH="12"BGCOLOR="red"><FONT SIZE="5" COLOR="white">4</FONT></TD>
<TD WIDTH="12"BGCOLOR="red"><FONT SIZE="5" COLOR="white">2</FONT></TD>
</TR>
</TABLE>
%
```

Here we asked for a red background with white letters, a border around the table of 1 pixel, a total width for the table of 112 pixels, and a font size of 5. If you're curious to see what the counter looks like, you can execute the counter.cgi program in this chapter's example directory, which displays the counter by itself as shown in Figure 7-1.

**Figure 7-1** Hit Counter

Well, we now have the top level Mortgage Calculator screen from the previous chapter and a Tcl package that dynamically generates the HTML code for our hit counter. The question is, how do we combine the two? In essence you need to turn your static HTML document into a CGI program. One of the easiest ways is to save the HTML code that has been generated by the Web editing tool of your choice and then simply output it at the appropriate place in your newly created CGI program.

The following mort.cgi program shows how this can be accomplished. Notice that the variable **doc_text** contains the HTML code created in the last chapter. The reason the text is contained in {} characters is to prevent the Tcl parser from performing any substitution on it. Remember that Tcl performs command and variable substitution on quoted strings but not on strings contained inside {} characters. This allows you to cut any type of HTML code from a static Web page and set a variable equal to the contents. Then when you are ready, you can simply output the contents of the variable with the **cgi_puts** command.

The reason that the header lines were excluded is that they will be recreated with the **cgi_header** routine in this program. This allows for the generation of the Content-Type: text/html line, which must precede the HTML output sent to the server. You could also place this at the beginning of the **doc_text** with a couple of blank lines after it. Either approach should get the job done.

```
#!/usr/local/bin/tclsh

package require cgi.tcl
package require counter.tcl

set doc_text {

<CENTER>
<TABLE BORDER="1" WIDTH="41%" BGCOLOR="#D8D8D8">
<TR>
<TD WIDTH="100%">
<TABLE BORDER="0" WIDTH="100%">
<TR>
<TD WIDTH="100%">
<P ALIGN="CENTER"><B><FONT SIZE="5">Mortgage Calculator</FONT></B>
</TD>
</TR>
<TR>
<TD WIDTH="100%">
<P ALIGN="CENTER">Please select one of the two options below:
</TD>
</TR>
</TABLE>
```

```
<BR>
<BR>
<TABLE BORDER="0" CELLSPACING="12" WIDTH="477">
<TR>
<TD WIDTH="39%"><A HREF="payment.html">Monthly Payment</A></TD>
<TD WIDTH="61%">This screen calculates your monthly payment based on
your principal balance, yearly interest rate, and the length of the
loan in years.</TD>
</TR>
<TR>
<TD WIDTH="39%"><A HREF="schedule.html">Amortization Schedule</A></TD>
<TD WIDTH="61%">This screen generates a full amortization schedule
based on your principal balance, yearly interest rate, and monthly
payment.</TD>
</TR>
</TABLE>
</TD>
</TR>
</TABLE>
}
cgi_header "Mortgage Calculator" {BACKGROUND="../images/oakbkgd.jpg"}
cgi_puts $doc_text
cgi_puts "You are number"
counter red white 1 112 4
cgi_puts "to visit this page"
cgi_puts "</CENTER></BODY> </HTML>"
```

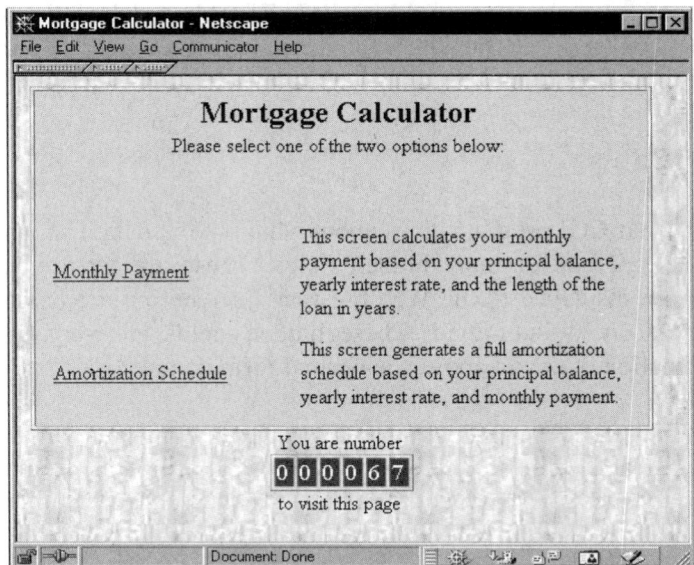

**Figure 7-2** Mortgage Calculator with Hit Counter Displayed

This cuts our CGI program down to just six lines of code! The first two lines generate the opening <BODY> and <HTML> tags with the appropriate background specified and then output the HTML text that we borrowed from our static HTML page. The last four lines print the counter greeting and the counter itself. This is the reason that the counter was written to output HTML-type tags directly so that it could be easily embedded in CGI programs. Figure 7-2 shows the new top level screen with the counter included.

# More Tricks

We now have a fully functioning program that contains three HTML files and three CGI programs, just as we did in the last chapter with the exception of the extra hit counter added to the top level screen. If you're like most programmers, you're probably already looking for ways to simplify and consolidate the code. Good! One of the ways you can do this is by combining the payment.cgi and the schedule.cgi programs into one CGI program that handles requests from both the payment.html form and the schedule.html form. How can this be done? The two forms submit different data. The schedule.html submits three form elements named AMOUNT, PAYMENT, and INTEREST, and the payment.html form submits three form elements named AMOUNT, TERM, and INTEREST. How will the combined cgi script know which form elements to expect? The answer is through the use of hidden fields.

## The Hidden Field

One way to pass your CGI program clues about what type of data it should expect is through the use of one or more hidden fields. These are form elements in HTML that are not displayed to the Web browser's screen but are passed to the server when the form is submitted. These hidden fields are very useful for conveying information over and above the normal form data.

We will use this hidden field concept to pass a key piece of information to the new combined.cgi program, which contains the two CGI programs from the last chapter rolled into one. The payment.html file and the schedule.html file each contain one additional line of HTML code that declares a hidden field. This hidden field is then used by the combined.cgi script to determine what type of request it received. The payment.html declares a hidden field named *MODE* with a value of *payment* with the following line.

```
<INPUT TYPE="HIDDEN" NAME="MODE" SIZE="-1" VALUE="payment"></P>
```

Likewise, the schedule.html declares a hidden field named ***MODE*** with a value of
***schedule*** with the following line.

```
<INPUT TYPE="HIDDEN" NAME="MODE" SIZE="-1" VALUE="schedule"></P>
```

Additionally, the action attribute of the form tag in each of these files was changed
to point to the new combined.cgi program. The combined.cgi program then
checks for the existence of the MODE field and switches off the value to perform
the appropriate calculation. The source code for the combined.cgi program
follows.

```
#!/usr/local/bin/tclsh

# This script will take the form data from the mortgage calculation
# form and calculate a payoff schedule and return it to the user.
# The required field names that this form will look for are shown
# below. These field names are case sensitive.
#
# AMOUNT     This is the amount of the loan to be amortized.
# TERM       This is the length of the loan in years.
# INTEREST   This is the annual interest rate.

package require cgi.tcl
package require mort.tcl

# Parse the cgi arguments to create the cgi() data array and check for
# the required cgi fields

if { [cgi_parse] } {
    cgi_print_message "mort.cgi received no input from form"\
                      "Back to Mortgage Calculator"\
                       mort.cgi
    return 1
}

# Verify that the MODE field was received
if { [cgi_validate_fields "MODE" err_msg] } {
    cgi_print_message $err_msg "Back to Mortgage Calculator" mort.cgi
    return 1
}

switch $cgi(MODE) {
    payment {
        # Calculate and print the monthly payment.
        if { [cgi_validate_fields "AMOUNT TERM INTEREST" err_msg] } {
            cgi_print_message $err_msg \
                    "Back to Mortgage Calculator" mort.cgi
            return
```

```tcl
        } else {
           set amount $cgi(AMOUNT)
           set term $cgi(TERM)
           set interest $cgi(INTEREST)
        }

        if {  ![mort::payment $amount $interest $term payment ] } {
           cgi_print_message $payment \
                   "Back to Mortgage Calculator" mort.cgi
           return 1
        }

        cgi_header "MONTHLY PAYMENT" {BGCOLOR=white TEXT=black}
        puts [cgi_link "Back to Mortgage Calculator" mort.cgi]
        cgi_pre
        puts "Loan Amount      \$$amount"
        puts "Term             $term"
        puts "Interest         $interest%\n"
        puts "Payment = \$$payment"
        cgi_pre_end
        return 0
    }

    schedule {
        # Calculate and print the amortization schedule
        if { [cgi_validate_fields "AMOUNT PAYMENT INTEREST" err_msg] } {
           cgi_print_message\
                   $err_msg "Back to Mortgage Calculator" mort.cgi
           return
        } else {
           set amount $cgi(AMOUNT)
           set payment $cgi(PAYMENT)
           set interest $cgi(INTEREST)
        }

        if {  [mort::schedule $amount $payment $interest\
                                 payoff cost months ] } {
           cgi_print_message $err_msg \
                   "Back to Mortgage Calculator" mort.cgi
           return
        }

        mort::format_schedule  $payoff output

        cgi_header "PAYOFF SCHEDULE" {BGCOLOR=white TEXT=black}
        cgi_h4 "AMORTIZATION SCHEDULE"
        cgi_h4 "Loan Amount = $amount; Payment = $payment;\
                            Interest = $interest%\n"
        cgi_form "default.cgi"
        cgi_text_area 15 60 textbox $output
        cgi_form_end
        cgi_h4 "Total Interest Paid = $cost  Total Months = $months\n"
```

```
        puts [cgi_link "Back to Mortgage Calculator" mort.cgi]
        cgi_end
        return 0
    }
}
```

This is just one possible use for the hidden field element in CGI programs. You can be the judge as to the value of this particular example, but it's easy to see how hidden fields can be used to communicate information to a CGI program that is not displayed to the client's Web browser.

Another typical use for hidden fields is to maintain state information. Oftentimes a CGI program may need to remember something about a particular client from one invocation to the next. This is different than our counter example, which only kept track of the number of times a Web page was accessed, regardless of who accessed it. For instance, you may want to keep track of a person's zip code as he or she traverses from one Web screen to the next so you can present the appropriate information, but you don't want it cluttering up every screen. This would be a perfect use for a hidden field.

## Chapter Summary

This chapter should have demonstrated the following points to you.

- Existing programs can be enhanced with relative ease by adding features such as a hit counter to display the number of people that have accessed the site.
- By creatively using tables you can avoid using fancier graphing programs to produce your counters.
- An external file can be used to maintain state information from one execution of a CGI program to the next.
- Hidden fields can be used to convey information to the CGI program that is not displayed to the client's Web browser screen.

# *Chapter 8*

## *Server Side Includes*

One of the lessons learned in the last chapter is that there are often times when we would like to include some dynamic content in our static HTML forms without having to convert them into CGI programs.

In the case of the mortgage calculator example, it would have been desirable to execute the counter.tcl program from within the HTML document at the point where we wanted the counter to be displayed without having to turn the document into a CGI program to do so. Other examples might include the ability to add a date and time stamp to a static HTML document or perhaps to insert some file characteristics such as the size of the file or the last time it was modified.

Some servers provide just this type of ability in a feature known as Server Side Includes, or SSI for short. Most servers provide this functionality, but not all. You must check the documentation for the particular Web server you are running to determine if Server Side Includes are available.

The code in this chapter again refers to the NCSA server but is generally representative of the types of features available on servers that include this feature.

## Understanding Server Side Includes

Server Side Includes are directives that can be embedded directly into your HTML documents. Figure 8-1 illustrates a typical transaction using Server Side Includes. When a Web browser requests a document that includes these directives, the Web server will process the document, evaluate the directives, replace them with the resulting HMTL code, and return the resulting document to the Web browser. Server Side Includes are not really CGI programming but can make a useful weapon in your arsenal of CGI programming tricks.

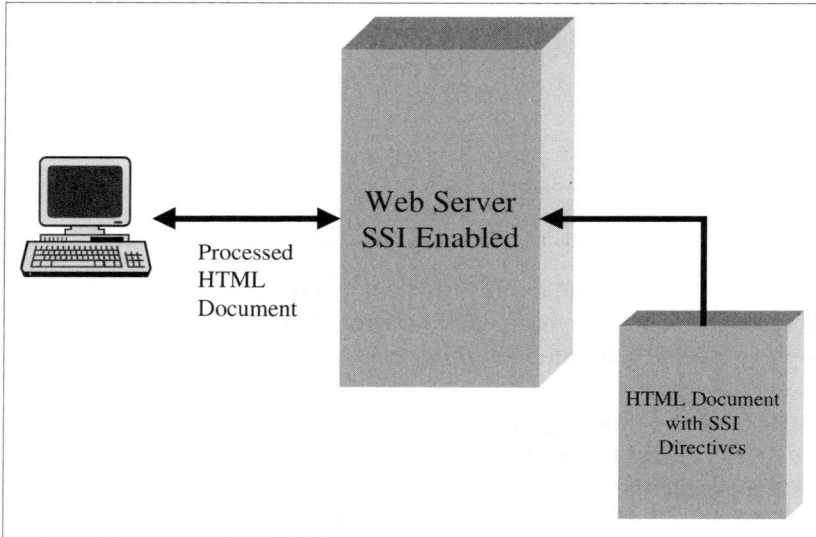

**Figure 8-1** SSI Document Flow

So how does the Web server know to process the HTML document? The answer is the same as for CGI programs—by the file extension. A common file extension for HTML documents containing SSI directives is .shtml. You establish the file extensions that will be processed as well as other characteristics of the Web server's behavior in the Web server's configuration file.

## Configuring Your Web Server

In order to take advantage of Server Side Includes, your Web server must be configured properly. In the NCSA Web server there are two configuration files you will need to edit in order to enable SSI processing and control its behavior. These files are srm.conf and access.conf.

The first thing you will probably want to do is configure your server for which file extensions the server will process for SSI directives. To do this you would add a line as follows to the srm.conf file:

```
AddType text/x-server-parsed-html .shtml
```

This line will instruct the server to parse any documents that end in .shtml. Alternatively, you could add the following line to instruct the server to parse all HTML documents:

```
AddType text/x-server-parsed-html .html
```

This makes the job of organizing a Web site easier, because you don't have two extensions for HTML-type documents, but it can be costly. Instructing the server to process all .html type documents will add a lot of overhead and degrade your server's performance if the majority of your documents don't have SSI directives embedded in them.

The server.conf file dictates which files the Web server will process by using the file extension, but you must also specify what type of processing is allowed on these documents. This is done in the access.conf file. This file tells the server which SSI directives to process. This file expects a directive named **Options**, which can have several arguments.

To enable processing of all SSI directives, you would simply use the All argument.

```
Options All
```

To enable parsing SSI directives that embed environment variables in your document, you would use the Includes argument to the **Options** command in one of two ways. If you also wish to be able to process external programs, you would use the following line:

```
Options Includes ExecCGI
```

To enable parsing SSI directives that embed environment variables in your document without enabling the execution of external applications, you would use the line:

```
Options IncludesNoExec
```

As usual, there are security considerations you must keep in mind when you enable a feature such as Server Side Includes. One such issue is providing novice users the ability to execute system commands from inside HTML documents. As an example, it would be easy for a novice user to execute system commands that might seriously degrade server performance or release confidential information to the clients who should not have access to it. In short, giving the ability to execute external programs from inside static HTML documents can place higher expectations on the typical Web page designer.

## Server Side Includes Directives

Despite the security risks and potential server overhead, Server Side Includes can be a useful feature. Table 8-1 shows the directives supported on the NCSA Web server. The remainder of this chapter will be devoted to examples of the usage of these different directives, but not necessarily in the order they are presented in the table.

So how do we actually go about inserting one of these SSI directives in our HTML document? Server Side Includes directives are inserted using what appears to be a comment field in the HTML document. The format for an HTML comment field is

```
<!-- Text of Comment -->
```

The format of a Server Side Includes directive is

```
<!--#command parameter="argument"-->
```

As you can see, this looks like a comment to the HTML document. An SSI enabled server will expand these directives before returning the page to the client's Web browser. Because the unprocessed directives look just like comments to the Web browser, the HTML document will still be interpreted properly on the client's Web browser if the document is executed on a server where SSI is not enabled. Of course, the additional functionality of the SSI directives won't be present.

The first directive we will look at is the echo directive. This directive is used to embed certain system variables inside of your HTML documents. Actually, these system variables show up as environment variables just as they would under the

CGI protocol. All of the environment variables available to a typical CGI program, such as REMOTE_HOST or REMOTE_ADDR, are also available when using the echo command. In addition to these variables, there are some additional system parameters available when using Server Side Includes.

**Table 8-1** SSI Directives

| Command | Parameter | Description |
| --- | --- | --- |
| config | | Modifies various aspects of SSI |
| | errmsg | Default error message |
| | sizefmt | Format for size of the file |
| | timefmt | Format for dates |
| echo | var | Inserts value of special SSI variables as well as other environment variables |
| exec | | Executes external programs and inserts output in current document |
| | cmd | Any application on the host |
| | cgi | CGI program |
| flastmod | file | Inserts the last modification date and time for a specified file |
| fsize | file | Inserts the size of a specified file |
| include | | Inserts text of document into current file |
| | file | Pathname relative to current directory |
| | virtual | Virtual path to a document on the server |

Table 8-2 lists the additional environment variables that may be displayed with the echo command and a short description of their meaning.

**Table 8-2** SSI Environment Variables

| Environment Variable | Description |
| --- | --- |
| DATE_GMT | Current date and time in GMT |
| DATE_LOCAL | Current date and time in the local time zone |
| DOCUMENT_NAME | The name of the current file |
| DOCUMENT_URI | Virtual path to the file |

**Table 8-2** SSI Environment Variables  (Continued)

| Environment Variable | Description |
| --- | --- |
| LAST_MODIFIED | Date and time the current file was last modified |
| QUERY_STRING_UNESCAPED | The non-decoded query string with all shell metacharacters escaped with a backslash (\) character |

# SSI Examples

Enough of the analysis; let's look at some examples. The first example is a remake of the Hello World program from Chapter 4. In this example we will modify the simple static HTML document that caused the words "hello world" to be displayed on the client's Web browser to now include some additional information about the file using the echo directive.

## Inserting System Variables into Your Documents

The goal in this first example is to use the echo SSI directive to print out the name of the file, the date and time the file was last modified, and the current local time. The format of the echo command is the same as for any SSI command:

```
<!--#echo parameter="argument"-->
```

The echo command accepts an argument containing the name of the variable to display. As you can see from the following code, three H4 tags were added to the document. Each of these header tags contains an SSI directive to echo the appropriate variable.

```
<!DOCTYPE HTML PUBLIC "-//W3C//DTD HTML 3.2//EN">
<HTML>
   <TITLE>SSI Hello World Page</TITLE>
<HEAD>
</HEAD>
<BODY>
<P><FONT SIZE="5"></FONT></P>
<P><FONT SIZE="5">Hello World</FONT>
<BR>
<BR>
The name of this document is <!--#echo var="DOCUMENT_NAME"-->
<BR>
```

```
It was last modified on <!--#echo var="LAST_MODIFIED"-->
<BR>
The current local time is <!--#echo var="DATE_LOCAL"-->
</BODY>
</HTML>
```

Figure 8-2 shows how this will appear on the client's Web browser. All of the echo directives have been replaced with the system value they represent. If you refresh the page several times, you will see that the document name and last modified date remain the same, while the system clock continues to be updated dynamically each time the page is loaded.

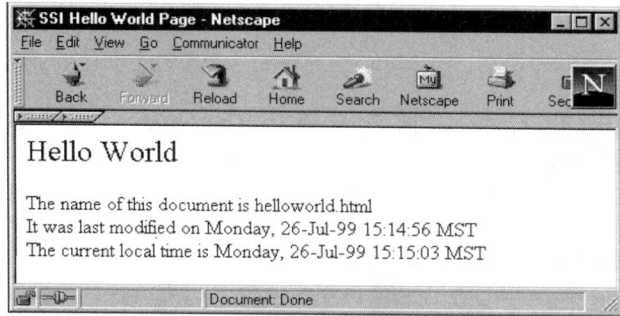

**Figure 8-2** SSI Formatted Web Page

## Inserting Text into Your Documents

In addition to including environment variables in your documents, you may also insert the text of another document using SSI directives. Let's say one of the pages on your Web site includes a joke of the day. Rather than changing the HTML document each day to include the new joke, you could simply place the joke in a text file and then include that file into your HTML page.

The joke.shtml and joke.txt documents under this chapter's example directory contain the code for this example. The joke.shtml file uses the include directive to include the text file joke.txt. The SSI directive is included inside of a <PRE> type tag to ensure that the formatting of the file is maintained.

```
<HTML>
<HEAD>
<TITLE> Joke of the Day </TITLE>
</HEAD>
<BODY>
<P><FONT SIZE="5"></FONT></P>
```

```
<P><FONT SIZE="5">Joke of the Day</FONT>
<PRE>
<!--#include file="joke.txt"-->
</PRE>
</BODY>
</HTML>
```

In this way the joke.txt file can be a simple text file with the joke of the day as shown:

```
Question:
    How many programmers does it take to
    change a light bulb?

Answer:
    None, it's a hardware problem.
```

The resulting screen display is shown in Figure 8-3. There are many places where the **include** directive can save you time and money. Another example would be to place a standard footer at the bottom of your HTML documents, specifying the person to contact with questions or comments concerning your Web site. Many people duplicate this information in each document. This is a lot of extra work and won't provide the same flexibility you can achieve with SSI.

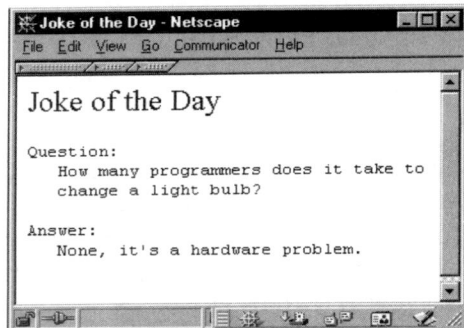

**Figure 8-3** File Inclusion with SSI Directives

As an example, let's say that your Web master's name is Billy Bob Bits. You hard code all of your HTML documents with some banner information at the bottom of the document that lets everyone know to contact Billy Bob with problems or questions about your Web site. Well, let's say that Billy Bob gets fed up with the constant stream of e-mail, faxes, and phone calls he gets from this banner and decides to quit. In comes Betty Beth Bytes to take his place, and suddenly you need to change every HTML document where you hard coded Billy Bob's information and replace it with Betty Beth's phone, fax, and other information. This is a lot of extra work that could have been eliminated by placing this information in a file and then simply including that file with the **include** directive at the bottom of each HTML document you create.

The files you include in your HTML documents with the **include** directive may contain HTML code and may even contain embedded SSI directives themselves. Consider the Web master banner that we just discussed. The joke1.shtml file is a modification of the joke.shtml file that not only includes the joke.txt file, which contains the joke of the day, but also includes a file called webmaster.shtml, which includes contact information for the Web master at the mythical site of magicweb.com. Only one line of code was added to the joke.shtml file to create the joke1.shtml file:

```
<!DOCTYPE HTML PUBLIC "-//W3C//DTD HTML 3.2//EN">
<HTML>
<HEAD>
<TITLE> Joke of the Day </TITLE>
</HEAD>
<BODY>

<P><FONT SIZE="5"></FONT></P>
<P><FONT SIZE="5">Joke of the Day</FONT>
<PRE>
<!--#include file="joke.txt"-->
</PRE>
<!--#include file="webmaster.shtml"-->

</BODY>
</HTML>
```

The webmaster.shtml file contains actual HTML code. The Web will replace the line

```
<!--#include file="webmaster.shtml"-->
```

with the contents of the webmaster.shtml file:

```
<HR>
<H4>If you have any questions or comments about this page,
<H4>please e-mail Betty Beth Bytes at
<A HREF="mailto:betty_bytes@magicweb.com">
<B>betty_bytes@magicweb.com</B></A>
<H5> This page last modified on <!--#echo var="LAST_MODIFIED"-->
```

The resulting HTML code returned to the Web browser by the SSI enabled Web server would look as follows:

```
<!DOCTYPE HTML PUBLIC "-//W3C//DTD HTML 3.2//EN">
<HTML>
<HEAD>
<TITLE> Joke of the Day </TITLE>
</HEAD>
<BODY>

<P><FONT SIZE="5"></FONT></P>
<P><FONT SIZE="5">Joke of the Day</FONT>
<PRE>
Question:
    How many programmers does it take to
    change a light bulb?

Answer:
    None, it's a hardware problem.

</PRE>
<HR>
<H4>If you have any questions or comments about this page,
<H4>please e-mail Betty Beth Bytes at
<A HREF="mailto:betty_bytes@magicweb.com">
<B>betty_bytes@magicweb.com</B></A>
<H5> This page last modified on Monday, 21-Sep-98 20:53:47 MST

</BODY>
</HTML>
```

As you can see from Figure 8-4, our Web page now contains the joke of the day as well as the contact information for the Web master. There is no need for anyone to edit the HTML document for the new joke of the day, which eliminates a potential source of error, and if the Web master's name should ever change again, only the webmaster.shtml document would have to be modified.

Notice that all of these documents contained the .shtml extension, which is the normal extension that you might expect to see for documents that contain Server Side Includes directives. Also notice that the documents that you include inside an .shtml type document may themselves be .shtml type documents with SSI directives, as was the case for the webmaster.shtml document.

If the srm.conf file had specified .html as the extension to be processed for SSI directives, then all of these files could have been named with the standard .html file extension and all of the examples would have worked the same. Just remember, this would also cause excessive server overhead because each .html file would be processed by the server, regardless of its content, which can degrade your server's performance.

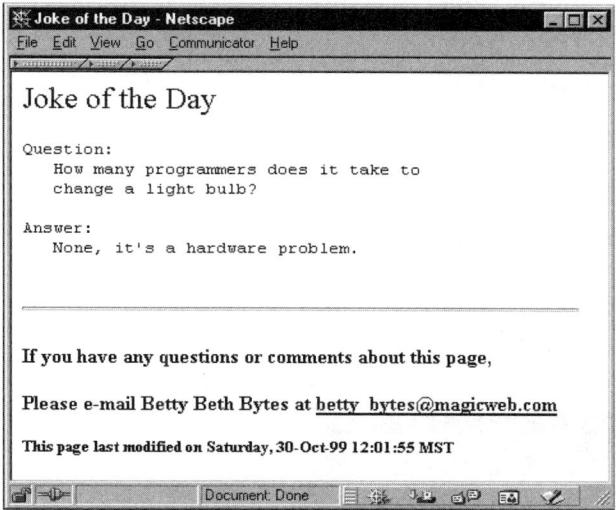

**Figure 8-4** Multiple File Substitutions with SSI

## File Statistics

Some other useful SSI directives are *fsize* and *flastmod*. These two directives may be used to display file statistics about other files in the system. This can be particularly useful if you are providing download services for documents on your Web server. In this case these two directives can be used to let your users know how big the file is and how current it is. This may effect their decision to download the file. The fstats.shtml file contains an example of this. This file lists the size and last modified date of the .shtml files in the same directory.

```
<HTML>
<HEAD>
<TITLE> File Statistics Example </TITLE>
</HEAD>
<BODY>
<P><FONT SIZE="5"></FONT></P>
<P><FONT SIZE="5">File Statistics for chapter8 examples</FONT>
<TABLE BORDER="1">
    <TR>
        <TD>File Name</TD>
        <TD>File Size</TD>
        <TD>Last Modified</TD>
    </TR>
    <TR>
        <TD>joke.shtml</TD>
        <TD><!--#fsize file="joke.shtml"--></TD>
```

```
        <TD><!--#flastmod file="joke.shtml"--></TD>
     </TR>
     <TR>
        <TD>joke1.shtml</TD>
        <TD><!--#fsize file="joke1.shtml"--></TD>
        <TD><!--#flastmod file="joke1.shtml"--></TD>
     </TR>
     <TR>
        <TD>webmaster.shtml</TD>
        <TD><!--#fsize file="webmaster shtml"--></TD>
        <TD><!--#flastmod file="webmaster shtml"--></TD>
     </TR>
  </TABLE>
  </BODY>
  </HTML>
```

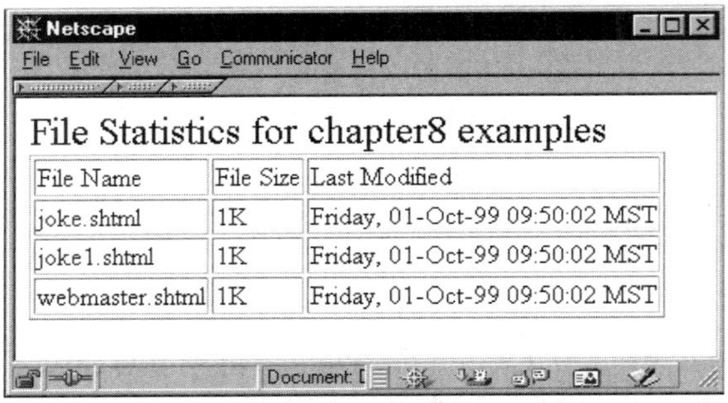

**Figure 8-5** Printing File Statistics with SSI Directives

The fstats.shtml file uses an easy-to-read table to arrange the data returned from the SSI directives (see Figure 8-5). A more meaningful page would be one that contains links to download the files rather than just listing the file name. The user can now see the file size and last modified date before downloading the file, which may impact his or her decision to download it.

## Executing External Programs

Until now, all the examples we have seen with Server Side Includes have involved the insertion of system variables or text files into your otherwise static HTML documents. There are, however, many cases where you might like to execute an external program from within your HTML documents.

The *exec* directive provides this ability. The format for the **exec** directive is

```
<!--#exec cmd="command_name"-->
```

This command syntax looks like any of the other SSI directives we have looked at so far. It consists of the directive name, in this case **exec**, followed by a single argument, in this case the name of the command to execute.

If you are executing a command that returns text, you should enclose the **exec** directive inside of the <PRE> </PRE> tags so that the formatting of the text is preserved. The ls.shtml file uses the **exec** directive to output a directory listing of this chapter's examples using the UNIX "**ls -1**" command.

```
<HTML>
<HEAD>
</HEAD>

<BODY>
<P><FONT SIZE="5"></FONT></P>
<P><FONT SIZE="5">Directory listing of chapter8 examples</FONT>
<PRE>
<!--#exec cmd="ls -1"-->
</PRE>
</BODY>
</HTML>
```

That's all there is to it! In this case, because the output of the **ls** command is simple text, the **exec** directive is executed inside of the <PRE> </PRE> tags so the formatting of the command is preserved. Figure 8-6 shows how this will appear to the user.

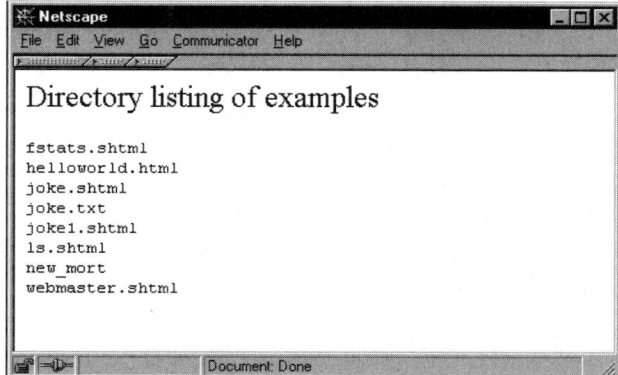

**Figure 8-6** Directory Listing with SSI Directives

Virtually any command that can be executed from the shell can be executed using the SSI **exec** directive. There are a couple of pitfalls that you can run into when trying to get your static HTML documents to execute an SSI directive. The first one to keep in mind is that the paths may be different than what you expect when the Web server processes the .shtml file, as opposed to executing commands from a shell when you are logged onto the server. Each user in the UNIX environment can have a unique set of search rules under the PATH environment variable. Commands that are located through your search path may not be found by the Web server operating with a different search path. When all else fails, you can specify the full path to the command when using the **exec** directive.

## The Mortgage Calculator Revisited

With all this in mind, it's time to once again revisit our mortgage calculator program to see how we can now use Server Side Includes to insert our page hit counter into the static HTML top level page. The new_mort subdirectory in this chapter's examples contains the modified mortgage calculator program. Only a few changes to the original code were necessary.

- The mort.html file was modified to execute the standalone counter.tcl program that outputs the code necessary to display the counter inside of an existing HTML document.
- Links that referenced the mort.html program were changed to reference the mort.shtml file.

Pointing your Web browser to the new mort.shtml file now produces the results shown in Figure 8-7.

The original mort.html file from Chapter 6 was modified in two ways. The first modification was to change the file extension to .shtml, causing the Web server to process it for SSI directives. The second change was to execute the count.tcl program using the **exec** command as shown in the following string. This line was inserted into the HTML code just prior to the closing </BODY> and </HTML> tags, causing the counter to be displayed at the bottom of the screen.

```
<!--#exec cmd="./count.cgi"-->
```

As you can see, this is much easier than converting the HTML document to a CGI program. The count.cgi program can now be used in any number of documents where you would like to provide a page hit counter without having to convert them to CGI programs.

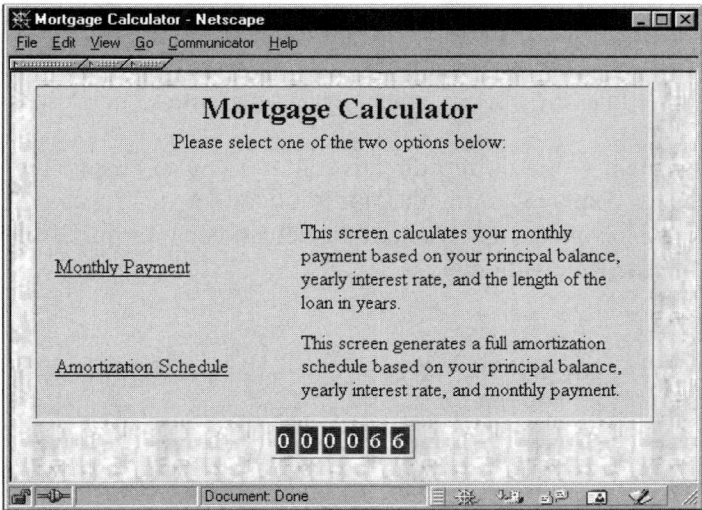

**Figure 8-7** Mortgage Calculator Using SSI Directives

The code for the count.tcl program follows. The program loads the counter.tcl package and executes the **counter_display** procedure with some hard-coded parameters to set up the display characteristics of the counter. For more information on the counter.tcl package, refer to Chapter 7.

```
#!/usr/local/bin/tclsh8.0
package require counter.tcl
counter_display counter_value red white 1 112 4
return 0
```

## Customizing the SSI Output

The final directive that will be discussed is **config**. This directive has three parameters as shown in Table 8-1 on page 155. These are **errmsg**, **sizefmt**, and **timefmt**. The **errmsg** parameter is used to change the default conditions for error messages associated with the processing of SSI directives. As an example, if you try to perform an **fsize** directive using a **filename** parameter that can't be found, you will normally receive an error that looks like this:

```
[an error occurred while processing this directive]
```

You may want to provide more information, such as the person to contact when SSI errors occur.

```
<!--#config errmsg="SSI error occurred, contact sys_adm@help.com-->
```

This directive will replace the default error message with one providing some contact information that doesn't leave the user feeling quite so helpless.

The sizefmt argument to the **config** directive allows you to change the way file size information is displayed from the **flastmod** directive. You can specify a string parameter inside quotes that changes the default behavior for displaying file size information. The following line:

```
<!--#config sizefmt="abbrev"-->
```

will cause the server to display the file size as the number of kilobytes. This is the default output. To display the file size as a byte count, you can specify bytes as the string parameter:

```
<!--#config sizefmt="bytes"-->
```

You can also change the way time-related information is displayed when using the **flastmod** directive. This is accomplished with the **timefmt** parameter to the **config** directive. There is a rather extensive list of time format parameters that you can use to customize the printing of time- and date-related information as shown in Table 8-3.

For example, if you wish to simply output the current date and not include the time, you could use the following directive prior to using the **flastmod** directive.

```
<!--#config timefmt="%D"-->\
```

Or, if you wish to display the time in 24-hour clock format after the date, you can change this line to include the %T format after the date:

```
<!--#config timefmt="%D %T"-->\
```

These format options can only be used as an argument to the **config** directive. You cannot embed them directly into the argument portion of any other SSI directives. For example you could not use these format specifiers with the **echo** directive. If you were to try the following:

```
<!--echo var="%D"-->
```

in an attempt to echo the current date, you would simply see the words (none) displayed in the place were this directive was evaluated, indicating that an

environment variable named %D was not found. The argument to the echo
directive must be a valid environment variable name.

Notice the similarity between the format codes in Table 8-3 and the UNIX date
command.

**Table 8-3**  Date and Time Format Codes

| Format | Value | Example |
| --- | --- | --- |
| %a | Day of the week abbreviation | Sun |
| %A | Day of the week | Sunday |
| %b | Month name abbreviation | Jan |
| %B | Month name | January |
| %d | Date | 1 (and not 01) |
| %D | Date as "%m/%d/%y" | 01/15/99 |
| %e | Date | 01 |
| %H | 24-hour clock hour | 13 |
| %I | 12-hour clock hour | 1 |
| %j | Decimal day of the year | 260 |
| %m | Month number | 01 |
| %M | Minutes | 08 |
| %p | am \| pm | a.m. |
| %r | Time as "%I:%M:%S AM \| PM" | 06:10:20 PM |
| %S | Seconds | 20 |
| %T | 24-hour time as "%H:%M:%S" | 18:20:20 |
| %U | Week of the year (also %W) | 32 |
| %w | Day of the week number | 02 |
| %y | Year of the century | 99 |
| %Y | Year | 1999 |
| %Z | Time zone | EST |

## Chapter Summary

Server Side Includes, though not really CGI programming, provide a convenient way to incorporate some dynamic content into otherwise static HTML documents. Here are some of the benefits of using SSI directives.

- You can display the contents of certain environment variables with the echo directive.

- You can include the contents of other files in your documents using the include directive. This makes it easy to add boiler-plate type information to your HTML documents, such as who to contact with questions or comments about your Web page. This gives you the ability to change the information by modifying one file instead of having to modify all of your HTML documents.

- You can use the fsize and flastmod directives to display the size of files and the dates they were last modified without the need to write CGI code to do this.

- The exec directive allows you to execute external programs directly from inside of your HTML documents. This allows you to add features, such as page hit counters, directly to HTML documents without having to convert them to CGI programs.

- You can use the config directive to customize the way the server displays error messages, file size parameters, or date- and time-related information.

# Chapter 9

## *Image Maps*

Web designers are constantly faced with the challenge of presenting information to users in a manner that makes it both aesthetically pleasing and easy to understand. Truly, "A picture is worth a thousand words"—for the Internet and intranets alike. This is the realm of the image map.

An image map is a pictorial way, rather than a textual way, to navigate the World Wide Web. Instead of having the user click on a text string to load a new HTML page, as most of the examples in this book have been so far, the user is presented with a picture that has one or more defined *hot spots* to click on. Hot spots are regions of the image that correspond to a URL. When the user clicks anywhere in this region, the browser responds just as if the user had clicked on an HTML link.

Though image maps are not a complex topic, you will need to understand them in order to create CGI code that handles input from these types of Web pages. In most cases these days, the browser does the majority of the work for you.

Image maps are probably used more predominantly on the Internet than on intranets, but as intranets gain in popularity, the use of pictures for navigation will no doubt continue to increase.

Even if you have never heard of image maps before, you have probably used them if you have spent any time browsing the Web. For example, they are popular for the display of dynamic maps that allow you to select areas of a city, zooming in on the regions you are interested in. Many sites include *clickable graphics*, which take you to different locations depending on the portion of the graphic you select. On intranets and the Internet alike, image maps can be useful for documenting your products. For instance, you might present the user with a picture of your product and allow him or her to click on various areas of the graphic to retrieve more detailed specifications about the selected region. Still others use image maps for providing information about building layouts, such as retrieving information about a particular room by clicking on it.

The main example in this chapter presents a hypothetical floor plan containing a number of conference rooms. By clicking on a conference room, you are presented with detailed information about the room, such as the number of people it can hold, if it has an overhead projector, and so on. The specific information covered will include:

- The difference between client side and server side image maps. This chapter will focus on client side image maps because they are rapidly replacing server side image maps for both efficiency and ease of use.
- The HTML tags for image maps and how to manually create an image map for your HTML documents.
- A short discussion on tools available to create image maps.
- A complete client side image map example.

## Server Side Image Maps

Even though this chapter will not present any examples of server side image maps, it is probably a good idea to at least be exposed to the concepts involved. A little history can provide a lot of insight.

With server side image maps, the person generating the Web page would normally start with a good, crisp graphic and then define the hot spots (areas where the user can click). He or she would have to generate a map file that contains one or more entries of the following format:

```
shape URL coordinate1, coordinate2, ..., coordinateN
```

where shape is either a *rectangle*, *polygon*, or *circle,* and *URL* is the URL to invoke when the user clicks anywhere in this region. This is followed by a list of coordinates specific to the shape selected that define the region in the graphic. Normally some external paint-type program would be used to determine these coordinates.

This map file would be placed on the server, usually as a subdirectory to the cgi-bin directory maintained by the Web master. The image is then inserted into the HTML file with the IMG tag. The <ISMAP> attribute is included to tell the browser that this graphic is an image map.

```
<A HREF="/cgi-bin/imagemap/floorplan"><IMG SRC="floorplan.gif"
ISMAP></A>
```

The associated HREF would reference the CGI program, which in this case is named *imagemap*. The name of the actual map file to be used is appended to the URL as extra path information, which in this case would be *floorplan*.

The ISMAP attribute causes the browser to send the coordinates of the user's selection, appended as query string information, to the CGI program specified in the HREF tag associated with the image. The CGI program, which is typically provided by the server environment, would then open the map file, check for a match to the coordinates provided, and call the associated URL. There is typically a default URL named in the map file for coordinates that don't fall inside any defined region.

The critical point here is that a CGI program is required, even if all the data retrieved is contained in static HTML documents. Also, several file accesses are required for each selection in the image map. The first access is to invoke the CGI program with the coordinates of the user's selection. The CGI program is then required to open the map file and search for a coordinate match. The destination URL is then loaded, based on the results of the coordinate search by the CGI program. This process is very inefficient, which is the reason most Web masters do not allow server side image maps anymore. However, there are still server side maps in existence, and you may run into them in your travels, which is why this cursory explanation of their functionality has been provided.

With client side image maps, the map information is contained inside the HTML file. The client's browser does all the work of converting the selected region directly to the URL to be loaded. If the URL specifies another static HTML file, no CGI program is required at all! This reduces the Web server's overhead, takes advantage of the processing power of the client's Web browser, and is easier to implement than server side image maps. These are the main reasons that most Web masters will encourage or even demand that application developers use client side image maps rather than their server side equivalents.

> Server side image maps always required a CGI program to process the coordinates that are sent from the Web browser to the Web server. These types of image maps, for the most part, have been replaced by client side image maps where the browser deciphers the coordinates directly.

# Client Side Image Maps

In the client side image map, the map is actually contained inside the HTML file, and the browser does the translation for you based on the area the user selects. This allows the Web page designer to associate particular links with specific areas of a graphic. When the user clicks in one of these areas, the desired URL is called directly.

For a URL that just references another static HTML document, this eliminates two file accesses on the server that would have been necessary in the case of a server side image map; the first being the CGI script that would have been called to process the coordinates and the second the actual accessing of the image map file that contained the coordinate map.

### A File for Every Shape

The simplest thing to do with a client side image map is to map the hot spots to static HTML documents. Consider the Web page shown in Figure 9-1. This page contains examples of the three shapes allowed for in the client side image map—the rectangle, the circle, and the polygon. Each one of these shapes is mapped to a static HTML document that tells you which shape you selected.

When you click on a shape, one of three static HTML documents is returned to the browser. As you can see, you are not restricted to a single image map in your HTML file. In this example we have three different image maps that cause three different HTML files to be displayed. You can also have a single image with multiple regions mapped, as shown in the conference room example in the following section.

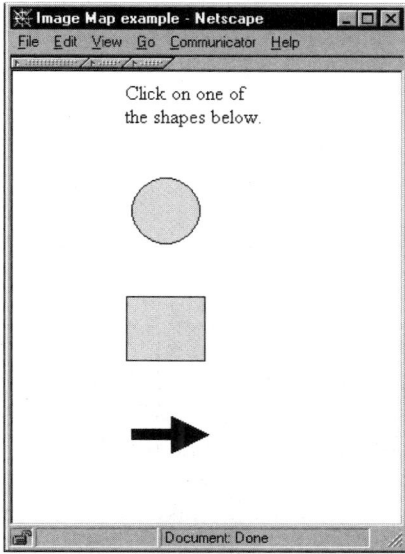

**Figure 9-1** Three Image Maps in One Document

The HTML code for Figure 9-1 follows.

```
<!DOCTYPE HTML PUBLIC "-//W3C//DTD HTML 3.2//EN">
<HTML>

<HEAD>
    <TITLE>Image Map example</TITLE>
</HEAD>

<BODY BGCOLOR="white">

<BLOCKQUOTE>
    <P>Click on one of <BR>
    the shapes below.</P>
    <P><BR>
    <IMG SRC="circle.gif" WIDTH="65" HEIGHT="59" ALIGN="BOTTOM"
         BORDER="0" USEMAP="#circle"></P>
    <P><BR>
    <IMG SRC="square.gif" WIDTH="64" HEIGHT="55" ALIGN="BOTTOM"
         BORDER="0" USEMAP="#square"></P>
    <P><BR>
    <IMG SRC="arrow.gif" WIDTH="72" HEIGHT="42" ALIGN="BOTTOM"
         BORDER="0" USEMAP="#arrow">
```

```
</BLOCKQUOTE>

<MAP Name="circle">
   <AREA Shape="Circle" coords = "31,29,26"  HREF="circle.html">
</MAP>

<MAP Name="square">
   <AREA Shape="Rect" coords = "2,3,62,53"  HREF="square.html">
</MAP>

<MAP Name="arrow">
   <AREA Shape="Polygon" coords =
   "5,16,36,16,36,6,66,21,36,37,36,25,5,25,5,16"  HREF="arrow.html">
</MAP>
</BODY>
</HTML>
```

There are two parts to a client side image map in your HTML documents. The first is the actual image itself, which is declared with the IMG tag, and the image map that defines the clickable regions of the image, which is declared with the MAP tag. The map is referred to inside the IMG tag through the use of the USEMAP attribute. The following code segments were taken from the map.html file in the example1 subdirectory of this chapter's examples.

```
<IMG SRC="square.gif" WIDTH="64" HEIGHT="55" ALIGN="BOTTOM" BORDER="0"
USEMAP="#square"></P>

<MAP Name="square">
<AREA Shape="Rect" coords = "2,3,62,53"  HREF="square.html">
</MAP>
```

The IMG tag defines the position of the graphic and the USEMAP attribute of the IMG tag specifies the MAP to use. The # symbol indicates that the map is contained inside the same HTML file.

The MAP tag actually defines the map, which contains the coordinates of the hot spots inside the image. Clicking anywhere inside the defined region will result in the URL defined by the HREF tag being loaded.

## Building the Map

The image map for the preceding HTML code was once again built with the aid of a Web publishing tool. Many such publishing tools provide support for image maps and allow you to simply draw an outline around the area you want to define as a *hot spot* inside your graphic, and the tool generates all the necessary HTML tags for your client side image map.

There are numerous shareware utilities that will perform the same function, including Mapedit (www.boutell.com) and LiveImage (www.liveimage.com). Most of these tools operate in a similar fashion, allowing you to select one of the three defined area types (circle, polygon, rectangle) and then trace the area that you want to define as a hot spot. The tool then modifies the HTML file, inserting all the proper codes for image and image map. Some of the tools, such as Mapedit, require that you have an existing HTML file already defined, while others will allow you to construct the entire HTML document, including the image map portion.

If you wish to do the job manually, you can use any number of drawing packages that display the coordinates as you edit an image. You then copy the coordinates into the AREA tag as you write the HTML code.

## The Gemstone Conference Room

The last example in this chapter will demonstrate how to process data from your image maps with a CGI program. The example is based on an imaginary company named Gemstone that has four conference rooms.

A simple text file contains information for each of the conference rooms. Clicking on one of the conference rooms will invoke a CGI program that will return a screen full of information detailing important information such as room size, intended occupancy, equipment in the room, and so on.

As opposed to our earlier example that contained three different image maps, this example contains a single image map with multiple regions defined for each of the conference rooms that we wish to provide information for. Once again, the top level file in this application is just a static HTML document named map.html that contains the image map. In this case, however, the URL defined by the HREF attribute inside your MAP tag points to a CGI program rather than a static HTML document. There is also some additional query string information in the URL that identifies the region selected to the CGI program. This additional information contained in the URL's query string is quite typical in client side image maps.

The map shown in Figure 9-2 is a simple floor plan showing just the layout of the conference rooms. In actual practice this floor plan could be much more detailed.

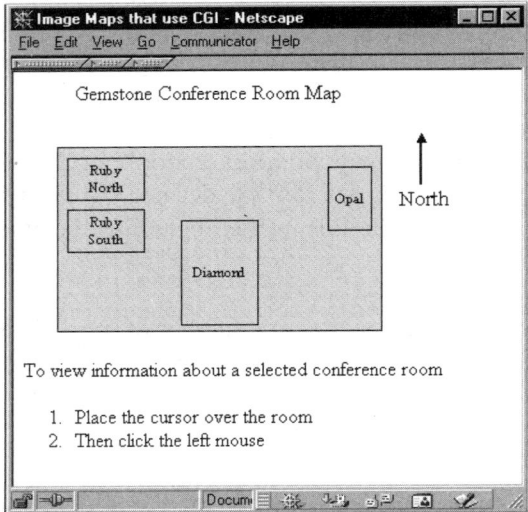

**Figure 9-2** The Gemstone Conference Room Example

The full text of the HTML document responsible for this Web page follows. Once again, the <MAP> </MAP> tags identify the image map that will be used by the Web browser. Each <AREA> tag in the image map will contain an <HREF> tag, which calls the map.cgi program with the name of the conference room selected in the query string portion of the URL.

```
<!DOCTYPE HTML PUBLIC "-//W3C//DTD HTML 3.2//EN">
<HTML>

<HEAD>
    <TITLE>Image Maps that use CGI</TITLE>
</HEAD>

<BODY BGCOLOR="white">

<BLOCKQUOTE>
    <P>Gemstone Conference Room Map</P>
</BLOCKQUOTE>

<P><IMG SRC="rooms.gif" WIDTH="339" HEIGHT="186" ALIGN="BOTTOM"
BORDER="0" USEMAP="#rooms">
<BR>
To view information about a selected conference room
```

```
<OL>
   <LI>Place the cursor over the room
   <LI>Then click the left mouse
</OL>

<MAP Name="rooms">
   <AREA Shape="Rect" coords = "34,25,94,58"
            HREF="map.cgi?room=ruby+north">
   <AREA Shape="Rect" coords = "35,67,95,101"
            HREF="map.cgi?room=ruby+south">
   <AREA Shape="Rect" coords = "124,76,183,159"
            HREF="map.cgi?room=diamond">
   <AREA Shape="Rect" coords = "239,33,272,83"
            HREF="map.cgi?room=opal">
</MAP>
</BODY>
</HTML>
```

Let's look at the first entry in the map, which identifies the Ruby North conference room. The AREA attribute of the map contains the coordinates of the shape, and the HREF attribute is the link that will be called when the user clicks in this area. The query string information in the HREF tells the CGI program which conference room the user selected. The AREA tag for the Ruby North conference room is

```
<AREA Shape="Rect" coords = "34,25,94,58"
            HREF="map.cgi?room=ruby+north">
```

The query string is delimited from the rest of the URL by the question mark character as required, which causes the name/value pair of room=ruby+north to be sent along with the request. The plus sign (+) is required in this case because the value contains a space character.

The HTML file for this display looks similar to the previous example with these few exceptions:

- There is only a single image map with multiple regions defined.
- The hot spots all reference a CGI program rather than a static HTML document.
- The room selected is contained as a name/value pair in the query string portion of the URL.

## Processing the Request

The map.cgi program parses the CGI data contained in the browser's request and returns information about the selected conference room. Figure 9-3 shows the reply generated by the CGI program when the user selects the Diamond conference room.

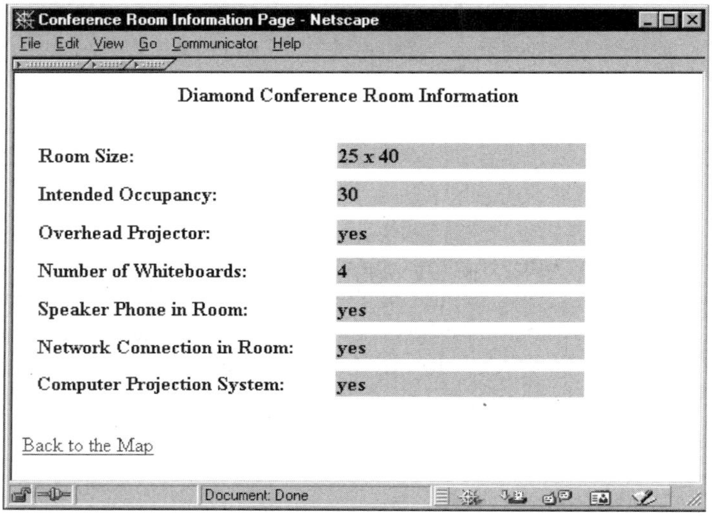

**Figure 9-3** Result from Map Selection

Information about the conference room is stored in a file named room.data. This file contains the Tcl code necessary to build an array called rooms with information about each of the conference rooms in the image map. By arranging the data in this fashion, the map.cgi program can use the Tcl **source** command to load the data file and build the array, all in one operation. This is a convenient way to store information separate from the program in a format that is easy to reload by the Tcl CGI program.

```
set rooms(opal,name) "Opal"
set rooms(opal,roomsize) "13 x 14"
set rooms(opal,occupancy) 10
set rooms(opal,overhead)  yes
set rooms(opal,speakerphone) yes
set rooms(opal,whiteboard) 2
set rooms(opal,network) no
set rooms(opal,projection) no

set rooms(ruby_north,name) "Ruby North"
set rooms(ruby_north,roomsize) "20 x 15"
```

```
set rooms(ruby_north,occupancy) 15
set rooms(ruby_north,overhead)   yes
set rooms(ruby_north,speakerphone) yes
set rooms(ruby_north,whiteboard) 3
set rooms(ruby_north,network) yes
set rooms(ruby_north,projection) yes

set rooms(ruby_south,name) "Ruby South"
set rooms(ruby_south,roomsize) "20 x 15"
set rooms(ruby_south,occupancy) 15
set rooms(ruby_south,overhead)   yes
set rooms(ruby_south,speakerphone) yes
set rooms(ruby_south,whiteboard) 3
set rooms(ruby_south,network) yes
set rooms(ruby_south,projection) yes

set rooms(diamond,name) "Diamond"
set rooms(diamond,roomsize) "25 x 40"
set rooms(diamond,occupancy) 30
set rooms(diamond,overhead)   yes
set rooms(diamond,speakerphone) yes
set rooms(diamond,whiteboard) 4
set rooms(diamond,network) yes
set rooms(diamond,projection) yes
```

In this example there is no real benefit to saving the information in a separate file.
In fact, you actually pay a bit of a penalty in terms of the processing time required
to source in the contents of the second file. This mechanism is just provided as an
example in case you want to create a more sophisticated version of this example at
your facility. For example, you could modify the HTML file to send the name of
the conference room map along with the name of the conference room selected to
the map.cgi program. That way you could provide separate HTML and data files
for each building in your facility with one CGI program. The code for the map.cgi
program follows.

```
#!/usr/local/bin/tclsh

package require cgi.tcl

set form_data {
<!DOCTYPE HTML PUBLIC "-//W3C//DTD HTML 3.2//EN">
<HTML>
<HEAD>
    <TITLE>Conference Room Information Page</TITLE>
</HEAD>
<BODY BGCOLOR="white">
<BLOCKQUOTE>
    <BLOCKQUOTE>
        <BLOCKQUOTE>
```

```
                <P><B>
                    $rooms($room_name,name) Conference Room Information
                </B></P>
            </BLOCKQUOTE>
        </BLOCKQUOTE>
    </BLOCKQUOTE>

<P>
<TABLE BORDER="0" CELLSPACING="10" WIDTH="450">
    <TR>
        <TD WIDTH="50%"><B>Room Size:</B></TD>
        <TD WIDTH="50%" BGCOLOR="silver">
            <B>$rooms($room_name,roomsize)</B>
        </TD>
    </TR>
    <TR>
        <TD WIDTH="50%" HEIGHT="21"><B>Intended Occupancy:</B></TD>
        <TD WIDTH="50%" HEIGHT="21"
            BGCOLOR="silver"><B>$rooms($room_name,occupancy)</B></TD>
    </TR>
    <TR>
        <TD WIDTH="50%"><B>Overhead Projector:</B></TD>
        <TD WIDTH="50%" BGCOLOR="silver">
            <B>$rooms($room_name,overhead)</B></TD>
    </TR>
    <TR>
        <TD WIDTH="50%"><B>Number of Whiteboards:</B></TD>
        <TD WIDTH="50%"
            BGCOLOR="silver"><B>$rooms($room_name,whiteboard)</B></TD>
    </TR>
    <TR>
        <TD WIDTH="50%"><B>Speaker Phone in Room:</B></TD>
        <TD WIDTH="50%"
        BGCOLOR="silver"><B>$rooms($room_name,speakerphone)</B></TD>
    </TR>
    <TR>
        <TD WIDTH="50%"><B>Network Connection in Room:</B></TD>
        <TD WIDTH="50%" BGCOLOR="silver">
            <B>$rooms($room_name,network)</B></TD>
    </TR>
    <TR>
        <TD WIDTH="50%"><B>Computer Projection System:</B></TD>
        <TD WIDTH="50%"BGCOLOR="silver">
            <B>$rooms($room_name,projection)</B></TD>
        </TR>
</TABLE>
<BR>
<A HREF="map.html">Back to the Map</A>
</BODY>
</HTML>
}
```

```
# Source in the room data, print an error if the source fails
if { [catch {source room.data} err] } {
   cgi_puts "Error sourcing room data was $err"
   return 1
}

# Parse the cgi data and validate the room field is present
cgi_parse

# Build room name by substituting spaces with underscores
regsub -all " " "$cgi(room)" "_" room_name

if { [cgi_validate_fields room err_msg] } {
      cgi_print_error $err_msg
} else {
   cgi_puts "Content-Type: text/html\n"
   cgi_puts "[subst -nocommands -nobackslashes $form_data]"
}
```

Notice the use of the **form_data** variable set at the top of the file. This variable contains the HTML code for the resulting display. This template page for the CGI program's output was generated with a Web publishing tool and assigned to the **form_data** variable. This eliminates the need to dynamically create it when the CGI program runs. A Tcl variable reference has been inserted at each location where we wish to return conference room specific data to the client. For example, the following line is used to provide the title to returned data.

```
<P><B>$rooms($room_name,name) Conference Room Information</B></P>
```

This line will substitute the name of the conference room from the array that was read from the rooms.data file previously shown. The **room_name** variable, obtained from the CGI data returned by the browser, is used to pick the appropriate elements from the rooms array. Once the data file has been loaded, to define the rooms array, the Tcl **subst** command is executed against the **form_data** variable to replace the references to the rooms array with the actual values they contain.

The Tcl **subst** command will execute the Tcl parser against the contents of a *string* and perform the indicated substitutions. The default is to perform backslash, command, and variable substitution on *string*.

subst *?options? string*

You may exclude specific types of substitution with the *-nocommands*, *-nobackslashes*, or *-novariables* options. In this example we have used two of these options to prevent backslash substitution and command substitution because we are only interested in replacing the rooms( ) array variables with the contents defined in the rooms.data file sourced in earlier.

The resulting value of the room_data variable is then returned directly to the client's browser. Because we did not call the cgi_header routine, it is important to write out the *Content-Type* HTTP header first as the form_data variable does not contain this. You could also add this as the first line of the form_data variable contents. In either case, if you use a publishing tool to create the HTML code to be used in this way, don't forget to send this line out first so the client's Web browser knows what to do with the incoming data.

So, the total program is about 20 lines of code, excluding the form_data variable containing the predefined HTML code. With only two or three conference rooms, you could have just as easily created two or three HTML files referenced directly from your top level image map and eliminate the CGI program altogether. However, in larger facilities where there may be 20, 30, or even more conference rooms, it is much easier to maintain a single data file and 20 lines of CGI code than trying to juggle 30 separate HTML files!

## Chapter Summary

This chapter showed you how image maps can provide a pictorial approach to navigating the World Wide Web. It also demonstrated the associated CGI code that may be required to make this approach work. Though image maps can provide useful content in you Web-based applications, they should not be abused. Oftentimes it is quicker and clearer to provide textual links. Still, there are many times when a picture is truly worth a thousand words.

This chapter should have provided you with the following information about image maps.

- An image map is a graphic embedded in an HTML file that provides hot spots, or clickable areas, that users may select to load some destination URL.
- Image map hot spots can be represented as either rectangles, polygons, or circles. The data that defines these hot spots are relative coordinates inside the graphic being displayed.

- The resulting URL may be another static document or a CGI program that may contain additional query string information appended to the URL that defines the selection that has been made.
- The earliest approach to image maps were server side image maps, which should be avoided in future development.
- Server side image maps required a CGI program and an associated map file to reside on the server. A minimum of two file accesses is typically necessary to resolve the user's selection into the destination URL to be loaded. This makes server side image maps less efficient and more difficult to implement than client side image maps.
- With client side image maps, the map is contained inside the HTML document and the client's browser does all the work of deciphering the user's selection. The resulting URL can be called directly without the need for an image map program or data file on the Web server.
- Client side image maps are more efficient and, in some cases, can eliminate the need for a CGI program altogether!
- Many off-the-shelf Web publishing tools provide tools for creating client side image maps as you edit your HTML document.

# Chapter 10

## Putting Data Behind Your Forms

As a CGI programmer, you will often be called on to provide database solutions for your client's needs. In fact, database applications are one of the most prominent uses of the client-server model—the basis for the World Wide Web environment today. There are many avenues that will lead you to similar solutions. A number of database vendors produce a myriad of products, all geared toward getting control of your data. The tools available to you are powerful, oftentimes expensive, and quite frequently overwhelming!

The purpose of this chapter is not to turn you into a database expert. There are volumes of information and numerous classes available for just this purpose. This chapter provides several examples that demonstrate how to place data behind your Web pages using Tcl as the only solution. The first example uses a simple flat file database to present a history of the Super Bowls beginning with the first Super Bowl in 1967. In this example the database is a simple text file that contains data for each Super Bowl. When first accessed, the CGI program reads the file and returns a form containing a list of Super Bowl numbers. When the user selects one of the numbers, the CGI program reads the file again to extract the information about the user's selection and returns information about the Super Bowl selected.

The next example introduces a database package that was developed just for this book and written entirely in Tcl in just over a week. The author now uses the resulting database package inside Motorola whenever a low-cost, small- to medium-size solution database is required. This second example maintains a database of NFL player statistics and allows users to generate more complex queries that may result in multiple records being retrieved and displayed from the underlying database. The database package is flexible enough to be used in either standalone programs or in client-server applications.

## The Flat File Database

The simplest form of a database is referred to as a flat file database. In a flat file database, all the data is generally contained in one simple ASCII text file that is operated upon directly by the application providing the data. This is so simple to implement in Tcl that it's not worth spending much time on but is a good springboard into the material that follows.

In the example1 directory under this chapter's examples, you will find a simple database that contains statistics about all the Super Bowls that have been played since Super Bowl I. The entire application consists of three files.

- superbowl.cgi is the main file that the user would point his or her browser to. It validates the CGI data and then uses the FUNCTION field to decide what action has been requested.
- procs.tcl contains the support procs that are called by the superbowl.cgi script to process the user's request.
- data.txt contains the actual data in an ASCII-delimited format.

The entire text of the superbowl.cgi program follows. This script validates the CGI data and then switches off the FUNCTION field to decide which procedure to call in the procs.tcl file. It is often useful to split up your CGI programs in this fashion to make it easier to test the standalone procedures using the Tcl shell program.

```
#!/usr/local/bin/tclsh8.0

# This is the CGI script for the NFL Super Bowl history page example.

package require cgi.tcl
source procs.tcl
```

```
# Parse the CGI data and check for the existence of the FUNCTION field.
# If it is not present, default the field to ENTRY.
cgi_parse
if { [cgi_validate_fields FUNCTION err_msg] } {
      set cgi(FUNCTION) ENTRY
}

# Switch off the FUNCTION field to decide what action to take.  (Values
are case sensitive!)
switch  -- $cgi(FUNCTION) {
   ENTRY {
      superBowlTopPage
      return 0
   }
   VIEW {
      superBowlSelection $cgi(SELECTION)
      return 0
   }
   default {
      cgi_print_error "Unknown FUNCTION '$cgi(FUNCTION)'\
            received by bugt.cgi"
      return 1
   }
}
```

## A Look at the Flat File

As mentioned earlier, the data file, or flat file, is a simple ASCII-delimited text file. An ASCII-delimited text file is a text file containing records, where each field in the record is separated by some specific ASCII character. Records are normally separated by a standard carriage return. The first record of the file normally contains the names of the fields and may contain the actual delimiting character as well. The first record of the data.txt file appears as follows:

```
~Number~Date~Winner~Loser~Score~Location~Attendance~MVP
```

Notice the first character in the line is the tilde (~) character. This indicates to the program processing the file the character used to delimit fields inside each record. The remaining fields show the names of the fields in the order in which they will appear in each data record. Once again, a data record is simply a single line in the file terminated by a standard carriage return. The rest of the file contains the data for each Super Bowl, beginning with Super Bowl I in 1967.

## The Selection Screen

When a user first clicks on the superbowl.cgi link, no field definition will exist for the FUNCTION field. The superbowl.cgi script checks for this condition. If no FUNCTION field is defined, it forces the cgi(FUNCTION) variable to be equal to ENTRY. The switch statement then calls the **superBowlTopPage** procedure as shown.

```
proc superBowlTopPage {} {

   # Read the data file into an array called stats.
   if { [catch {set stats [readAsciiDelimitedFile data.txt]} err] } {
      cgi_print_error $err
      return 1
   }
   # Disregard the first record and extract the Super Bowl
   # number from each remaining record.
   foreach year $stats { lappend year_list [lindex $year 0] }
   lreplace $year_list 0 0
   cgi_header "NFL SUPER BOWL HISTORY" {bgcolor=white TEXT=black}
   cgi_h4 "Choose the Super Bowl you're interested in."
   cgi_form superbowl.cgi
   cgi_select SELECTION $year_list 1 10
   cgi_br
   cgi_h4 "Then click the view button."
   cgi_submit FUNCTION VIEW
   cgi_form_end
   cgi_end
}
```

The **superBowlTopPage** reads the ASCII-delimited text file and extracts the Super Bowl number from each record in the file. It then uses a few calls in the cgi.tcl library to dynamically build the page shown in Figure 10-1.

The screen produced by the **superBowlTopPage** procedure contains an HTML form with a selection field containing the Roman numeral designation for each Super Bowl played, along with a submit button. The submit button field is named FUNCTION. When the user clicks on the VIEW button, the superbowl.cgi script is called again, only this time with the FUNCTION field set to VIEW. Now, the switch statement in the superbowl.cgi script will call the **superBowlSelection** procedure to display the statistics for the selected Super Bowl.

The **readAsciiDelimitedFile** procedure is used to process the ASCII-delimited data file. The routine is pretty generic and can be easily adapted to parse any ASCII-delimited file into a Tcl list.

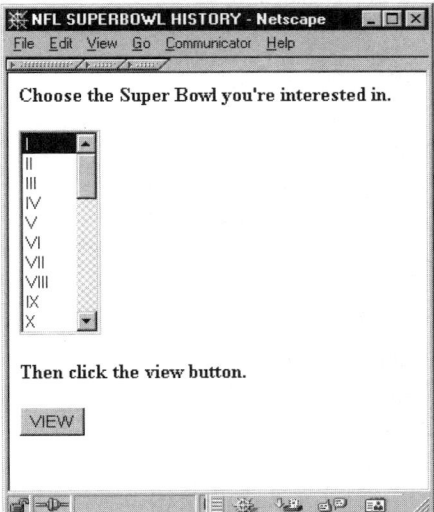

**Figure 10-1** Super Bowl Selection Screen

```
proc readAsciiDelimitedFile { file_name } {

    # Read the file_name passed in from the caller.
    if { [catch { set fptr [open $file_name r] } err] } {
       error "error opening file '$file_name' was $err"
    } elseif { [catch { set text [read $fptr] } err] } {
       catch { close $fptr }
       error "error reading file '$file_name' was $err"
    } else {
       # Trim any leading spaces
       string trimleft $text " "
       set delimiter [string index $text 0]
       set list [split $text \n]
       foreach record $list {
          lappend stats [split $record $delimiter]
       }
    }
    return $stats
}
```

## The Results Screen

This procedure will generate the HTML code to display the statistics for the selected Super Bowl, as shown in Figure 10-2. I've picked the results of Super Bowl XXXIII to display here.

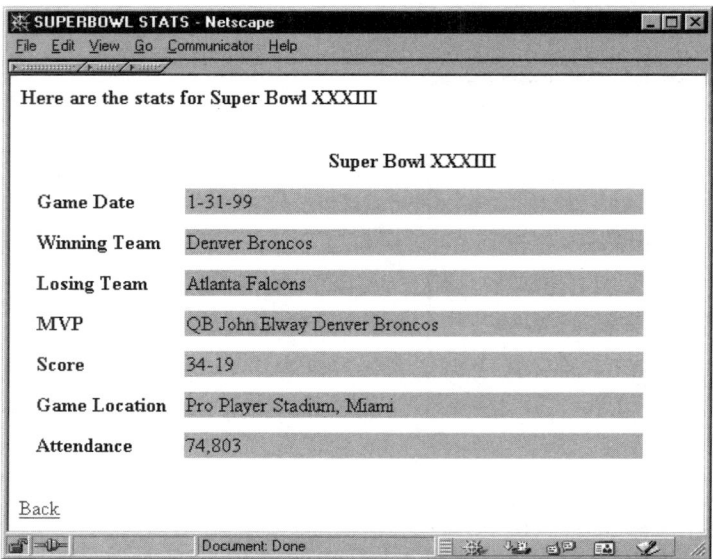

**Figure 10-2** The Super Bowl Results Screen

The **superBowlSelection** procedure contains an interesting trick you can use to build many such displays quickly. Notice in the following code that the variable **form_code** contains HTML code with a few Tcl variables in strategic places. The basic screen for this display was created using an off-the-shelf Web editing package. This quickly takes care of generating the HTML code that contains tables, text formats, field names, and so forth. The resulting HTML code is then edited to contain a Tcl variable in all the places where the dynamic data must go. In this case you will see an array variable named **stats( )** placed in all the locations where the Super Bowl statistics will be.

In our example the **superBowlGetGameStats** procedure is called to get the statistics for the selected Super Bowl. This procedure returns an array variable with the fields expected by the **form_code** variable. The **subst** command is then run against the **form_code** variable to substitute the variables with the data just before the HTML code is sent to the requesting client. This eliminates the need to generate the HTML code on the fly and can prevent a lot of headaches in form design.

```
proc superBowlSelection { selection } {

set form_code {
```

```
<TABLE BORDER="0" CELLSPACING="12" WIDTH="500">
    <TR>
        <TD WIDTH="21%"> </TD>
        <TD WIDTH="79%">
        <P ALIGN="CENTER"><B>Super Bowl $selection </B>
        </TD>
    </TR><TR>
        <TD WIDTH="21%"><B>Game Date</B></TD>
        <TD WIDTH="79%" BGCOLOR="silver">$stats(date)</TD>
    </TR><TR>
        <TD WIDTH="21%"><B>Winning Team </B></TD>
        <TD WIDTH="79%" BGCOLOR="silver">$stats(winner)</TD>
    </TR><TR>
        <TD WIDTH="21%"><B>Losing Team</B></TD>
        <TD WIDTH="79%" BGCOLOR="silver">$stats(loser)</TD>
    </TR><TR>
        <TD WIDTH="21%"><B>MVP</B></TD>
        <TD WIDTH="79%" BGCOLOR="silver">$stats(mvp)</TD>
    </TR><TR>
        <TD WIDTH="21%"><B>Score</B></TD>
        <TD WIDTH="79%" BGCOLOR="silver">$stats(score)</TD>
    </TR><TR>
        <TD WIDTH="21%"><B>Game Location</B></TD>
        <TD WIDTH="79%" BGCOLOR="silver">$stats(location)</TD>
    </TR><TR>
        <TD WIDTH="21%"><B>Attendance</B></TD>
        <TD WIDTH="79%" BGCOLOR="silver">$stats(attendance)</TD>
    </TR>
</TABLE>

}

    superBowlGetGameStats $selection stats
    cgi_header "SUPER BOWL STATS" {bgcolor=white TEXT=black}
    cgi_h4 "Here are the stats for Super Bowl $selection"
    cgi_puts [subst -nobackslashes -nocommands $form_code]
    cgi_br
    # Generate a link to go back to the selection screen
    cgi_puts [cgi_link "Back" "superbowl.cgi"]
    cgi_end
    return 0
}
```

This simple example is fine for a read-only database, which is all that is necessary in many situations. The code is straightforward and the data file is easy to maintain. Each year as the Super Bowl is played out, only a single line of data needs to be added to the data.txt file to update the Web pages. The access permissions of the data file can be restricted so that only authorized individuals can write the file, while anyone can read it.

If you wish to provide the ability to write new data or update existing data in your database, things become a bit more complicated. There are several problems associated with read-write access to this type of flat file database. One of problems is concurrent access to the data.

As you can see from Figure 10-3, there is the possibility of multiple clients trying to access the data simultaneously. Because you cannot control when the execution of any particular task may be preempted in a multitasking operating system, you cannot guarantee that the client 1 operation will be complete before the client 2 operation begins. If the code that accesses the data is written carefully, you can avoid problems, but it is more difficult than serializing the requests to the data to ensure operations are atomic—meaning they cannot be preempted by other clients trying to access the data at the same time.

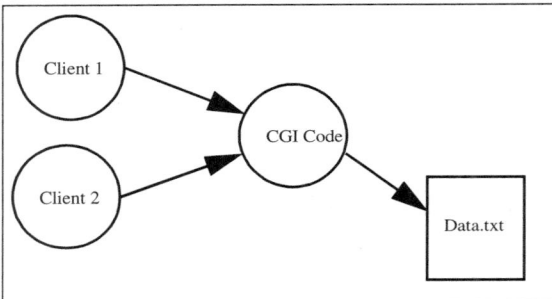

**Figure 10-3** Concurrent Access through CGI Program

A second issue is security. It can be difficult to allow the CGI script to access the data file while preventing unauthorized users from accessing it. In a typical UNIX system, for example, the CGI code is normally run as user "nobody." In order for the CGI code to be able to access the data file, the file must either be created as user nobody or its permissions must be set such that user nobody can access the data. In either case you run the risk that nonauthorized users may be able to access your data.

A third issue is performance. Because the HTTP protocol is a stateless protocol, the CGI script has no inherent memory from one invocation to the next as to what the client did in the last transaction. This requires extra code to maintain the state of any intermediate results that may be needed from one invocation to the next. Also, because the CGI code is not persistent from invocation to invocation, all files that may have been open will be closed, and any information gathered about the file must be regenerated every time the file is accessed. This results in increased latency associated with each access.

An alternate solution is to allow the CGI script to act as intended—a gateway to an external resource that stays resident between transactions. This is the typical model used for many of the Web-based database applications on the Internet today. In this case a Database Management System (DBMS) is run as a persistent process in the background that manages the data. The CGI code then makes calls to the DBMS system. Clients make their requests through the CGI code to the DBMS, which takes care of adding, deleting, and updating data in the database (see Figure 10-4).

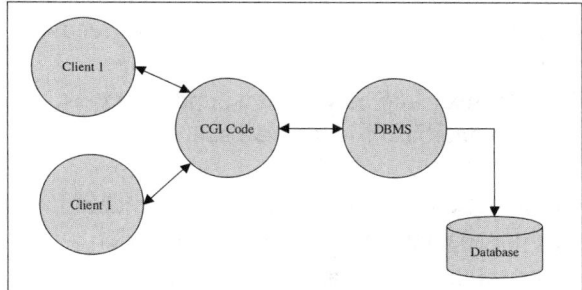

**Figure 10-4** Concurrent Access through DBMS

Here, the CGI code is simply a gateway to the DBMS system. This will become apparent in one of the later chapters where we use an actual Oracle database as the DBMS and use a package called OraTcl to access the database from the CGI code. Here and in Chapter 12 we will use a simple homegrown database written entirely in Tcl to act as our DBMS system.

## The db.tcl Package

The package in this case is simply referred to as **db.tcl** and exists in the packages directory of the enclosed CD. A command summary is provided on page 203. If you have not already installed the Tcl packages and examples that came with this book, please see Chapter 3, Getting Started, on page 59.

Here again, the **db.tcl** package is written as a standard Tcl package with its procedures wrapped in a Tcl namespace. Programs that wish to use the **db** package do so by issuing the **package require db.tcl** command. If you are not familiar with packages or namespaces, now would be a good time to take a break and review some of your other Tcl documentation or refer to Appendix B at the back of this book.

Here are some of the features of the db.tcl package:

- The package is written entirely in Tcl.
- The same package may be used to build multiuser client-server implementations or single-user standalone applications.
- Database files are text files that may be easily processed by other Tcl programs.
- The package provides an account-based security scheme that associates a user with a particular account. Each account may contain multiple database files. The user is assigned access permissions that allow for reading, writing, or creating new database files.
- Commands are provided for inserting new records, updating existing records, and deleting records from a database file, as well as the ability to create new database files.
- Ability to generate automatic sequence numbers for each record in a database file is provided through the special @recno column identifier.
- The command syntax is straightforward and easy to follow.

The db.tcl package contains the following procedures to create and manipulate database files.

```
connect      Used to connect as a client or a server
create       Creates a database table file
delete       Deletes records from the database
getFields    Returns field names for a specified database
insert       Adds new records to a database file
logon        Used to log in to a database
logoff       Used to log off from a database
select       Reads records from the database
trace        Outputs a debug message if tracing is enabled
traceOn      Turns on embedded debugging information
traceOff     Turns off embedded debugging information
update       Updates an existing record in the database
```

These exportable procedures will be discussed in this chapter. The db.tcl package also contains numerous support procedures that are intended to be local to the package and are therefore not exported. You can review the support procedures if you desire by referencing the source code for the package on the enclosed CD.

The **db.tcl** package is designed to be used in standalone, single-user applications requiring a database or in a client/server environment where multiple users require concurrent access to the same data. This chapter will discuss both configurations.

## Using db.tcl in Standalone Applications

This section discusses the single-user configuration of the **db.tcl** package and shows how easy it is to create simple standalone database applications. This first example creates a database containing NFL player names, what teams they played for in a particular year, and what position they played. The code for this example is contained in the example2 subdirectory of this chapter's examples.

```
#!/usr/local/bin/tclsh

package require Tcl 8.0
package require db.tcl 1.1

# Optional call to db::connect, the db package defaults to local
# (standalone program)
db::connect local
set handle local

# Delete any existing table and then create and open the database
db::create $handle nfl "team year player position"
catch {exec rm tables/nfl.tbl}

# Fill the database with some records.
db::insert $handle nfl "Dallas Cowboys" 1998 "Troy Aikman" QB
db::insert $handle nfl "Dallas Cowboys" 1998 "Emmit Smith" RB
db::insert $handle nfl "Dallas Cowboys" 1998 "Michael Irvin" WR
db::insert $handle nfl "Arizona Cardinals" 1998 "Jake Plummer" QB
db::insert $handle nfl "Arizona Cardinals" 1998 "Larry Centers" RB
db::insert $handle nfl "Arizona Cardinals" 1998 "Rob Moore" WR
db::insert $handle nfl "Denver Broncos" 1998 "John Elway" QB
db::insert $handle nfl "Denver Broncos" 1998 "Terrel Davis" RB
db::insert $handle nfl "Denver Broncos" 1998 "Rod Smith" WR

# Read all records from the database
puts "\nReading all records from the database"
set view [db::select $handle nfl team * ]
foreach record $view { puts $record }

# Find all the Quarterback positions
puts "\nReading all Arizona Quarterbacks from the database"
set view [db::select $handle nfl "team position" "Arizona* QB"]
foreach record $view { puts $record }
```

```
# Find all the Running Back positions
puts "\nReading all Running Backs from the database"
set view [db::select $handle nfl position RB "team player"]
foreach record $view { puts $record }

# Delete all the Running Back Positions
puts "\nDeleting all Running Backs from the database"
set count [db::delete $handle nfl position RB]
puts "Deleted $count records from the database"

# Update Jake to 1999
puts "\nUpdating Jake Plumber to 1999"
set count [db::update $handle nfl player "'Jake Plummer'" 1999 year]
puts "Updated $count records in the database"

# Read all records from the database
puts "\nReading all records from the database"
set view [db::select $handle nfl team * ]
foreach record $view { puts $record }
```

As you can see, the program is short and easy to follow. The program creates a database file named nfl.tbl, populates it with numerous records, selects records, deletes records, and updates records—all in less than a page of code!

For standalone applications the model is straightforward. The application includes the **db** package directly and uses it to manipulate the data files. In this mode of operation, the data files are not meant to be shared among concurrently executing applications (see Figure 10-5).

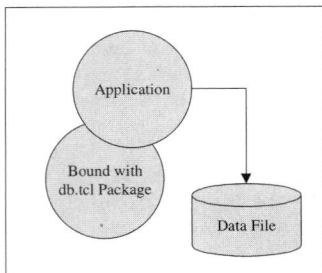

**Figure 10-5** Standalone Model

Notice that the program uses the following line to ensure that the proper version of Tcl exists:

```
package require Tcl 8.0
```

This points out an interesting fact. Tcl itself is a package. Specifying the version number in this way allows you to ensure the proper version number of Tcl is installed. The reason for doing this is because the **namespace** command used in this program does not exist in pre 8.*x* versions. Here we have specified that 8.0 is the minimum version number required to run this program. Because the **-exact** flag is not used, the package facility will load any 8.*x* version.

If you require the **db.tcl** package to run under earlier versions of Tcl, you would need to remove the namespace references in the source file.

## Including the db.tcl Package

The first few lines of this application requests the **db** package from the Tcl interpreter using the **package require** command.

```
package require db 1.1
```

The **namespace import** command could be used to import all the commands declared exportable by the **db.tcl** package as follows:

```
namespace import db::*
```

This is an approach preferred by some Tcl coders so they don't have to type the fully qualified name each time they call a procedure from one of their loaded packages. If you do not use the **namespace import** command to import the commands into the global namespace, then you must specify the fully qualified name to invoke the procedure from outside the db namespace. This is how the example code works and is the method preferred by this author for several reasons. The first reason is code readability. If you always reference procedures by their fully qualified name, it's easy to determine what package a given procedure resides in. This makes it much easier to debug the code should you encounter problems.

The second reason is demonstrated perfectly in this example. It would be a mistake to import all the commands in the db namespace, because one of the command names is **update**, which will conflict with the Tcl **update**. In this case you would receive the following error:

```
% namespace import db::*
can't import command "update": already exists%
```

You could add the -force option to the namespace import command to prevent the error from being generated, but this would have the effect of silently redefining the standard Tcl update command; definitely not a good habit to get into!

Once the db.tcl package has been loaded, the db::connect command is called to tell the package it is being used in a standalone application. The single argument local indicates this. Actually, this call is optional because the default mode is to operate as a standalone application.

```
# Optional call to db::connect, the db package defaults to local
# (standalone program)
db::connect local
set handle local
```

The handle variable is set to the value of local and is included in all subsequent calls made to the db.tcl package. The value is actually irrelevant because the package ignores it when connected in the local mode. The value of this field is only utilized when running in the client-server mode of operation, which will be discussed later in this chapter.

## Creating and Populating the Database

The next portion of code creates the actual database file and populates it with several records.

```
# Delete any existing table and then create and open the database
catch {exec rm tables/nfl.tbl}
db::create $handle nfl "team year player position"

# Fill the database with some records.
db::insert $handle nfl "Dallas Cowboys" 1998 "Troy Aikman" QB
db::insert $handle nfl "Dallas Cowboys" 1998 "Emmit Smith" RB
db::insert $handle nfl "Dallas Cowboys" 1998 "Michael Irvin" WR
db::insert $handle nfl "Arizona Cardinals" 1998 "Jake Plummer" QB
db::insert $handle nfl "Arizona Cardinals" 1998 "Larry Centers" RB
db::insert $handle nfl "Arizona Cardinals" 1998 "Rob Moore" WR
db::insert $handle nfl "Denver Broncos" 1998 "John Elway" QB
db::insert $handle nfl "Denver Broncos" 1998 "Terrel Davis" RB
db::insert $handle nfl "Denver Broncos" 1998 "Rod Smith" WR
```

The db::create call creates the database file, which will also be referred to as the database table. The db::create call requires three arguments: 1) the database handle, which in this case is simply the word "local"; 2) the name of the database file to be created; and 3) a list of field names for each record in the database file.

In this case the name of the database file will be "nfl" and the fields for each record will be

```
team year player position
```

All tables created in the local mode of operation are placed into a tables subdirectory. The **db** package automatically appends the .tbl extension to data files, so you must not specify an extension when providing a name to any of the commands in the **db** package. The **exec rm** command, performed inside the **catch**, is there to ensure that the old table is removed before the new one is created. Attempting to create a table name that already exists will result in an error.

Once this first section of code executes, a file named nfl.tbl will be created in the tables subdirectory of the directory where the program is executing. The contents of the file will appear as follows.

```
 team year player position
{Dallas Cowboys} 1998 {Troy Aikman} QB
{Dallas Cowboys} 1998 {Emmit Smith} RB
{Dallas Cowboys} 1998 {Michael Irvin} WR
{Arizona Cardinals} 1998 {Jake Plummer} QB
{Arizona Cardinals} 1998 {Larry Centers} RB
{Arizona Cardinals} 1998 {Rob Moore} WR
{Denver Broncos} 1998 {John Elway} QB
{Denver Broncos} 1998 {Terrel Davis} RB
{Denver Broncos} 1998 {Rod Smith} WR
```

Notice that the first line contains the field names, and the remaining lines contain the data that was entered using the **db::insert** call. The data in each line is recorded as a simple Tcl list. This makes it easy for the **db.tcl** package to manipulate the file with native Tcl commands.

## Reading Records from the Database

The **db::select** call is used to read records from the database. The following lines read and display all records in the database.

```
# Read all records from the database
puts "\nReading all records from the database"
set view [db::select $handle nfl team * ]
foreach record $view { puts $record }
```

The db::**select** procedure allows you to extract records by specifying a field and a pattern. In this case the **field** argument is team and **pattern** is *. The pattern argument follows the same glob-style pattern matching as the string match command in Tcl. This allows you to easily match one or more records by specifying the exact pattern to be found or by specifying a pattern containing wildcard characters. The results of these lines will appear as follows on your screen.

```
Reading all records from the database
{Dallas Cowboys} 1998 {Troy Aikman} QB
{Dallas Cowboys} 1998 {Emmit Smith} RB
{Dallas Cowboys} 1998 {Michael Irvin} WR
{Arizona Cardinals} 1998 {Jake Plummer} QB
{Arizona Cardinals} 1998 {Larry Centers} RB
{Arizona Cardinals} 1998 {Rob Moore} WR
{Denver Broncos} 1998 {John Elway} QB
{Denver Broncos} 1998 {Terrel Davis} RB
{Denver Broncos} 1998 {Rod Smith} WR
```

The db::**select** procedure can accept multiple field/pattern combinations to make it easier to extract exactly the records you want. The next few lines of code in the program again use the db::**select** procedure to extract the desired records, but this time the program specifies two fields, team and position, and two patterns, Arizona* and QB.

```
# Find all the Quarterback positions
puts "\nReading all Arizona Quarterbacks from the database"
set view [db::select $handle nfl "team position" "Arizona* QB"]
foreach record $view { puts $record }
```

This has the effect of finding all quarterback positions in any team that begin with the string Arizona. The result of this selection returns only one record.

```
Reading all Arizona Quarterbacks from the database
{Arizona Cardinals} 1998 {Jake Plummer} QB
```

The db::**select** call is used a second time to extract all the running back positions from the database. The code is similar to the first db::**select** call, but this time an exact value is given to the field and pattern arguments. Here, only a single field and pattern is required to get the job done. Also, the filter argument is used to restrict the return records to just the team and player fields.

```
# Find all the Running Back positions
puts "\nReading all Running Backs from the database"
set view [db::select $handle nfl position RB "team player"]
foreach record $view { puts $record }
```

In this case three records match the field and pattern combination specified by the application program. Notice that only the team and player fields were returned in the selection set as these were the specific fields requested in the filter argument. This makes it possible to extract a subset of the fields in each record of the database.

```
Reading all Running Backs from the database
{Dallas Cowboys} {Emmit Smith}
{Arizona Cardinals} {Larry Centers}
{Denver Broncos} {Terrel Davis}
```

## Deleting Records from the Database

Deleting records from the database is just as easy as reading them. The **db::delete** command is used to remove unwanted records from your database files. The calling sequence is nearly identical to the **db::select** procedure, with the exception of the filter argument. Because it only makes sense to delete whole records, no filter argument exists for the **db::delete** procedure.

In the example program the **db::delete** call is used to delete all running back positions from the database. Here, it is simply a matter of specifying the position field and the pattern of RB as shown in the following code.

```
# Delete all the Running Back positions
puts "\nDeleting all Running Backs from the database"
set count [db::delete $handle nfl position RB]
puts "Deleted '$count' records from the database.
```

The **db::delete** procedure returns the number of records deleted, as you can see from the screen output.

```
Deleting all Running Backs from the database
Deleted 3 records from the database.
```

## Updating Records in the Database

The last operation to look at in the example program is updating records in the database. This is done with the **db::update** procedure. This command has similar arguments to the **db::select** call. In the example program the **db::update** call is used to update the year field for Jake Plummer, because he stayed as quarterback for the Arizona Cardinals in 1999.

```
# Update Jake to 1999
```

```
set count [db::update $handle nfl player "'Jake Plummer'" 1999 year]
puts "Updated $count records in the database."
```

Here, the filter field has been used to restrict the changes to just the year field in the record, so only one update is specified in the call—1999. Notice that this field is enclosed in single quotes because it contains white space.

This operation, like the delete operation, returns a count of the number of records that were successfully updated in the database.

```
Updated 1 records in the database.
```

The last operation we perform on the database file before closing it is to read all the records in the database. This is done so you can see that all the changes made actually occurred.

```
 Reading all records from the database
{Dallas Cowboys} 1998 {Troy Aikman} QB
{Dallas Cowboys} 1998 {Michael Irvin} WR
{Arizona Cardinals} 1999 {Jake Plummer} QB
{Arizona Cardinals} 1998 {Rob Moore} WR
{Denver Broncos} 1998 {John Elway} QB
{Denver Broncos} 1998 {Rod Smith} WR
```

This is a good time to emphasize a point about the actual database file. If you freeze execution at this point, you would see it in the following state:

```
{     3} team year player position
{Dallas Cowboys} 1998 {Troy Aikman} QB

{Dallas Cowboys} 1998 {Michael Irvin} WR
{Arizona Cardinals} 1999 {Jake Plummer} QB

{Arizona Cardinals} 1998 {Rob Moore} WR
{Denver Broncos} 1998 {John Elway} QB

{Denver Broncos} 1998 {Rod Smith} WR
```

Notice that each of the deleted records show up as a blank line. This is the way the db.tcl package deletes records from the database. This is much faster than actually consolidating the file each time a record is deleted while the database file is open. Not to worry—the package takes care of removing these blank lines for you in the background.

# db.tcl Command Summary

`db::connect` *type {host {}} {port {}}*

This call is used to determine if the **db.tcl** package runs as a client or a server. In this case the *type* argument must be either the word *client* or *server*. The *host* argument will define the name of the host and the *port* argument will contain the port number used for the underlying socket communication. This call is only required when running in client-server mode. The default configuration for the package is to run as a standalone program. You may supply the word *local* in the *type* field when running as a standalone program, but it is not necessary.

`db::create` *dbhandle dbname fields*

This call creates a database file named **dbname**. When executed as a client, *dbhandle* must have been obtained by a previous call to **db::logon**. When executed as a standalone application, the dbhandle argument is ignored and any string value may be supplied but "local" is used by convention.

The name provided by **dbname** must not contain a file extension. The file extension for a data file is always .tbl and will automatically be appended to the file name by the **db** package. If a file extension is provided, it will be ignored.

Each record in the database will contain the fields defined by the *fields* argument. If the special field designator @recno is specified as one of the fields in the *fields* argument, it directs the **db.tcl** package to tag all records with a unique record number. This provides a convenient way to ensure a unique field in each record, which can make it easier to specify a particular record in the database to delete or update.

If this call is successful, it returns 0. If the call fails for any reason, an error is raised with an appropriate error message defining the failure.

`db::delete` *dbhandle dbname fields patterns*

This command deletes one or more records from the database file identified by *dbname*. The argument *dbhandle* is the handle returned by the **db::logon** call if operating as a client or may simply be set to "local" if operating as a standalone program.

The *fields* and *patterns* arguments are used to identify the records to be deleted. The database is searched looking for records where all *fields* match all *patterns*. When *fields* contains multiple field names, they should be enclosed in quotes: "field1 field2 field3". Field names may not contain white space.

When *patterns* contains multiple patterns to match, the whole string must be enclosed in quotes, and any patterns that contain white space must be delimited with single quote characters; "pattern1 'pattern 2' pattern3"; *patterns* may use glob-style pattern matching syntax.

All records where all *fields* match all *patterns* will be deleted from the database file. The procedure returns the number of records deleted from the database file.

`db::getFields` *dbhandle dbname*

Returns the field names defined for the database name contained in the *dbname* argument. If operating as a client, *dbhandle* should be the handle returned by the **db::logon** call. If operating as a standalone application, *dbhandle* should be set to a value of "local." The procedure returns the field names as a standard Tcl string.

`db::insert` *dbhandle dbname args*

The **db::insert** procedure inserts records into the database file identified by *dbname*. The argument *dbhandle* is the handle returned by the **db::logon** call if operating as a client or may simply be set to "local" if operating as a standalone program. The record to add to the database is contained in the remaining arguments as individual fields. The fields must appear in the same order as defined by the **db::create** call when the database file was created. The number of arguments must match the number of fields defined for the database. If a field contains white space, it must be enclosed in parentheses.

`db::logon` *username password*

This procedure is used to authenticate users when operating in the client-server mode of operation. If the call is successfully made with a valid user name and password, a connection handle is returned, which must be used in all subsequent database commands.

If the program is a standalone application, then this call need not be made.

db::logoff *dbhandle*

> Closes the connection identified by *dbhandle*, returned by the db::logon command, ending the user's session. This call is only required by the client when operating in client-server mode.

db::select *dbhandle dbname fields patterns {filter {}}*

> This command returns as a Tcl list all records where all *fields* match all *patterns*. The records are read from *dbname*, which is the name of the database file as specified in the original db::create call. When operating in client-server mode, the *dbhandle* argument must contain the handle returned by the db::logon call. When operating as a standalone program, *dbhandle* should be set to the value "local."

> When *fields* contains multiple field names, they should be enclosed in quotes: "field1 field2 field3". Field names may not contain white space.

> When *patterns* contains multiple patterns to match, the whole string must be enclosed in quotes, and any patterns that contain white space must be delimited with single quote characters: "pattern1 'pattern 2' pattern3"; *patterns* may use glob-style pattern matching syntax.

> If *filter* is defined, then only the fields specified in *filter* will be returned for each record read. If *filter* is not defined or it is a null string, then all fields for each matching record will be read from the database.

db::update *dbhandle dbname fields patterns updates*
*{filter {}}*

> This call is used to update records in a database file. The name of the database file to update is contained in the *dbname* argument. The *fields* argument contains the fields that will be tested against *patterns*. If all *fields* match all *patterns*, the record will be updated with the new field information contained in *updates*.

> As was the case with the db::delete and db::select procedures, glob-style expressions may be used in the *patterns* argument. This provides the capability of updating multiple records with a single call.

> If *filter* is defined, then only the fields specified in *filter* will be updated. In this case *updates* must contain the same number of fields as *filter*. If *filter* is not defined or it is a null string, *updates* must contain the same number of fields as the original record definition defined by the db::create call.

# Using db.tcl in Client-Server Applications

The db.tcl package may be used in client-server applications, which is the preferred method for building CGI applications that must provide read-write access to data. It is easy to convert a standalone program to the client-server model. In fact our previous example can be converted to a client-server application by the addition of just two lines of code!

```
set handle [db::logon $username $password]
db::connect client localhost 5031
```

The db::connect command instructs the db.tcl package to act as either a client, a server, or a local (standalone application). The default mode for the package is to act as a standalone application. This eliminates the need to actually call the db::connect procedure when used in the standalone configuration.

If the application specifies client as the connection type, then the db.tcl package does not execute the code that acts on the database file, but instead it packs up the procedure call as a message and sends it to the server. The server address is specified by the *host* and *port* arguments, which in this case are *localhost* and *5031*. The *localhost* argument has special meaning to the socket command in Tcl and indicates the same machine the code is executing on.

The port number in this example is arbitrary and needs to be agreed upon between you and your system administrator. Normally, ports below the number 1024 are reserved for system resources and controlled by your system administrator. You can normally use higher number ports for your applications without a problem. Still, you need to decide on the method by which the port will be made known to client applications. In the case of writing CGI programs, this is simply a specific port number, agreed upon by you and your system administrator. The port number will be used in both the CGI program that accesses your db server and the db server applications itself.

## The Database Server Program: dbserver.tcl

In order to execute an application as a client, it is necessary to first have a server running. The dbserver.tcl application in the dbserver subdirectory of the examples directory is just such a server. This program wraps the db.tcl package in a server. This program is small and can be used as a model for many such applications where you want a persistent server for your CGI applications to communicate with.

The code for the server application follows. Notice that the server application references the same **db.tcl** package with the **package require** command, just as was done in the previous standalone example.

```
#!/usr/local/bin/tclsh8.0

#<:-----------------------------------------------------------------
# PACKAGE dbserver.tcl
#  This application provides a simple database server using the db.tcl
#  package. It will establish a callback procedure associated with the
#  server port and call this routine whenever a message is received
#  from a client application. The message is expected to be in the
#  form of a procedure call that is executed using the eval command.
#  The results of the execution are returned to the client. Any errors
#  raised are trapped and communicated back to the client as well.
#:>-----------------------------------------------------------------


#<:-----------------------------------------------------------------
# PROC dbProcess
#  This is the callback for messages from the client. Whenever
#  the server socket accepts a socket connection from the client,
#  this procedure will be called to process the client's message. The
#  message is simply passed on as a procedure call, and the results
#  are returned to the client.
#
#  Arguments
#     sock
#         The socket associated with the client. This process must
#         read the data associated with the client socket.
#  Returns
#     0  if successful, followed by the results of the call
#     1  if the call resulted in an error followed by the error message
#:>-----------------------------------------------------------------
proc dbProcess { sock } {
   set cmd_name dbProcess

   if { [eof $sock] || [catch {gets $sock line} ] } {
      db::trace "socket eof or abnormal termination,\
                      closing socket $sock"
      close $sock
   } elseif { $line == "" } {
      # Ignore blank lines
   } else {
      set rvalue ""
      db::trace "($cmd_name) cmd from client was '$line'"
      if { [catch {eval $line } err] } {
         lappend rvalue 1
```

```
        } else {
           lappend rvalue 0
        }
        # Now append the results message to the return value
        lappend rvalue "$err"
        db::trace "($cmd_name) returning '$rvalue'"
        puts $sock $rvalue
        #close $sock
    }
}
#<:------------------------------------------------------------------
# PROC dbAccept
#   This is the callback for the server socket. It configures the
#   new socket connection from the client to be buffered and sets up
#   dbProcess as the call to handle socket I/O. The arguments are the
#   standard socket, address, and port parameters passed to the
#   callback procedure designated by the socket command.
#   Arguments
#       sock    The socket associated with the server.
#       host    The host responsible for the socket connection.
#       port    The port associated with this socket connection.
#   Returns
#       0   always
#:>------------------------------------------------------------------
proc dbAccept { sock host port }

    db::trace "(dbAccept) Accept $sock from $host port $port"
    fconfigure $sock -buffering line
    fileevent $sock readable [ list dbProcess $sock ]
    return 0
}

package require db
namespace import db::*
db::traceOn

# Set up a receive loop for messages to this server
db::trace "DB server running"
set dbSocket [socket -server dbAccept 5031]
vwait   forever
```

If you remove the verbose comments, you'll see the code is very short. How can you build a database server so small? The real magic is in the **db.tcl** package itself, so let's take a look at how a typical command is written before returning to our discussion of the server application. Each of the exportable routines in the **db.tcl** package is written in such a fashion that the code can be executed either locally or remotely. To see how this works, let's examine the **db::insert** command. This is one of the shortest commands in the package and is, therefore, a good candidate for study. The code for the **db::insert** command follows:

```
proc db::insert { handle name args } {

    variable connect_type
    trace "(db::insert) entered\nname=$name\nargs=$args"

    # Send the command to the host if executing as a client.
    if { $connect_type == "client" } {
        if { [catch {socketSend "db::insert $handle $name $args "} err]} {
            error "$err"
        } else { return $err }
    }

    # Validate the database handle and name and open it.
    if { [validateAccess $handle $name w path err] } {
        set fptr [open $path a+]
    } else {
        error $err
    }
    # Ensure the number of args submitted matches the number of fields
    # in the database. If the recno field exists, replace it with the
    # next number in the sequence.
    seek $fptr 0
    set fld_names [gets $fptr]
    if { [set recno_index [lsearch $fld_names @recno]] != -1 } {
        set field_count [expr [llength $fld_names] -1]
        incr recno_index -1
    } else {
        set field_count [llength $fld_names]
    }
    if { [llength $args] != $field_count } {
        error "(insert) Wrong number of fields for database '$name'"
    }
    if { $recno_index != -1 } {
        set new_recno [dbincRecno $fptr]
        set fields [lreplace $args $recno_index $recno_index $new_recno]
    } else {
        set fields $args
    }

    writeRecord $fptr end $fields
    close $fptr
    return 0
}
```

The first thing this code does is to check the **connect_type** variable. If the value of this variable is equal to *client*, the code calls the **socketSend** with a string that represents the **db::insert** call made by the caller. The **socketSend** command sends this string to the *host* and *port* arguments supplied to the **db::connect** call.

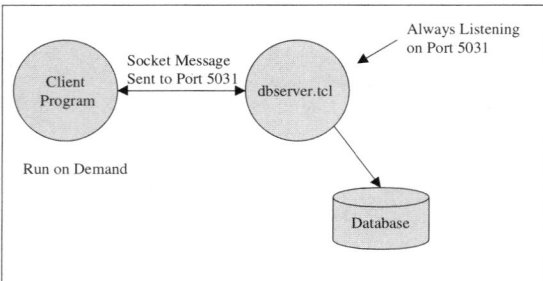

**Figure 10-6** The db.tcl Remote Procedure Call

This is similar in concept to remote procedure calls provided for in some operating systems, but the beauty and power of the socket command makes it even easier to implement in Tcl. Figure 10-6 illustrates this type of remote procedure call being sent to the dbserver.tcl program from a client program.

Every exportable call in the **db.tcl** package is written in this fashion. This allows you to quickly turn a standalone application into a client-server application by simply adding the **db::connect** command with the *type* argument set to client. In this way you can prototype your application in a standalone environment and then convert it to operate as a client with just one line of code.

Of course, to run your applications in client-server mode, you must first have the server running. On a UNIX machine, you may execute the sample database server program that comes with this book by just typing the command dbserver.tcl from the command line while in the dbserver subdirectory of the examples directory. This executes the server in the foreground, meaning that no other input will be accepted by the shell where you run the program. Any message output by the **dbserver** command will be sent to this console. You can alternately execute the program in the background with the special & character as shown in the following command line argument.

```
dbserver.tcl &
```

This causes the program to be executed in background mode. When programs are executed in background mode, you can still execute other command line arguments from the same shell. Any messages sent by the dbserver.tcl program will also show up in this same shell.

When the dbserver.tcl program first executes, it establishes a socket connection on the specified port using the Tcl socket command. This can be seen in the first few executable lines at the bottom of the dbserver.tcl script.

These few lines of code set up the **dbAccept** call back procedure as the routine to call anytime the server accepts a socket connection from a client. The **dbAccept** procedure configures the new socket connection to run in the line buffering mode and then establishes a file event handler procedure named **dbProcess** to be called whenever the socket connection becomes readable. It is the **dbProcess** procedure that does all the work.

```
proc dbProcess { sock } {
    set cmd_name dbProcess

    if { [eof $sock] || [catch {gets $sock line} ] } {
        db::trace "socket eof or abnormal termination,\
            closing socket $sock"
        close $sock
    } elseif { $line == "" } {
        # Ignore blank lines
    } else {
        set rvalue ""
        db::trace "($cmd_name) cmd from client was '$line'"
        if { [catch {eval $line } err] } {
            lappend rvalue 1
        } else {
            lappend rvalue 0
        }
        # Now append the results message to the return value
        lappend rvalue "$err"
        db::trace "($cmd_name) returning '$rvalue'"
        puts $sock $rvalue
        #close $sock
    }
}
```

Notice that the first few lines of this procedure attempt to read the socket and check for an end of file condition. If an end of file condition is found, the procedure closes the socket. It is important to check for this end of file condition and, if found, close the socket connection. If you don't do this, the socket connection will appear to be readable all the time, causing the **dbProcess** command to be executed continuously until you close the connection. Closing the socket connection established for an incoming client message does not prevent the server from listening to the port.

As previously mentioned, the message from the client is expected to be in the form of a Tcl procedure call. This is an easy way to make a remote procedure call in Tcl. The client simply sends the call that it would have tried to make locally to the server and the server then executes it using the Tcl **eval** command.

```
if { [catch {eval $line } err] } {
    lappend rvalue 1
} else {
    lappend rvalue 0
}
```

The **eval** command is executed inside a catch so if the procedure raises an error, it does not kill the server. The err argument will contain the result of the executed procedure, whether an error was raised or not. The remaining code packs up the results into a message and sends it back to the client.

The result is a simple Tcl list containing two elements. The first element indicates if an error was raised by the calling procedure. If this first element contains a 1, it indicates the calling procedure raised an error. In this case the second element contains the error message caught by the **catch** command. If the call completed successfully, the first element of the result will contain a value of 0 and the second element will contain the results from the procedure called.

The **db::socketSend** in the **db.tcl** package takes care of sending messages to the server and receiving responses when the program is acting as a client. The procedure is only intended for internal use by the **db.tcl** package.

```
proc dbSocketSend { str } {

    variable dbSock
    variable dbType

    # Send the request to the server and get the response.
    puts $dbSock $str
    set rvalue [gets $dbSock]
    if { [lindex $rvalue 0] } {
       error [lindex $rvalue 1]
    } else { return [lindex $rvalue 1]}
}
```

This routine writes the message to the socket connection established by the **db::connect** call and then reads the results that come back from the client. If an error was raised by the procedure executing under the server, the **db::socketSend** follows suit and raises the error on the client side when the transaction is complete. If no error is raised, it simply returns the results back to the caller.

It is the combination of these two procedures that do all the remote communication between the client and the server. This is considerably simpler than the same task might be in other languages, such as C. Once again, the power of Tcl is clearly visible here.

Before discussing CGI implementations, let's first turn our simple standalone NFL application into a client-server application. As mentioned before, this is accomplished with the addition of just two lines of code to the client side program.

```
db::connect client localhost 5031
set handle [db::logon buba fumble]
```

The **db::connect** call, with the *type* argument set to client, instructs the **db.tcl** package to send all commands to the server specified by the *host* and *port* argument. In this example the host is set to localhost—the same computer the client is running on—and port is set to 5031, which was picked arbitrarily. That's all there is to it. The commands in the program will now be sent to the server program running in the background. The data files operated on will be the files under the server's control rather than in the local subdirectory of the standalone application. The access permissions of these files could be set in such a manner that the client could not read them at all. The only access would be through the database server program.

## Authentication in the Client-Server Model

Another consideration when turning a local application into a client program is authentication of the client. When the **db.tcl** package is operated in the client-server model, a user name and password are required to access files in the database. A file named db.acc is used to contain the user names and their associated passwords. This one file is used to maintain all the user names and passwords. This file should have the same set of permissions as the database server program and should be maintained by the administrator of the database. This access file lists the authorized users, their access level, and the *account* they are authorized for. An account is an area where one or more database files may reside.

The **db** package actually maintains these accounts as a directory structure that is rooted relative to the location the database program is executed from. Underneath the top level is a *tables* directory, which contains all the tables used in the client-server configuration.

When the program is run in the client-server configuration, each account exists as a subdirectory under the tables tree, which itself is a subdirectory of the directory that the dbserver.tcl program is invoked from.

You can see from Figure 10-7 that the nfl account is a subdirectory under the tables directory and contains a single file named nfl.tbl. This is the database file containing the example data for this chapter's example. The bugt directory contains the database file that will be used in Chapter 12.

```
G:\PUBLIC_HTML\BOOK\EXAMPLES\DBSERVER
    dbserver.tcl
    db.acc

   tables
        account_2
        nfl
             nfl.tbl
        account_n
        bugt
             problems.tbl
```

**Figure 10-7** The Tables Subdirectory

The account_2 and account_n are fictitious directories to further clarify the point that any number of additional accounts may appear as subdirectories in this location. There may be any number of accounts, but each account name must be unique because it maps directly to a directory structure.

The db.acc file is the access file that specifies user names and passwords for each of the account subdirectories. The format is simple:

```
baby fumble c nfl
```

As you can see, each line of the access file consists of a user name, an associated password, the permission level of the user, and the account that the user is being granted access to. An r signifies read-only access, a w allows read-write access to the file, and a c allows the ability to create tables as well as to read and write them. In this case the account is nfl. This maps to a subdirectory of the tables directory.

Any number of database files can be maintained in an account directory. A user that has access to a given account directory has access to all the database files in that account. This is certainly not as flexible as authentication in an off-the-shelf database like Oracle, but it's small and free!

## Real CGI

Now that we have a server application that uses the **db.tcl** package, it's fairly simple to let your CGI code talk to it. This is the real essence of CGI code—to act as a gateway to an external resource! In this example the external resource is the dbserver.tcl program running in the background.

Next we will take the NFL statistics database created in the last example and make it available via a Web page. This whole process took less than an hour and resulted in just a couple of pages of code: about one page of HTML code for the user selection screen and one page of CGI code to process the query and extract the requested records from the database server.

The static HTML page named top.html acts as the query screen for the client. Figure 10-8 shows what the selection screen looks like for this example. Once again, this page was built with the help of a Windows-based Web development package and took less than 15 minutes to construct.

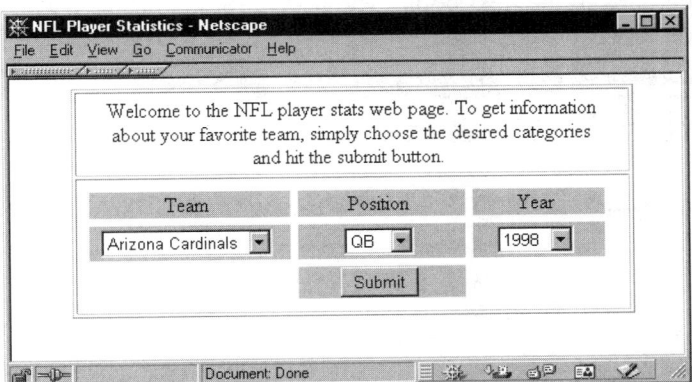

**Figure 10-8** The Selection Screen for the NFL Statistics Database

This form has three list boxes that map to the field names TEAM, YEAR, and POSITION. The form sends its contents to the nfl.cgi program when the Submit button is clicked on. Here again, the CGI script is not interested in the name or value of the submit button. It simply has to be there to allow the form to be submitted.

Of course you would probably like to jazz up your screens with dazzling graphics and other cosmetics that make the response slower—but for the sake of simplicity, let's stick to the basics!

We won't bother looking at the HTML code for this page. It is available in the example3 subdirectory of this chapter's examples. By now you should be familiar with HTML forms and realize the only important point from a CGI perspective is which CGI program is called and what form data is sent to it.

The form was designed with the database content in mind so the field values submitted correspond directly to the values needed in the db::select call used to read the requested data from the database. This made it easy to just plug the values received from the HTML form into the db::select call to retrieve the requested data.

The only exception to this is the ALL selection that is available for each field in our HTML form. Because the db.tcl package expects a * character to signify ALL, and this character could have been confusing to the user, it was decided to translate the ALL value to a * before submitting the query to the database. Because this would be a common request in most query screens, it suggests that maybe the db.tcl package should be enhanced to accept the word ALL in place of a * character. Perhaps in the next book! The results of submitting your query are shown in Figure 10-9.

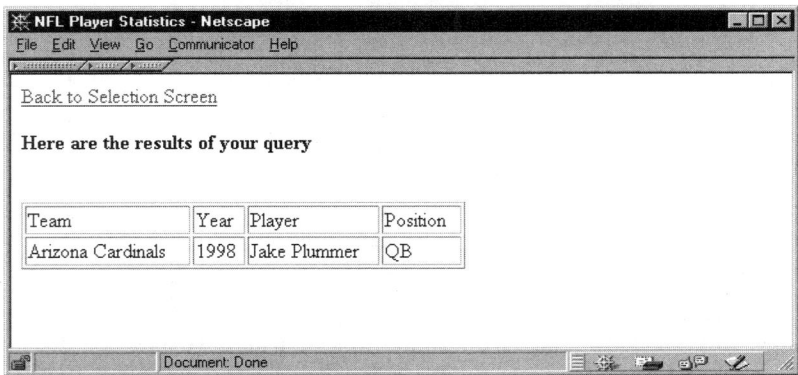

**Figure 10-9** Results of the Submitted Query

The CGI script that processes the form data and returns the requested data is quite short. This is a result of leveraging off of the cgi.tcl package and the db.tcl package. The CGI code performs the following basic steps.

- Parse the form input and validate that the proper fields are present.
- Convert any field values containing ALL to the * character required by the db package.

- Connect to the server with the **db::connect** call. If an error occurs, bail out and return an error screen.
- Open the NFL database with the **db::logon** call and save the returned handle. If an error occurs, bail out and return an error screen.
- Execute a **db::select** command using the values obtained from the form data submitted. If an error occurs, bail out and return an error screen.
- Convert any field values containing the * character back to ALL for display.
- Display the results of the query.

Simple, basic programming! Remember as you review this code that it is necessary to first have the dbserver.tcl application running before any client requests can be processed. If the CGI script cannot connect to the server, it will simply return an error message.

```
# This is the cgi script for the NFL Super Bowl history page
# example.

package require Tcl 8.0
package require cgi.tcl
package require db.tcl

# Parse the cgi arguments and check for the required cgi fields
cgi_parse
if { [cgi_validate_fields "TEAM YEAR POSITION" err_msg] } {
    cgi_print_message $err_msg "Back to Main Screen" nfl.cgi
    return
} else {
    set team $cgi(TEAM)
    set year $cgi(YEAR)
    set position $cgi(POSITION)
}

if { $team == "ALL" } { set team * }
if { $year == "ALL" } { set year * }
if { $position == "ALL" } { set position * }

# Connect to the server
if { [catch {db::connect client localhost 5031} err] } {
    cgi_print_error "Error connecting to the database server was\n$err"
    return 1
}

# Open the NFL database
if { [catch { set handle [db::logon buba fumble] } err] } {
    cgi_print_error "Error opening nfl database was \n$err"
    return 1
}
```

```
# fields are team year player position
# Open the NFL database
if { [catch { set view [db::select $handle nfl \
        "team year position" "'$team' '$year' '$position' " ] } err] } {
   cgi_print_error "Error reading records from nfl database was \n$err"
   return 1
}

if { $team == "*" } { set team ALL }
if { $year == "*" } { set year ALL }
if { $position == "*" } { set position ALL }

cgi_header "NFL Player Statistics" {BGCOLOR=white TEXT=black}
puts [cgi_link "Back to Selection Screen" top.html]
if { $view == "" } {
   cgi_h4 "No records found matching the following query"
   cgi_h4 "Team = $team;  Year = $year;  Position = $position"
} else {
   cgi_h4 "Here are the results of your query"
   cgi_br
   cgi_build_table 1 60% [list "Team"  "Year"  "Player" "Position"]
$view
}
cgi_end
return 0
```

## Off-Line Maintenance of Your Data

There is another added benefit to running the database as a server that your CGI programs query. You can use off-line, command-driven scripts to query or update the database while the server is on-line and servicing real clients! As an example, let's say that you decide to add more historical data to your database and provide player positions for the year 1996. You could write a simple little script, similar to our first example in this chapter, that would add these records. Of course, it is not a good idea to run ad hoc scripts against a production database. With a little extra work you could easily generate a tool with a nice Tk graphical interface that would safely add records to the database without the risk of corrupting the data.

This example was limited to a Web site that provided your clients with read-only access to the on-line database. Users were not able to insert new records or update existing records. This actually represents a large portion of the on-line databases available on intranets and the World Wide Web today, but it is certainly not adequate for all occasions. Oftentimes you want to provide your clients with the ability to modify the contents of the database rather than just read it.

Providing users with read-write capability to an on-line database requires a little more thought and a lot more caution. You don't want to blindly allow untrusted clients the ability to modify or delete your mission-critical data files. The next couple of chapters will deal with some of the issues in providing an on-line read-write database. Chapter 11 will first show you how to use magic *cookies*. This is a mechanism that can be used to maintain state information from one invocation to the next inside a CGI program. This technique will be used in Chapter 12 to track authenticated users, so their login remains persistent for some specific period of time, eliminating the need for them to reenter their user name and password every time they change screens.

Chapter 12 will build an interactive database that provides clients with the ability to update records. Here you will learn the types of activities you should and should not allow, as well as explore some of the other provisions of the db.tcl package that can help you get your job done.

## Chapter Summary

This chapter showed several examples of how to put read-only data behind your Web pages. Read-only databases are common methods of conveying information to clients and represent a large portion of the database technology available on the Web today.

The following key topics were covered in this chapter.

- Flat file databases are nothing more than ASCII text files containing information that may be read by your CGI programs.
- ASCII-delimited files are simple line-oriented text files, where each line is a record and each field in the record is separated by some specific ASCII character, such as the ~ character.
- ASCII-delimited files are ideal for flat file databases and are very easy to process with short Tcl procedures.
- The db package provided with this book may be used to create small databases quickly. The package allows for the development of client-server database applications through a socket-based connection scheme.
- Using a database server that provides serialization of client can help eliminate a lot of potential conflicts that arise when multiple clients are trying to access the same data simultaneously.

- Using the db package to build a back-end database server significantly simplifies CGI applications that want read access to the database file. In most cases the CGI code involved will be less than a page or two!

# Chapter 11

## Cookies Anyone?

The last chapter showcased a database server written entirely in Tcl. A Web-based application was then constructed that provided read-only access to the database. Clients were allowed to query the database but not update or insert new data. Though many client requirements may be fulfilled by this type of read-only database, it is often necessary to provide a more complete interface, allowing users to update records or create new ones.

The next chapter contains just such an application allowing users read-write access to a problem-reporting database that may be used to track issues that arise during product development. Before putting such a system together, it is important to explore some of the issues involved in allowing clients read-write access to your data.

As you might expect, one of the main concerns is security. How do you allow authorized users access to your data while denying those who are unknown or untrusted? A typical solution to this age-old problem is to provide your trusted clients with a user name and password. Indeed, this is still the accepted method today.

The database application in the next chapter will use the simple authorization system, built into our homegrown Tcl database. Users will be supplied with a login screen, in which they must enter a user name and password. Simple enough, but once your user has logged in, how do you maintain this information in a stateless protocol like HTTP? You don't want your users to have to log in every time they use the Back button on their browser to return to your Web site!

## Cookies Anyone?

In many CGI applications this type of tracking is done with *cookies*. No, not the chocolate chip kind! *Cookies* is a scheme developed by Netscape to provide state information to the otherwise stateless protocol of the World Wide Web. I apologize up front for any humorous remarks in this section, but with a subject title like this, it's sometimes hard to resist!

Before reading this book's interpreted version, you should become familiar with some resources available to investigate cookies on your own. One of the first places that you can start is with Netscape. As of the writing of this book, the preliminary Netscape cookie specification is available at the following Web site:

http://home.netscape.com/newsref/std/cookie_spec.html

There are also some RFCs that pertain to cookies. Recall that RFC (Request For Comment) is the method used to document Internet standards. For more information on this subject, refer to The RFC Series on page 25. The following link contains an index of currently published RFCs:

http://nic.mil/RFC/

If you're interested, go to this site and look up RFC 2109, entitled "HTTP State Management Mechanism," which precisely details the cookie specification.

The concept of cookies is a fairly simple one. When a CGI program receives a request from a client, it has the option to embed some information in its response using a predefined HTTP header type. The Web browser then maintains this information on the client machine for future use by the CGI program. You can think of it as an identification packet. The next time the Web browser is used to contact the same URL, this packet of information, or magic cookie as some people like to call it, is automatically sent back to the Web server along with the client's new request. The CGI program then reads the cookie and uses its contents to determine what transpired during the last transaction. Remember that the HTTP protocol is a stateless protocol, and, therefore, the CGI program generally has no knowledge about previous transactions. Cookies provide a way for the CGI program to maintain state information from one transaction to the next.

Cookies are in wide use today, and most commercial browsers support them. One of the principal uses of cookies is in shopping cart applications, which seem to be popping up everywhere on the Web today.

In the case of an electronic shopping cart, the client contacts a Web site that offers the ability to purchase products on-line. A CGI program then processes the initial request, which usually involves some type of registration, and returns a response to the user. This response contains a cookie, which is just some type of text string used to uniquely identify this customer (see Figure 11-1).

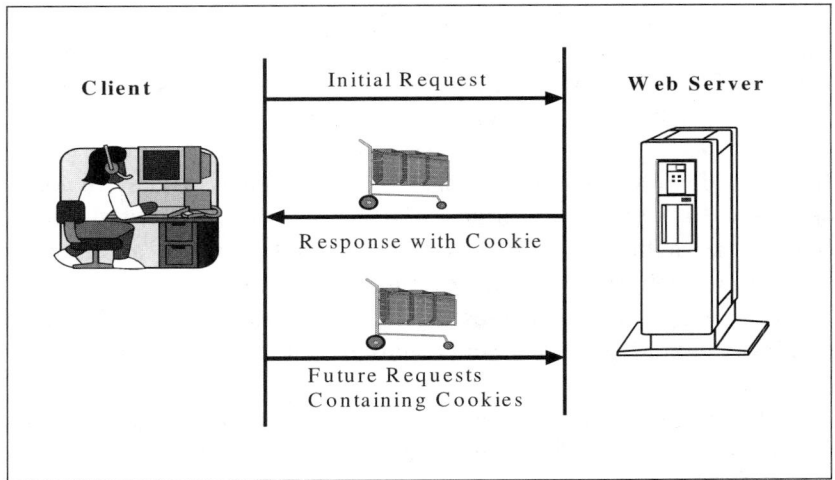

**Figure 11-1** Shopping Cart Application Using Cookies for the Shopping Basket

In this case the cookie acts like a shopping cart. Each time a user selects another item, some more information is added to the cookie, just like dropping another product into your shopping cart at the supermarket. When the user is ready to check out, the Web server inspects the contents of the shopping cart and processes the order.

Another practical use for cookies is to provide a persistent connection to a service that requires user authentication. Here's how it works. The first request the client makes of a specific Web server will generally contain no cookies. The Web server determines this and returns a login screen. The user enters the appropriate user name and password and submits the form to the Web server. The Web server authenticates the user and returns a reply that contains a cookie. The browser then saves this cookie and automatically returns it to the Web server on subsequent requests. The cookie lets the CGI program know that the client has already been authenticated, allowing it to grant access to the resources the user is interested in without going through the login process again.

## The Cookie Controversy

If you do some browsing on the Web, you will find that the subject of electronic cookies seems to be full of controversy. There are numerous articles that link cookies with everything from an invasion of privacy to the fall of civilization as we know it! Many people claim that cookies are the ultimate Big Brother tool for invading your privacy—tracking your every move on the electronic superhighway that we affectionately call the World Wide Wait. Others feel certain that cookies are a means for malicious hackers in cyberspace to secretly spy on the contents of their hard drive, revealing their most trusted secrets!

Well, the good news is they're not that bad! The bad news is they're not that good! Cookies serve a very useful purpose. We have already discussed two, shopping carts and user authentication. You have probably already accepted numerous cookies from Web sites you have contacted without even knowing it. Most legitimate sites use these cookies for legitimate reasons. Of course, like most everything else in life, cookies can be abused. But to what extent?

First of all, cookies cannot be used to read your hard drive. The cookie is simply a packet of data maintained by the browser on some CGI program's behalf. As such, it has no ability to read your hard drive or do damage to your system. To the best of this author's knowledge, there is no computer in the sky, run by Big Brother, using cookies to track your every move on the Internet. So why all the concern?

Cookies are information packets. The information they contain is generally linked in some fashion to you. When you contact a Web site, that site may require you to fill out a registration form. The information may be placed into a database along with a user id that uniquely identifies you. When the Web site replies to your registration form, it may send along a cookie to your Web browser that contains this unique user id. The next time you contact this site, it can use this user id to look you up in its database and log the time and date that you contacted the server.

The site may furnish this information to advertisers, who are always hungry for this type of demographics information.

If you consider this to be an invasion of your privacy, you can instruct most current browsers to refuse cookies, or at least inform you when one is about to be placed on your system. You may be surprised, however, at the number of sites that use cookies and quickly find yourself annoyed by all those irritating messages.

In general cookies are a way to provide a more rewarding experience on the World Wide Web by helping CGI programs, trapped in an otherwise stateless existence, to remember something about you to help provide better content in your transactions.

## How to Bake Cookies

Now that you know what a cookie is—how do you make one? A cookie is created via a Set-Cookie header embedded in an HTTP response. According to Netscape's preliminary specification, the syntax of a Set-Cookie header is:

```
Set-Cookie: NAME=VALUE; expires=DATE; path=PATH; domain=DOMAIN_NAME;
secure
```

Let's examine the arguments to the Set-Cookie header, one at a time.

NAME=VALUE

This is the only required attribute of a Set-Cookie header. It is a name/value pair similar to those used for CGI fields that identifies the name of the cookie and its value. This string may contain any sequence of characters excluding semicolons, commas, and white space.

expires=DATE

This field specifies an expiration date, after which the cookie will no longer be valid. The browser will not return expired cookies to the server. This is an optional attribute. If it is not specified, the cookie will expire when the user's session ends. The date string has a very specific format that must be exactly followed.

Wdy, DD-Mon-YYYY HH:MM:SS GMT

The only legal time zone is GMT. (Don't worry, Tcl makes this easy.) There is a bug in Netscape Navigator version 1.1 and earlier. Only cookies whose path attribute is explicitly set to / (forwardslash) will be properly saved between sessions if they have an expires attribute.

`path=PATH`

The path attribute is used to specify the subset of URLs in a domain for which the cookie is valid. If a cookie has already passed domain matching, then the pathname component of the URL is compared with the path attribute. If there is a match, the cookie is considered valid and is sent along with the URL request. The path /foo would match /foobar and /foo/bar.html. The path / is the most general path.

If the path is not specified, it is assumed to be the same path as the document being described by the header that contains the cookie.

`domain=DOMAIN_NAME`

When the browser is searching its cookie list for valid cookies, a comparison of the domain attributes of the cookie is made with the Internet domain name of the host from which the URL will be fetched. If there is a tail match, then the cookie will go through path matching to see if it should be sent. *Tail matching* means the domain attribute is matched against the tail of the fully qualified domain name of the host. A domain attribute of acme.com would match host names anvil.acme.com as well as shipping.crate.acme.com.

Only hosts within the specified domain can set a cookie for a domain, and domains must have at least two (2) or three (3) periods in them to prevent domains of the form .com, .edu, and va.us.

Any domain that falls within one of seven special top level domains only requires two periods. Any other domain requires at least three. The seven special top level domains are com, edu, net, org, gov, mil, and int.

The default value of domain is the host name of the server that generated the cookie response.

`secure`

If the cookie is marked secure, it will only be transmitted if the communications channel with the host is a secure one. Presently, this means that secure cookies will only be sent to HTTPS (HTTP over SSL) servers. If secure is not specified, a cookie is considered safe to be sent over unsecured channels.

## The Cookie Viewer

This section contains a small utility to create cookies from your own Web browser. The code in this example should prove useful in understanding how to create cookies, as well as how to delete them.

In this chapter's examples you will find a program named cookie.cgi. Once the code is installed on your server, you just access the cookie.cgi URL from your Web browser to create and delete cookies.

The cookie viewer screen contains two sections separated by horizontal lines. The top section will display any cookies sent from the Web browser. Only cookies that match the path and domain under which the cookie.cgi program is running will appear in this window because these are the only cookies the browser will send to this CGI program. In other words, if a cookie was created by some other application running on another host, it won't show up on this screen. The first time you point your Web browser at this CGI program, no cookies should be found (see Figure 11-2).

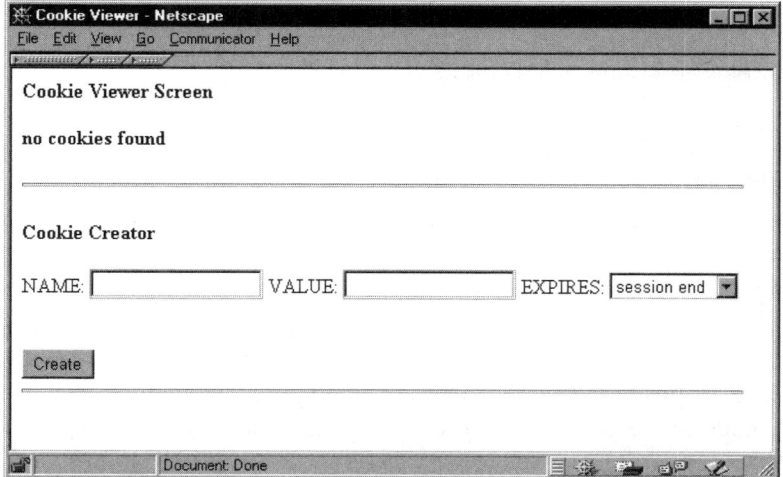

**Figure 11-2** The Cookie Viewer Screen with No Cookies Found

The bottom portion of the screen contains form fields that let you create a new cookie. It contains two text boxes that allow you to enter the name and value of the cookie you want to create and a drop down list box that provides several selections for when you want the cookie to expire.

The methodology of the CGI code is the same as previous examples in this book. The first thing the code does is to use the **cgi_validate_fields** procedure to ensure that the request contains a required field named FUNCTION. The program then switches off the FUNCTION field to decide how to process the request. If the FUNCTION field has not been defined, which would be the case for the initial request from the client, it is forced to a value of View, which calls the **cookieView** procedure that creates this screen.

There are three cases in the switch statement for viewing, creating, and expiring cookies.

```
#!/usr/local/bin/tclsh
package require cgi.tcl
source procs.tcl
global cgi_cookies

cgi_parse
cgi_parse_cookies

if { [cgi_validate_fields FUNCTION err_msg] } {
     set cgi(FUNCTION) View
}

# Switch off the function argument to decide which action to take.
# Values are case sensitive.
switch  -- $cgi(FUNCTION) {
   View { cookieView }
   Create { cookieCreate }
   Expire { cookieExpire }
   default {
      cgi_print_error "Unknown FUNCTION '$cgi(FUNCTION)' received by
bugt.cgi"
      return 1
   }
}
```

In this case the program sources in a file named procs.tcl, which contains the three support functions responsible for processing the client's request. We will examine the **cookieView** procedure first.

The **cookieView** procedure is called anytime there is no form data associated with the browser's request. This will occur the first time you point the browser at the cookie.cgi program or anytime you click on one of the links created by this program that return you to the main screen. In these cases the **cookieView** procedure will return the screen shown in Figure 11-2.

The code for the cookieView procedure follows. Notice that the **cookieView** procedure uses the **info exists** command to check for the existence of a cookies array. The cgi_cookies array is built as a result of the **cgi_parse_cookies** call in the cookie.cgi program. If the cgi_cookies array exists, the array is converted to a list and displayed as a HTML selection field using the **cgi_select** call. The first time this routine is called, you will see the "no cookies found" message, indicating that the browser did not send along any cookies when it made its initial contact with the cookie.cgi program. This is to be expected.

The procedure then creates the three form fields used to create or expire cookies at the bottom of the form.

```
proc  cookieView {} {

   global cgi
   global cgi_cookies

   # Write out the HTML header information
   cgi_header "Cookie Viewer" {BGCOLOR=white TEXT=black}
   cgi_h4 "Cookie Viewer Screen"
   cgi_form cookie.cgi

   # Display any existing cookies in the top half of the form
   if { [info exists cgi_cookies] } {
      # convert cookies array to a list for display
      foreach crumb [array names cgi_cookies] {
         lappend cookie_list "$crumb=$cgi_cookies($crumb)"
      }
      cgi_select SELECTION $cookie_list 1 5
      cgi_br
      cgi_br
      cgi_submit FUNCTION Expire
   } else {
      cgi_h4 "no cookies found"
   }

   # Build the form for creating and expiring cookies
   cgi_hr
   cgi_h4 "Cookie Creator"
   cgi_text "NAME: " 3
   cgi_text_field NAME 15
   cgi_text "VALUE: " 3
   cgi_text_field VALUE 15
   cgi_text "EXPIRES: " 3
   cgi_select EXPIRES [list +1minute +1hour "session end"] 3 1
   cgi_br
   cgi_br
   cgi_submit FUNCTION Create
   cgi_hr
```

```
        cgi_form_end
        cgi_end
        return 0
}
```

## Creating a Cookie

To create a cookie you simply fill in the NAME and VALUE fields, select an expiration option, and then click on the Create button. The NAME and VALUE fields must not contain any white space. If you need white space in a cookie, it will have to be encoded, in much the same fashion as form data from a standard HTML form. This simple cookie viewer program is not set up to automatically encode white space, so you must encode white space characters yourself.

Figure 11-3 shows the drop down list box used to set the expiration attribute of the cookie. The expiration options are limited but should serve to demonstrate the expires attribute of the Set-Cookie header field. The expires attribute determines how long the browser will continue to return the cookie. In this example you can choose 1 minute, 1 hour, or session end. The session end selection signifies that the cookie will remain valid until the client's browser is closed and reopened. The EXPIRES selection box defaults to the session end option. This is a very common way to create cookies. We will examine each of these options and see the difference it makes in the HTTP response returned from the server.

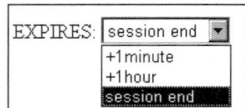

**Figure 11-3** The Expires Field

Let's say you decide to make a cookie named test_cookie and give it a value of 12345. You choose the session end option to have the cookie expire whenever the client shuts down the Web browser. When you hit the Create button, an acknowledgment screen is generated, as shown in Figure 11-4.

This acknowledgment screen indicates that a cookie has been created with the name you requested. If your browser options are set up to notify you about cookies, you will also get a notification message from the browser. This is because the act of sending the acknowledgment screen is really what created the cookie! To understand this let's examine the HTML code that was returned to the browser for this request by the cookie.cgi program.

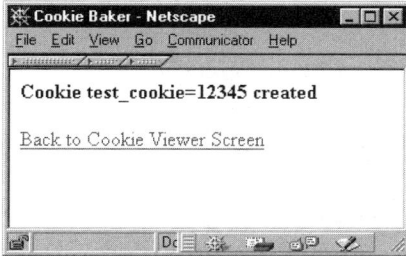

**Figure 11-4** Acknowledgment Screen

The following HTML code was generated by the **cookieCreate** procedure:

```
Content-Type: text/html
Set-Cookie: test%5fcookie=12345; path=/

<HTML>
<HEAD>
<TITLE>Cookie Baker</TITLE>
</HEAD>
<BODY>
<H4>Cookie test_cookie=12345 created</H4>
<A href="cookie.cgi">Back to Cookie Viewer Screen</A>
</BODY>
</HTML>
```

Notice the response now contains two HTTP header lines. There is the normal Content-Type header line that we have seen in previous examples and an additional Set-Cookie header that we have not seen before. This was created by an additional argument supplied to the **cgi_header** procedure. Also notice that the underscore character in the original test_cookie name was converted to its escaped equivalent of %5f. This conversion is done in the routine that creates the cookie with a call to **cgi_encode**, which replaces characters as specified by the HTTP specification with their escaped equivalents.

You don't see the HTTP header lines when you view the source HTML on your browser because it has already been processed and is not displayed as part of the source code. This makes the creation of cookies invisible to clients, unless users have enabled options on their browser to inform them of such activities.

Figure 11-5 diagrams a typical transaction involving a cookie. When the client makes a request to some Web server, the CGI program on the Web server embeds a cookie in the reply. The browser then stores that cookie and returns it as part of the request anytime it contacts the same Web server in the future.

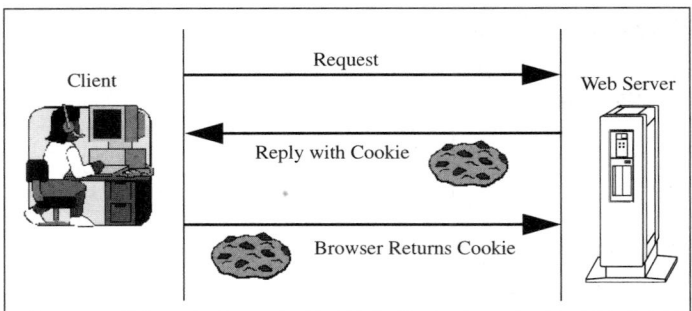

**Figure 11-5** Cookie Transactions

Clicking on the Back to Cookie Viewer Screen link in the response screen will simply call the cookie.cgi screen again, just as it did the first time. No form data has been submitted and there is no query data appended to the link, yet this time the screen looks different, as shown in Figure 11-6.

You now see one cookie with the name test_cookie and a value of 12345. This is because the **cookieView** procedure checks for the existence of cookies and displays them if they exist as shown in the following code segment.

```
if { [info exists cgi_cookies] } {
   # Convert cgi_cookies array to a list for display
   foreach crumb [array names cgi_cookies] {
      lappend cookie_list "$crumb=$cgi_cookies($crumb)"
   }
   cgi_select SELECTION $cookie_list 1 5
   cgi_br
   cgi_br
   cgi_submit FUNCTION Expire
} else {
   cgi_h4 "no cookies found"
}
```

Remember the **cgi_parse_cookies** procedure is called early on by the cookie.cgi script, so if any cookies were passed to the cookie.cgi program, the global variable **cgi_cookies** will already exist. All the **cookieView** procedure has to do is check for its existence, turn the array into a list, and display it with the **cgi_select** procedure.

If you examine the **cookieCreate** function, you will see a new wrinkle in the **cgi_header** procedure that we have not used as of yet. This procedure accepts a third argument, *headerparams*, which is used for generating additional header information in the HTTP response. As you can see from the following code, the **cookieCreate** procedure first validates that the cgi array contains the field names NAME, VALUE, and EXPIRES. It then creates an HTML acknowledgment screen and embeds the Set-Cookie header in the response.

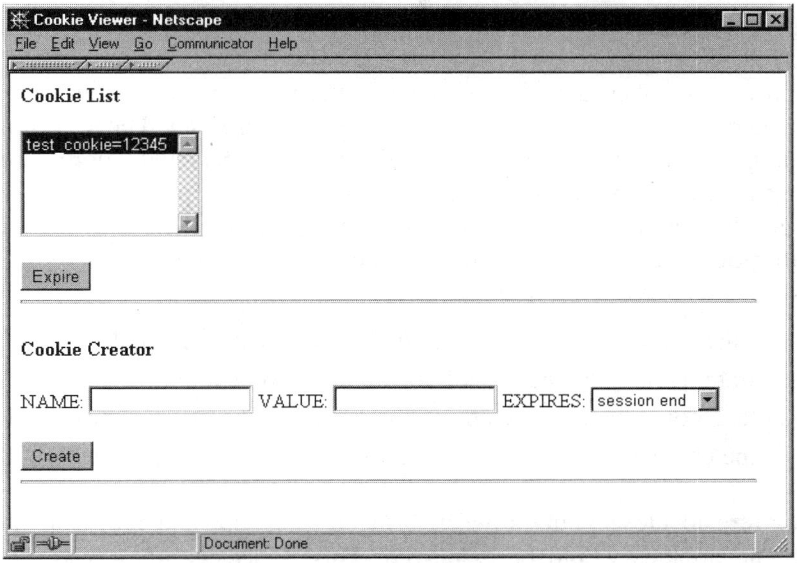

**Figure 11-6** Cookie Viewer Screen with Cookies Found

```
proc cookieCreate {} {
   global cgi

   # Create the cookie in the acknowledgment screen
   if { [cgi_validate_fields "NAME VALUE EXPIRES" err_msg] } {
      cgi_print_error $err_msg
   }

   set cookie_str [cgi_encode $cgi(NAME) $cgi(VALUE)]

   if { $cgi(EXPIRES) == "session end" } {
      cgi_header "Cookie Baker" "" "Set-Cookie: $cookie_str\; path=/"
      cgi_h4 "Cookie $cookie_str created"
   } else {
      set expiration [clock format [clock scan $cgi(EXPIRES)] \
                          -format "%A, %d-%b-%Y %H:%M:%S GMT" -gmt T]
      cgi_header "Cookie Baker" "" \
          "Set-Cookie: $cookie_str\; expires=$expiration\; path=/"
      cgi_h4 "Cookie [cgi_decode $cookie_str] created,\
              will expire on $expiration"
   }
   puts [cgi_link "Back to Cookie Viewer Screen" cookie.cgi]
```

```
        cgi_end
        return 0
    }
```

Notice the use of the **cgi_encode** procedure to create the variable **cookie_str**.

    cgi_encode *args*

This procedure takes a series of name/value pairs, in *args*, and generates an appropriate encoded string that is acceptable to the browser. The encoding is done according to the same rules used in the QUERY STRING portion of HTTP messages. The **cgi_encode** procedure actually calls a procedure from the *http* package that comes with the Tcl release to accomplish the encoding. The **cgi_encode** procedure will handle any number of name/value pairs. It converts according to the following rules:

- Separate name and value in name/value pairs with an equal sign
- Separate name/value pairs with the ampersand character
- Replace nonalphanumeric characters with their hex code equivalents
- Escape characters that have special meaning to the Tcl parser

If you were to close your browser, bring it back up, and return to the cookie viewer, no cookies would be displayed. This is because the cookie was set to expire when the browser session ended. The next section will show how to make the cookie persistent so that it remains, even when the browser application is closed and then reopened.

## Creating Cookies with an Expiration Date

The cookie named test_cookie that we just created had no specific expiration date. When cookies are created in this manner, the browser will automatically expire them when the user session ends, which is normally marked by the user shutting down the browser application. This works well for most cases. In fact, for security reasons this is the preferred method anytime a cookie is used for user authentication. One reason is the log in will only remain active for the life of the current browser session. As soon as the user closes his or her browser, the cookie is discarded and the user will be required to log in again the next time he or she contacts the site. Another reason is the cookie name and value are maintained in memory rather than being written out to the local disk as they are with cookies that have a defined expiration date. This prevents the client from examining the local cookie file maintained by the Web browser to decipher how the cookie is structured.

So, it sounds like the session end attribute is the only way to create authentication-related cookies. Well, not necessarily! Looking at it from another perspective, you may be concerned with leaving a cookie on the user's browser for an indeterminate period of time as occurs with the session end attribute. After all, the user may stay logged in for weeks and never shut down the browser. This is typical behavior in much of corporate America. If you want to place a specific expiration date on the cookies you create, the Set-Cookie header must include the *expires* attribute set with an appropriately formatted time and date.

In general the expires attribute is not used to restrict the life of a cookie but to extend it. Remember that the first cookie that we created had no expires attribute. In this case the cookie persists for the length of the client's session. Once the client shuts down the browser, the cookie is lost.

To verify this, shut down your browser, bring it back up, and return to the cookie.cgi page URL. The Cookie Viewer screen should now display the message "no cookies found." The cookie named test_cookie is gone. The reason is that when a browser, such as Netscape Navigator, receives a cookie that does not contain an expiration date, it saves it in its cache memory. When you shut down the browser application, it checks each cookie for an expiration date. If none was specified, the browser discards the cookie. So what do you do if you want more persistent cookies?

To force the cookie to be persistent for a specified period of time, even if the user closes his or her Web browser, you just supply the *expires* attribute in the Set-Cookie header along with an expiration date.

To demonstrate this point let's create a new cookie called chocolate_chip with a value of tasty. This time we will select the +1 hour expiration time in the EXPIRES field of the Cookie Viewer screen. When you click on the Create button, the sequence of events is the same as the last cookie that we created. The difference is in the content of the Set-Cookie header that is returned to the browser. This time an expires attribute is added that contains a string representing the GMT time, one hour in the future.

```
Content-Type: text/html
Set-Cookie: chocolate%5chip=tasty; expires=03-Aug-1999 22:46:00 GMT;
path=/
```

```
<HTML>
<HEAD>
<TITLE>Cookie Eater</TITLE>
</HEAD>
<BODY>
<H4>Cookie chocolate_chip=tasty created, will expire on 03-Aug-1999
22:46:00 GMT</H4>
<A href="cookie.cgi">Back to Cookie Viewer Screen</A>
</BODY>
</HTML>
```

This is nearly identical to the HTML code produced for the first cookie we created. The only difference is the addition of the expires attribute in the Set-Cookie header.

```
Set-Cookie: persistent%5fcookie=keep%5fme; expires=03-Aug-1999
22:46:00 GMT; path=/
```

This gives the client browser a specific expiration time and date. The browser will no longer return this cookie after the time and date specified by the expires attribute. The acknowledgment screen also displays the fact that the cookie was created with an expiration date and time (see Figure 11-7).

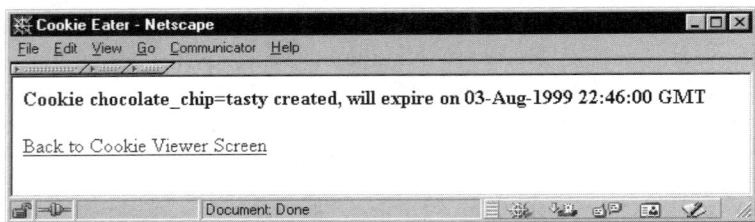

**Figure 11-7** Cookie Creation Acknowledgment Screen

The code required to add the expiration date is simple, thanks to Tcl's **clock** command. The **cookieCreate** procedure uses this code to generate the expires attribute, if it determines the session end selection has not been selected. If either the +1 minute or +1 hour selection has been selected, the CGI program uses the value directly in the **clock scan** command to generate the appropriate time string. This is possible due to the convenient *relative time* option available for this command, as shown in the following code segment:

```
set expiration [clock format [clock scan $cgi(EXPIRES)]  \
                            -format "%d-%b-%Y %H:%M:%S GMT" -gmt T]
    cgi_header "Cookie Eater" "" \
        "Set-Cookie: $cookie_str\; expires=$expiration\; path=/"
    cgi_h4 "Cookie $cookie_str created, will expire on $expiration"
```

If you return to the Cookie Viewer screen, you will now see two cookies in the top section of the window, as shown in Figure 11-8. You see the previous test_cookie that was created with the session end attribute and the chocolate_chip cookie that we just created with the +1 hour attribute.

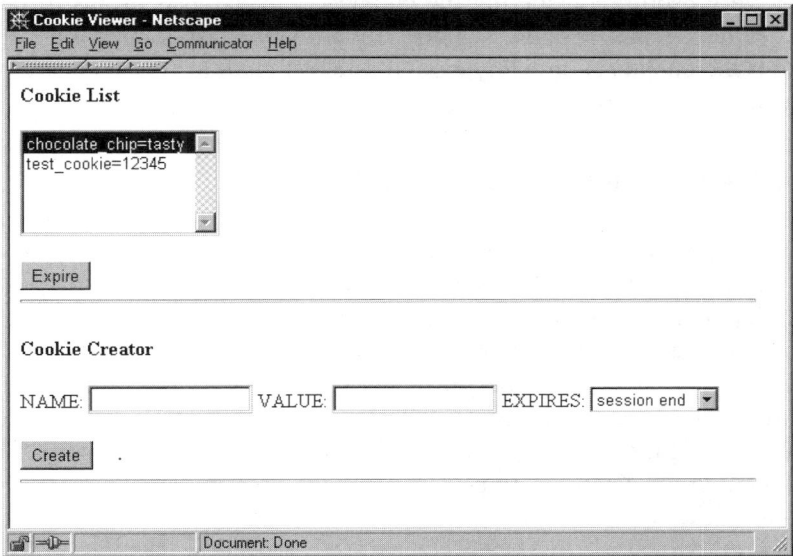

**Figure 11-8** Cookie Viewer Screen wtih Two Cookies Found

Now shut down your browser application and bring it back up. If you get back to the cookie.cgi URL in less than an hour after restarting your browser application, you will still see the cookie you created listed in Cookie Viewer Screen. The reason is simple. When you closed your browser, it searched for cookies that contained an expiration date. These cookies were then saved to a cookie file before the browser application was closed. When you bring the browser back up, it reloads its cookie file. This is how cookies are made persistent from one browser session to the next. This is the only way that cookies cause activity to your hard disk, and it is completely under the control of the hosting browser.

If you return to this screen more than an hour later, the chocolate_chip cookie will disappear automatically. The reason? The browser expired the cookie once the specified time and date elapsed. The browser will no longer return cookies once they have expired.

Even though the EXPIRES field in our Cookie Viewer contains a +1 minute attribute in the drop down list box, it's probably not a good idea to create a cookie with such a short expiration time. There could easily be this much difference between the clock on the server and the local time set in the client's browser. It is also not very useful, considering the cookie is created as a means of helping to automate the client's session, which will probably last longer than a minute. Half-hour increments is probably a good rule of thumb for those cookies that you feel need a short expiration.

## Where Are Persistent Cookies Kept?

So how does the browser keep track of persistent cookies in between invocations? They are kept in a file on the local hard drive. You can examine the contents of this cookie file, but you must first determine its location. For example the Netscape cookie file, when Netscape is running under Windows NT, is kept in a subdirectory of the Netscape installation directory. The folder is named Users/*username*, where *username* is the user name under which you operate the browser application. Netscape maintains all the cookie information in a file named cookie.txt; Internet Explorer maintains a separate text file for each persistent cookie.

If you examine your cookie files, you may be surprised at the number of cookies currently being maintained by your browser. You may also notice that many of these cookies have very long expiration dates! It is not possible to create a cookie that never expires, but you can achieve the same results by tagging the cookie with an expiration date that is very far in the future.

## Manually Expiring Cookies

Oftentimes your CGI program must have the ability to expire a cookie before it reaches its normal expiration time. As an example, let's consider the Bug Tracker database that we will discuss next. In this application we allow the user to log into one database at a time. A persistent connection is maintained by a cookie that contains the connection information to the specified database. The cookie is actually created without an expires attribute in the Set-Cookie header, which has the effect of keeping the cookie persistent for the duration of the client's current Web browser session. Before the client may access a separate database, the user must log out of the first one. In this case, we want to expire the cookie before the user terminates the browser session in preparation for logging into a different database.

Fortunately, it's just as easy to expire a cookie as it is to create it. You simply send the same Set-Cookie header you used to create the persistent cookie but supply an expiration date that is in the past. The **cookieExpire** procedure accomplishes this task.

```
proc cookieExpire {} {

    global cgi

    # Validate that the fields received are correct
    if { [cgi_validate_fields "SELECTION" err_msg] } {
        cgi_print_error "ERROR: No SELECTION field defined"
        return 1
    } else {
        # Return a reply with the Set-Cookie header embedded
        set expiration [clock format [clock scan "yesterday"] \
                               -format "%A, %d-%b-%Y %H:%M:%S GMT" -gmt T]
        cgi_header "Cookie Eater" "" \
               "Set-Cookie: $cgi(SELECTION)\; expires=$expiration\; path=/"
        cgi_h4 "Cookie $cgi(SELECTION) expired"
        puts [cgi_link "Back to Cookie Viewer Screen" cookie.cgi]
        cgi_end
        return 1
    }
}
```

The HTML code that the **cookieExpire** procedure creates is nearly identical to the code that the **cookieCreate** procedure creates, with the exception of the expires attribute. Notice in the following code the expiration date is set to yesterday's date and time. This causes the browser to immediately expire this cookie.

```
Content-Type: text/html
Set-Cookie: persistent_cookie; expires=Monday, 02-Aug-1999 23:25:35
GMT; path=/

<HTML>
<HEAD>
<TITLE>Cookie Eater</TITLE>
</HEAD>
<BODY>
<H4>Cookie persistent_cookie expired</H4>
<A href="cookie.cgi">Back to Cookie Viewer Screen</A>
</BODY>
</HTML>
```

The next time you return to the cookie.cgi program, you will again see the "no cookies found" message displayed, indicating that the persistent cookie was successfully expired.

### How Many Cookies Per Box?

The last point that should be made about cookies is that you shouldn't use too many of them. There are limitations on the number of cookies that a client can store at any one time. The numbers that follow are taken from Netscape's preliminary specification on HTTP Cookies, which you can reference at

> http://home.netscape.com/newsref/std/cookie_spec.html

This document contains a specification for the minimum number of cookies that a client should be prepared to receive and store.

- 300 total cookies
- 4K per cookie, where the name and the OPAQUE_STRING combine to form the 4K limit.
- 20 cookies per server or domain (Note that completely specified hosts and domains are treated as separate entities and have a 20-cookie limitation for each, not combined)

Servers should not expect clients to be able to exceed these limits. When a cookie larger than 4K is encountered, the cookie should be trimmed to fit, but the name should remain intact as long as it is less than 4K. When the 300-cookie limit or the 20 cookies per server is exceeded, clients should delete the least recently used cookie.

## Chapter Summary

This chapter covered the use of cookies, or magic cookies, as they are referred to by some. Cookies are a way to provide state management in the otherwise stateless mechanism of the HTTP protocol. In English this means that cookies provide a convenient way for CGI programs to remember what happened during the previous transaction. This is not a normal capability of the HTTP protocol. The following major points were covered in this chapter:

- Cookies are packets of information that Web browsers will maintain on behalf of the CGI program that creates them.
- Cookies may be written to the client's hard drive. This provides for a persistent cookie that is still present after the client's Web browser application has been shut down and restarted.
- Cookies are created with the Set-Cookie header in the HTTP response returned from the Web server to the requesting Web browser.
- Cookies may be created with specific expiration dates. The browser will no longer return an expired cookie—one that is older than its expiration date.
- If a cookie is created without an expiration date, the cookie will be discarded by the browser when the user session ends. This is normally when the user closes the browser application.
- Cookies are deleted with the same Set-Cookie header that is used to create them. When deleting a cookie, the expiration date and time are set to a value in the past.
- Cookie uses are varied. A typical example of cookie usage would be a shopping cart application. In this type of application, cookies are generally used to track the user's purchases from one screen to the next. Another example would be persistent connections to services that require a log in.

# Chapter 12

## The Bug Tracker

This chapter ties together the concepts presented in Chapters 10 and 11 by presenting an on-line database system that can be used for tracking problems as they occur anywhere throughout your product development cycle. The program is simply referred to as Bug Tracker and can be used as is or to provide a sound basis for developing an even more sophisticated system.

When developing a product, it is often useful to have a way to record problems discovered during development. This system should allow designers to log suggestions for enhancements and keep track of fixes as they occur. For distributed access it's nice to provide a Web-based interface to this information. With this type of system in place, you are less likely to forget issues that arise during the development of your products.

The Bug Tracker leverages off of the cgi.tcl package as well as the db.tcl package, which was designed for this book. The db.tcl package is explained in detail in Chapter 10. This chapter shows how to build an on-line database that provides read-write access to its clients. The Bug Tracker also allows you to restrict some users to read access while granting other users read-write access. Limited security is provided through the use of plain text passwords built into the db.tcl package.

User authentication will be remembered from one transaction to the next through the use of *cookies*, discussed in Chapter 11. This prevents the user from having to log in each time he or she wishes to access the database. In addition to cookies, *hidden fields* will also be used to maintain state information about current filter selections that a specific user has imposed on his or her view into the database. Hidden fields are HTML form fields that contain a value but do not appear on the browser's screen. They are useful for remembering information from one screen to another.

Though the security provided here is simple and straightforward, it should prove sufficient for most environments, particularly on an intranet. However, no matter how safe the lock, someone can always pick it. A very profound saying is "Locks keep honest people honest." It can be very difficult to keep a truly talented hacker at bay. It is something you should never attempt alone.

The realm of Internet security is confusing, rapidly changing, and filled with holes. Security is a complicated issue. Don't take it lightly, and don't assume that you have the time or resources to answer all the questions yourself. Trust in your system administrators and seek out new information whenever possible. Most of us are not UNIX gurus, nor are we experts in cryptography. Unfortunately, security is something that will probably never be mastered by most of us, so accept your deficiencies and always weigh on the side of caution! My main intent in this chapter is to expose you to some of the issues and show you some solutions to protecting your data. You must ultimately decide what methods are appropriate for your data.

It will soon become obvious that all these issues can greatly overshadow the complexity of the rest of your CGI code. As you saw in Chapter 10, providing read access to our back-end Tcl database was not that difficult. In fact, the CGI code was less than a couple of pages. Providing read-write access adds another layer of complexity, especially when you factor in the security issues, but it did not significantly increase the code size. Most of the work is done by the two reusable packages, and just three or four pages of code drives this whole application.

## Authenticating Bug Tracker Users

This **db.tcl** package is built around a simple scheme for validating users. This is the authentication scheme used in the Bug Tracker application. In this application, as with most applications in this book, the CGI code is running in a UNIX-like environment (AIX) on an NCSA Web server. However, the principles will apply to most environments you will encounter, which is the reason for the security scheme used in the **db.tcl** package. It's portable, simple, and effective.

The authentication scheme for the Bug Tracker program relies on the fact that the code is run in a client-server arrangement. Why is the client-server arrangement critical to this authentication scheme? Because it easily allows for the creation of an access file with a different set of permissions than those of the CGI program that accesses the data.

The dbserver.tcl program is executed with the same permissions as those of the access file, so it is able to read and write the access file. On the other hand, because the CGI program is normally executed as nobody, or some other form of restricted user, it will be denied access to this file should it attempt to read or write it. So how does the client authenticate a user? Through the use of network sockets. The network socket interface to the dbserver program provides a narrow, tightly controlled interface to the dbserver program from the CGI code. This combination of a tightly controlled interface and the standard UNIX file permissions makes it easy for an application programmer on the UNIX side to administer the access file without fear of corruption by client programs that need authenticated access.

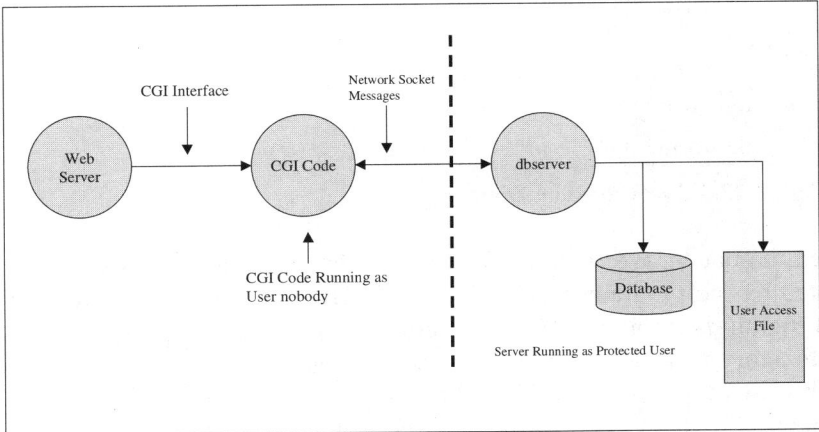

**Figure 12-1** Isolation with Tcl Sockets

Figure 12-1 illustrates the architecture of this client-server model used in the Bug Tracker application program. Here, the dbserver.tcl program is executing with a different set of permissions than the CGI program that requests data from it. The CGI code can easily communicate with the dbserver program through a network socket while having a very limited set of permissions. The dbserver program, on the other hand, can be executing as root, or any other protected user, and as such has access to the database access file, which is created under the same set of user permissions. This concept uses the network socket layer as a kind of firewall, providing isolation between the CGI applications and the user access file maintained for the database.

## User Accounts in the db.tcl Package

The dbserver.tcl program has the ability to maintain multiple database files due to the construction of the **db.tcl** package. One access file is used to maintain all the user names and passwords. This file would normally have the same set of permissions as the database server program and would typically be maintained by the administrator of the database. The access file lists the authorized users, their access level, and the *account* they are authorized for. An account is an area where one or more database files may reside.

The **db.tcl** package actually maintains these accounts as a directory structure that is rooted relative to wherever the database program is executed. Underneath the top level is a tables directory that contains all the tables that will be used in either the client-server configuration or the single-user configuration.

```
G:.
├──account_2
├──nfl
│       nfl.tbl
│
├──account_n
└──bugt
        problems.tbl
```

**Figure 12-2** db.tcl Account Directories

When the database program is running in the single-user configuration, all files created by the program will be placed directly under the tables directory. When the program is run in the client-server configuration, each account will exist as a subdirectory under the tree. You can see in Figure 12-2 that the bugt account is a subdirectory under the tables directory and contains a single file named problems.tbl. This is the database file containing the example data for this chapter's example. The account_2 and account_n are fictitious directories to further clarify the point that any additional accounts will appear as subdirectories in this location. There may be any number of accounts, but each account name must be unique because it maps directly to a directory structure.

The db.acc file is the access file that specifies user names and passwords for each of the account subdirectories. As you can see from the following example lines, the format is straightforward. Each line of the access file consists of a user name, an associated password, the permission level of the user, and the account that the user is being granted access to. An r signifies read-only access, a w allows read-write access, and a c allows the ability to create and delete tables as well as to read and write them.

```
dogbert woof c bugt
dilbert openup w bugt
wally letmein r bugt
```

There may be multiple database files in any given account directory. A user has the same access level to any file in the account. This provides the ability to assign different access levels to different users for different accounts. Inside the same account, you cannot assign a user different permissions for each table. This simplifies the administration of the password file and should be adequate for most situations.

The example in this chapter does not show tables being created through the Web interface. For now our example will be limited to creating the tables manually with the script file named seed.tcl, in the same directory that creates the initial problems.tbl file in the bugt account. This script deletes the problems.tbl file, if it exists, and then creates a new table by the same name. The code for this simple script follows.

```
#!/usr/local/bin/tclsh8.0

package require db.tcl 1.1
catch {exec rm ../dbserver/tables/bugt/problems.tbl}

# Connect to the database server and create the database file
db::connect client localhost 5031
set db_handle [db::logon dogbert woof]
db::create $db_handle problems "@recno date_entered originator\
    product shortdesc fulldesc status engineer_assigned\
    date_assigned date_complete action"

# Logoff
puts "\nLogging off"
```

```
if { ![db::logoff $db_handle] } {
   puts "Error logging off from database"
} else {
   puts "Successfully logged off"
}
```

Prior to running this script, you need to ensure that the dbserver.tcl program is running already. This program is in the book/dbserver directory, along with the sample databases used in the various examples that deal with the **db.tcl** package. You will want to ensure that access to the files in this directory is restricted to access by the database administrator. This could be anyone with the knowledge to maintain the database.

When you run the seed.tcl script, it communicates directly with the database by establishing a network socket connection on port 5031 of the local host. This was an acceptable port number on the platform where this application was developed but may not be suitable for your environment. You should check with your system administrator to determine which ports may be used on your Web server.

Using this same network socket connection principle, it would be easy to create a Tk console for communicating directly with the database while it is on-line and servicing clients over an Internet or intranet connection. Because the client-server interface serializes requests to the database files, there is no need to worry about contention when utilizing off-line tools in this fashion. You can even access the database with the standard Tcl shell while it is operational and servicing clients.

The database on the enclosed CD is shipped with a few sample records. To access it once the dbserver.tcl program is running, you can connect to it in the following manner.

```
> tclsh
% package require db.tcl
1.1
% db::connect client localhost 5031
0
% set handle [db::logon dogbert woof]
c:db11-934179510
% set view [db::select $handle problems @recno 1 "product shortdesc"]
{{db.tcl 1.1} {Encoded Passwords}}
%
```

This code connects to the database, logs in with an authorized name and password, and then executes a **db::select** to retrieve all the problems reports that currently exist in the database. Notice that a filter is provided so that only the *date_entered* and *shortdesc* fields are returned from the database. When you are done, log off with the db::logoff command.

```
% db::logoff $handle
1
```

Logging into the database from the Tcl shell is easy. Trying to create a persistent connection to the database through a Web interface is a little more involved and is the next topic of our discussion of the Bug Tracker application.

## The bugt.cgi Program

The main entry point to the Bug Tracker system is the CGI program named bugt.cgi. This is where users wishing to use the Bug Tracker program would point their Web browser. Here, as in previous examples in this book, the CGI program has been split into two separate files: the bugt.cgi program and a support file named procs.tcl. The procs.tcl file contains the code necessary to process the form data. The bugt.cgi program does the initial parsing and validation and then calls one of the procedures in the procs.tcl file to further process the request. The bugt.cgi file is reproduced here.

```
#!/usr/local/bin/tclsh

# This cgi script is the entry point for the bug tracker database.
# The input is checked for the presence of authentication cookie
# which is returned when user logs in. If the cookie is not found the
# login screen is returned to the caller. Each input screen contains
# a FUNCTION field, used below to determine how to process the request.

package require cgi.tcl
package require db.tcl
source procs.tcl

global cgi env cgi_cookies

# Parse the form data and cookies. Select the appropriate action
# depending on the value of the FUNCTION field and the presence of
# or absence of the authentication cookie.
cgi_parse
cgi_parse_cookies

set cookie_found 0
set bugt_handle ""
if { [cgi_validate_fields FUNCTION err_msg] } {
    set cgi(FUNCTION) Authenticate
```

```tcl
} elseif { [cgi_validate_cookies BUGTDBHANDLE err_msg] } {
    set cgi(FUNCTION) Login
} else {
   set cookie_found 1
   set bugt_handle $cgi_cookies(BUGTDBHANDLE)
   if { [cgi_validate_fields FUNCTION err_msg] } {
      set cgi(FUNCTION) Browse
   }
}


# Assign the hidden field variable used to maintain the filter
# selections. Both fields default to the 'All' value
if { ![cgi_validate_fields "STATUS_FILTER" err_msg] } {
   set bugt_status_filter $cgi(STATUS_FILTER)
} else {
   set bugt_status_filter "All"
}


if { ![cgi_validate_fields PRODUCT_FILTER err_msg] } {
   set bugt_product_filter $cgi(PRODUCT_FILTER)
} else {
   set bugt_product_filter "All"
}


# Connect to the server as a client
if { [catch {db::connect client localhost 5031} err] } {
   cgi_print_error "Error connecting to database server was\n$err"
   return 1
}


# Switch off the function argument to decide which action
# to take. Values are case sensitive.
switch  -- $cgi(FUNCTION) {
   "Add Entry"         { bugtAddEntry }
   "Authenticate"      {
      cgi_dump_html_file login.html
   }
   "Back to Browser" { bugtBrowser 0 }
   Browse            { bugtBrowser 0 }
   "Cancel Entry"    { bugtBrowser 0 }
   "Edit Entry"      { bugtEditScreen $cgi(SELECTION) }
   Filter            { bugtBrowser 0 }
   Login             { bugtBrowser 1 }
   Logoff            { bugtLogoff }
   "New Entry"       { bugtEntryScreen }
   "Update Entry"    { bugtUpdateEntry }
   "View Entry"      { bugtViewEntry $cgi(SELECTION) }
   default {
      cgi_print_error "Unknown FUNCTION '$cgi(FUNCTION)'\
         received by bugt.cgi"
   }
}
```

This program is responsible for deciphering what the client's request is and calling the appropriate procedure in the procs.tcl to handle the request. This code performs the following functions:

- Calls the **cgi_parse** procedure to build the global cgi array containing any name/value pairs sent by the client's browser.

- Calls the **cgi_parse_cookies** procedure to build the global cgi_cookies array containing any cookies sent by the client's Web browser. The program uses a cookie named BUGTDBHANDLE to uniquely identify each individual client.

- Checks for the presence of two hidden fields named PRODUCT_FILTER and STATUS_FILTER. These hidden fields are used to maintain state information about the current settings for a particular user.

- Creates a client socket connection with the database using the **db::connect** call. This is necessary before any transactions can be made with the database.

As with other CGI programs in this book, a field named FUNCTION is submitted by every form in the application and is used to determine what processing needs to be performed.

### The Login Screen

The client's initial call to the bugt.cgi link will contain no cookie and no FUNCTION field. The bugt.cgi program senses this condition in the first few lines of code and calls **cgi_dump_html_file** to return the login.html file to the requesting browser, resulting in the login screen shown in Figure 12-3.

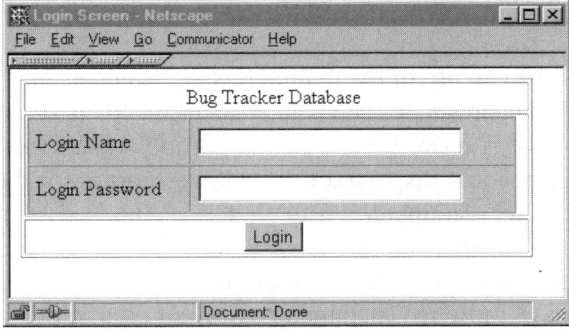

**Figure 12-3** The Login Screen

This is the only time the CGI program does not actually create a client connection to the Bug Tracker database. It simply returns the static login screen that accepts a user name and password. Clicking on the Login button causes the fields shown in Table 12-1 to be sent to the bugt.cgi program. This time the FUNCTION field will be present containing a value of Login. The USERNAME field and the PASSWORD field must contain a user name and password that correspond to a valid entry in the db.acc file.

**Table 12-1** Name/Value Pairs from Login Screen

| Name | Value |
|------|-------|
| FUNCTION | contains the value LOGIN |
| USERNAME | contains the user-supplied name |
| PASSWORD | contains the user-supplied password |

The bugt.cgi program will now call the **db::connect** command to establish a client socket connection with the dbserver.tcl program. If the connection cannot be established, the CGI program will return an HTML-formatted error message to the requesting client. If the connection is successful, the bugt.cgi program switches off the FUNCTION field, which results in a call to the **bugtBrowser** procedure. This in turn brings up the main database Browser Window from which the user may perform various operations against the database, depending on his or her specific access level privileges defined in the db.acc file.

## The Browser Window

Figure 12-4 contains a screen capture of the main Browser Window. This window allows the user to select the records he or she is interested in and choose an action to perform. The screen is split into two parts. The top portion contains a filter that may be used to restrict the records displayed by the lower portion of the screen. There are two selectable filter parameters. The first is a Status parameter that allows you to choose open records, closed records, or all records. The second portion of the filter allows you to select an individual product or choose all products. The combination of these two parameters allows you to quickly display just the records you are interested in.

One of the lessons in this chapter will be how to remember these filter selections from one transaction to the next. For example let's say a user selects a particular record to edit. This sends the user to the edit screen, where he or she is free to make changes to certain fields. After making the edits and submitting the changes, the program automatically returns the user to the browser screen. This seems like one cohesive application to the user, however, in terms of the CGI program, returning to the browser is a completely separate transaction. So how does the CGI program remember the previous filter selections for this particular user when another user may have selected a different set of filter criteria? The answer is through the use of hidden fields. Each screen returned to the user contains two hidden fields that specify the current user's filter selection. The CGI program checks these hidden fields before returning to the browser window and presents the appropriate view. This allows many users accessing the Bug Tracker application in parallel to have their own unique view of the data.

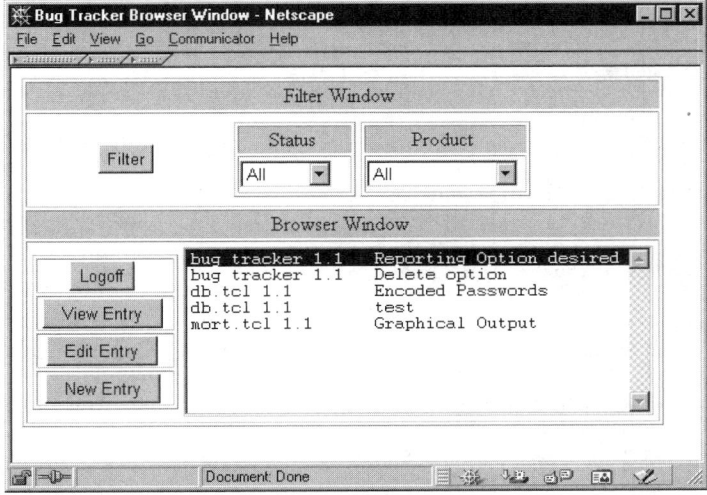

**Figure 12-4** The Database Browser Window

The lower portion of the screen contains the Browser Window, which presents a list of the records in the database that match the current filter criteria. Each record contains several fields. Two of these fields are the product name and a short description of the problem reported. These two fields are presented in the Browser Window as a quick summary of each record that matched the filter requirements. The user highlights one of the records and then chooses one of several actions, such as viewing, editing, or adding records. The last option is to log off from the database, which will automatically return the user to the login screen.

Another unique aspect of this application is the actions available in the Browser Window depending on the user's access privileges. The screen in Figure 12-4 will be returned for a user who has either write (w) or create (c) access privileges. If the user has read-only permissions, the EDIT ENTRY and NEW ENTRY buttons will not appear on the form.

The code for this procedure follows. We will examine each piece in detail throughout the rest of this section.

```
#<:------------------------------------------------------------------
# PROC bugtBrowser
#
#   Description
#       This procedure builds the browser screen for the database.
#       If the procedure is called with the login_flag true, it will
#       remove the login cookie, if present, and then call the db::login
#       procedure and return the login cookie as part of the browser
#       screen.
#
# Arguments
#    login_flag
#        set to a positive value to log in user
#  Return Values
#:>------------------------------------------------------------------

proc bugtBrowser { login_flag } {

    global cgi cgi_cookies bugt_handle
    global bugt_status_filter bugt_product_filter

    # If the login_flag is set, validate the USER and PASSWORD fields
    # and call db::logon procedure to get a handle to the database.
    if { $login_flag == 1 } {
        # Validate input fields and then attempt to open the database.
        if { [cgi_validate_fields "USER PASSWORD" err_msg] } {
            bugtErrorLogout $err_msg
            return 0
        } elseif { [catch {set bugt_handle\
                [db::logon $cgi(USER) $cgi(PASSWORD)] } err] } {
            cgi_print_error "ACCESS DENIED: error was $err"
            return 0
        }
    }

    # Substitute the All selection, if present, with the * symbol
    # and then select all records matching the two filters.
    regsub All $bugt_status_filter * status_filter
    regsub All $bugt_product_filter * product_filter
    if { [catch {set view [db::select $bugt_handle problems\
        "product status" "'$product_filter' '$status_filter' "\
        "@recno product shortdesc" ]} err ]} {
```

```
      bugtErrorLogout $err
      return 0
}


# Sort the list by product and get the user's access level
# from the cookie to determine which HTML template to use.
set view [lsort  -index 1 $view]
set access [string index $bugt_handle 0]
if { $access == "w" || $access == "c" } {
   set screen wbrowser.html
} else {
   set screen rbrowser.html
}


# Read the products and build the two filter lists.
set products [concat [bugtGetProducts] All]
set product_filter [bugtBuildSelection "PRODUCT_FILTER" \
                    $products 1 $bugt_product_filter]
set status_filter [bugtBuildSelection "STATUS_FILTER" \
                   "Open Closed All" 1 $bugt_status_filter]


# Determine the maximum tabbing space required to separate the
# product field from the description field.
set tabSize 0
if { $bugt_product_filter == "All" } {
   foreach item $view {
      set size [string length [lindex $item 1]]
      if { $size > $tabSize } {
         set tabSize $size
      }
   }
} else {
   set tabSize [string length $bugt_product_filter]
}
incr tabSize 3


# Build the browser_list variable containing the HTML code for the
# selection list that will be substituted into the static HTML form.
if { $view == "" } {
   set browse_list "No records in database"
} else {
   set index 1
   append browse_list "<SELECT NAME=\"SELECTION\" SIZE=10>\n"
   foreach item $view {
      # Generate the appropriate number of nonbreaking spaces to
      # tabularize the output.
      set space ""
      for { set i 0}\
        { $i < [expr $tabSize - [string length [lindex $item 1]]] }\
        { incr i } {
            append space "\ \;"
      }
```

```
        if { $index == 1 } {
           append browse_list \
              "<OPTION VALUE=[lindex $item 0] SELECTED>\
              [lindex $item 1]$space[lindex $item 2]</OPTION>\n"
        } else {
           append browse_list "<OPTION VALUE=[lindex $item 0]>\
              [lindex $item 1]$space[lindex $item 2]</OPTION>\n"
        }
        incr index
     }
  }
  append browse_list "</SELECT>\n"

  # Read the template file, perform variable substitution on
  # it, and send it back to the user. If the login flag is set,
  # check to see if a cookie already exsits.  If one does, then
  # expire it first and then generate a new one.
  set fptr [open $screen]
  set txt [read $fptr]
  close $fptr
  puts "Content-Type: text/html"
  if { $login_flag == 1 } {
     if { ![cgi_validate_cookies BUGTDBHANDLE err_msg] } {
        set expiration [clock format [clock scan "yesterday"] \
                            -format "%A, %d-%b-%Y %H:%M:%S GMT" -gmt T]
        puts "Set-Cookie: BUGTDBHANDLE=$bugt_handle\;\
                            expires=$expiration\; path=/"
     }
     puts "Set-Cookie: BUGTDBHANDLE=$bugt_handle\; path=/"
  }
  puts [subst -nobackslashes -nocommands $txt]
  return 1
}
```

This procedure presents the main database Browser Window. The procedure accepts a single argument, which is a flag indicating if a login is required. The first time the database is accessed after the user logs in, this flag will be set true, causing the procedure to ensure that the USERNAME and PASSWORD fields have been received from the browser and then log in to the database using the db::login procedure.

## Logging into the Database

The db::logon command validates the supplied user name and password and returns a connection handle. This handle is necessary for all subsequent accesses to the database. The connection handle is of the form

```
access:count-datestring
```

The *access* field may contain an r (read), w (write), or c (create). The *count* field will be the letters db followed by an incrementing number that defines how many connections have been made since the server was started, and the *datestring* makes the handle unique to this specific user and adds some randomization that makes it harder to hack.

The *login_flag* argument is set true the first time the procedure is called, so when the bugtBrowser procedure returns the main Browser Window, it will also send the HTTP Set-Cookie header field necessary to create the cookie containing the handle returned from the login.

The bugt.cgi code makes use of this information by looking at the first character to decide what the user's access privileges are. If r is detected as the first character, then all functions that would require write access are disabled. The server keeps track of these handles and requires a valid handle for all transactions following the db::logon call, so it would be reasonably difficult to hack into the database. You would have to guess all three fields correctly, which would be most difficult with the randomization provided by the *datestring* fields.

### Creating the Authentication Cookie

The connection handle is used in this command to retrieve the records to display in the main Browser Window, but it will also be required by other routines in the Bug Tracker application. So how does the program, executing in a stateless environment, remember this connection handle from one transaction to the next? The answer here is with a *magic cookie*. Magic cookies are discussed in detail in Chapter 11 on page 221.

Notice the code at the bottom of this procedure that checks the value of the *login_flag* argument.

```
if { $login_flag == 1 } {
    if { ![cgi_validate_cookies BUGTDBHANDLE err_msg] } {
        set expiration [clock format [clock scan "yesterday"] \
            -format "%A, %d-%b-%Y %H:%M:%S GMT" -gmt T]
        puts "Set-Cookie: BUGTDBHANDLE=$bugt_handle\;\
            expires=$expiration\; path=/"
    }
    puts "Set-Cookie: BUGTDBHANDLE=$bugt_handle\; path=/"
```

This code serves a dual purpose. First it checks to see if a cookie by the name of BUGTDBHANDLE already exists. At this point, the cookie should not exist, but if it does, it will be expired before creating the new cookie. Remember that cookies are expired by sending an *expires* attribute with an expiration date set to some time in the past. The Tcl clock command comes in handy here and is used to set the variable expiration to the current time with yesterday's date, using the format required by the browser when setting a cookie.

The new cookie is created by writing out the Set-Cookie header with no *expires* attribute. Now anytime the client Web browser makes a request to the URL pointing to the bugt.cgi program, it will return the BUGTDBHANDLE cookie that supplies the connection handle received from the log in.

### The HTML Template

As with some of the examples in earlier chapters, this procedure starts with an existing static HTML page containing a few embedded Tcl variables. The screen capture in Figure 12-5 shows what the static HTML form looks like before it is processed by the bugt.cgi program.

**Figure 12-5** The Static HTML Form

The three variables contained in the static HTML page are named **status_filter**, **product_filter**, and **browse_list**. The **bugtBrowser** procedure defines these variables and then uses the Tcl **subst** command to substitute the variables before returning the page to the requesting client. Each of these variables will be substituted with the HTML code required to produce a selection list.

We will look at how the **browse_list** variable is substituted first and then follow this with a discussion of the two filters used to restrict which records are retrieved from the database.

### Building the Browse List

The following code calls the **db::select** command to retrieve the records to be displayed in the Browser Window. The first argument is the handle to the database that was returned by the **db::logon** command. The second argument is the name of the table to access, which in this case is "problems." The third argument specifies the fields that will be used as the selection criteria, and the fourth argument contains the patterns to be matched against those fields. The last argument is a filter to apply to before returning the records. Only those fields specified in the filter will be returned by the **db::select** command. In this case only three fields are returned. They are the **@recno** field, the product field, and the short description field.

```
if { [catch {set view [db::select $bugt_handle problems\
      "product status" "'$product_filter' '$status_filter' "\
      "@recno product shortdesc" ]} err ]} {
    bugtErrorLogout $err
```

The **db::select** call will return any records where all patterns match all fields. Once the list of records is retrieved from the database, it is sorted with the *-index* options to the **lsort** command. This is a new feature in Tcl 8.X and is handy for sorting lists of lists. With this feature, you can specify which column you want to sort on and let Tcl do the rest.

This view, returned by the **db::select** call, is used to create the HTML selection list inside the Browser Window. You will notice in Figure 12-4 that the unique number assigned to each record is not displayed. This is intentional. The value of the **@recno** field is embedded inside each OPTION line using the VALUE tag. The contents of the VALUE tag do not appear on the Web browser's window but are passed back to the CGI program as part of the form data. This allows the CGI program to easily determine which record, by record number, was selected.

Once the proper records specified by the current filter settings have been selected, the only job remaining is to convert them into a selection list that will take the place of the **browse_list** variable. The **cgi_select** call is not appropriate here because it does not utilize the option attribute and has no way to redirect its output to a variable. So we'll just have to do it the old-fashioned way and build the

HTML code directly with a few Tcl commands. The code segment is duplicated here for convenience.

```
# Build the browser_list variable containing the HTML code for the
# selection list that will be substituted into the static HTML form.
if { $view == "" } {
   set browse_list "No matching records in database"
} else {
   set index 1
   append browse_list "<SELECT NAME=\"SELECTION\" SIZE=10>\n"
   foreach item $view {
       # Generate the appropriate number of nonbreaking spaces to
       # tabularize the output.
       set space ""
       for { set i 0}\
          { $i < [expr $tabSize - [string length [lindex $item 1]]] }\
          { incr i } {
              append space "\ \;"
       }
       if { $index == 1 } {
          append browse_list \
            "<OPTION VALUE=[lindex $item 0] SELECTED>\
            [lindex $item 1]$space[lindex $item 2]</OPTION>\n"
       } else {
          append browse_list "<OPTION VALUE=[lindex $item 0]>\
            [lindex $item 1]$space[lindex $item 2]</OPTION>\n"
       }
       incr index
   }
}
append browse_list "</SELECT>\n"
```

The code first checks to see if the view is empty, in which case it simply sets the browse_list variable equal to the message "No matching records in database." If records have been found, then each record is converted into a line in an HTML selection list. The for loop iterates through the records and assigns the @recno field to each line as the VALUE tag. This value is sent to the CGI program in place of the text displayed. When the form is submitted, the unique record number can then be used to recall the selected record. The loop defaults the first item in the list to being selected.

As the OPTION statements are being built, nonbreaking space characters are inserted to align the column. The code just before this had calculated a tab size based on the maximum field size and placed the result in a variable named tabSize. This tabSize variable is then used to calculate how many spaces to add between the two columns. A word of caution when using this type of approach to align columns in a selection box: You must ensure that the font used in the selection box is a fixed width font, otherwise the columns won't align properly. This is taken care of in the HTML template file by setting the font to Courier as shown:

```
<FONT SIZE="1" FACE="courier">$browse_list</FONT>
```

## Building the Filter

The filter window contains two drop down list boxes that are just HTML selection fields with the display size set to one. The first, labeled Status, allows the user to quickly select open reports, closed reports, or all reports. The second list box is labeled Products and allows the user to select an individual product type or see all products.

```
# Read the products and build the two filter lists.
set products [concat [bugtGetProducts] All]
set product_filter [bugtBuildSelection "PRODUCT_FILTER" \
                    $products 1 $bugt_product_filter]
set status_filter [bugtBuildSelection "STATUS_FILTER" \
                    "Open Closed All" 1 $bugt_status_filter]
```

Both of these selection boxes are built by a common procedure named **bugtBuildSelection**. This procedure returns the HTML code for a selection box. The arguments are the field name to be used, an array of options to display, the size of the display window, and the initial selection. The initial selection argument is optional; the procedure will default to the first element in the array of options if no initial selection is specified. The code for this procedure follows:

```
#<:-------------------------------------------------------------------
# PROC bugtBuildSelection
#
#   Description
#       This procedure returns the HTML code for a selection list.
#       If name of an element is provided in the selection argument,
#       then that element is selected, otherwise the default is to
#       select the first element.
#
# Arguments
#     name
#         The name to be assigned to the selection field.
#     list
#         The list of elements to appear in the selection field.
#     selection
#         A string selection to match for the item initially selected.
#         If not supplied, the first item in list will be selected
#
#   Return Values
```

```
#        1 if successful
#        0 if an error occurs. If an error occurs, an HTML screen is
#        displayed containing the error message.
#:>--------------------------------------------------------------------
proc bugtBuildSelection {name list size {selection {}} } {

    # Ignore empty elements
    regsub -all \{\} $list "" list

    # Write out the select attribute with the supplied name and size
    append filter "<SELECT NAME=\"$name\" SIZE=$size>\n"
    set counter 1

    # Iterate through the supplied list and generate the HTML OPTION
    # statement for each element.
    foreach item $list {
        if { $selection != "" && [string match $item $selection] ||
            $selection == "" && $counter == 1 } {
          append filter "<OPTION SELECTED>$item</OPTION>\n"
        } else {
            append filter "<OPTION>$item</OPTION>\n"
        }
        incr counter
    }
    append filter "</SELECT>\n"
    return $filter
}
```

## The View Entry Screen

When the user selects a record from the Browser Window and clicks on the View Entry button, an HTML page is returned displaying the contents of the selected record, as shown in Figure 12-6.

This screen just presents the current contents of the selected record. The user has no ability to edit the record contents or modify the underlying database. When done reviewing the contents of the record, the user may press the Back to Browser button to return to the main Browser Window. The reason that a button is used here rather than an HREF is the screen actually contains some hidden fields that are used to maintain the current filter settings when returning to the main Browser Window. If a link was used, these hidden fields would not be sent to the CGI program.

The code for this routine is short:

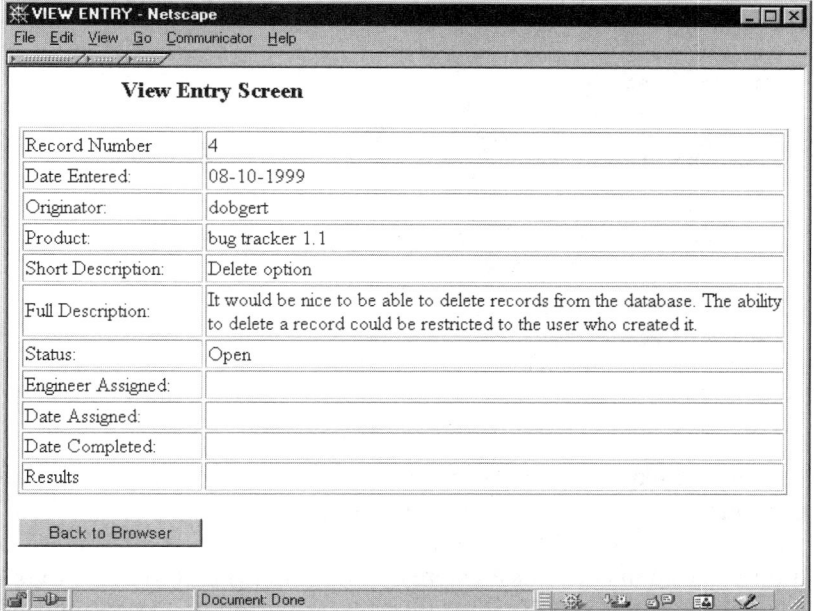

**Figure 12-6** The View Entry Screen

```
#<:-------------------------------------------------------------------
# PROC bugtViewEntry
#
#   Description
#       Displays, in read-only mode, a record from the database.
#       The screen is built using a prebuilt html file and
#       command substitution.
#
# Arguments
#       selection
#           The record number to view
#
#   Return Values
#       1 if successful
#       0 if an error occurs.
#:>-------------------------------------------------------------------
proc bugtViewEntry { selection } {

    global bugt_handle bugt_status_filter bugt_product_filter

    # Read the record from the database.
    if { [catch {set view\
        [db::select $bugt_handle problems @recno $selection]} err] } {
        bugtErrorLogout "(bugtEntryScreen) error from dbSelect was $err"
        return 0
```

```
    }

    # Because db::select returns a list of records, select
    # the first record.
    set record [lindex $view 0]
    set fptr [open view.html]
    set txt [read $fptr]
    close $fptr

    # Substitute any empty fields with a nonbreaking space so
    # the table outlines show up.
    regsub -all \{\} $record \\ \; record

    puts "Content-Type: text/html\n"
    puts [subst -nobackslashes $txt]
    return 1
}
```

It first reads the requested record from the database into a variable named record.
The contents of the view.html file is then read from the same directory. The static
HTML code in the view.html file has been modified to contain a Tcl command
substitution string in each place where a field from the record needs to be inserted.
For example the two HTML lines that define the Short Description row in the
returned table appear as follows:

```
<TD WIDTH="137">Short Description:</TD>
<TD WIDTH="448">[lindex $record 4]</TD>
```

## Using Hidden Fields

The subst command is then used to make the substitution, causing the values of
the different elements in the record list to be substituted into the HTML file. As
previously mentioned, there are hidden fields named STATUS_FILTER and
PRODUCT_FILTER used to preserve the top screen filter selections. These
hidden fields are assigned the contents of two variables named bugt_status_filter
and bugt_product_filter, respectively.

```
<INPUT TYPE="HIDDEN" NAME="STATUS_FILTER"
     SIZE="-1" VALUE="$bugt_status_filter">
<INPUT TYPE="HIDDEN" NAME="PRODUCT_FILTER"
     SIZE="-1" VALUE="$bugt_product_filter">
```

These fields are set by the main code in the bugt.cgi file and then just declared
global in this procedure so they automatically get substituted, along with the
record values, when the subst command is executed. Because the cookie is
maintained by the browser and not by the CGI program, the value of each user's

cookie can be different. This allows each user to define his or her own view into the database. This same technique of using hidden fields to maintain the current state of the filter settings is used in each of the screens in the Bug Tracker application.

Once the substitution has been performed, the translated HTML template file is sent back to the requesting browser after the correct HTTP header has been prepended to it.

Notice that the subst command is issued with the *-nobackslashes* argument and the *-novariables* argument. This enables only command substitution, which is all that is required to translate the view.html template file into the screen returned to the requesting Web browser.

## The Edit Entry Screen

If the user has write or create access privileges, the Edit Entry and New Entry buttons will be displayed on the Browser screen. When the user clicks on the Edit Entry button, the FUNCTION field will be set to "Edit Entry," which is just the name of the button pressed. The bugt.cgi program will switch off this value and call the bugtEditEntry procedure.

The bugtEditEntry procedure will read the selected record from the database using the db::select command and perform command substitution against a template HTML file, named edit.html, just as was done with the View Entry screen. This will generate the screen shown in Figure 12-7.

The method for producing the Edit Entry screen is identical to producing the View Entry screen. The main difference between this screen and the View Entry screen is that some of the database fields are now displayed in text entry boxes allowing the user to modify those fields and resubmit the form. A few of the fields may not be modified because it does not make sense to do so. It would cause confusion to allow fields such as the record number or originator to be changed. This information should be preserved throughout the life of the record. For these fields the data is written out as text in the table cells rather than as form input elements.

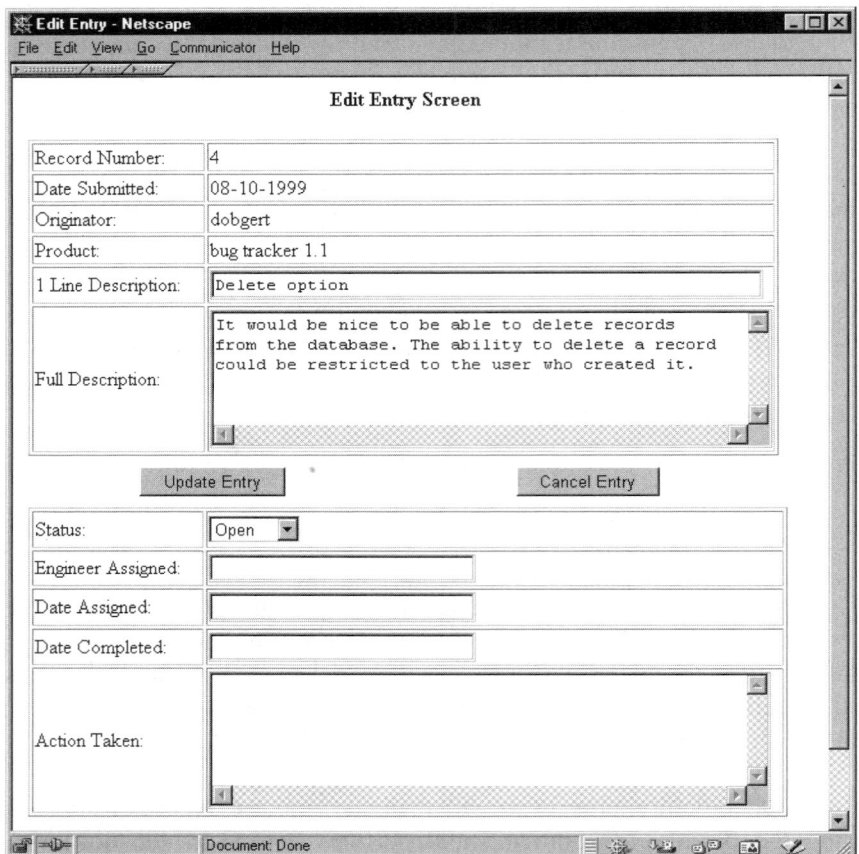

**Figure 12-7** The Edit Entry Screen

The code that produces the Edit Entry screen follows.

```
#<:----------------------------------------------------------------
# PROC bugtEditScreen
#
#  Description
#     This procedure generates the input screen for updating
#     an existing record. The screen is built using a prebuilt html
#     file and command substitution.
#
# Arguments
#     bugt_handle
#         The handle to the database returned by the dbLogon procedure.
#     selection
#         The record number to be updated. This number is embedded in
#         the form data received from the browser window.
```

```
#   Return Values
#       1 if successful
#       0 if an error occurs. If an error occurs, an HTML screen is
#       displayed containing the error message.
#:>------------------------------------------------------------------
proc bugtEditScreen { selection } {

    global bugt_handle bugt_status_filter bugt_product_filter

    # Read the record to be edited.
    if { [catch {set view\
       [db::select $bugt_handle problems @recno $selection]} err] } {
       bugtErrorLogout $err
       return 0
    }
    set record [lindex $view 0]

    # Read in the HTML template file.
    set fptr [open edit.html]
    set txt [read $fptr]
    close $fptr

    # Build the status selection field.
    set status [bugtBuildSelection "status" \
       "Open Closed" 1 $bugt_status_filter]
    append status "<SELECT NAME=\"status\">\n"

    # Substitute the variables and return the HTML page.
    puts "Content-Type: text/html\n"
    puts [subst -nobackslashes $txt]
    return 1
}
```

Once again, this code is nearly identical to the **bugtViewEntry** procedure. The real difference is in the HTML file used to create the screen. These two procedures could easily be combined into one with the name of the file being passed in as an argument to the procedure. However, having them as separate procedures does reduce the complexity just a bit.

As you can see in Figure 12-7, the Edit Entry screen contains buttons named Update Entry and Cancel Entry. Clicking the Update Entry button will return the FUNCTION field with a value of "Update Entry." This will cause the bugt.cgi program to update the record by calling **bugtUpdateEntry**.

```
#<:------------------------------------------------------------------
# PROC bugtUpdateEntry
#
#   Description
#       This procedure takes the form data from the edit entry screen
```

```
#       and updates the specified record.
#
# Arguments
#
#  Return Values
#    1  if successful
#    0  if an error occurs. If an error occurs, an HTML-formatted
#       error message will be returned.
#:>----------------------------------------------------------------
proc bugtUpdateEntry {} {

    global cgi bugt_handle

    if { [cgi_validate_fields "shortdesc fulldesc status\
        engineer_assigned date_assigned date_complete\
        action" err_msg] } {
      bugtError "$err_msg"
      return 0
    }

    if { [catch {db::update $bugt_handle problems @recno $cgi(recno)\
      "'$cgi(shortdesc)' '$cgi(fulldesc)' '$cgi(status)'\
       '$cgi(engineer_assigned)' '$cgi(date_assigned)'\
       '$cgi(date_complete)' '$cgi(action)'"\
       "shortdesc fulldesc status engineer_assigned\
        date_assigned date_complete action" } err_msg] } {
      bugtErrorLogout $err_msg
    }
    bugtBrowser 0
    return 1
}
```

This procedure takes the data submitted from the Edit Entry screen and supplies it
to the **db::update** command to update the record in the database. Notice the value
of the **@recno** field is used to identify which record will be updated, but the Edit
Entry screen displays this value as text and not as a form element. So how does
the record number get communicated to the CGI program? Here again, the answer
is in a hidden field. The edit.html form contains a hidden field that is used to hold
the value of the **@recno** field.

```
<TD WIDTH="147">Record Number</TD>
<TD>[lindex $record 0] <INPUT TYPE="HIDDEN" NAME="recno" SIZE="-1"
VALUE="[lindex $record 0]"></TD>
```

If the user changes his or her mind about the update, he or she may cancel the
update by hitting the Cancel Entry button. This will return the FUNCTION field
set to a value of "Cancel Entry." This results in the **bugtBrowserEntry** procedure

being called to display the main Browser Window again. This has the effect of discarding the changes made in the Edit Entry screen.

As you can see from the following code segment, the *login_flag* argument to the **bugtBrowser** procedure call is set to 0, for the Cancel Entry case statement. This is because the user is already logged in. The Cancel Entry button is just another case statement, by the same name, in the switch command contained in the bugt.cgi program.

```
switch  -- $cgi(FUNCTION) {
    "Add Entry"       { bugtAddEntry }
    "Back to Browser" { bugtBrowser 0 }
    Browse            { bugtBrowser 0 }
    "Cancel Entry"    { bugtBrowser 0 }
    "Edit Entry"      { bugtEditScreen $cgi(SELECTION) }
    Filter            { bugtBrowser 0 }
    Login             { bugtBrowser 1 }
    Logoff            { bugtLogoff }
    "New Entry"       { bugtEntryScreen }
    "Update Entry"    { bugtUpdateEntry }
    "View Entry"      { bugtViewEntry $cgi(SELECTION) }
    default {
        cgi_print_error "Unknown FUNCTION '$cgi(FUNCTION)'\
            received by bugt.cgi"
    }
}
```

## The New Entry Screen

The last operation to be discussed is adding a new entry to the database as shown in Figure 12-8. Here again, the user must have write access. This form allows the user to enter values into every field excluding Date Submitted. This field is automatically filled in by the Bug Tracker application to ensure proper history. Once the date field has been entered into the database, it is never allowed to be changed by the user.

This code, as with other procedures discussed so far, returns an HTML template file to the requesting Web browser after performing variable substitution on it. The variable substitution serves to fill in the Date Submitted field as well as the Product field, which is a drop down list box that presents the user with a selection of product names. The Date Submitted field in the HTML template contains the variable form_date, which will be set to contain the current date (see Figure 12-8).

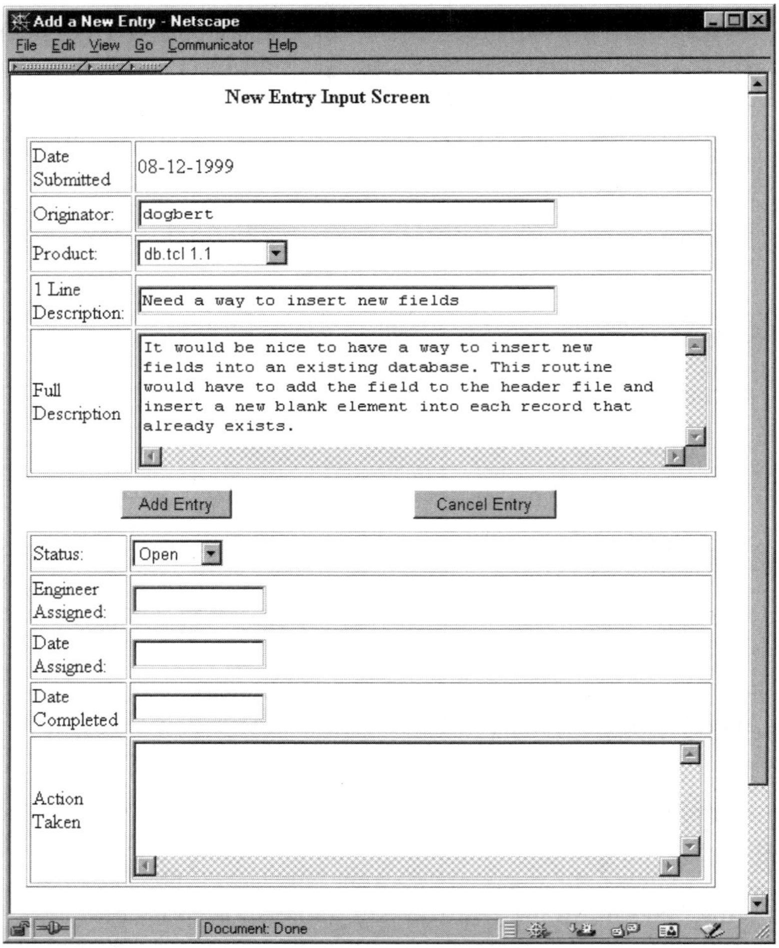

**Figure 12-8** The New Entry Screen

Here again, the user has two action buttons to choose from. The Add Entry button will submit the record to the database, and the Cancel Entry button will discard the entries and return the user to the main Browser Window. The Cancel Entry operation is identical to the one discussed in the preceding section.

If the user selects the Add Entry button, the FUNCTION field is set to the value "Add Entry," which results in the bugtAddEntry procedure being called to add the entry to the database. If the user selects the Cancel Entry button, the FUNCTION field is set to "Cancel Entry," which returns the user to the main Browser Window without saving the record.

The code first calls the cgi_validate_fields procedure to ensure that all the required fields were received from the browser. If an error occurs, a call is made to bugtError to return an HTML-formatted error to the requesting Web browser. If the validation passes, the db::insert command is called to insert the record into the database.

```
#<:-------------------------------------------------------------------
# PROC bugtAddEntry
#
#   Description
#       This procedure calls the db::insert function to add a new
#       record to the database. The current cgi form data should contain
#       all the record fields in the database.
#
# Arguments
#       none
#
#   Return Values
#       0 if an error occurs
#       1 if the call is successful
#:>-------------------------------------------------------------------
proc bugtAddEntry {} {

    global cgi bugt_handle

    if { [cgi_validate_fields\
            "date_entered originator product shortdesc\
             fulldesc status engineer_assigned date_assigned\
             date_complete action" err_msg] } {
        bugtError "$err_msg"
        return 0
    }

    if { [catch {db::insert $bugt_handle problems @recno\
         "$cgi(date_entered)" "$cgi(originator)" "$cgi(product)"\
         "$cgi(shortdesc)" "$cgi(fulldesc)" "$cgi(status)"\
         "$cgi(engineer_assigned)" "$cgi(date_assigned)"\
         "$cgi(date_complete)" "$cgi(action)" } err ] } {

        bugtErrorLogout $err
    }
    bugtBrowser 0
```

```
        return 1
    }
```

## Chapter Summary

This chapter presented an example database that allows users to read and write records in the database using a Web browser interface. The db.tcl package was used for both the client (CGI program) and server ends of this application.

The entire application is just 300–400 lines of commented code plus a couple of template HTML files! The reason the program is so small is due to the earlier investment in the db.tcl package and the cgi.tcl package. Just another reason to pay attention to reusability when writing your code modules.

This chapter reinforced several of the concepts that have been presented earlier in this book, and also introduced several new strategies for establishing persistent connections. The following key concepts were presented in this chapter.

- CGI programs may often communicate with an external server running in the background, such as the dbserver.tcl program discussed in this chapter.
- Sockets are a convenient way for a CGI program to connect with an external service. The Tcl socket command makes it easy to build socket-based clients or servers.
- The socket interface provides a layer of security that can be used to control access to data sources by forcing the CGI program to access the data through an external server.
- Hidden fields are HTML form fields that do not print on the client's Web browser screen. Hidden fields are a good way to maintain user-dependent state information from one transaction to the next. In this chapter hidden fields were used to maintain the current database filter settings for a particular user.
- Cookies are useful for maintaining persistent connections with some external resource, such as the Bug Tracker database. In this chapter the cookie contained the database handle returned from the log in, eliminating the need to log in to the database each time the user needs to access the data.

# Chapter 13

## Building Gateways to Your Data

Until now the database solutions in this book have utilized relatively simple ASCII files for storing data. These types of databases, generally referred to as flat file databases, are highly suited to a great many applications but provide limited capabilities for relating one type of data to another. Still, flat file databases are oftentimes adequate for the day-to-day requirements of a CGI programmer. They are inexpensive, can be developed quickly, and can get interactive Web sites up and running quickly.

On the flip side of the coin, you may encounter problems that demand you interface with more sophisticated, off-the-shelf products to get your job done. In these cases you may require a true *Relational Data Base Management System* (RDBMS) for maintaining your data. In a relational database you have the ability to maintain data in more than one file or table and build relationships between the tables through the use of common fields. This approach provides capabilities far beyond those of a simple flat file database.

There are a number of RDBMSs available on the market today. A few common ones are Oracle, Informix, and Microsoft's SQL Server. One of the realities of being a CGI programmer is that you often have to know as much about how databases work as your database administrator (if you're lucky enough to have one). This level of knowledge is required to write CGI programs that interface with the database. Fortunately, there is a free extension to Tcl that makes interfacing to several of the mainstream RDBMSs quite easy.

This chapter will demonstrate how to write the CGI code necessary to put an Oracle database behind your Web pages. The example used in this chapter is a small database containing information about a number of hard drive manufacturers and the products they produce. The CGI program uses a package named *OraTcl* to access the Oracle database.

Among other things, the OraTcl package provides the ability to connect to an Oracle database and execute SQL statements against the database. SQL stands for Structured Query Language and is a standardized language whose principal purpose is to create and manipulate relational databases. This chapter is not meant to be a tutorial for SQL. There are a great number of books that cover this topic in depth.

Still, it is impossible to demonstrate how to build CGI programs that take advantage of OraTcl's features to communicate with an Oracle database without some discussion of SQL. So, this chapter will discuss SQL as necessary to comprehend the example being presented. Fortunately, SQL is easy to learn and can be a great deal of fun once you understand its basic command set.

The principal intent of this chapter is to demonstrate OraTcl being used inside of a CGI program to access an Oracle database. Though this chapter provides a great deal of information in using OraTcl to execute SQL queries against an Oracle database, it is not meant as a replacement for the OraTcl documentation or a good Oracle reference book. If you find that you will be involved in using OraTcl to interface with an Oracle database, you should read the OraTcl documentation that comes with the most current release and obtain a good SQL reference manual because OraTcl's primary purpose is to let you execute SQL statements against an Oracle database.

## Database Overview

In order to understand why you might want to use a relational database for saving your Web-based data, let's review the flat file database architecture used in previous chapters and contrast it with the relational database model.

## The Flat File Database

In a typical flat file database, all the information is contained in a single file consisting of line-oriented records. These line-oriented records are normally referred to as rows. Each row consists of a number of fields, also referred to as columns, with some type of ASCII character delineating one field from another.

Figure 13-1 shows how the data in a simple flat file database is organized. Each line contains a number of comma-separated fields. Actually, any character can be used to separate the columns in a row. Each line, or row, is typically terminated with a standard carriage return character.

| Row1 | Column1,Column2,Column3,Column4,ColumnN |
|------|------------------------------------------|
| Row2 | Column1,Column2,Column3,Column4,ColumnN |
| Row3 | Column1,Column2,Column3,Column4,ColumnN |

**Figure 13-1** Data Organization in Flat File Databases

Flat file databases work well when all the records can be contained inside a single file. Our simple NFL statistics database in Chapter 10 was a good example of this. All of the information was contained in a single file containing rows terminated with a standard carriage return character (see Figure 13-2). The columns in each row were separated with the ~ character.

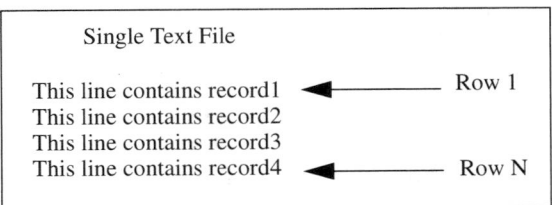

**Figure 13-2** Flat File Databases Are Normally a Single File

There is a great deal of data that can be effectively organized in simple ASCII delimited files. If the data you have to represent fits this model, go ahead and use it. As you begin to expand the types of data contained in your databases, or find the need to add new information dynamically, you will see that it is not always efficient or desirable to save all the information in a single record, or in a single file for that matter. This is where the relational model comes into play.

## The Relational Model

In the relational model information is saved in different files, also called tables, and logically grouped according to the type of data being described. The actual data in each table is used to build relationships between the different tables. This is a key concept in the relational model—there are no special indexes created in the table by the database system!

The data in a relational database is typically saved in rows and columns, just as with the simple ASCII flat file. However, in the relational model it is customary to have more than one table's worth of data. Additionally, the tables are intended to be related to each other through the data contained in their rows, as shown in Figure 13-3.

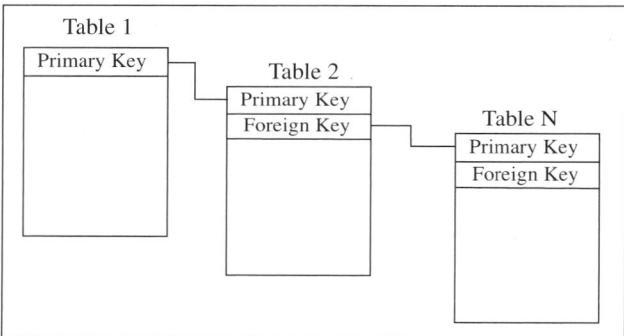

**Figure 13-3** The Relational Model

Normally, one of the columns in a table is chosen to be a *primary key* and a corresponding column in a different table is chosen to be a *foreign key*. The data values in the primary key column must be unique. The primary key acts as a unique identifier for each record in the table. Each record in a given table must contain a unique primary key value. A foreign key, on the other hand, does not have to be unique. Foreign keys are used to relate a row in one table with a corresponding row in another table that contains a primary key. Because foreign keys do not have to be unique, there may be multiple rows in any given table that contain the same foreign key value.

One of the principal benefits of the relational model is that it lets you eliminate the storage of redundant data. For instance this chapter's example will show a simple database that contains hard drive parameters by a number of hard drive manufacturers. You can extract information about a particular drive make and model, or get some generalized information about the manufacturer, such as its address, telephone number, or the URL to its Web site. If we were to try and put all this information in one table, we would have to duplicate the company information in each row containing the hard drive parameters. As the number of records grows, this becomes increasingly inefficient.

The logical place to split this data is to put the manufacturers' data in one table and the drive data in another table. The challenge then becomes to determine how to relate the data in the first table to the second table. There are several approaches that can be used. One approach is to use the company name as the primary key in the company table and use it as a foreign key in the other tables. As long as two hard drive manufacturers never have the same name, this approach will work fine. However, to be safe, we can assign each hard drive manufacturer a unique number and use this unique identifier as the primary and foreign keys. This is not quite as clear when you look at the tables, but the database takes care of most of the tedious details for us. This approach has three distinct advantages:

1. You can accommodate hard drive manufacturers with the same name. Not terribly important in this chapter's example—but if you are building a database where duplicate names will be encountered, you will need to construct the data in this fashion.

2. The data stored is smaller because the id number will typically consume less space than the actual company name. This might not seem important if you only have a few records in your database, but if you are building databases with millions of records, it has a significant impact on your system resources and performance.

3. The company name exists in just one place so if it changes, it is much easier to update your database than it would have been if the name had been embedded in each record in the database.

This process of reducing your data sets to the best fit is referred to as *normalizing* your data and can take years to master. The art and science of designing relational databases involves designing these tables and relationships so that the database is both efficient and easily expandable as you discover new types of data that need to be included in your database.

Though this chapter's example application is simple compared with some of the databases that exist on the Internet today, it demonstrates a classic case where you would like to split information into more than one table. It also demonstrates most of the points that you must concern yourself with when trying to provide a Web interface to more complex databases.

## The Entity Relationship Diagram

An entity relationship diagram shows the relationships between tables in a relational database. In addition the fields for each table are called out. Figure 13-4 shows the entity relationship diagram for the sample application contained in this chapter.

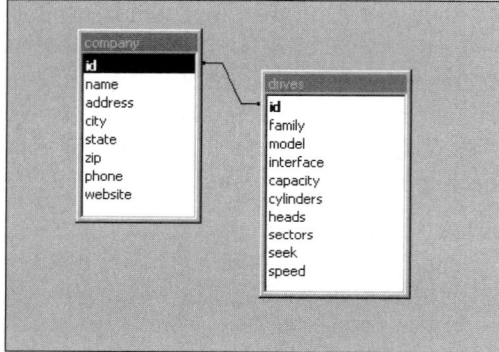

**Figure 13-4** Disk Drive Database Entity Relationship Diagram

Our database contains two tables, appropriately named company and drives. The company table is used to contain information about the hard drive manufacturer, such as its address and the URL of its Web site, if it has one. This table also contains a unique id number for the manufacturer. This id number will be used to locate information contained in the drives table about the drives it manufactures.

The drives table contains parameters for an individual hard drive. These parameters include the CMOS setup parameters necessary to install the hard drive on Windows-based workstations. Each hard drive manufacturer generally has this information available at its Web site, but having it all together in a single database could be an advantage to companies that need to deal with a lot of different types of hard drive manufacturers.

You may hear the words "database schema" when dealing with relational databases. A schema is just the definition of a particular database solution including the field definitions for each table, the type of data those fields contain, the primary and foreign key relationships, and so on.

## The OraTcl Package

The OraTcl Package is an extension to Tcl that provides a number of commands for interfacing with an Oracle database. OraTcl was created by Tom Poindexter and is available from the Tcl archives at www.neosoft.com/tcl. He has also written a package for interfacing to a Sybase database with Tcl.

OraTcl is a compiled library and, as such, its installation is a little more difficult than installing a simple Tcl script package. Fortunately the directions are fairly straightforward and the process is relatively painless. In general, under UNIX, you would perform the following steps:

1. Locate the current release of the package and download it into the directory that you would like to build from. It is easiest if this is at the same level as the source directories for Tcl.

2. Run the configure script that comes with the package. This builds a make-file that is specific to your installation. There are a number of options that can be supplied to the **configure** command that allow you to customize the OraTcl configuration to suit your particular installation requirements. You should reference the included README and INSTALL files that come with the distribution for a detailed description of these options.

3. Execute **make** to compile the source code into object code.

4. Execute **make install** to install the binaries into their proper directories.

Getting the right options to the **configure** command is the trick to making the installation smooth, just as is the case with the standard Tcl/Tk releases, so take a little time to review the options in the INSTALL file.

If you're running on a UNIX-based platform and have compiled a Tcl release, you should have no problems getting OraTcl up and running. Otherwise, you may want to contact your system administrators for a little help. There are also DLLs (Dynamic Link Libraries) and an install script available for Windows-based machines. I have not personally tried OraTcl in a Windows environment.

Once you have a version of Tcl built with OraTcl installed, you can bring up the Tcl shell and check out the new commands installed by the OraTcl package. The easiest way to see all the OraTcl commands is with the Tcl **info** command:

```
% info commands ora*
oralogon oraplexec oraopen oracancel orapoll oracols orawritelong
oracommit orareadlong orabreak oralogoff orafetch oraclose oraautocom
orabindexec orasql oraroll
%
```

You can see that OraTcl added 17 new commands to the standard Tcl interpreter. These commands allow you to connect to an Oracle database, create new databases, or manipulate existing databases. Before you can connect to your Oracle database, you will most likely have to set the environment variables specified in Table 13-1.

**Table 13-1** Oracle Environment Variables

| Name | Function |
| --- | --- |
| ORACLE_SID | specifies the Oracle server id |
| ORACLE_HOME | specifies the Oracle home directory |

Check with your Oracle database administrator for the values to be placed in these environment variables as well as any additional setup that might be necessary to get you up and running.

## Connecting to the Oracle Database

The first thing you must do when trying to access your database is to connect to the Oracle server with the **oralogon** command. This command requires a single argument.

> oralogon *connect_string*

The *connect_string* argument can take one of several forms. The most common form and the one that will be used consistently in this chapter's examples is

```
username/password
```

For a description of the other options, see the supporting OraTcl documentation that comes with the OraTcl release. Typically, the id and password sections required for the connection string would be contained in a couple Tcl variables passed in on the command line or perhaps submitted by a Web form. In any case it is good practice to never embed actual passwords in your script files. Exceptions to this might be a public user name and password that have been specifically set up to allow read-only access for a large group of people. Check with your administrator before ever embedding a user name or password in your CGI scripts and avoid it whenever possible.

For the purposes of simplicity, several examples in this chapter do use an embedded password or, in the case of the script that builds the test database, an exposed password, which is passed in on the command line. If you intend to execute the sample code in this chapter, you should have your Oracle administrator set you up with a test account where the password can be exposed in this fashion.

The **oralogon** command returns a connection *handle* in the form of a simple text string. The first handle returned will be oratcl0 with subsequent connections incrementing the number at the end of the string.

```
% oralogon $id/$password
oratcl0
```

More than one Oracle connection may be opened at the same time. Successful completion of the **oralogon** command results in a connection handle being returned. If the connection fails for any reason, the **oralogon** command will raise a Tcl error. This is true of most of the OraTcl commands. Information on the nature of the failure can be obtained from the array variable **oramsg(errortxt)**.

Several other OraTcl commands that operate at a connection level require the handle returned by the **oralogon** command. This is similar to the Tcl **file** command, which returns a file handle to be used with commands like **gets** and **puts**.

## Oracle and Cursors

The next thing to be done after establishing a connection with the Oracle database using the **oralogon** command is to open one or more *cursors*. Oracle cursors are work areas in memory used to store information about the current SQL transaction being performed against the database. You create a cursor in OraTcl using the **oraopen** command. This command requires a single argument, the connection string returned from the **oralogon** command. Cursors returned by the **oraopen** command are equal to the connection string with .# appended to the end of the string, where # is a zero-based number indicating the specific cursor. You may have multiple cursors opened against any database. The following code uses the

**oralogon** command to connect to the Oracle server and then creates a cursor with the **oraopen** command.

```
% set handle [oralogon $id/$password]
oratcl0
% set cursor [oraopen oratcl0]
oratcl0.0
%
```

You close the cursor with the **oraclose** command. This command takes just one argument, the name of the cursor returned by the **oraopen** command. Once you have closed all your open cursors, you can log out from the Oracle database using the **oralogoff** command.

```
% oraclose $cursor
% oralogoff $handle
```

You should always close any open cursors and log out from the database before exiting your applications.

## Using SQL under OraTcl

Once you have a cursor established, you may use SQL commands to manipulate your database. The **orasql** command is provided for executing SQL statements and is the command used to do most of the work in your CGI scripts that utilize the OraTcl package. This command takes a single argument, which is the SQL command, to execute. Any valid SQL command can be executed with the **orasql** command, but you may only execute one command at a time. You will, in all probability, spend the majority of your time executing just a couple of the more common SQL commands described in Table 13-2.

**Table 13-2** Basic SQL Commands

| Command | Description |
|---------|-------------|
| CREATE  | Creates new tables in the database; also used to create primary and foreign keys in those tables |
| DROP    | Deletes a table from the database |
| INSERT  | Used to insert new rows into an existing database table |

**Table 13-2** Basic SQL Commands  (Continued)

| Command | Description |
|---------|-------------|
| SELECT | Used to query the database and extract information from one or more tables based on some defined selection criteria |
| UPDATE | Used to modify existing rows in one or more database tables |

After building the test database that will be used in the example CGI code, we will investigate a few of these commands by executing them from inside the Tcl shell. If you find that you will be involved in writing embedded SQL commands in your CGI scripts, pick up one of the many excellent references to SQL available on the market today.

## Building the Test Database

The examples in this chapter use a test database that contains some information about various hard drives and the companies that manufacture them. A small Tcl script is provided to build the test database. You will need to successfully execute this script before you can execute the rest of the examples that remain in the chapter. The script to build the test database is called seed.tcl and requires the Oracle connection string as an argument.

seed.tcl *connection_string*

WARNING: The password will be exposed as it is typed on the command line so make sure that you have a valid test user name and password that can be used in this fashion.

The code for the seed.tcl script follows.

```
#!/usr/local/bin/tclsh

if { $argc != 1 } {
    puts "\nYou must supply the Oracle connection string on the"
    puts "command line in the form of username/password."
    puts "The password will be exposed as it is typed."
    exit 1
}
set drive_data {
    {'1','Caviar','AC14300','EIDE',
```

```
                  '4.3GB','8912','15','63','9.5','5400' }
             {'1','Caviar','AC26400','EIDE',
                  '6.4GB','13328','15','63','9.5','5400'}
             {'1','Caviar','AC28400','EIDE',
                  '8.4GB','16383','16','63','9.5','5400'}
             {'1','Caviar','AC310100','EIDE',
                  '8.4GB','16383','16','63','9.5','5400'}
             {'1','Caviar','AC310200','EIDE',
                  '8.4GB','16383','16','63','9.5','5400'}
             {'1','Caviar','AC313000','EIDE',
                  '13GB','16383','16','63','9.5','5400' }
             {'2','Marathon','ST94030AG','ULTRAATA',
                  '4.1GB','993','128','63','12','4500'}
             {'2','Medalist','ST310230A', 'ULTRAATA3',
                  '10.24GB','1023','256','63','12','5400'}
             { '2','Medalist','ST310240A','ULTRAATA4',
                  '13.02GB','1023','256','63','9','5400' }
             { '2','Medalist','ST310364A','ULTRAATA3',\
                  '13.6GB','1023','256','63','12','5400' }
             { '2','Medalist','ST317240A','ULTRAATA4',
                  '17.25GB','1023','256','63','9','5400' }
}
set handle [oralogon $argv]
set cursor [oraopen $handle]

orasql $cursor {CREATE TABLE company
          (id SMALLINT, name VARCHAR(20), address VARCHAR(40) NULL,
          city VARCHAR(20) NULL, state CHAR(2) NULL,
          zip VARCHAR(10) NULL, phone CHAR(15) NULL,
          website VARCHAR(60) NULL,
          PRIMARY KEY (id))
}


orasql $cursor {CREATE TABLE drives
          (id SMALLINT, family VARCHAR(20) NULL,
          model VARCHAR(20) NOT NULL,
          interface VARCHAR(20) NOT NULL,
          capacity VARCHAR(10) NOT NULL,
          cylinders SMALLINT NOT NULL,
          heads SMALLINT NOT NULL,
          sectors SMALLINT NOT NULL,
          seek SMALLINT NOT NULL,
          speed SMALLINT NOT NULL,
          FOREIGN KEY (id)
          REFERENCES company)
}


orasql $cursor {
   INSERT INTO company
   VALUES (1,'Western Digital','8105 Irvine Center Drive',
          'Irvine','CA','92618','(949) 932-
5000','www.westerndigital.com')
```

```
    }

    orasql $cursor {
        INSERT INTO company
        VALUES (2,'Seagate','920 Disc Drive','Scotts Valley','CA',
                '95066','1-831-438-6550','www.seagate.com')
    }

    foreach drive $drive_data {
        orasql $cursor "INSERT INTO drives VALUES ($drive)"
    }

    orasql $cursor { select * from company }
    orafetch $cursor {lappend companies @0}
    foreach company $companies { puts $company }

    orasql $cursor { select * from drives }
    orafetch $cursor {lappend drives @0}
    foreach drive $drives { puts $drive }

    oraclose $cursor
    oralogoff $handle
```

This script builds two Oracle tables named company and drives. In order to
successfully execute the script, you must have the necessary Oracle permissions
to allocate resources because it creates two tables. Information about the
manufacturer is placed in the company table while the hard drive parameters are
placed in the drives table. The first line of the script must point to a copy of Tcl
that includes the OraTcl package. We will examine the SQL statements in this
table and try a few additional commands from the Tcl shell once the test database
is built.

This script expects a command line argument, which is the Oracle connect string
that will be used in the **oralogon** command to connect to the database. Once
again, the password will be exposed as you type it.

The supplied username/password string is used by the script to create a connection
handle, *handle*, using the **oralogon** command and then a cursor named *cursor*
with the **oraopen** command. These two steps will be necessary anytime you wish
to execute SQL commands against a table. The script then uses the **orasql**
command to create the two new tables with the SQL CREATE command.

You will notice that the SQL commands and data types are shown in capital letters
in all the examples. In actuality these key words are case insensitive under SQL,
so you may use either lower or upper case letters. In practice you will encounter

nearly every combination of upper and lower case in existing programs and SQL documentation. The main thing to keep in mind is that the data specified for insertion into tables is case sensitive!

## Retrieving Query Results with the orafetch Command

Once the tables are created with the SQL CREATE command, the orasql command is used to execute the SQL SELECT command to select all the companies from the company table. The orafetch command is then used to retrieve the results for display.

```
orasql $cursor { select * from company }
orafetch $cursor {lappend companies @0}
foreach company $companies { puts $company }
```

Whenever an SQL SELECT command is executed against the Oracle database, the results are stored in an internal buffer. You must explicitly ask for the contents of this buffer, one row at a time. The orafetch command is used to return the next row from this internal buffer. The row is returned as a Tcl list. The procedure prototype for the orafetch command is

orafetch *cursor_handle ?commands? ?substitution_character?*
        *?tclvarname column ...?*

The *cursor_handle* argument must be a valid handle previously opened with oraopen and is the only required argument to the orafetch command. When used in this fashion, orafetch will return the next row available from the previously executed query (SELECT command). The row is returned as a valid Tcl list. A null string is returned if there are no more rows in the current set of results. The Tcl list returned by the orafetch command contains the values of the selected columns in the order specified by the SELECT command. Each execution of the orafetch command will return the next row from the query result. If no more rows are available, the orafetch command returns a null string.

Because queries often return multiple rows, the optional *commands* argument is provided to allow orafetch to process all rows returned with a single call. The presence of the *commands* argument tells the orafetch command to execute the command contained in the *commands* argument against each row of the query result. Any valid Tcl command(s) can be specified in the *commands* argument.

The *substitution_character* argument is provided to identify specific columns to be operated on. This substitution is performed for each row processed. The default substitution character is @, where @1 refers to the first column, @2 refers to the second column, and so on. The special case of @0, used in the previous example, refers to all the columns contained in the query result. In our example the line

```
orafetch $cursor {lappend companies @0}
```

uses the Tcl **lappend** command to build a list where each element is itself a Tcl list containing one row from the initial query. When the *commands* argument is provided in this fashion, the **orafetch** command remains in a loop, retrieving one row at a time from the query result and executing the Tcl code contained in the *commands* argument against the returned row. In this case the **lappend** command is executed for each row retrieved, generating a list of rows matching the query.

## Examining the Database from the Tcl Shell

If you want to examine the database that was just built using the seed.tcl program, you can execute OraTcl commands directly from the Tcl shell. The following code logs into the database, creates a cursor, and then executes an SQL SELECT command to retrieve all the rows from the company table.

```
% oralogon $username/$password
oratcl0
% oraopen oratcl0
oratcl0.0
% orasql oratcl0.0 { select * from company }
0
% orafetch oratcl0.0 {lappend companies @0}
% set companies
{1 {Western Digital} {8105 Irvine Center Drive} Irvine CA 92618 {(949)
932-5000 } www.westerndigital.com} {2 Seagate {920 Disc Drive} {Scotts
Valley} CA 95066 {1-831-438-6550 } www.seagate.com}
%
```

If you execute the same query again and then invoke the **orafetch** procedure with no *commands* argument, you will see that the rows returned from the query are retrieved one at a time.

```
%  orasql oratcl0.0 { select * from company }
0
% orafetch oratcl0.0
```

```
1 {Western Digital} {8105 Irvine Center Drive} Irvine CA 92618 {(949)
932-5000 } www.westerndigital.com
% orafetch oratcl0.0
2 Seagate {920 Disc Drive} {Scotts Valley} CA 95066 {1-831-438-6550 }
www.seagate.com
% orafetch oratcl0.0
%
```

If you want to build a list of just the company names, you can replace @0 with @1 to specify the first column, which is the company name.

```
% unset companies
% orasql oratcl0.0 { select * from company }
0
% orafetch oratcl0.0 {lappend companies @2 }
% set companies
{Western Digital} Seagate
%
```

Substitution columns may appear in any order or more than once in the same command. Substituted columns are inserted into the commands string as proper list elements (i.e., one space will be added before and after the substitution, and column values with embedded spaces are enclosed by {} if needed).

The optional *substitution_character* argument can be used to specify a different substitution character. If this argument is not specified, the substitution character defaults to the @ character. If you specify a null string for the substitution character, no column substitutions are performed. For example, we can rewrite one of the previous examples to use the tilde (~) character as the substitution character by specifying it as the third argument to the **orafetch** command. We will **unset** the companies variable, to be sure we are building the list from scratch, and execute the same query. This time the *commands* argument of the **orafetch** command is written to use the ~ character as the substitution character. The same results are obtained as before.

```
 unset companies
% orasql oratcl0.0 { select * from company }
0
% orafetch oratcl0.0 {lappend companies ~2} ~
% set companies
{Western Digital} Seagate
%
```

The remaining arguments to the **orafetch** command allow Tcl variables to be set for commands on each row that is processed. The arguments consist of matching pairs of Tcl variable names and a column number. The column number may be 0, in which case the Tcl variable is set to display the entire result row as a Tcl list. Column numbers must be less than or equal to the number of columns in the SQL result set.

If a **break** command is executed in the commands string, processing is interrupted. Remaining rows may be fetched with a subsequent **orafetch** command. If the commands execute **return** or **continue**, the remaining commands are skipped and **orafetch** execution continues with the next row. Commands should be enclosed in " " or { }.

**Orafetch** will raise a Tcl error if evaluation of the commands string causes an error to be generated. Additionally, the **orafetch** command will raise a Tcl error if the cursor handle specified is not open or a column substitution number greater than the number of columns is used in the commands string.

The **oracols** command will return as a standard Tcl list the names of the columns retrieved by the **orafetch** command. The **oracols** command requires one argument, the cursor used by the **orafetch** command.

```
% orasql oratcl0.0 { select * from company }
0
% orafetch oratcl0.0 {lappend companies @2 }
% oracols oratcl0.0
ID NAME ADDRESS CITY STATE ZIP PHONE WEBSITE
%
```

Because the SELECT command used the * character to signify that all columns should be returned in the query, the **oracols** command returned the names of all columns defined for the company table. If we narrow the column selection to just the NAME column, the list returned by the **oracols** command will also be narrowed to the selected column.

```
% orasql oratcl0.0 { select name from company }
0
% orafetch oratcl0.0 {lappend companies @1 }
% oracols oratcl0.0
NAME
%
```

## OraTcl Inside Your CGI Scripts

It's just as easy to embed OraTcl commands inside your CGI scripts as it is to execute them from the command line. This chapter's example application provides a Web interface to the hard drives database built with the seed.tcl program. The entry URL is named drives.cgi and exists in the chapter13 examples directory on the enclosed CD. This is where users of the database would point their browsers to access the information. Figure 13-5 shows how the screen will appear when you first access the program with your browser.

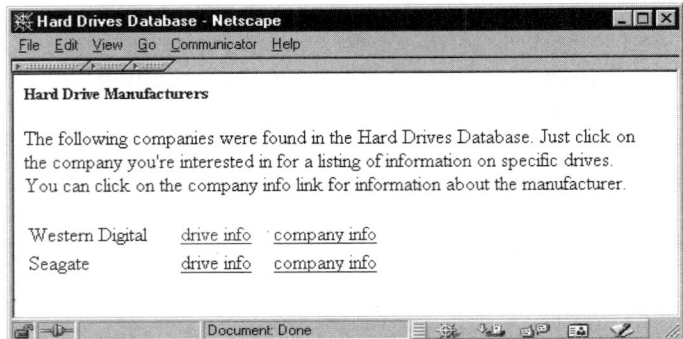

**Figure 13-5** Top Level Screen for the Hard Drives Database

The first thing the CGI code does is to access the Oracle database to retrieve the current names of hard drive manufacturers stored there. It then produces the page shown in Figure 13-5 containing two links for each manufacturer. The drive info link will return a listing of the hard drive models on file for the specified manufacturer. The company info link returns a page of information about the selected manufacturer.

The links, which are built dynamically by the drives.cgi program, contain query string information about the selection that was made. As with some of the other examples in this book, the drives.cgi program is called repeatedly from the different browser screens and is the only CGI program used to process all the various requests that come from the client Web browser. The query string portion of each URL contains a field named function and is used to decide how to process the request. For example if the user selects the drive info link for Western Digital, the query string portion of the URL sent to the Web server would appear as follows:

```
?function=drives&company=Western+Digital
```

If the function field is not defined, as will be the case for the first access from the client Web browser, it will be forced to a default value of "companies," which returns the top level page shown in Figure 13-5. If the function field is defined, as would be the case when selecting the drive info link, the CGI program will switch off the function field to determine what action to take.

Also, just as with many of the other examples in this book, the main CGI program sources a file called procs.tcl, which contains the actual code to process the requests from the various Web pages. The drives.cgi program is responsible for detecting what value, if any, is contained in the function field and calling the appropriate procedure to process the request. A slight performance improvement can be obtained by consolidating all the code into the drives.cgi program, eliminating one file access. This is acceptable when the total code is fairly small. Ultimately, it is up to the CGI programmer to decide where to split files.

The code for the drives.cgi program uses the cgi.tcl package and sources in the procs.tcl file. Here again, it is important to remember that the version of Tcl referenced in the first line of the script must be compiled with the OraTcl package and the proper version of Oracle must be up and running with the hard drives database already created (by running the seed.tcl program).

The entire program, including the procs.tcl program that is sourced in, is just a few pages of commented code: not bad for a gateway program to an Oracle database! The code for the drives.cgi program is reproduced here:

```
#!/usr/local/bin/tclsh

# This CGI script acts as a gateway to the Oracle database containing
# the hard drives database example. This program must be executed with
# a version of Tcl that includes OraTcl.

lappend auto_path /usr/local/lib
package require cgi.tcl
source procs.tcl

global cgi
global env

#cgi_dump_fields
#return

# Parse the CGI data and extract the function
cgi_parse
if { [cgi_validate_fields function err_msg] } {
   set cgi(function) companies
```

```
     }

     set env(TWO_TASK) MAGI
     set env(ORACLE_SID) MAGI
     set env(ORACLE_HOME) /wrk/oracle

     # Connect to the server
     if { [catch {set handle [oralogon dmaggian/dmaggian]} err ] ||\
          [catch {set cursor [oraopen $handle] } err ] } {
        cgi_print_error "Can't connect to the database; error was $err"
        return 1
     }

     # Switch off the function argument to decide which action to take.
     # Values are case sensitive.

     switch  -- $cgi(function) {
        companies { drivesGetCompanies $cursor }
        profile { drivesGetProfile $cursor $cgi(company) }
        drives {
           if { [cgi_validate_fields company err_msg] } {
              cgi_print_error "Missing company field in search request"
              return 0
           } else {  drivesGetDrives $cursor $cgi(company) }
        }
        stats {
           if { [cgi_validate_fields drive err_msg] } {
              cgi_print_error "Missing drive field in search request"
              return 0
           } else {  drivesGetStats $cursor $cgi(drive) }
        }
        default {
           cgi_print_error "Unknown FUNCTION '$cgi(FUNCTION)'\
              received by bugt.cgi"
           return 1
        }
     }

     # Close the database connections
     oraclose $cursor
     oralogoff $handle
```

Once again, the **cgi_parse** routine is used to parse the CGI input and then the **cgi_validate_fields** function is used to check for the existence of the function field. If the function field is not found, it is defaulted to companies, which will cause the top level selection screen to be returned to the calling Web browser.

The global env array is used to set up the three environment variables required for accessing the Oracle database. This is necessary for the **oralogon** command to work properly. If the user environment, under which your CGI programs run, already has these environment variables defined, these few lines of code are not necessary.

At this point, the **oralogon** command is executed with an embedded connection string. Because the user name in the connection string is restricted to read-only access and intended for general use by a large number of people, it is acceptable to embed this user name and password in the CGI code. This saves anyone interested in accessing the database from having to know a login id and go through a login screen.

If you wish to restrict access to the database, you'll need to utilize a login screen that lets the user enter his or her name and password. A *cookie* would most likely be used to identify the user once the login is successfully completed, creating a persistent connection that only requires the user to log in once during any browser session. Once the connection to the Oracle server is successful, the drives.cgi program will switch off the function field to decide how to process the request.

Table 13-3 shows the values that are acceptable for the function field and the names of the additional fields expected for each of these function field values.

**Table 13-3** CGI Field Usage in drives.cgi Program

| Function Value | Action | Additional Required Fields |
|---|---|---|
| companies | Returns a list of manufacturers in the database | none |
| profile | Returns information about the chosen company | company |
| drives | Returns a list of the hard drive models available for the selected manufacturer | company |
| stats | Returns hard drive parameters for the selected hard drive model | drive |

In each case the **cgi_validate_fields** function will be used to ensure that additional required fields were sent along by the requesting Web browser. The drives.cgi program will then call one of the procedures defined in the procs.tcl file to process the request. This will typically involve querying the database for the requested information and then dynamically generating an appropriate HTML page containing the requested information.

## Getting the Company Profile

Now let's take a look at what happens when the user selects the Western Digital link from the top level screen and receives the screen shown in Figure 13-6.

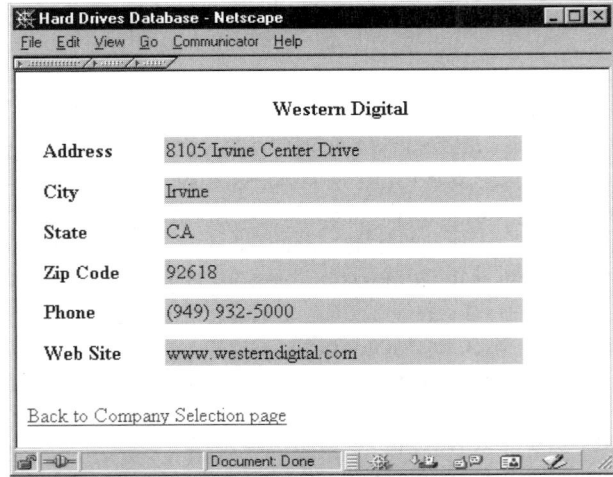

**Figure 13-6** The Company Information Screen

The Western Digital link contains a query string that defines the function and company fields:

```
?function=profile&company=Western+Digital
```

Because the function field is set to profile the drives.cgi program that will call the drivesGetProfile procedure, the screen is produced as shown in Figure 13-6. The company's address, phone number, and Web site address are displayed along with a link that returns the user to the top level Company Selection page.

The code for the drivesGetProfile procedure is shown below the screen capture. The code uses a variable, named form_code, which contains the actual HTML code required to produce the company information page. This code was produced with a Web publishing tool and then copied into the form_code variable. Notice that in each place where data is to be filled in from the resulting query, a Tcl command substitution string has been placed. For example the first line of the table appears as follows:

```
<P ALIGN="CENTER"><B>[lindex $profile 1]</B>
```

The profile variable will contain the matching record as a Tcl list after the database query is executed. The subst command then replaces these Tcl variables with the information retrieved from the Oracle database. This approach of substituting variables embedded inside HTML code has been used in many examples throughout this book. The remaining few lines of code execute an SQL query against the database to retrieve the requested information. Here's the code that returns the company profile information. You can reference the entire listing in this chapter's examples directory on the enclosed CD.

```
#<:---------------------------------------------------------------------
# PROC drivesGetProfile
#
#  Description
#      Returns information for requested company.
# Arguments
#      cursor
#          The oracle cursor returned from oraopen call.
#      company
#          The name of the company for which the profile was requested.
#
#  Return Values
#          0 always
#:>---------------------------------------------------------------------
proc drivesGetProfile { cursor company } {

set form_code {
<TABLE BORDER="0" CELLSPACING="12" WIDTH="400">
    <TR>
        <TD WIDTH="21%"> </TD>
        <TD WIDTH="79%">
        <P ALIGN="CENTER"><B>[lindex $profile 1]</B>
        </TD>
    </TR><TR>
        <TD WIDTH="21%"><B>Address</B></TD>
        <TD WIDTH="79%" BGCOLOR="silver">[lindex $profile 2]</TD>
    </TR><TR>
        <TD WIDTH="21%"><B>City</B></TD>
        <TD WIDTH="79%" BGCOLOR="silver">[lindex $profile 3]</TD>
    </TR><TR>
        <TD WIDTH="21%"><B>State</B></TD>
        <TD WIDTH="79%" BGCOLOR="silver">[lindex $profile 4]</TD>
    </TR><TR>
        <TD WIDTH="21%"><B>Zip Code</B></TD>
        <TD WIDTH="79%" BGCOLOR="silver">[lindex $profile 5]</TD>
```

```
        </TR><TR>
           <TD WIDTH="21%"><B>Phone</B></TD>
           <TD WIDTH="79%" BGCOLOR="silver">[lindex $profile 6]</TD>
        </TR><TR>
           <TD WIDTH="21%"><B>Website</B></TD>
           <TD WIDTH="79%" BGCOLOR="silver">[lindex $profile 7]</TD>
        </TR>
     </TABLE>
   }
      cgi_header "Hard Drives Database" {BGCOLOR=white TEXT=black}
      orasql $cursor "select * from company where name = '$company'"
      set profile [orafetch $cursor]
      cgi_puts [subst -nobackslashes $form_code]
      cgi_br
      cgi_puts [cgi_link "Back to Company Selection page" drives.cgi]
      cgi_pre_end
      cgi_end
   }
```

The **orasql** command is used to execute the following SQL statement against the database:

```
select * from company where name = '$company'
```

In plain English this query says return all columns from the table named company where the "name" column is equal to the contents "Western Digital." Because the company column is a primary key for the company table, this query is guaranteed to return a single row, if the company name exists in the database. Because the * character was used to specify the columns, the query will return all columns for the retrieved record. Once the query has been executed, the **orafetch** command is used to retrieve the results.

```
        set profile [orafetch $cursor]
```

Only a single record is expected from the database so no *commands* option string is necessary. The return value of the **orafetch** command is assigned directly to the profile variable.

Finally, a link is placed at the bottom of the page that calls the drives.cgi program to reproduce the top level listing of company names.

## Obtaining the Drive List

Clicking on the drive info link from the top level Web page will produce a list of hard drive models contained in the database for the given manufacturer as shown in Figure 13-7.

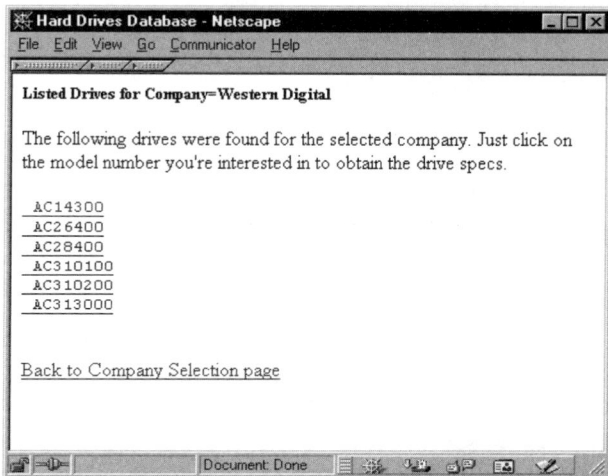

**Figure 13-7** Hard Drive Models for the Selected Manufacturer

The process for obtaining the drive list for a given manufacturer is similar to obtaining the company profile described in the previous section. The principal difference is the actual query used to interrogate the database. Also, because this action produces a variable list of hard drive model numbers, the HTML page is created dynamically with no predefined HTML source. The lines of code for this operation are less than the previous version even though the HTML code is being generated dynamically through the use of cgi.tcl library calls.

```
#<:-------------------------------------------------------------------
# PROC drivesGetDrives
#
#  Description
#      Returns an HTML page listing the drives for a given company.
# Arguments
#      cursor
#          The oracle cursor returned from oraopen call made by
#          the main CGI program.
#
#  Return Values
#      0 always
# :>-------------------------------------------------------------------
```

```
proc drivesGetDrives { cursor company } {

    cgi_header "Hard Drives Database" {BGCOLOR=white TEXT=black}
    cgi_h5 "Listed Drives for Company=$company"
    cgi_p
    cgi_puts "The following drives were found for selected\
        company. Just click on the model number you're interested\
        in to obtain the drive specs."
    orasql $cursor "select model from company,drives where\
        company.name = '$company' and company.id = drives.id"
    orafetch $cursor {lappend drives @0}
    cgi_pre
    foreach drive $drives {
        set txt [lindex $drive 0]
        cgi_puts [cgi_link $txt\
          "drives.cgi?function=stats&drive=[cgi_encode $txt]"]
    }
    cgi_pre_end
    cgi_br
    cgi_puts [cgi_link "Back to Company Selection page" drives.cgi]
    cgi_end
    return 0
}
```

In this example the SQL select statement will perform a *join* of the company table and the drives table. A join is an operation performed for you by the database in which related rows from multiple tables are retrieved and combined into an intermediate table. Your query is then executed against the intermediate table. The primary and foreign keys, defined when you create the tables, are used as the join criteria. Remember that the primary key for the company table was the id column that contained a unique number assigned to each drive manufacturer. This id column was then used as a foreign key in the drives table.

```
orasql $cursor "select model from company,drives where
            company.name = '$company' and company.id = drives.id"
```

This join builds an intermediate table consisting of all rows where the id in the drives table is equal to the id of the selected company. The query returns just the model column, which is converted into a list of links as shown in Figure 13-7. Because multiple rows will typically be returned from this query, the *commands string* argument to the **orafetch** command is used to concatenate all the rows into a single Tcl list named *drives*.

```
orafetch $cursor {lappend drives @0}
```

The @0 characters select all the columns returned from the query, which have already been narrowed to just the model column by the SQL statement itself. The drives list is then displayed as a Web page where each model is a clickable link containing a query string that defines the function field to be equal to *stats* and the drive field to contain the drive model selected.

## Getting the Drive Statistics

Selecting one of the drive model links will cause the screen in Figure 13-8 to be produced for the selected drive.

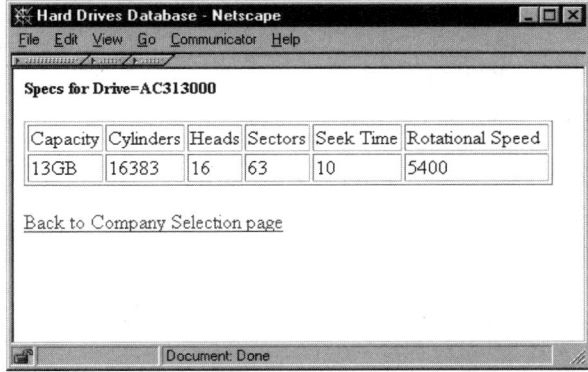

**Figure 13-8** Drive Statistics Page

This screen contains specific information about the drive selected. The query used to extract this information selects the six columns, shown in Figure 13-8, from the record in the drives table where the model number is equal to the one selected from the previous Web page.

```
orasql $cursor "select capacity,cylinders,heads,sectors,seek,speed\
                       from drives where model = '$drive'"
```

The **orafetch** command is then used to retrieve the resulting row from the database. The columns that will exist in the query results will contain only the headings that were requested with the **orasql** command. Furthermore, this procedure assumes that only one record will correspond to the selected model number, so only a single record is read with the **orafetch** command.

The code for the **drivesGetStats** procedure follows.

```
#<:------------------------------------------------------------------
# PROC drivesGetStats
#
#  Description
```

```
#       Returns the stats for the selected drive.
# Arguments
#     cursor
#         The oracle cursor returned from oraopen call made by
#         the main CGI program.
#
#   Return Values
#       0 always
#:>----------------------------------------------------------------
proc drivesGetStats { cursor drive } {

    cgi_header "Hard Drives Database" {BGCOLOR=white TEXT=black}
    cgi_h5 "Specs for Drive=$drive"
    orasql $cursor "select capacity,cylinders,heads,sectors,seek,speed\
      from drives where model = '$drive'"
    orafetch $cursor {lappend drives @0}
    set headers [list Capacity Cylinders Heads Sectors "Seek Time"\
      "Rotational Speed"]
    cgi_build_table 1 100% $headers $drives
    cgi_br
    cgi_puts [cgi_link "Back to Company Selection page" drives.cgi]
    cgi_pre_end
    cgi_end
    return 0
}
```

The last action performed by the drives.cgi program before it exits is to close the cursor that was opened with the **oraopen** command and to log off from the database.

```
# Close the database connections
oraclose $cursor
oralogoff $handle
```

Thus far, you have seen how to access data stored in an Oracle database with just a few of the commands available in the OraTcl package. The OraTcl package provides additional commands, such as the ability to roll back transactions performed against the database or cancel an SQL transaction before it has completed.

For information on these remaining OraTcl commands, consult the OraTcl documentation or check out the chapter on OraTcl in the book *Tcl/Tk Tools* by Mark Harrison. Harrison's book does an excellent job of explaining each of the OraTcl commands. He also includes additional information on some of the included applications that come with OraTcl, such as Wosql, a Windows-based SQL processor that lets you interactively execute SQL commands against an Oracle database.

Table 13-4 summarizes all of the OraTcl commands.

**Table 13-4** OraTcl Command Summary

---

`oraautocom` *logon_handle { on | off }*

This command enables (on) or disables (off) automatic commit of SQL transactions that manipulate data in the database. Cursors opened with *logon_handle* will be affected by this command.

`orabindexec` *cursor ?-async? ?:varname value ...?*

Used to execute an SQL statement that was previously parsed by the **orasql** command using the **-personally** option. The statement is not re-parsed by the **orabindexec** command.

`orabreak` *cursor*

Causes the currently executing SQL statement, running against cursor, to be interrupted.

Note: This command is only available when OraTcl is compiled with Oracle version 7.2 or higher libraries and connected to an Oracle server of 7.2 or higher.

`oracancel` *cursor*

Cancels any pending results from a prior **orasql** command executed with the same cursor. An error is raised if cursor is not valid.

`oraclose` *cursor*

Closes the cursor created with a call to **oraopen**. Cursors should be closed before the application terminates.

`oracols` *cursor*

Returns as a Tcl list the names of the columns retrieved by the last **orafetch** command against the specified Oracle cursor.

`oracommit` *connection_handle*

This command commits any pending transactions for the cursor specified by *connection_handle*. The *connection_handle* must have been opened previously with a call to **oralogon**.

**Table 13-4** OraTcl Command Summary (Continued)

`orafetch` *cursor ?tcl_statements?*

The **orafetch** command is used to fetch results generated by executing SQL statements executed against the database. Oracle holds the results in an internal buffer after SQL execution until the application asks for them. The **orafetch** command retrieves the results, one row at a time, from the database view specified by *cursor*, which must have been opened previously with the **oraopen** command.

Normally the **orafetch** command retrieves only the next row available from the query result. It is often desirable to retrieve all the rows and process them as they are being retrieved. The *tcl_statements* argument is provided for just this purpose. This argument allows you to specify a body of code to be executed against each row in the query result. By providing the *tcl_statements* argument, you are instructing the **orafetch** command to iteratively loop until all rows available have been retrieved and processed.

`oralogon` *connection_string*

Connects to a running Oracle server and returns the connection handle required by many of the other OraTcl commands. The *connection_string* argument may be any of the following forms:

```
name
name/password
name@n:dbname
name/password@n:dbname
```

where *n* = the type of network connection (typically T for TCP/IP) and dbname = the name of the Oracle server; name and password are those assigned by the Oracle administrator.

`oraopen` *logon_handle*

Returns an SQL cursor against the database identified by *logon_handle*. The connection to the database must have been made previously with a call to **oralogon**.

Multiple cursors may be opened, one at a time, against the same database.

**Table 13-4** OraTcl Command Summary (Continued)

oraplexec *cursor pl_block ?:varname1 value1
:varname2 value2 ...?*

Used to execute a PL/SQL procedure, *pl_block*. PL/SQL is a procedural language that can be used for transactional processing. This is where an entire group of SQL statements are executed as an atomic unit. The group of statements may be sent to the server or stored in the database for execution at a later time.

orapoll *cursor ?-all?*

Returns a Tcl list containing all the cursors that currently have results waiting to be processed.

Note: This command is only available when OraTcl is compiled with Oracle version 7.2 or higher libraries and connected to an Oracle server of 7.2 or higher.

orareadlong *cursor rowid table column filename*

Reads the contents of a LONG or LONG RAW *column* from the row identified by rowid in the table identified by *table*. The results of the read are written into *filename*.

The read is performed against the database pointed to by the *cursor* argument. The *rowid* must be in the proper form for an Oracle *rowid* data type. This command generates the appropriate SQL command, based on the input arguments, to extract the requested long column.

If the command completes successfully, the number of bytes read from the LONG column is returned. A Tcl error is raised if any of the arguments are invalid.

oraroll *logon_handle*

This command can be used to roll back any pending transactions from prior **orasql** commands using a cursor opened with *logon_handle*. The *logon_handle* must have been previously opened with the **oralogon** command.

**Table 13-4** OraTcl Command Summary  (Continued)

`orasql` *cursor sql_statement* ?*-parseonly*? ?*-async*?

Sends *sql_statement* to the Oracle server identified by *cursor*. Any valid SQL statement may be executed, but only a single statement may be executed with each call.

The **-parseonly** option causes the statement to be parsed but not executed. You may execute the statement at a later time with the **orabindexec** command.

The **-async** option specifies that the SQL statement should be executed asynchronously.

Note: This command is only available when OraTcl is compiled with Oracle version 7.2 or higher libraries and connected to an Oracle server of 7.2 or higher.

`orawritelong` *cursor rowid table column filename*

Writes the contents of *filename* to a LONG or LONG RAW *column* in *rowid* contained in *table*.

The number of bytes written to the file is returned upon successful completion. A Tcl error is raised if any of the input arguments is invalid, such as a cursor that does not exist or an improper *rowid* or *table* name.

## Chapter Summary

This chapter demonstrated how to use the OraTcl package to access an Oracle database from inside your CGI programs. Here are some of the key points to remember from this chapter.

- OraTcl is a compiled library extension to Tcl. The package includes the necessary support to compile it under UNIX and provides a number of DLLs (Dynamic Link Libraries) that allow it to function under the Windows environment as well.
- OraTcl provides a rich set of commands for working with an Oracle database. The package provides the ability to connect to multiple databases at the same time. In addition to this the package allows multiple views into the same database by opening multiple Oracle cursors.

- The **orasql** command is the principal command for acting upon existing databases or creating new ones. This command allows any standard SQL statement to be executed against the database. Only one SQL statement may be executed at a time.
- Anytime a query is executed against the database the results are stored in an internal Oracle buffer. The **orafetch** command is used to retrieve the results, one row at a time.
- OraTcl commands may be embedded in your CGI programs just like any other Tcl command.

# Chapter 14

## Expect in CGI Scripts

This chapter is aimed at individuals programming in more complex environments on an intranet. In this type of environment, it may be necessary to have your CGI programs communicate with another process. A process is just another running program, such as the shell you execute commands from or a running telnet or ftp application. You normally communicate with these processes by typing commands on the command line. There are many circumstances where it is desirable to automate communication with a running process.

As an example, you may want to give your employees the ability to log in and remotely extract source files from a configuration management system like SCCS or allow a gateway to a telnet service on the other side of your company's firewall. The solutions to these types of problems may require your CGI program to log in with a different user id, launch a program, such as a telnet application, and then communicate with the telnet server to accomplish the desired task. Providing interactive communication with a secondary process through a CGI interface is not a trivial task.

Certainly you can use the Tcl file facility to open a channel to another process. You can even use it to execute an rlogin command on your host server, but interactively communicating with that channel, once it is open, is tedious at best. If you simply wish to execute a task and get the results, the file facility or the Tcl

**exec** command work fine. If you are interested in having more extensive interactive communication with another process, I recommend that you look at Expect.

Expect is an extension to Tcl and is the brainchild of Don Libes of the National Institute of Standards and Technology (NIST). The Expect extension is perfectly suited for interactive communication with one or more running processes. Because Expect is layered on top of Tcl, you still have the full Tcl command set available, as well as some additional commands geared specifically for interactive process communication.

One of the principal reasons I became involved with Tcl was because of Expect. I was hired into the Motorola Computer Group to develop complex automated test suites that interact with the embedded firmware on a variety of VME and Compact PCI-based hardware. The communication is normally accomplished through a telnet connection to a serial console port on the board under test. Expect made this job a breeze compared with any other environment I could imagine. We also use Expect to communicate with power control modules, X10 controllers, and even change our passwords on the many servers that we work with.

This chapter will first present a quick overview of the main features of Expect with a few command line examples. The attention will then shift to an example CGI program that allows you to log in to the Web server and execute a few different commands as that user. The UNIX **su** (substitute user) command is used by the CGI program to log in as the requested user. One of the commands you may then execute is the UNIX **whoami** command to verify that you have actually logged in as the designated user. Of course you must have a login account on the Web server's computer before using the example application.

Once again, this application could be accomplished with the normal file commands in Tcl but would prove to be more tedious when it comes to detecting the various responses that are possible from the server. It would also be more tedious to implement some form of time-out if the server did not respond as you expected. Expect does all this for you.

# A Quick Tour of Expect

Expect offers a rich set of commands that deal with interactive communication with another running process. This chapter will not attempt to cover all the commands or options to the commands. It is designed to give you a taste of Expect's power. If you are interested in more information on Expect, check out the Expect home page at

http://expect.nist.gov/

or get a copy of Don Libes's book, *Exploring Expect*. It is very well written and makes it easy to master the many capabilities of Expect.

There are three principal commands that you will need to understand before proceeding. They are **spawn**, **send**, and **expect**. We will save our discussion of the **spawn** command until last and first talk about the **send** and **expect** commands.

## The send Command

The **send** command is used to send a string to another running process. Its closest cousin is Tcl's **puts** command, which can also send a string to another process. The **send** command accepts a number of possible options followed by the string to send

send *?options? string*

You may execute Expect commands from the command line, just as you can with the Tcl shell. The following code sends "Hello World" to standard out, normally assigned to your computer's video display.

```
expect1.1> send "Hello World\n"
Hello World
expect1.2>
```

Notice the use of the \n characters. This caused the next Expect prompt to appear on a new line. Without these characters, the prompt would have appeared immediately after the "Hello World" string. This is contrary behavior to the Tcl **puts** command, which normally appends a new line character to the end of the string.

So, if this command does everything the Tcl **puts** command does, why not just use **puts**? When simply sending characters to your video display, there is very little difference. Once we connect to another running process with the **spawn** command, explained later, it will be necessary to use the **send** command, because the connections created by the **spawn** command will not be understood by the **puts** command.

Additionally, the **send** command provides much more control over how characters are sent, which can be useful when communicating with another process. For example the **-s** option to the **send** command can be used to send characters at a predefined rate of speed. Most programs will not accept input as fast as Expect can send it, and some may not provide adequate buffering, allowing Expect to overrun their buffers. This can cause unexpected results. The **send slow** option can eliminate this problem. As an example, the following code would send our "Hello World" string at a rate of one character per second.

```
set send_slow {1 1}
send -s "Hello World"
```

The **send_slow** variable is used by the **send** command to determine the rate at which to send the characters. The **send_slow** variable is just a normal Tcl list with two elements. The first number determines how many characters to send at one time, and the second number specifies a time delay between each transmission.

In this case we will send one character every second. To send two characters every tenth of a second, you would set **send_slow** to {2 .1}. You must set the **send_slow** variable before specifying the **-s** option. Other options to the send command are summarized in Table 14-1.

**Table 14-1** Send Command Options

| Option | Description |
|--------|-------------|
| -- | Indicates the end of the option; the next argument is the string to send |
| -i process_id | Send string to the process identified by process_id |
| -h | Send humanly: inserts some randomness into the sending process |
| -s | Send slowly, according to the values defined in the send_slow variable |
| -null | Send a null character |

**Table 14-1** Send Command Options (Continued)

| Option | Description |
| --- | --- |
| -raw | Do not insert returns |
| -break | Send a break character |

## Matching Input with Expect

The **expect** command does just what its name implies. It expects input from another running program. The **expect** command gives you the ability to match input against a predefined pattern. The pattern may be an exact string to match; a glob_style pattern, such as the type used in most shell environments; or a regular expression. The default is glob-style pattern matching. We will talk more about these pattern types in a moment.

Just as the **send** command defaults to sending its information to *standard out*, the **expect** command defaults to expecting its input from *standard in*, which is normally assigned to your console's keyboard. The following example will wait for you to type **HELLO** on the keyboard.

```
expect1.1> expect "HELLO"
HELLO
expect1.2>
```

One of the problems with expecting input from another process is what to do if you don't get any! Expect provides a time-out that defaults to ten seconds on **expect** commands. Had we not typed **HELLO** in the preceding example, Expect would have returned on its own after a specified time-out period.

```
expect1.1> expect "HELLO"
expect1.2>
```

You can change the default time-out to any value necessary. If you're not the fastest typist in the world, you could rewrite the preceding example to wait 30 seconds before timing out.

```
expect1.1> set timeout 30
30
expect1.2> expect "HELLO"
HELLO
expect1.3>
```

There, now we have plenty of time to enter the required input. The **expect** command allows for performing different actions based on the data that was received from the running process. The following code will respond "HELLO" if you type **hi** and then continue waiting for more input. If you type **bye**, the program responds with "Goodbye" and exits. If you wait longer than ten seconds to respond, the program will print the string "Time-out waiting for user input" and exit.

```
expect {
   hi { puts "HELLO" ; exp_continue }
   bye { puts "Goodbye" ; exit }
   timeout { puts "Time-out waiting for user input" }
}
```

The format for an **expect** command with multiple actions is

```
expect {
   pattern action
   pattern action
   ...
}
```

Normally the **expect** command will match the pattern specified, perform the associated action, and then return. You may cause the **expect** command to repeat with the **exp_continue** as we did in the preceding example. This command tells the **expect** command to execute again. This has the effect of wrapping the **expect** command in a loop but is easier and produces more concise code. The use of the **exp_continue** command is the reason the program continues to wait for input after you type **hi**.

The pattern is the string to match and the action can be any Tcl type script, including the additional Expect commands added by the Expect extension. You can write Expect scripts in the same manner that you write Tcl scripts. The main difference is the first line that tells the shell which interpreter to use when running the script. We can easily turn the previous code into an executable script named test.exp as shown:

```
#!/usr/local/bin/expect

expect {
   hi { puts "HELLO" ; exp_continue }
   bye { puts "Goodbye"  }
   timeout { puts "Time-out waiting for user input" }
}
```

Now, let's run the script and type **hi** followed by the word **bye**:

```
> test.exp
hi
HELLO
bye
Goodbye
>
```

Notice that we used the Tcl **puts** command inside the Expect statement. You can mix and match Tcl commands in the same file because Expect is just an extension to Tcl.

## The spawn Command

So how does Expect know where to send output and look for input? Expect uses the terminology of a *spawn id* to define a running process. This is analogous to a channel identifier in Tcl. Just like the Tcl **puts** and **gets** commands, if you don't specify a channel to talk to, the command defaults to reading and writing to its normal standard input and output streams.

If you do not explicitly specify which process to communicate with, Expect will communicate with the process that is currently identified by a global variable named **spawn_id**. Expect has three predefined spawn id variables, as listed in Table 14-2, that do not correspond to actual processes but can be used as if they do.

**Table 14-2**  Predefined Spawn ID Variables

| Name | Description |
| --- | --- |
| user_spawn_id | Standard input and output |
| error_spawn_id | Standard error |
| tty_spawn_id | Controlling terminal |

When Expect is first started, the **spawn_id** variable is set equal to the value of **user_spawn_id**, which has the effect of defaulting all input and output operations to standard input and standard output.

If you wish to create a new process and talk to it with the **send** and **expect** commands, you use the **spawn** command to create the process. The **spawn** command is similar to opening a process with Tcl's **file** command. The first argument to the **spawn** command is the *name* of the program to execute. Any remaining arguments are passed to the program as command line arguments.

> spawn *name args*

The **spawn** command starts the process running and returns a process identifier. The process identifier cannot be used directly to communicate with the process and will be disregarded in this discussion. Of more importance to us is the global variable **spawn_id**. Whenever you execute a **spawn** command, the **spawn_id** variable is set to the value that identifies the new process. Any **send** and **expect** commands executed after **spawn** will now talk to the new running process.

```
expect1.1> send hello\n
hello
expect1.2> spawn sh
spawn sh
48686
expect1.3> send hello\r
expect1.4> expect -re .+
> hello
sh: hello: not found
expect1.5>
```

Consider the preceding code. The first command executed sends the word "hello" to standard out, which is printed on the user's console. The word "hello" is not interpreted as a command because it is being sent to standard out—the default value of the **spawn_id** variable when Expect is first started. Therefore, the word "hello" is simply echoed on the user's console.

Notice the use of the \n characters after the **send hello** command. The **send** command sends the data exactly as it appears. If we had not specified the new line character, the next Expect prompt would have appeared immediately after the word "hello," as shown:

```
expect1.1> send hello
helloexpect1.2>
```

The next command in our example spawns a new shell and replaces the value of the underlying **spawn_id** variable with one that points to the newly spawned shell. Any **send** and **expect** commands executed at this point will operate on the new shell. If you wish to communicate with some other process, you may use the -i option (discussed later) to the **send** and **expect** commands to specify which process to communicate with. Before doing this, you must have first created a running process with the **spawn** command.

## The Web Login Application

In this chapter's example application, the **spawn** command is used to open another shell that is used to log in as a different user. The **send** and **expect** commands are then used to talk to the shell that was just created. You can use this principle to open telnet or ftp sessions as well. The *Exploring Expect* book, listed in the bibliography, contains many excellent examples along these lines.

Figure 14-1 shows what the login screen for our example application looks like. This Web page is just a static HTML file, named login.html, and is available under this chapter's example directory on the enclosed CD. This screen allows you to supply a user name and password and select a UNIX command for execution.

**Figure 14-1** The Login Screen

When the user clicks on the Submit button, the CGI program will first spawn a new shell, then execute the selected command as the user executing the CGI program, which in a typical UNIX environment is "nobody." The CGI script will then use the UNIX **su** command to log in to the shell with the supplied user name and password and execute the command a second time. The results of the two command executions are then displayed to the screen.

In Figure 14-2 you can see that the **whoami** command returned the user name "nobody" for the first execution. This is the user under which CGI scripts are executed on the system where this application was developed on. The second time the command is executed, the **whoami** command returned the user name "dmaggian" which was the one supplied to the login screen. This indicates that the command was indeed executed in a shell that was operating as the new user.

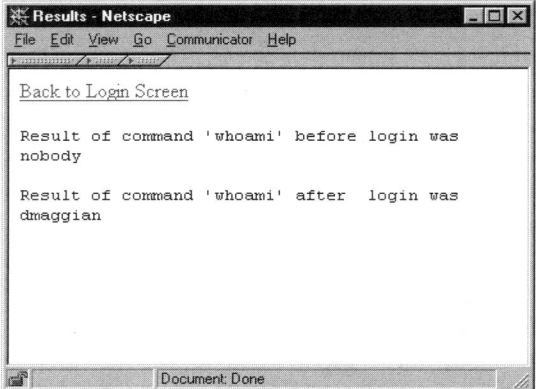

**Figure 14-2** The Results of Both Command Executions

The code for the login.cgi program follows. Notice that the first line tells the shell to use the Expect interpreter rather than the Tcl interpreter, which has been the case in most of the examples throughout this book.

```
#!/usr/local/bin/expect

#<:-----------------------------------------------------------------
#  PROC login
#
#      This procedure will execute the su command and log in the user
#      with the specified user name and password arguments, giving this
#      script the permissions that go along with the user's login.
#      If any error is encountered, it is returned in err_buff.
#
#>:-----------------------------------------------------------------
proc login {  username password err_buff} {

    global spawn_id
    upvar $err_buff err

    set working_dir [pwd]
    set prompt "(%|#|>|\\\$) $"

    set timeout 10

    send "su $username\r"
    expect {

        "$username*Password:" {
            send "$password\r"
            exp_continue
        }
```

```
            "User*does not exist" {
                set err "User $username does not exist"
                return -1
            }

            "*Authentication is denied" {
                set err "Authentication is denied"
                return -1
            }

            -re $prompt {
                set err ""
                return 0
            }

            timeout {
                expect -re ".+"
                set err "Time-out while logging in as $username\
                        expect_out(buffer) contained '$expect_out(buffer)'\
                        working dir = [pwd]"
                return -11
            }
        }
    return 0
}

package require cgilib.tcl
set prompt "(%|#|>|\\\$) $"
global spawn_id

#cgi_dump_fields
#return

cgi_parse

if { [cgi_validate_fields "username password cmd" err_msg] } {
    cgi_print_error $err_msg
    return 1
}

# Turn off logging to prevent corrupting the HTTP stream
log_user 0

# Spawn a shell and wait for the prompt
spawn sh
expect {

    -re $prompt {}
    timeout {
        set err "time-out waiting for prompt from su command"
        return -1
    }
```

```
}

# Send the command without logging in and get the results.
set cmd $cgi(cmd)
send "$cmd\r"
expect {
    -re ($cmd\r\n)(.*)(\r\n.*$prompt) {
      set result1 $expect_out(2,string)
    }
    timeout { set result1\
      "Time-out waiting for first command to execute"}
}

# Now log in and execute the command again.
if { [login $cgi(username) $cgi(password) err] == -1 } {
   cgi_print_error "Error logging in was $err"
   return 1
} else {
   set cmd $cgi(cmd)
   send "$cmd\r"
   expect {
      -re ($cmd\r\n)(.*)(\r\n.*$prompt) {
         set result2 $expect_out(2,string)
      }
      timeout { cgi_print_error\
       "Time-out waiting for second command to execute"}
   }
}

# Print both results
cgi_header "Results" {BGCOLOR=white TEXT=black}
cgi_puts [cgi_link "Back to Login Screen" login.html]
cgi_br
cgi_pre
cgi_puts "Result of command '$cmd' before login was \n$result1\n"
cgi_puts "Result of command '$cmd' after  login was \n$result2"
cgi_pre_end
cgi_end
return 0
```

The main body of the program creates a new shell with the **spawn sh** command and waits for the system to return a prompt. Successful completion of the **spawn** command will automatically change the value of the global **spawn_id** variable to point to the new shell that was started. Any **send** and **expect** commands executed after this point will talk to this process, rather than the standard in and standard out streams of the CGI program.

The program first executes the command selected in the newly created shell without changing to the new user name and saves the results. The program then calls the login procedure to change the user name supplied to the HTML login screen and executes the same command again to contrast the difference.

The login procedure executes the UNIX su command to log in with the supplied user name and password. The single expect command looks for a number of possible patterns that could be returned from the su command. The procedure returns 0 if the login fails and 1 if it succeeds. After the user is logged in, the program will execute the same command a second time and record the new results. An HTML page is then created that shows the results of executing the selected command before and after the login (see Figure 14-2).

Notice that the results of the whoami command returned "nobody" prior to changing the user id with the su command. This means that on this Web server CGI programs are set up to execute as the user named nobody, which coincidentally, is usually restricted from most critical system resources. After execution of the su command, the whoami command returned the user id of "dmaggian," indicating the CGI program is now acting as a gateway to a different user account on the system.

## Chapter Summary

Expect is an add-on to Tcl that provides a powerful tool set for programmatically dealing with interactive processes. This chapter's example provided a simple Web page that allows users to execute commands under their own UNIX account rather than the default account assigned to CGI programs. Here are the key points to remember from this chapter.

- Because Expect is an extension to Tcl, you can create Expect-based CGI programs in exactly the same manner you create Tcl-based CGI programs. Expect programs have access to the entire Tcl command set as well as a number of additional commands provided by the Expect extension.
- Expect is most ideally suited for automating communication with interactive processes, such as you would expect to find in many automated test environments, but can be useful for isolated CGI-related programming problems.
- The main aspects of Expect are encompassed in three commands: send, expect, and spawn. The spawn command creates a new running process and establishes a communication channel with that process. The send command sends information to a process created with the spawn command. The

expect command reads information from processes created with the spawn command.

- By using the spawn command inside your CGI scripts, you can build dynamic Web pages that allow authenticated users access to resources that would not normally be accessible. This can be useful for allowing access to source control systems, such as SCCS, or providing a telnet link to some equipment that is only available inside your company's firewall. The author has used Expect for both of these scenarios.

A single chapter cannot possibly do justice to the true beauty of the Expect extension. I highly recommend the book *Exploring Expect* by Don Libes if you are interested in learning more about Expect.

# Chapter 15

## The Tcl Browser Plug-In

Until now, all the examples given in this book have used CGI code running on a Web server with relatively simple HTML-based Web forms providing the user interface. Many operations that would be left up to the user interface in a conventional program are handled by the CGI program. As an example, the CGI program is responsible for validating the form data submitted from an HTML form before processing the request. This means the CGI program is forced to deal with both valid and invalid data.

When the CGI form receives invalid data, it must generate the appropriate error message formatted as an HTML document and return it to the client. The client must then submit the corrected data, which results in another query to the server. This generates extra work for the Web server and results in delays and increased traffic over the Internet. This model also violates standard user interface design conventions for the client-server model.

Providing field validation directly on the client's Web browser would be a twofold improvement. First, it would decrease the response time if the browser could validate the input data and generate messages indicating the form data is incorrect. Second, it would reduce traffic on the Internet. Because no message is sent until the user has input valid data, extra messages over the Internet are avoided. This may seem insignificant when you view it from the scope of one program, but when you multiply it by the tens of millions of users, it represents a significant amount of traffic on the Web that is very nonproductive.

Local field validation is just one example where it is desirable to take advantage of the local processing capability of the client machine. In reality a great many tasks performed by CGI programs could be done by the client Web browser if it had the intelligence to perform these tasks.

This is where the Tcl Web browser plug-in comes into play. The browser plug-in is a Tcl interpreter running inside the client's Web browser that allows you to execute Tcl programs on the client machine. This opens up a whole new world of processing capabilities that are not available under HTML.

A large portion of the industry uses Java for this purpose. Java allows code segments, known as applets, to be embedded directly into HTML documents. These embedded programs are executed on the client's Web browser by a Java interpreter that is built into the browser. Though Java is by far the most widely used language for executing applets on the client machine, learning another language is not always an exciting prospect! For individuals familiar with Tcl, there is an alternative—the Tcl Web browser plug-in.

The Tcl browser plug-in, like Java, runs an interpreter inside the client's Web browser that allows for execution of Tcl/Tk code directly on the client's machine. This chapter discusses the Tcl browser plug-in, tells you where to obtain it, and shows you how to write some simple Tcl applets, which are typically referred to as Tclets.

## What Is a Browser Plug-In?

A browser plug-in is an external program that extends the capabilities of the native Web browser program. A typical use of a plug-in is to provide display abilities for file types not directly supported by the browser itself. Plug-ins are used to extend the browser's capabilities. Because it would be impossible to take into account all the different data formats that might need to be displayed by the Web browser, the plug-in concept was introduced to make the browsers more easily extensible.

A good example of this is Adobe Acrobat Reader, which allows for the viewing of PDF files from inside the browser. Browsers, such as Netscape and Internet Explorer, are not designed to display these file types directly, so Adobe provides a browser plug-in that does. This is just one example of the many cases where browser plug-ins are currently in use. In fact, according to the FAQ at Sun's Tcl Web site, there are more than 170 plug-ins currently available on the market today.

What the Tcl browser plug-in does is to allow Tcl code to be executed directly on the client machine. This allows for numerous programmatic activities to be performed locally, once the initial HTML document is loaded. The Tcl plug-in is not limited to just Tcl code. It also allows for Tk widgets to be placed inside your documents as well. Tk is a graphical toolkit for building screen objects such as menus, radio buttons, text boxes, and so forth. If you are not familiar with the Tk extension to Tcl, there are several excellent reference books available on the subject, including *Tcl and the Tk Toolkit,* written by the inventor of the language, John Ousterhout, and also published by Addison-Wesley. See the bibliography at the end of this book for more information about Tcl/Tk literature.

## The Pros and Cons of Using the Browser Plug-In

Like most things in life, there are trade-offs to be considered when deciding whether or not to use the Tcl browser plug-in when designing your Web-based applications. This section highlights some of the advantages to using the browser plug-in as well as some of the disadvantages.

Here are some of the advantages.

- It is easy to obtain and install the Tcl browser plug-in, and it works with both Netscape and Internet Explorer.
- You don't have to learn another language. If you are already familiar with Tcl and the Tk extension to it, you can start designing complex Web interfaces right away.
- The browser plug-in provides a strong security model that can be used to provide varying degrees of access to the client's system resources depending on the origin of the embedded program.
- Powerful GUI widgets are available for building user interface screens. The Tk toolkit provides a complete set of widgets for building any type of custom GUI.

- You will most likely find Tcl/Tk easier to learn than Java.

Here are some of the disadvantages of using the Tcl Web browser plug-in.

- Users must obtain and install the browser plug-in. Although this is a very easy process, it still requires an extra step on the part of users. This generally means that the plug-in is found more commonly in intranet activities rather than on the Internet as a whole.

- The user may be reluctant to load the plug-in without understanding the security issues. The browser plug-in does have good security, but it is a separate layer that you will most likely not be familiar with. This will result in a certain learning curve before you can be truly productive.

- There is still precious little documentation available using the Tcl browser plug-in. There are manual pages on the Scriptics Web page at http://www.scriptics.com, but I don't believe they qualify as a user manual at this point in time.

- Most of the demo programs available are centered around standalone applications running under the browser plug-in and do not demonstrate using the plug-in to act as a more sophisticated user interface to CGI programs running on some other server. This book does include examples that show the browser plug-in used in conjunction with CGI programs running on a remote Web server's computer.

- There are still a lot of bugs. There is a good list of known bugs, which helps, but the plug-in is not the stable environment that you have come to know and love with Tcl. Unfortunately, Sun Microsystems, the inventor of the plug-in, does not seem to be actively pursuing its development anymore.

## Obtaining and Installing the Plug-In

The Tcl Web browser plug-in, like Tcl, is free and there are versions that run on multiple operating systems including Solaris, Mac, and Windows-based platforms. It is easy to acquire and lets you, as the CGI programmer, provide more powerful applications without having to learn another language like Java.

To obtain the Tcl Web browser plug-in, you can download it free from the following link:

http://www.scriptics.com

In Netscape version 4.*x* you can check to see which plug-ins are available by clicking on the Help menu selection and then selecting About Plug-Ins. This will display a list of the currently installed plug-ins.

One of the issues with using the plug-in is dealing with browsers that do not have the plug-in installed. One solution is to have your HTML documents check for the plug-in and let the user know how to obtain it if it is not found. The following code segment can be embedded in your HTML documents for this purpose. This code was adapted from a similar example contained in the plug-in FAQ at the Scriptics URL just listed.

```
<P>
<FONT SIZE="2"> If you do not see a </FONT>
<FONT SIZE="2" COLOR="lime">green</FONT>
<FONT SIZE="2"> ball here-&gt;
    <EMBED SRC="http://www.scriptics.com/products/tcltk/plugin/
        javascript/upgrade.tcl"
        WIDTH="22" HEIGHT="22" ALIGN="BOTTOM"
        type="application/x-tcl" align="absbottom" bg="#ffffff">
    <BR>You need to
</FONT>
<A HREF="http://www.scriptics.com/software/plug-in.html"
target="_top">
    <FONT SIZE="2">download</FONT>
</A>
<FONT SIZE="2"> the latest </FONT>
<A HREF="http://www.scriptics.com/plug-in/" target="_top">
    <FONT SIZE="2">Tcl Plug-in</FONT></A>
<FONT SIZE="2">!</FONT>
```

This HTML code produces the following display and provides an easy way for users to determine if they have the latest Tcl browser plug-in. The green ball is a small executable Tcl program that produces a green sphere and flashes the version digits, one at a time, whenever the mouse is positioned over the ball. If the Tcl plug-in is not installed, a broken image graphic will appear in its place. If the browser plug-in is installed, the embedded application will be loaded and executed in place. An embedded Tcl application is typically referred to as a Tclet.

If you do not see a green ball here-> ●
You need to download the latest Tcl Plug-in !

## Your First Tclet

As with our earlier CGI programming examples, we will start by generating a simple Hello World application utilizing the Tcl browser plug-in. Writing applications for the plug-in is very similar to writing normal Tk applications with a few exceptions. One of the exceptions is that your application is not guaranteed to run because the hosting Web browser may not have the Tcl browser plug-in installed. The best way to handle this situation is to provide a way for the user to easily download the plug-in as previously described. Another exception is that certain commands, for security reasons, are unavailable to the default configuration of the browser plug-in. A Tclet that requires the use of these commands must first request the appropriate *security policy* from the browser plug-in. Security policies are described in detail in Appendix D. For now we will limit the scope of our examples so they will run under the default configuration.

There are two ways to embed Tcl scripts inside of your Web pages. The first way is to place the Tcl/Tk code right inside of the HTML page itself, sometimes referred to as an in-line Tclet. The second way is to reference a script file that contains the code for the Tclet. In the second case the browser will retrieve the script file after the Web page is loaded.

The hello.html file in this chapter's examples directory contains a simple Web page with an in-line Tclet. In this case the code for the Tclet is contained inside the Web page itself and does not have to be loaded separately from the Web page. The screen produced by the Tclet is shown in Figure 15-1.

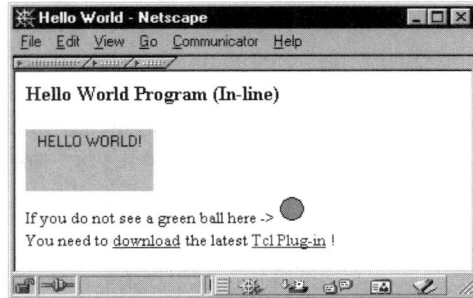

**Figure 15-1** Hello World In-line Tclet

In this example the code for the Tclet is contained inside of the HTML **EMBED** tag. If the code is embedded directly inside the EMBED tag, then the **SCRIPT** attribute is used to tag the source code. If a reference to a file containing the code is provided rather than the code itself, the SRC attribute is used. The SRC attribute is covered later in this chapter. For an embedded Tclet, the TYPE argument must be *application/x-tcl*, which tells the browser to use the Tcl Web browser plug-in to execute the embedded code. The HTML code for the hello.html page is shown here.

```
<!DOCTYPE HTML PUBLIC "-//W3C//DTD HTML 3.2//EN">
<HTML>
<HEAD>
        <TITLE>Hello World</TITLE>
</HEAD>
<BODY BGCOLOR="white">
<H4>Hello World Program (In-line)</H4>
<EMBED TYPE="application/x-tcl" SCRIPT='
  label .l -text "HELLO WORLD!"
  pack .l
'
WIDTH=100 HEIGHT=50>
<BR>
<FONT SIZE="2">If you do not see a green ball here -&gt;
    <EMBED SRC="http://www.scriptics.com/products/tcltk/plug-in/
       javascript/upgrade.tcl" WIDTH="22" HEIGHT="22" ALIGN="BOTTOM"
       type="application/x-tcl" align="absbottom" bg="#ffffff">
<BR>
You need to </FONT>
<A HREF="http://www.scriptics.com/software/plug-in.html"
target="_top">
    <FONT SIZE="2">download</FONT></A>
<FONT SIZE="2"> the latest </FONT>
<A HREF="http://www.scriptics.com/plug-in/" target="_top">
    <FONT SIZE="2">Tcl Plug-in</FONT></A>
<FONT SIZE="2">!</FONT>
</BODY>
</HTML>
```

The EMBED tag requires a WIDTH and HEIGHT attribute, which tell the hosting Web browser the amount of screen space in pixels to set aside for the embedded application. In Figure 15-1 you can see that the words "HELLO WORLD!" reside inside a gray rectangle. This is the default background color for an executing Tclet. The size of this rectangle is defined by the WIDTH and HEIGHT attributes.

## Referencing Script Files with the SRC Attribute

If you do not wish to include the Tclet in-line, you can simply reference the script using the SRC attribute of the EMBED tag.

```
<EMBED SRC="hello.tcl" TYPE="application/x-tcl" WIDTH=100 HEIGHT=50>
```

The **SRC** attribute gives the name of the script file to be retrieved from the server. This is a relative pathname. In this case it will cause the file hello.tcl to be retrieved from the same directory at the same URL that the original Web page was loaded from. The **TYPE, HEIGHT,** and **WIDTH** attributes perform just as they did in the previous example.

The hello.tcl file simply contains the two lines that were previously contained in the in-line Tclet. These two lines create a label widget that contains the words "HELLO WORLD!" and places the label on the screen using the Tk **pack** command.

```
label .1 -text "HELLO WORLD!"
pack .1
```

The first thing the hosting Web browser does in this example is to load the hello1.html Web page. The **EMBED** tag directs the browser to load the hello.tcl file from the same location the hello1.html Web page was retrieved from. After retrieving the hello.tcl file, it then executes the script under the control of the Tcl Web browser plug-in. As you can see in Figure 15-2, the results look identical to the in-line example.

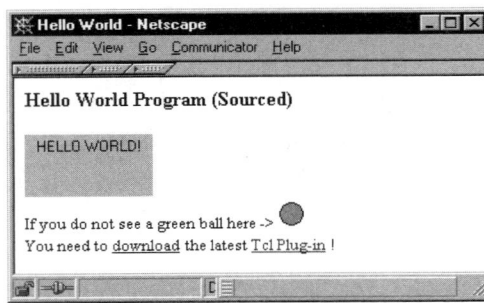

**Figure 15-2** Script-Based Hello World Tclet

Notice that there are no differences in writing Tk code for a Tclet than for an equivalent standalone program. As an example, let's say that you don't want your Tclet to stand out quite so boldly as it does with the default gray background color. Simply change it as you would any Tk application:

```
. config -bg white
label .1 -text "HELLO WORLD!" -bg white
pack .1
```

This code configures the top level frame to have a white background rather than the default gray color. The background of the label containing the HELLO WORLD text has been changed to white as well. This makes it blend in with the white background of the browser window, so you can't even tell the Tclet is separate from the browser page.

Most of the standard Tk commands work with the plug-in just as most of the standard Tcl commands work with the plug-in. However, just as some of the standard Tcl commands are unavailable in the default configuration of the plug-in, some of the Tk commands are also hidden from the Tclet. The Tk commands listed in Table 15-1 are disabled by default.

**Table 15-1**  Disabled Tk Commands

| | | | |
|---|---|---|---|
| bell | clipboard | grab | menu |
| selection | send | tk | tk_chooseColor |
| tk_getOpenFile | tk_getSaveFile | tk_messageBox | toplevel |
| wm | | | |

Here again, these commands have been disabled for security reasons, mostly to prevent annoyance attacks at the user interface level. However, commands such as the clipboard command have been disabled to prevent real security risks. The clipboard command could allow a mischievous Tclet to spy on information that was placed in the clipboard by other applications. Unfortunately, the browser plug-in does not provide a method for exposing the hidden Tk commands like it does for the hidden Tcl commands.

## The "HELLO WORLD" Form Application

This example uses the plug-in to duplicate the form-based Hello World program introduced in Chapter 4. The Tclet uses Tk widgets, rather than HTML form fields, to allow the user to input a text string and select a size for it to be displayed in the returned HTML Web page. The resulting screen is shown in Figure 15-3.

As shown in Chapter 4, this exercise can be accomplished with nothing but an HTML form, so there is no magic here! The main purpose for this example is to show an alternate solution using the browser plug-in. This is often the best way to gain confidence in a new environment. Fear not, we will build rapidly on this simple example to illustrate the power of the plug-in versus simple HTML forms.

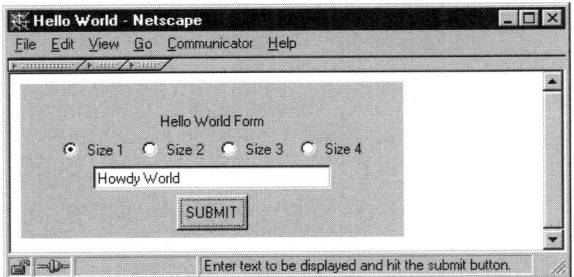

**Figure 15-3** The Hello World Form

The HTML code for this example follows. Here again, the EMBED tag in this example contains the **SRC** attribute rather than the **SCRIPT** attribute. This tells the browser to load the file named helloform.tcl from the same URL the Web page was loaded from. The width and height attributes tell the Web browser to construct a window 300 pixels wide by 125 pixels high and execute the Tclet inside this region of the screen.

```
<!DOCTYPE HTML PUBLIC "-//W3C//DTD HTML 3.2//EN">
<HTML>
<HEAD>
    <TITLE>Hello World</TITLE>
</HEAD>
<BODY BGCOLOR="white">
<H4>Hello World Form </H4>
<EMBED SRC="helloform.tcl" TYPE="application/x-tcl" WIDTH=300
HEIGHT=125>
</BODY>
</HTML>
```

The Tclet contains a Tk text entry widget, where the user can input the text to be displayed. A set of radio buttons allows the user to select the size for the displayed text, and a submit button allows the user to submit the form. After entering the text and choosing one of the size selections, the user hits the Submit button to send the form data to the CGI script running on the Web server. The CGI program will process the form data and return a formatted HTML page, resulting in the submitted text being displayed in the requested size.

The status window of the Web browser displays the message "Enter text to be displayed and hit the submit button." This ability is also provided for through the use of the **home** security policy. In our preceding example, the user has entered the words "Howdy World" and selected the size 1 option. When the Submit button is clicked, the screen shown in Figure 15-4 is returned to the user's Web browser.

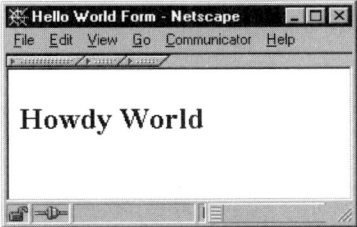

**Figure 15-4** The Returned Web Page

The Tclet in this example acts just as an HTML form would. It accepts user input and then sends an HTTP-formatted message to a CGI program on the remote Web server. This performance is identical to its HTML predecessor in Chapter 4. The Tclet also displays a status message to the user, which is something our previous HTML form did not do.

The CGI program that processes this message is exactly the same as the helloform.cgi script in the Chapter 4 examples and produces the resulting screen shown in Figure 15-4.

The code for the helloform.tcl file follows.

```
#!/home/dmaggian/usr/local/bin/wish8.0

proc submit { } {
    global text size
    ::browser::displayForm "helloform.cgi" _current\
        "[list TEXT $text SIZE $size ]"
}

set size 1
set msg ""

message .m -textvariable msg
pack .m -side top

if { [catch {policy home} err]} {

    set ::msg "($err)\n\nAn error occured while loading\
            the home security policy. You're using version\
            $plugin(patchLevel) of the Tcl plug-in."
} else {
    ::browser::status "Enter text to be displayed\
        and hit the submit button."
    frame .title
    frame .bottom
    frame .size -relief flat
```

```
        frame .text
        label .title.name -text "Hello World Form"
        pack .title.name -side top
        foreach i { 1 2 3 4} {
            radiobutton .size.$i -variable size -text "Size $i" -value $i
            pack .size.$i -side left
        }
        entry .text.text -width 30 -textvariable text
        pack .text.text -side top
        pack .title -side top
        pack .size -side top
        pack .text -side top
        button .bottom.submit -text "SUBMIT" -command { submit }
        pack .bottom.submit -pady 5 -padx 10
        pack .bottom -side top

    }
```

The submit procedure is called when the Submit button is clicked. Inside the submit procedure, ::browser::displayForm is used to send the form data to the helloform.cgi script. The ::browser namespace is just one of several namespaces provided in the browser plug-in. The displayForm procedure takes three arguments: the URL of the CGI program to call; a window type, in this case _current, which causes the returned Web page to be displayed in the existing window; and a list of name/value pairs to be sent as the form data. The list will be properly encoded as part of the HTTP message by the ::browser::displayForm procedure. You may also supply name/value pairs that are already encoded. For more information on the use of the ::browser::displayForm procedure, see The URL Feature on page 499 in Appendix D.

## Security Policies

Notice the use of the policy command in the preceding code. This command is unique to the browser environment and is used to request a specific *security policy* from the plug-in. Security policies are predefined configurations that limit a Tclet's access to system resources on the client machine, preventing untrusted scripts from accessing critical system resources. This level of protection, as illustrated in Figure 15-5, is accomplished by executing the Tclet inside a slave interpreter.

Slave interpreters are created with the Tcl interp command and provide a convenient mechanism for imposing security restrictions on untrusted scripts.

This is done by either hiding certain Tcl commands from the slave interpreter or redefining them to reduce their functionality.

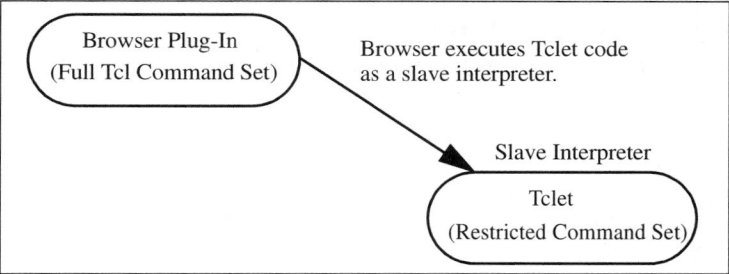

**Figure 15-5** Tclet Executes as a Slave Interpreter

Each security policy defines a different set of restrictions for the slave interpreter, thereby providing differing abilities depending on the level of trust assigned to the Tclet. The browser plug-in comes with several predefined security policies, as shown in Table 15-2 below:

**Table 15-2** Policy Overviews

| Policy Name | Policy Overview |
| --- | --- |
| Home | Allows access to resources on the host from which it was loaded |
| Inside | Allows access to resources inside a site's intranet |
| JavaScript | Allows access to arbitrary resources via HTTP and sockets; it also enables the Tclet to effect frames managed by the hosting application, call JavaScript functions, and send electronic mail |
| Outside | Allows access to resources outside a site's intranet |
| Trusted | Removes all restrictions from the Tclet, allowing it to perform any action a regular, trusted Tcl program could have performed |

You may also define your own security policy if the predefined policies do not fit your needs. For a more thorough discussion of these security policies and other browser plug-in features, see Appendix D on page 487.

In our preceding code example, the policy command first checks to see if the home security policy is allowed for the executing Tclet. It does this by looking at the section entitled *policies* in the plugin.cfg file, which is installed in the same directory as the security policies when you install the browser plug-in. If the home security policy is allowed, the restrictions defined by the home policy will be loaded into the slave interpreter.

It is possible to loosen these restrictions by editing the url section of the home security policy. For example, changing the allow statement in the url section to be allow *, as shown here, would allow any URL to be used.

```
# What URLs are allowed?
section urls
    # Expected format (by the url feature):
    # allow <urlPattern>
    allow   *
```

This would allow the Tclet to access any URL it desired. You will have to decide if this would be appropriate for your environment. If the home security policy is not allowed by the current plug-in configuration or another security policy that has already been loaded, this command will raise an error. This brings up an interesting subject. How do you handle errors in the browser plug-in?

## Default Error Handling

At this point, it is worth spending a moment to talk about how errors are handled in the plug-in environment. By default, the plug-in defines the Tcl bgerror procedure to display errors in a scrolling window that occupies the same screen region as the Tclet. If you have not been exposed to the bgerror command before, it is called by the Tcl interpreter for background errors that occur during the processing of a Tcl script. You may change the way errors are handled by redefining the bgerror command, which is exactly what the browser plug-in does to display errors, as shown in Figure 15-6.

As an example, let's say that you misspelled the first label command in the helloform.tcl program. This will result in the premature termination of your Tclet. The error will be caught by the bgerror procedure and displayed in a scrolling text window as shown in Figure 15-6.

This special bgerror graphical user interface installed by the plug-in will pop up to show the error to the user. The window covers the original Tclet window. This graphical interface has minimal interactive debugging capabilities and can be summoned anytime during the execution of the Tclet by pressing the hot-key combination Control-Shift-C.

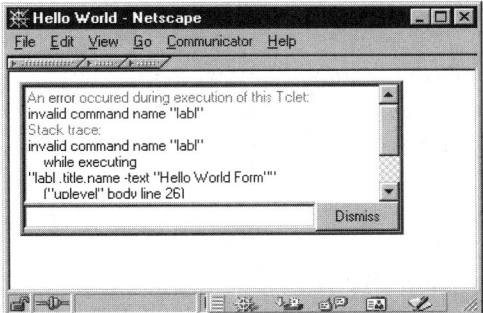

**Figure 15-6** Displaying Errors in the Plug-In

## Building Your Own Error Handling

Of course it is not always desirable to have such a dramatic error display generated for the user! In cases where you can anticipate possible errors, it is better to provide a more readable error message to the user. Because you know the Tcl plug-in may not have a certain security policy enabled, you should check for this case.

Figure 15-7 shows the error generated by the helloform.tcl file if it encounters an error while requesting the home security policy. The approach taken here reuses the existing top level window built for the Tclet by the plug-in. Remember, as a security precaution, the Tclet is prevented from creating its own top level windows and the tk_dialog procedure is also not available. If you write the message to the status bar using the ::browser::status procedure, the message may not be seen or may be overwritten.

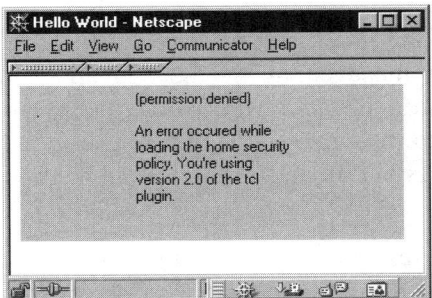

**Figure 15-7** An Application-Generated Error

The code builds a message widget that takes advantage of the screen area allocated to the Tclet and assigns it equal to a text variable. The **catch** command captures any error returned from the policy command and writes the error message to the text variable associated with the text widget. This has the advantage of printing out a clear error message to the user as shown in Figure 15-7.

## Streams and the JavaScript Policy

This next example applies only to code running on Netscape browsers. The application presents the same interface used in the Hello World form example, except that the SUBMIT button is now labeled SEND and the program is called Stream Talker (see Figure 15-8). When the user enters a text string and clicks on the SEND button, the application opens a new browser window and displays the text in the specified size inside the new frame.

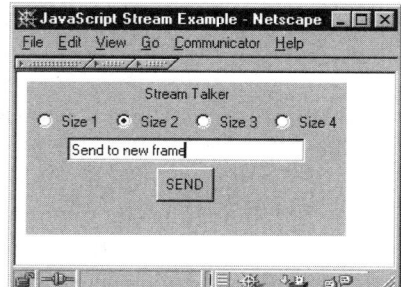

**Figure 15-8** The Stream Talker Panel

This functionality is provided for by the JavaScript security policy, which allows Tclets to communicate with frames managed by the hosting application, call JavaScript commands, and send electronic mail. The JavaScript security policy also provides the ability to connect to resources via HTTP and network sockets. This policy enables dangerous features but, if used properly, can be used to build powerful Web applications.

This example is contained in the example2 subdirectory of this chapter's examples. The application required only a slight modification to the previous example. Once again, the application consists of a simple HTML file containing the HTML **EMBED** tag and a Tcl source file containing the application.

The HTML file is nearly identical to the Hello World Form example. The EMBED tag instructs the Web browser to load the talk.tcl application and execute it using the Tcl Web browser plug-in.

```
<!DOCTYPE HTML PUBLIC "-//W3C//DTD HTML 3.2//EN">
<HTML>
<HEAD>
    <TITLE>JavaScript Stream Example</TITLE>
</HEAD>
<BODY BGCOLOR="white">
<H4>Stream Talker</H4>
<EMBED SRC="talk.tcl" WIDTH="250" HEIGHT="125" ALIGN="BOTTOM"
        type="application/x-tcl" align="absbottom" bg="#ffffff">
</BODY>
</HTML>
```

The talk.tcl code is nearly identical to the helloform.tcl code discussed for the Hello World application. The main difference is the SUBMIT button has now been labeled SEND and the **submit** procedure has been renamed to **talk_to_stream**. This procedure calls **browser::openStream** to create the new window and **browser::writeToStream** to send text to the new window. When the text has been sent, the stream is closed with the **browser::CloseStream** call.

```
proc talk_to_stream {str size} {
    # Open the new window and send the text in the designated size.
    set stream [browser::openStream _blank]
    browser::writeToStream $stream <H$size>$str</H$size>
    # Close the stream
    browser::closeStream $stream
}
```

When the user clicks on the SEND button, the window in Figure 15-9 is displayed. The new browser window is created with the same size and attributes of the parent window executing the Tclet.

**Figure 15-9** Text Displayed in New Frame

In this particular example the user has to close the newly created window manually. Clicking on the SEND button a second time will result in another new window being created. This example works only on Netscape browsers because some of the JavaScript support is not available for Microsoft's Internet Explorer.

If you wish to have more control over the window you create, you could use the ::browser::javascript procedure to call the window.open( ) javascript command. This would allow you to specify the size of the window as well as the other attributes allowed for under this command. You can also use the ::browser::email procedure to send e-mail from inside of your Tclets.

## The Mortgage Calculator Revisited

The mortgage calculator example in Chapter 6 used CGI code running on the Web server's computer to perform field validation, calculate the payment and amortization schedules, and dynamically generate the returned Web pages. In reality the entire application can be executed on the client's Web browser using the Tcl browser plug-in.

This chapter will show you how to restructure the earlier mortgage calculator example to take advantage of the Tcl browser plug-in. Two solutions will be presented. The first example will use the browser plug-in for just the user interface. A CGI program running on the Web server's computer will still be used to perform the necessary calculations and return the results as an HTML-formatted Web page.

In the case of the mortgage calculator, there is no real reason to communicate with the server once the initial Web page has been loaded. Using the browser plug-in, it is possible to embed the entire mortgage calculator application inside a Web page. This means only one access is required to the Web server for the entire duration of the application. This chapter shows how to accomplish this as well.

Many people might suggest that the mortgage calculator example is not really CGI programming, especially when the entire application is embedded in a Tclet running on the client's Web browser. This may be true, but the more proficient you become with providing sophisticated, client-side user interfaces, the more easily you will be able to build complex applications that include client-side processing, as well as server-side CGI processing. These two goals go hand in hand, and in this day and age, it is almost impossible to survive by doing only one or the other. You need to be well versed in both aspects to fare well against the competition!

## The Client-Server Approach

In this example we use the Tcl browser plug-in to provide a more sophisticated user interface than could be achieved with HTML. The remainder of the processing is still done with a CGI program running on the Web server's computer. In order to accomplish the same functionality without the use of the browser plug-in, you would have to become well versed in Java.

The Tclet will be used to gather the user's input, validate the data, and then send the form data off to a CGI script. This eliminates any traffic associated with invalid responses and speeds up the overall response to invalid input. The CGI script then processes the data and returns the results as an HTML-formatted page. The HTML Web page for this example is short and simply embeds the name of the Tclet to be loaded from the Web server's computer.

```
<HTML>
<HEAD>
    <TITLE>Mortgage Calculator</TITLE>
</HEAD>
<BODY BGCOLOR="white">
<H4>Mortgage Calculator</H4>
<EMBED SRC="calc.tcl" WIDTH="250" HEIGHT="200" ALIGN="BOTTOM"
    type="application/x-tcl" align="absbottom" bg="#ffffff">
</BODY>
</HTML>
```

The EMBED tag instructs the Web browser to load the Tclet named calc.tcl into a region of the screen that is 250 pixels wide by 200 pixels tall. The first screen that is presented to the user is the main screen shown in Figure 15-10. This screen contains two buttons that will allow the user to select the monthly payment screen or calculate an amortization schedule.

You may notice a short delay before this screen appears, while a message on your Web browser's status bar indicates the Tcl browser plug-in is being loaded. In Netscape, for example, each time the browser exits a page that contains an embedded Tclet, it will close down the Web browser plug-in. This means that each time you return to a page containing an embedded Tclet, you will experience this short delay as the plug-in is reloaded. This is expected but can be a bit annoying.

**Figure 15-10** The Main Screen

Several things happen in the global code prior to presenting the main screen. The
following code segment shows the executable code outside of any procedures in
the calc.tcl script.

```
# Create a message widget that can be used for error reporting
message .m -textvariable msg -bg white
pack .m -side bottom -fill x -expand 1

# Request the home security policy
if { [catch {policy home} err]} {
    set msg "($err)\n\nSorry, your current Tcl plug-in configuration\
        does not allow the javascript security policy. You must\
        enable this policy in your plug-in configuration before this\
        script can run.\n\nYou're using version $plugin(patchLevel)\
        of the Tcl plug-in."
} else {
    # Print a message to the status bar, set up trace variables used
    # for field validation, on the globals amount, term, interest,
    # and payment variables. The traces call the calc_make_dollar
    # routine to validate the user's input in real time.

    set msg ""
    ::browser::status "Enter the numeric values\
                       requested and hit the submit button."

    set amount {}; set term {}; set interest {}; set payment {}
    trace variable amount w calc_make_dollar
    trace variable term w calc_make_dollar
    trace variable interest w calc_make_dollar
    trace variable payment w calc_make_dollar
    set amount {}; set term {}; set interest {}; set payment {}

    calc_main_screen
}
```

This code requests the home security policy, calls the calc_main_screen routine, and sets up a trace on four different variables that will be used to input the data in the Mortgage Calculation screen and the Amortization Schedule screen. An important point to mention here is that for write traces to work properly, a valid value must be established both before and after the trace is established.

## Screen Validation with the trace Command

The Tcl trace command provides the ability to automatically call a Tcl procedure whenever a variable is accessed in your program. This example takes advantage of this feature and uses it to restrict the user input to decimal digits when entering the information requested in either the Mortgage Calculation screen or the Amortization Schedule screen.

The following lines at the bottom of the file set up traces on the variables amount, term, interest, and payment.

```
trace variable amount w calc_make_dollar
trace variable term w calc_make_dollar
trace variable interest w calc_make_dollar
trace variable payment w calc_make_dollar
```

This code will cause the calc_make_dollar procedure to be called whenever the variables amount, term, interest, or payment are written to. The syntax for the trace command is shown here:

```
trace variable name ops command
```
The trace command arranges for *command* to be executed whenever the variable *name* is accessed in one of the ways defined by *ops*. The values for *ops* may be as listed in Table 15-3.

**Table 15-3** Valid Values for the *ops* Argument

| | |
|---|---|
| r | Execute *command* whenever the variable is read. |
| w | Execute *command* whenever the variable is written to. |
| u | Execute the *command* whenever the variable is unset. |

When the variable is accessed in the manner specified by the *ops* argument, the command is called with the following arguments:

command *variable_name element_name op*

If the variable being traced is a scalar, *variable_name* contains the name of the variable and *element_name* contains the empty string. If the variable being accessed is an array, then *variable_name* contains the name of the array and *element_name* contains the element name used as the index into the array. The *op* argument contains the letters r, w, or u as just defined to indicate the type of access to the variable.

So, when any of the four variables (amount, term, interest, or payment) are accessed in the calc.tcl program, the calc_make_dollar procedure is called. This procedure was adapted from code contained in the *Entry Widget Validation Demo* Tclet by Jeff Hobbs at

> http://www.hobbs.wservice.com/tcl/tclet

Once again, this procedure will be called each time a character is entered into an entry widget that is tied to one of these four variables. The regexp command is used to ensure that the variable contains a positive number with no more than two digits after the decimal point. If the variable value is acceptable, then the value of the variable is updated with the new value. If the value is not acceptable, the variable is returned to its previous value. To the user this makes it appear as though the entry widget simply ignores any characters that are not positive integers or more than two significant digits after the decimal point. This is the majority of the screen validation required for the mortgage calculator program.

```
# This routine is called by the trace command for the
# variables set up at the bottom of the file.
proc calc_make_dollar {var_name element op} {
    global $var_name ${var_name}_real
    if [string comp {} $element] {
        set old    ${var_name}_real\($element)
        set var_name $var_name\($element)
    } else { set old ${var_name}_real }
    if ![regexp {^[+]?[0-9]*\.?[0-9]?[0-9]?$} [set $var_name]] {
        set $var_name [set $old]
        return
    }
    set $old [set $var_name]
}
```

## The Monthly Payment Screen

Figure 15-11 shows the screen produced when the user selects the Monthly Payment button from the top level screen. This screen allows the user to enter an amount to be financed, the term of the loan (in years), and an annual interest rate.

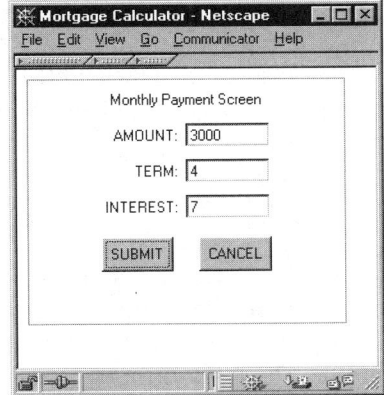

**Figure 15-11** The Monthly Payment Screen

The user may press the SUBMIT button to send the form data to the CGI program or hit the CANCEL button to return to the main screen. The code for the calc_payment_screen procedure follows.

```
proc calc_payment_screen {} {

    # Build the user interface for the monthly payment calculation

    frame .top -bg white
    frame .top.data -bg white
    frame .top.ctrl -bg white
    label .top.name -text "Monthly Payment Screen" -bg white
    pack .top.name -pady 5
    foreach i {amount term interest} {
        global $i
        frame .top.data.$i -bg white
        pack .top.data.$i -side top -pady 5 -padx 10 -anchor e
        label .top.data.$i.l$i -text "[string toupper $i]: " -bg white
        entry .top.data.$i.e$i -textvariable $i -width 10 -relief sunken
        pack .top.data.$i.l$i .top.data.$i.e$i -side left
    }
    button .top.ctrl.submit -text "SUBMIT" -command {
        destroy .top ; calc_submit payment  }
    button .top.ctrl.cancel -text "CANCEL" -command {
        destroy .top; calc_main_screen  }
    pack .top.ctrl.submit -side left -pady 5 -padx 10
    pack .top.ctrl.cancel -pady 5 -padx 10
    pack .top.data -side top
    pack .top.ctrl -pady 5
    pack .top -side top -fill y -anchor center
}
```

The bulk of the code is just the necessary Tk statements to build the screen. Each of the fields is built with a white background. The plug-in will default to a gray background on widgets unless you specify otherwise. Notice the SUBMIT button calls the calc_submit procedure with an argument of *payment*. This will be used by the calc_submit procedure to determine which CGI program to call. The CANCEL button simply calls the calc_main_screen procedure again to return the user to the main screen.

The code for the calc_submit procedure follows. The procedure accepts one argument, which is used to choose between a monthly payment calculation or an amortization schedule. You will notice a couple of other checks are made by the Tclet when the user clicks the SUBMIT button. The calc_submit procedure will make these checks based on the type of calculation being made. A term of 0 is disallowed for the monthly payment calculation and a *negative amortization* situation is disallowed for the case of an amortization calculation. *Negative amortization* results when the monthly payment being made is less than the interest portion of the payment. In this case the principal will never be payed off, and the interest owed will increase over the life of the loan. These checks are made inside the calc_submit procedure, which is called whenever the SUBMIT button is clicked in either input screen.

```
proc calc_submit { mode } {
    # This procedure processes the submit button and calls either
    # the payment.cgi script or the schedule.cgi script depending
    # on the value of mode.
    global amount term interest payment
    switch -- $mode {
        payment {
            if {$term == 0}  {
                ::browser::status "TERM must be a positive number\
                    greater than 0"
                set term ""
                calc_payment_screen
            } else {
                ::browser::displayForm "payment.cgi" _current\
                "[list AMOUNT $amount TERM $term INTEREST $interest]"
            }
        }
        schedule {
                ::browser::displayForm "schedule.cgi" _current\
                "[list AMOUNT $amount PAYMENT $payment INTEREST $interest]"
        }
    }
}
```

After the checks are made, the calc_submit procedure uses the ::browser::displayForm to send the request to the Web server. For the monthly payment calculation, the payment.cgi script is called with a list of name/value pairs that contain the amount, term, and interest variables entered by the user. For the amortization schedule calculation, the schedule.cgi script is called with the list of name/value pairs containing the amount, payment, and interest variables entered by the user in the Amortization Schedule input screen. For a complete description of the ::browser::displayForm procedure, see The URL Feature on page 499 in Appendix D.

Because the ::browser::displayForm procedure is called with the window type set to _current, the results of the CGI scripts will be displayed in the current window, overwriting the Web page that contains the Tclet.

The payment.cgi and schedule.cgi scripts are nearly identical to those used in Chapter 4. The only modification involved changing the return link to point to the mort.html Web page rather than the mort.cgi script, as was the case in the earlier examples in Chapter 4.

### Reusing the Tclet's Main Window

Another observation to be made about the code in this example is that it reuses the Tclet's main window for each of the user input screens. Because the Web browser plug-in restricts our ability to pop up new top level windows, the code in this example is written to easily reuse the top level window. A good example of this technique is in the calc_main_screen procedure.

```
proc calc_main_screen { } {
    # Build the top level interface that calls either the payment_screen
    # or schedule_screen routines for the different calculation options.

    frame .main
    label .main.title -text "Main Screen"
    button .main.payment -text "  Monthly Payment  " -command {
        destroy .main
        calc_payment_screen
    }
    button .main.schedule -text "Amortization Schedule" -command {
        destroy .main
        calc_schedule_screen
    }
    pack .main.title -pady 5
    pack .main.payment -pady 5
    pack .main.schedule -pady 5
```

```
        pack .main
    }
```

Notice that a frame called .main is created to contain all the widgets that are displayed in the screen. Clicking on either the Monthly Payment button or the Amortization Schedule button causes the .main frame to be destroyed, which also destroys all of the descendants of the frame for you. This leaves a blank slate for the next procedure to write on.

## The Client-Side Application

In the preceding sections we adapted the mortgage calculator example of Chapter 4 to use an embedded Tclet to accomplish local screen validation. For some applications it is just as easy to embed the entire application inside the initial home page. Because the monthly payment calculations and the amortization schedule can be calculated on the client side just as easily as on the server, there is really no reason to have any CGI programs on the Web server at all.

This example will embed the entire application inside the initial home page (see Figure 15-12). The example is located under the example4 subdirectory of this chapter's examples. Only two files are required for the entire application. The mort.html file is almost the same as in the previous example. The main difference is the size of the screen area allocated for the Tclet, which has been increased to allow enough room for the amortization schedule to be displayed inside the Tclet's window.

The main difference between this code and the earlier CGI-based example is that several of the routines that used to be inside the separate mort.tcl package have now been moved inside the Tclet. The reason is that it is not possible to source files from the hosting Web server, with the Tcl source command, so it is necessary to place the code inside this Tclet. Three following routines were previously contained in the mort.tcl package and have now been included inside the Tclet.

| | |
|---|---|
| mort_calculate_payment | calculates a monthly payment |
| mort_schedule | calculates the amortization schedule |
| mort_format_schedule | formats the mort_schedule output |

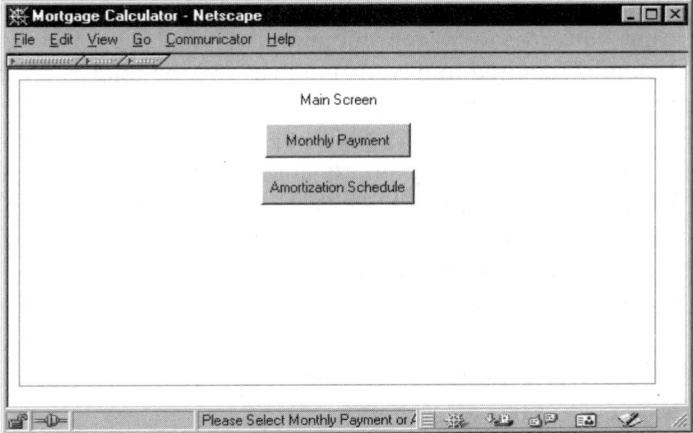

**Figure 15-12** Mortgage Calculator Tclet Top Screen

The user now has the complete mortgage calculator displayed on a single page. We will not examine the entire application here because the bulk of the code is the same as previous examples. For comparison's sake, we will examine the Amortization Schedule screen to contrast it with the earlier example.

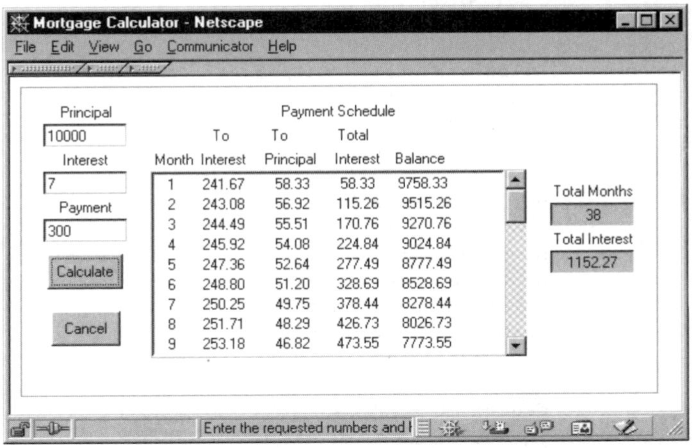

**Figure 15-13** The New Amortization Schedule Screen

Figure 15-13 shows what the new Amortization Schedule calculator looks like. The parameters, Principal, Interest, and Payment, are entered on the left side of the screen. The user inputs these parameters and hits the Calculate button to display the amortization schedule. Field validation is still accomplished by the same calc_make_dollar procedure that was shown on page 342. The middle of the screen contains a scrolling list box that will be used to display the amortization schedule. The right side of the screen contains two read-only fields that will contain the total months required to pay off the loan and the total interest charges accrued during the life of the loan.

All calculations required to build the amortization schedule are now performed locally, inside the hosting Web browser application. This makes it very quick to try different scenarios because the response is almost instantaneous. Your user will be much happier with the performance, especially if he or she wants to try many different combinations of parameters.

The following code segment shows the **calc_schedule** procedure.

```tcl
proc calc_schedule {} {

    global amount payment interest months cost

    # Build the high-level frames that will contain the
    #  widgets for this screen.
    frame .top -bg white
    frame .top.middle -bg white
    frame .top.left -bg white
    frame .top.right -bg white

    # Set up the Calculate and Cancel buttons.
    button .top.left.calculate -text "Calculate" -command {
        if { [mort_schedule $amount $payment $interest\
           schedule cost months] } {
          mort_format_schedule $schedule formatted_schedule
        } else {
          set formatted_schedule $schedule
        }
        # Clear the list of any entries and write the new values out.
        .top.middle.schedule delete 0 end
        foreach i [split $formatted_schedule "\n"] {
           .top.middle.schedule insert end $i
        }
    }
    button .top.left.cancel -text " Cancel " -command {
       destroy .top;  calc_main_screen
    }

    # Create the entry fields that will be used in this program.
    entry .top.left.principal -width 10  -textvariable amount
    entry .top.left.interest -width 10   -textvariable interest
    entry .top.left.payment -width 10   -textvariable payment

    # Create the listbox and scrollbars used to
    # display the payment schedule.
```

```
listbox .top.middle.schedule -width 45 -yscrollcommand\
   ".top.middle.schedule_scroll set" -bg white
scrollbar .top.middle.schedule_scroll -command \
  ".top.middle.schedule yview"

#Create all of the labels for the various UI widgets.
label .top.middle.schedule_label -bg white -text "Payment Schedule"
label .top.middle.line1 -bg white -text  \
   "            To          To            Total"
label .top.middle.line2 -bg white -text \
    "Month  Interest      Principal       Interest     Balance"
label .top.left.principal_label -bg white -text "Principal"
label .top.left.interest_label -bg white -text "Interest"
label .top.left.payment_label -bg white -text "Payment"
label .top.right.total_months_label -bg white -text "Total Months"
label .top.right.total_interest_label -bg white\
   -text "Total Interest"
label .top.right.total_months -relief sunken  -width 10\
   -justify left -textvariable months
label .top.right.total_interest -relief sunken -width 10\
   -justify left -textvariable cost

# Pack all of the widgets into the user front panel.
pack .top.left -side left -padx 3m -pady 3m
pack .top.middle -side left -padx 3m -pady 3m
pack .top.right -side right -padx 3m -pady 3m
pack .top.left.principal_label .top.left.principal\
    .top.left.interest_label .top.left.interest \
    .top.left.payment_label .top.left.payment -side top

pack .top.left.calculate -side top -pady 3m
pack .top.left.cancel -side top -pady 3m
pack .top.middle.schedule_label -side top
pack .top.middle.line1 -anchor w
pack .top.middle.line2 -anchor w
pack .top.middle.schedule  -side left
pack .top.middle.schedule_scroll -side left -fill y
pack .top.right.total_months_label .top.right.total_months \
    .top.right.total_interest_label .top.right.total_interest\
    -side top
pack .top
::browser::status "Enter the requested numbers and\
    hit the Calculate button"
}
```

Notice the Calculate button calls the **mort_schedule** procedure. This procedure is contained locally inside the Tclet, providing very quick response time. The same is true of the monthly payment calculation. Try the example for yourself and compare the response time to that of the earlier version that used CGI scripts running on the Web server.

By now you should realize that there is very little difference between writing this type of application and generating a standard wish application. We will not cover the entire application in this chapter, but the complete code is available on the enclosed CD.

Though adequate, the screen display for the amortization calculator is not nearly as impressive as it could be. For example you could use the power of Tk to plot the amortization schedule. This would dramatically show the relationship between the amount being paid to interest versus the amount being paid to principal each month. The possibilities are endless! The entire embedded application is less than 250 lines of code, and the performance is much better than could be hoped for in the client-server approach.

## Chapter Summary

This chapter showed you how to use the Tcl Web browser plug-in to provide more robust user interfaces than is possible with HTML. You also learned how to embed an entire application inside a Tclet, eliminating the need for any CGI code at all. Embedding an entire application inside a Tclet is a good way to easily make an application available to a large audience. It is not always necessary to have a CGI program executing on the server. More and more applications are heading in this direction due to the popularity of the Internet and the limitations of HTML. Java is by far the most popular vehicle for this type of application programming, but don't overlook the capabilities of the Tcl Web browser plug-in for doing exactly the same type of jobs.

The following topics were covered in this chapter:

- The Tcl browser plug-in allows for the execution of Tcl/Tk code from inside a client's Web browser. A Tcl application embedded inside an HTML Web page is referred to as Tclet.
- Similar functionality to a typical HTML form can be easily achieved with the browser plug-in.
- The browser plug-in makes use of the Tcl interp command to execute the untrusted Tclet inside a slave interpreter which, by default, is prevented from accessing critical system resources. This master/slave concept is how the plug-in achieves a high degree of security when executing untrusted Tclets.

- Tclets may regain some of the functionality that is denied the slave interpreter by requesting a security policy using the policy command. The policy command is provided by the plug-in environment and is not a standard Tcl command.
- The browser plug-in provides five default security policies entitled home, inside, JavaScript, outside, and trusted. Each policy is intended to provide a specific level of access to system resources on either the client machine, the hosting Web server from where the Tclet was loaded, or both.
- The screen area that a Tclet is executed in is specified by the width and height attributes of the HTML EMBED tag. The allocated size cannot be changed by the Tclet.
- With a few minor exceptions, most of your Tcl code should run under the plug-in environment. Existing Tk code will most likely not run due to restrictions in the widget set available in the plug-in environment.
- A number of Tk commands are disabled for security reasons. These include bell, clipboard, grab, menu, selection, send, tk, tk_chooseColor, tk_getOpenFile, tk_getSaveFile, tk_messageBox, toplevel, wm.
- The home security policy provides a Tclet access to its home system. This is the system from which the original Web page that contained the Tclet was loaded.
- The JavaScript security policy allows a Tclet to create and manipulate browser windows when the plug-in is running under Netscape. In addition to this capability, the JavaScript policy allows a Tclet to send electronic mail.
- The Tcl trace command can be used very effectively to perform local field validation inside a Tclet.
- An entire application can be embedded as a Tclet inside a simple HTML Web page. This eliminates the need to access the server after the initial Tclet is loaded.
- Browser cache settings, particularly in the current version of Netscape, can interfere with the ability to get an updated version of a given Tclet. If the Tclet changes while it is still in the browser's cache, the updated version may not actually be pulled from the server.

# Chapter 16

# A Tcl Chat Room

This chapter will focus on the network capabilities of both Tcl and the Tcl browser plug-in. The example presented in this chapter will make use of the socket command to provide a connection between a chat room server written entirely in Tcl and a Web-based client program that is used as the interface to the chat room.

The Web-based client program will again take advantage of the Tcl Web browser plug-in. The reason for this? With the extensive collection of widgets available and the underlying support for socket communications, it is easy to construct a Web-based user interface that is both functional and efficient. In actuality the browser is only used to make the initial connection to the chat room server. Once the connection is made, the remaining communication will actually be accomplished by lower-level network socket communication. In this fashion the Web browser simply acts as a convenient container for the chat room client as well as provides an easy way to initially connect to the chat room server via a CGI script.

This chapter will provide a good example of utilizing a CGI program to connect directly to an external resource without having to go through the Web server or a CGI program. All that is needed is a small HTML program to initially load the Tclet.

For those of you that might be familiar with the Internet Relay Chat (IRC) protocol (RFC 1459), this chapter is not about IRC. Internet Relay Chat protocol is a method of client-to-client communication on the Internet that was developed back in the 1993 time frame. There are numerous software packages, some Web-based, that allow you to connect to the IRC network. This chapter will show you how to construct a server-based chat room that allows anyone with access to your URL to log in and carry on discussions with other clients who may be logged in at the same time.

The maximum number of users in our chat room is arbitrarily restricted to ten. This is more of a limitation on the number of people who can constructively have a conversation than being a limitation of the software capabilities of the network socket layer in Tcl.

The Web browser plug-in is ideal for this application. Having a Tcl interpreter available inside your Web application allows you to establish a callback procedure to handle incoming messages from the chat room server. The callback procedure can then update the user interface widgets directly inside the Web application page. You could just as easily construct the chat room as a standalone Tcl/Tk program, but the Web interface makes it easy for people to get connected from any Web browser.

## Understanding Tcl Sockets

Though the code for the chat room is reasonably small, there are some underlying issues with serial data streams that can make your understanding of the code difficult. This section will break these concepts down into an understandable level, using a scaled-down, command line driven version of the chat program.

The example1 directory of this chapter's examples contains two programs entitled client.tcl and server.tcl. The server.tcl program creates the scaled-down chat room server used for explaining the underlying Tcl socket communication. The client.tcl program is the client that talks to the chat room server. Only one instance of the server will be running at any one time, whereas multiple instances of the client program can be run.

We will look at the server.tcl program first to understand its use of the Tcl **socket** command. The code for the server is just over a page, including comments. The full text of the server program is reproduced here:

```tcl
#!/usr/local/bin/tclsh

#<:------------------------------------------------------------------
# PROC process_sock
#   Description
#       This program is a simplified chat server. It accepts up to
#       ten connections from clients and maintains their connection
#       information in a socket stack. Anytime a new message is
#       received, it's broadcast to any clients connected at the time.
#:>------------------------------------------------------------------

#<:------------------------------------------------------------------
# PROC process_sock
#       Description
#           This procedure is called whenever one of the client sockets
#           becomes readable.
#       Arguments
#           sock  The channel identifier sock is used to read the socket.
#       Return Values
#           0  always
#:>------------------------------------------------------------------
proc process_sock { sock } {

    global sockets

    if { [eof $sock] || [catch { gets $sock line}] } {
       puts "closing socket $sock"
       close $sock
       set index [lsearch $sockets $sock*]
       set sockets [lreplace $sockets $index $index]
    } elseif { $line != "" } {
       foreach connection $sockets {
            puts [lindex $connection 0] $line
       }
    }
    return 0
}


#<:------------------------------------------------------------------
# PROC accept_sock
#   Description
#       This proc is called whenever a client socket is opened.
#       It configures the new socket connection from the client to be
#       line buffered and sets up the process_sock procedure as
#       the callback to be called whenever the client's socket becomes
#       readable.
```

```
#   Arguments
#      sock  The channel identifier sock is used to read the socket.
#   Return Values
#      0   always
#:>------------------------------------------------------------------
proc accept_sock { sock addr port} {

    global sockets

    if { [info exists sockets] && [llength $sockets] >=10 } {
        puts "Reject socket connection; too many open sockets"
        fconfigure $sock -buffering line
        puts $sock "Too many clients open, try again later"
        close $sock
        return
    } else {
        puts "Accept $sock from $addr port $port"
        lappend sockets "$sock $addr $port"
    }
    fconfigure $sock -buffering line
    fileevent $sock readable [ list process_sock $sock ]
    return 0
}


# Program code starts here

puts "Chat server started"
socket -server accept_sock 5020
vwait forever
```

## Creating the Server

The best place to start analyzing the code is with the last three lines of the file, which are outside any procedure. The first line prints a message to standard out indicating that the chat server has been started. The next two lines:

```
socket -server accept_sock 5020
vwait  forever
```

establish this program as a server, set up the **accept_sock** procedure as a *callback* for the client connections, and then enters the Tcl event loop to wait for client connections. Quite a bit of work for just two lines of code!

The Tcl **socket** command has two standard forms:

socket ?options? host port
socket -server command ?options? port

We will concern ourselves with the second form because it is the one used to establish the server connection. You will see the first form, used in a moment, when we shift our discussion to the client-side program.

When the socket command is invoked with the -server option, it creates a server for the specified *port*. This causes Tcl to automatically accept connections to this port number. Each time a connection is made, *command* will be executed with three additional arguments: the name of the new channel, the address of the client's host, and the client's port number. The *command* to be called is referred to as a callback procedure. It's just a command to be executed when some future event happens.

Notice that in our example port number 5020 is specified. This is the port that Tcl will monitor for new connections. The number was arbitrarily picked and has no special meaning. In most Web server environments, port numbers through 1024 are reserved for the operating system and standard resources that need to run under the operating system, such as the Web server. Many of these programs act as servers themselves and require a dedicated port to listen to. In order to join in the fun, you simply need to negotiate a port number, usually above the number 1024, with your system administrator and use it for your own server-based applications.

Notice the vwait *forever* command at the bottom of the program file. This command is necessary to enter the Tcl *event loop*, which must be active in order for the server to wait on socket connections. The vwait command accepts a single argument, which is a variable name:

    vwait varname

When the vwait command is executed, it causes the program to enter what is known as an event loop, processing *events* as they become available and *blocking* the application if no events exist. It continues processing events until some event causes the value of the variable *varName* to change. Once *varName* has been set, the vwait command will return. In this program the vwait command never returns! The variable *forever* is never intended to be modified. The whole purpose of the vwait command is to cause the program to enter the *event loop*.

The Tcl event loop is similar to many other Windows-based programming environments, including Tk programs. It allows your applications to respond to asynchronous events, and block (sleep) when there are no events to process. This is much more efficient than spinning in a loop, checking to see if the event has happened. This type of polling is costly in terms of processing power, hogging execution time that other applications could be using to accomplish their objectives.

> The vwait command is used to enter the Tcl event loop, which allows the program to suspend execution until some external event happens. This is more efficient than polling and is the expected application behavior in a preemptive multitasking environment like UNIX or Windows. *The best thing for a program to do, when it has nothing to do, is to do nothing!*

In our example an event is a message from one of the client programs. The event could be a first-time connection or messages sent to the server after the connection has been established.

## Accepting Client Connections

In the previous section we said that an arbitrary limit of ten connections was placed on our scaled-down chat server. This is done in the accept_sock procedure by examining the *sockets* variable to see if the number of elements in the sockets list is greater than or equal to ten:

```
if { [info exists sockets] && [llength $sockets] >=10 } {
    puts "Rejecting socket connection; too many open sockets"
    fconfigure $sock -buffering line
    puts $sock "Too many clients open, try again later"
    close $sock
    return
} else {
    puts "Accept $sock from $addr port $port"
    lappend sockets "$sock $addr $port"
}
```

If there are more than ten connections already, the message *"Too many clients open, try again later"* is sent to the client and the socket connection is immediately closed with the standard close command. If less than ten connections exist, the socket id, client address, and port number are appended to the global sockets list with the lappend command.

## Configuring the Client Connection

If the client connection is accepted, the next few lines in the accept_sock procedure configure the socket connection and set up the procedure to be called whenever a message is received from the client.

```
fconfigure $sock -buffering line
fileevent $sock readable [ list process_sock $sock ]
```

The fconfigure command is used to configure the client's socket connection. The prototype for this command looks like this:

fconfigure *channelId ?option value option value ...?*

and configures *channelId* with the specified options. Our procedure uses only one option, -buffering with a value of *line*. The -buffering option affects the way the underlying device deals with *output*. It has no effect on the way the device deals with input; this is configured on the client's side.

The Tcl fconfigure command provides three choices for the -buffering option: *line*, *full*, or *none*. With line buffering, Tcl will buffer output until it detects line terminator characters (usually \n) and then write the data to the device. With *full* buffering, all output is kept internal until the current buffer size is exceeded and then the data is written out to the device. With *no* buffering, data is written out to the specified device as soon as it becomes available. Our application has set this option to -line, which will cause output to be buffered on a line-by-line basis.

## Establishing the Callback Procedure

The fileevent procedure is used to establish a callback procedure, process_sock, to be called whenever the client sends the server a message. The fileevent command has two standard forms:

fileevent *channelId readable ?script?*
fileevent *channelId writable ?script?*

This Tcl command will execute script when *channelId* becomes readable or writable, depending on which form you use. You can use a separate *script* for readable and writable states, have one script handle both, or, in our case, only define one. In the accept_sock procedure, the fileevent readable command is used to establish **process_sock** as the callback to be used whenever the client's socket connection becomes readable.

```
fileevent $sock readable [ list process_sock $sock ]
```

A brief explanation of the use of the list command is warranted here. When the socket connection becomes readable (the client has sent a message), we would like the **process_sock** to be called with the *$sock* argument. The list command is used here to concatenate the two words **process_sock** and *$sock* into a single command that can be executed when the channel becomes readable. The reason the list command is used rather than simply enclosing the two words in braces is to ensure that variable substitution is performed on the *$sock* argument. Most socket id's will look something like sock4 or sock5. Let's say that the particular socket connection results in a socket id of sock4. The result of the [list process_sock $sock] will produce the command **process sock5** as the callback for this particular connection. The next socket connection would most likely result in an id of sock6 and a callback command of **process sock6**. When the socket becomes readable, these callbacks are executed in the global namespace. This is not a problem because the socket id has been reduced to its string representation. If you eliminated the list command and used curly braces:

```
fileevent $sock readable { process_sock $sock }
```

no variable substitution would be performed and the callback command would be **process_sock $sock**. This would result in an error because the $sock variable would not be resolved in the global namespace. This approach allows one callback routine, **process_sock**, to handle all the client connections, because each callback will contain the proper socket id for the connection that has become readable.

## Servicing the Client Connection

The **accept_sock** procedure sets up the **process_sock** procedure as the callback for client connections that become readable. When we say "becomes readable," it simply means that the client has sent the server a message. This is the text message that you type on the command line to broadcast to any other clients that might be connected. Notice that the **process_sock** procedure checks for an end-of-file condition as well as any other error condition that might occur during the **gets** command.

```
proc process_sock { sock } {
```

```
        global sockets

        if { [eof $sock] || [catch { gets $sock line}] } {
            puts "closing socket $sock"
            close $sock
            set index [lsearch $sockets $sock*]
            set sockets [lreplace $sockets $index $index]
        } elseif { $line != "" } {
            foreach connection $sockets {
                    puts [lindex $connection 0] $line
            }
        }
        return 0
    }
```

It is important to check for this end-of-file condition. Should the client socket be closed, the connection will appear readable and continue in that state until the server detects the end-of-file condition and closes the socket. This causes the process_sock procedure to be called continuously until the socket connection is closed by the server. The result is that your server will wake up, repeatedly attempt to read the socket, which will have no data, and go back to sleep. Needless to say, this is a real drain on system resources!

If a valid message has been received from the client, the server will broadcast the message received to all other clients connected. Figure 16-1 shows a server communicating with three clients. In this simple chat room example, the clients are simply identified by their socket id strings.

You can see the "Chat server started" message on the chat server screen, followed by three lines that indicate accepted socket connections from each client. Each time the server accepts a socket connection, it saves the connection in the sockets list. Each time a message is received from a client, the server traverses its list of sockets and broadcasts the contents of the received message to each of the connected clients.

Each message begins with name, where name is the name supplied on the command line of the client. The client then prepends this id to each message that it sends to the server. A similar approach will be used in the Web-based client.

## The Client

The client side of this first example is even shorter than the server. The client.tcl file contains the code for the client. The current server.tcl file will support up to ten client.tcl programs executing at one time. Once again, this is an arbitrary limit that may be adjusted up or down as desired. The only limitation is the number of ports available, system memory, and performance considerations if you try to broadcast to too many ports.

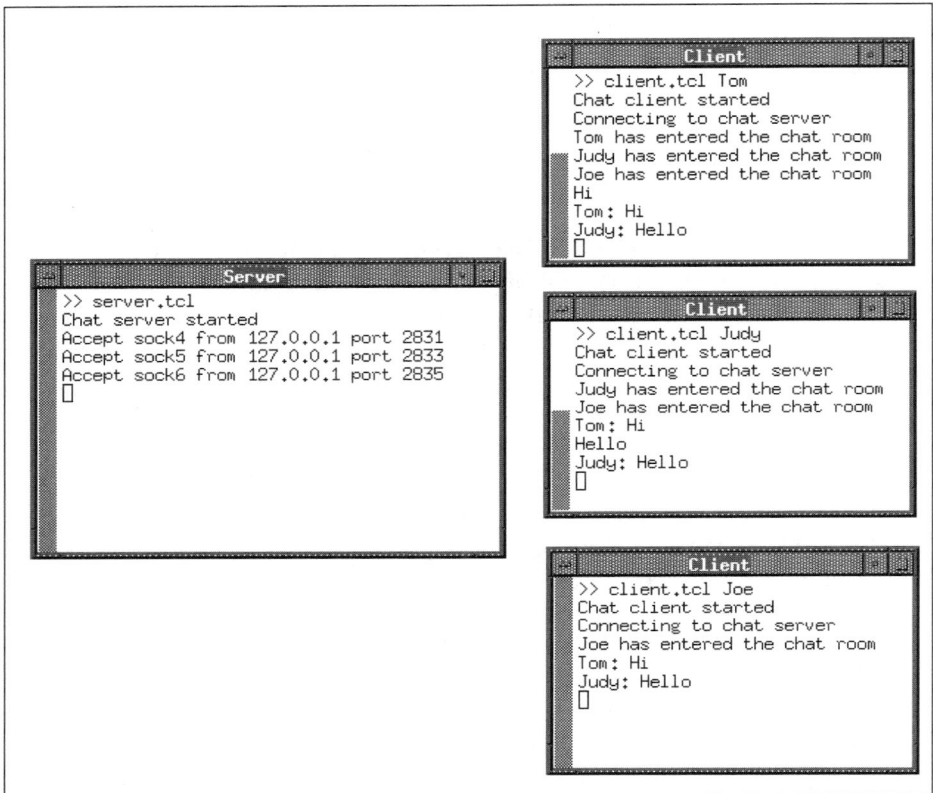

**Figure 16-1** Three Clients Talking to One Server

```
#!/usr/local/bin/tclsh

#<:-----------------------------------------------------------------
# PROGRAM client.tcl
#  Description
#      This program is a simplified chat client. It connects to the
#      server, which must be up and running on port 5020, reads
#      strings from standard in, and sends them to the server. This
#      program also sets up an event handler on the socket connection
#      and displays any messages received from the server on standard
#      out.
#:>-----------------------------------------------------------------
```

```
#<:------------------------------------------------------------------
# PROC process_stdin
#  This procedure sends the string typed by the user to the channel
#  defined by the channel argument. This procedure is called by
#  the fileevent handler whenever standard in becomes readable.
#:>------------------------------------------------------------------
proc process_stdin { channel chat_alias} {
   global sock

   puts $sock "$chat_alias: [gets $channel]"
   return 0
}


#<:------------------------------------------------------------------
# PROC process_sock
#  This procedure is called by the file event handler whenever the
#  socket connection with the server becomes readable. The sock
#  argument is the channel identifier that should be read.
#:>------------------------------------------------------------------
proc process_sock { sock } {

   if { [eof $sock] || [catch { gets $sock line}] } {
      puts "Server socket closed, exiting"
      close $sock
      exit
   } elseif { $line != "" } {
      puts $line
   }
   return 0
}

if { $argc != 1 } {
   puts "You must supply your chat room alias on the command line!"
   exit
}
set chat_alias [lindex $argv 0]
set sock [socket localhost 5020]
fconfigure $sock -buffering line
puts "Chat client started"
puts "Connecting to chat server"
puts $sock "$chat_alias has entered the chat room"
fileevent stdin readable [ list process_stdin stdin $chat_alias]
fileevent $sock readable [ list process_sock $sock]
vwait forever
```

Here, once again, the last few lines of the file get the ball rolling. In this case the
**socket** command is executed without the **-server** option. This opens a client
connection to the server specified. When using the socket command to create a
client connection, you must specify a *host* and a *port* argument as shown:

socket *?options? host port*

*Port* is an integer number that defines the port that the destination server is listening to. *Host* is a domain-style name, such as www.scriptics.com, or a numerical IP address, such as 127.0.0.1. You may also use *localhost* to refer to the host on which the command is invoked. Our example uses *localhost* for the *host* argument and 5020 as the *port* number, which is the arbitrary port number picked for the server.tcl program to use.

Now any text that you type at the command line is sent to the chat server, which broadcasts to each client that is connected at the time.

## Putting Your Clients on the Web

This section details the workings of a Web-based chat room. The server program is identical to the one presented in the previous section. The client has been enhanced a bit and the code has been modified to run under the Tcl Web browser plug-in. Once again, the lower-level communications are based on the Tcl socket command, but in this case the client will not be restricted to the local host computer. It may exist anywhere in the World Wide Web!

All of the code for this example exists in the example2 directory of this chapter's examples on the enclosed CD.

The client takes advantage of the home security policy provided in the plug-in distribution. The Tcl Web browser plug-in and security policies are discussed in Chapter 15. The home security policy is intended to let Tclets communicate with their home server. The main feature of the home security policy that interests us here is the network capability restored to the otherwise safe interpreter of the plug-in. This enables the Tclet to use a somewhat restricted version of the Tcl socket and fconfigure commands, allowing our Tclet to communicate directly with the chat server using Tcl sockets. The browser is used to load the Tclet, but once it is loaded the remaining communication is all handled by the embedded Tclet. This is similar to a Java applet running inside a Web page. In fact one of the only ways to duplicate this application is with an embedded Java applet!

The chat room Tclet, shown in Figure 16-2, is used to send and receive messages to anyone that may be in the chat room at the time. The messages are actually sent to the chat server, which then broadcasts them back to all the chat room members. The chat server is nearly identical to the chat server in the last section, and will be discussed in a moment. To enter the chat room you must first define a chat room alias, in the upper left corner of the screen, and then enter the chat room by clicking on the Enter button. You will not be allowed to connect without defining a chat room alias first. If you try, a message will be displayed in the large message window indicating the error of your ways. In fact all error messages are sent to this window, because you will spend most of your time looking here.

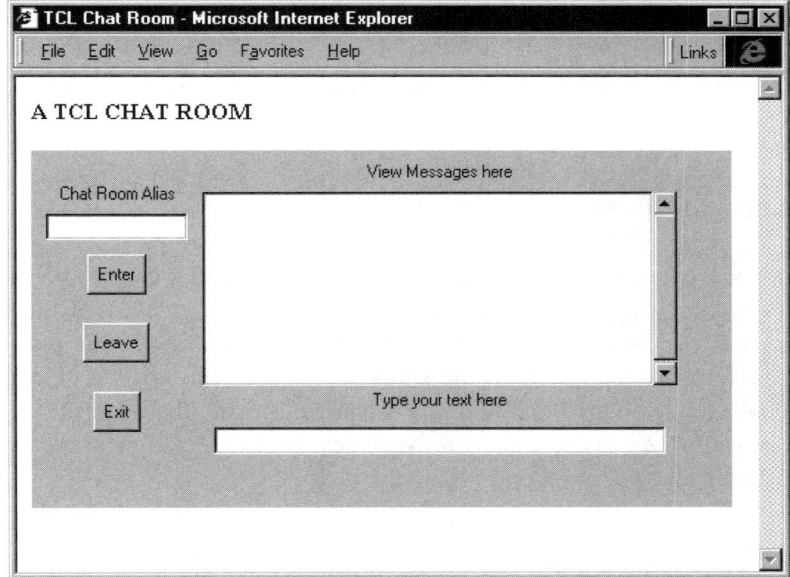

**Figure 16-2** The Chat Room Tclet

When you enter the chat room, a message is automatically sent to the chat server indicating that you have joined the chat room. This eliminates Peeping Toms! Once you have entered the chat room, you send messages by typing them on the single line at the bottom of the screen and read messages in the larger window above. You may leave the chat room at any time by clicking on the Exit button. Here again, a message is sent to the chat server indicating that you have left the chat room. Once you have left the chat room, you will no longer see messages from the chat room. Clicking on the Exit button terminates the Tclet and the screen will disappear from the browser window. This entire application is less than 200 lines of code!

To connect to the chat room, you would point your browser at the following chat.html file. This short HTML file contains the EMBED tag that causes the browser to load the client.tcl program. When the browser detects that the embedded program is a Tcl application, it launches the Tcl Web browser plug-in, retrieves the application specified by the EMBED tag, and executes the Tclet.

```
<!DOCTYPE HTML PUBLIC "-//W3C//DTD HTML 3.2//EN">
<HTML>
<HEAD>
    <TITLE>TCL Chat Room</TITLE>
</HEAD>
<BODY BGCOLOR="white">
<H4>A TCL CHAT Room</H4>
<P><EMBED SRC="client.tcl" WIDTH="475" HEIGHT="250" ALIGN="BOTTOM"
    type="application/x-tcl" align="absbottom" bg="#ffffff">
</BODY>
</HTML>
```

## Examining the Tclet

The Tclet is written as a Tk application, keeping in mind some of the limitations placed on such an application by the plug-in environment. One of the foremost limitations is the inability to create new top level windows. This is the reason error messages are displayed in the same window as the normal chat messages because we can't pop up a dialog box. Of course, it would be just as easy to create a separate status box to contain error messages, but the message window seems to work just as well.

Fundamentally this Tclet is the same as the command line version of the client that we looked at in the beginning of this chapter. The program opens a socket connection to the chat server and sets up a callback procedure to handle the messages broadcast from the chat server.

The main difference is the ability to connect and disconnect from the server at will and the code for the Tk widgets that comprise the user interface. The entire code of the Web-based Tclet is duplicated on the next few pages, following which is a discussion of how it works.

```
#!/usr/local/bin/tclsh

#   PROGRAM client.tcl
#   This program is a simplified chat client. It connects to a server
#   that must be up and running on port 5020 and gets strings from
#   the entry widget and sends them to the server. This program also
#   sets up an event handler on the socket connection and displays
```

```
#    any messages received from the server to the text widget.

#<:-------------------------------------------------------------------
#  PROC chatConnect
#      This procedure will connect to the chat server, if not already
#      connected. It will also enable the entry line for user input.
#:>-------------------------------------------------------------------
proc chatConnect {} {
   global connected sock chat_alias

   if { [string trim $chat_alias] == "" } {
      chatPuts "----You must enter a chat alias before connecting----"
      return
   }

   if { !$connected } {
      set host [getattr originSocketHost]
      if { [catch {set sock [socket $host 5020]} err ] } {
        chatPuts "Can't connect to server right now, try again later"
        return
      }
      fconfigure $sock -buffering line
      fileevent $sock readable [ list chatProcessSock $sock ]
      set connected 1
      puts $sock "$chat_alias: has entered the chat room"
   }
}

#<:-------------------------------------------------------------------
#  PROC chatDisconnect
#      This procedure disconnects from the server, if connected. It
#      will also disable the user line for input.
#:>-------------------------------------------------------------------
proc chatDisconnect {} {
   global connected sock chat_alias
   if { $connected } {
      puts $sock "$chat_alias: has left the chat room"
      close $sock
      set connected 0
      # Echo the exit message because the server won't
      chatPuts "$chat_alias: has left the chat room"
   }
}

#<:-------------------------------------------------------------------
#  PROC chatExit
#      This procedure disconnects from the server, if connected,
#      and then exits.
#:>-------------------------------------------------------------------
proc chatExit {} {
   global connected sock
```

```
      if { $connected } { close $sock }
      exit
   }


   #<:----------------------------------------------------------------
   #  PROC chatMainScreen
   #     Build the top level interface for the chat room
   #:>----------------------------------------------------------------
   proc chatMainScreen { } {
      global sock

      frame .ctrls
      frame .screens
      frame .msg
      label .ctrls.lalias -text "Chat Room Alias"
      entry .ctrls.alias -width 15 -textvariable chat_alias
      button .ctrls.enter -text Enter -command { chatConnect }
      button .ctrls.leave -text Leave -command { chatDisconnect}
      button .ctrls.exit -text Exit -command { chatExit}
      pack .ctrls.lalias -side top -pady 5
      pack .ctrls.alias -side top
      pack .ctrls.enter -side top -pady 10
      pack .ctrls.leave -side top -pady 10
      pack .ctrls.exit -side bottom -pady 10

      label .screens.title -text "View messages here"
      text .msg.text -width 50 -height 10 -yscrollcommand\
         ".msg.text_scroll set"
      scrollbar .msg.text_scroll -command ".msg.text yview"
      label .screens.lentry -text "Type your text here"
      entry .screens.entry -width 50
      pack .screens.title -pady 5
      pack .msg.text -side left
      pack .msg.text_scroll -side left -fill y
      pack .msg -in .screens -side top
      pack .screens.lentry -side top
      pack .screens.entry  -side top -pady 10
      bind .msg.text <KeyPress> { break }
      bind .screens.entry <KeyPress-Return> {
         chatProcessEntry .screens.entry
      }

      pack .ctrls -side left -padx 10
      pack .screens -side left
      ::browser::status "Welcome to the Tcl chat room."
      focus .ctrls.alias
      bind .ctrls.alias <KeyPress-Return> { focus .ctrls.enter }
      bind .ctrls.enter <KeyPress-Return> {
         chatConnect;focus .screens.entry
      }
      bind .ctrls.enter <ButtonRelease-1> {focus .screens.entry}
   }
```

```
#<:-------------------------------------------------------------------
#  PROC chatMainScreen
#  This procedure is called by an event handler and will send the
#  string typed by the user to the socket connection.
#:>-------------------------------------------------------------------
proc chatProcessEntry {widget} {
   global connected sock chat_alias

   set line [$widget get]
   $widget delete 0 end
   append str $chat_alias ": " $line
   if { $connected } {
      puts $sock $str
   } else {
      chatPuts "You must enter the chat room first"
   }
   return 0
}


#<:-------------------------------------------------------------------
#  PROC chatProcessSock
#     This procedure is called by the file event handler whenever the
#     socket connection with the server becomes readable. The sock
#     argument is the channel identifier that should be read.
#:>-------------------------------------------------------------------
proc chatProcessSock { sock } {
   global connected

   if { [eof $sock] || [catch { gets $sock line}] } {
      chatPuts "Server socket closed, exiting"
      close $sock
      set connected 0
   } elseif { $line != "" } {
      chatPuts $line
   }
   return 0
}


#<:-------------------------------------------------------------------
#  PROC chatProcessSock
#     This proc simply writes out str to the message monitor window.
#:>-------------------------------------------------------------------
proc chatPuts { str } {
   .msg.text insert end $str\n
   .msg.text see end
}


#-------------------------------------------------------------------
#                      global code starts here
#-------------------------------------------------------------------
```

```
set connected 0
set chat_alias ""

message .msg -textvariable err_msg
pack .msg -side bottom -fill x -expand 1

if { [catch {policy home} err]} {

    set err_msg "($err)\n\nSorry, your current Tcl plug-in\
        configuration does not allow the home security policy.\
        You must enable this policy in your plug-in configuration\
        before this script can run.\n\nYou're using version\
        $plug-in(patchLevel) of  the Tcl plug-in."

} else {
    set err_msg ""
    chatMainScreen
}
```

As with most Tcl/Tk programs, the best place to start analyzing the code is in the global space (the code outside any procedures) located at the bottom of the listing. This code sets up a message widget used to display an error message if the **home** security policy can't be loaded for any reason. If the policy is loaded successfully, this widget remains unused throughout the remainder of the program. Once the **home** security policy is loaded, the chatMainScreen procedure is called, which is responsible for building the user interface console.

The chatMainScreen procedure simply builds the interface and binds the controls to the necessary procedures. No socket connections are made at this time. Table 16-1 lists the bindings for each of the controls. We will investigate each one of these in the following text.

The first action you must perform to enter the chat room is to enter a chat room alias in the Chat Room Alias (.ctrls.alias) entry widget located in the upper left corner of the user interface screen. This is just an ordinary Tk entry widget that is tied to the global variable chat_alias through the use of the **-textvariable** option. The chatConnect procedure will verify this variable has been set by the user before allowing a connection to the chat server.

The next action you perform is to click on the Enter button (.ctrls.enter) to get connected to the chat server. The Enter button is bound to the chatConnect procedure through the use of the **-command** option. The first thing this procedure does is ensure that the chat_alias global contains a valid chat room alias. Actually a valid alias is any string that is not null or just white space. If no alias has been entered, a message instructing you to enter one is displayed in the large message window by calling the **chatPuts** procedure. If a chat alias does exist, this procedure creates the socket connection to the chat server, configures it for line buffering, and establishes the **chatProcessSock** procedure as the procedure to call anytime the socket becomes readable. The last thing the procedure does is to send a message to the chat server indicating that you have just joined the chat room. That's it! You are now connected to the chat room and will see all messages sent by anyone in the chat room.

While in the text entry widget (screens.entry) at the bottom of the screen, the keyboard Return key is bound to the **chatProcessEntry** procedure. When you type in a message in this area and hit the return key the **chatProcessEntry** procedure is called to send the message to the chat server. The chat server then relays the message to any clients that are currently connected to the chat room.

The large window at the top of the chat room panel (.msg.text) does not have any specific key bindings but is used inside the **chatProcessSock** call back procedure to display any messages received on the socket connection. It does this by writing the messages to the .msg.text widget.

**Table 16-1** client.tcl Control Binding Table

| Name | Type | Function | Command Binding |
|------|------|----------|-----------------|
| .ctrls.alias | entry | Enters chat room alias | None, -textvariable = chat_alias |
| .ctrls.enter | button | Connects to the chat server | chatConnect |
| .ctrls.leave | button | Disconnects from the chat server | chatDisconnect |
| .ctrls.exit | button | Disconnects and terminates Tclet | chatExit |
| .screens.entry | entry | Enters chat messages | Key binding to chatProcessEntry |
| .msg.text | text | Displays chat messages | |

To leave the chat room you click on the Leave button (.ctrls.leave), which is bound to the **chatDisconnect** procedure. This procedure sends a final message to the chat server indicating that you have left the chat room. It then closes the socket connection that was established earlier when the Enter button was pressed. The server will detect the fact that you have closed your socket connection and remove you from the list of active clients.

Finally, the Exit button (.ctrls.exit) closes the socket connection if it is open, and then the Tclet is exited.

## Chapter Summary

This chapter showed you how to create a complete, Web-based chat room application in less than 300 lines of commented code! The chat room uses the Tcl socket facility for its underlying communication and the Web-based client uses the Tcl Web browser plug-in to provide the user interface. The only way to duplicate the functionality of this chat room would be to write a Java applet, possibly with more lines of code!

The key features of this application are summarized in the following list:

- The chat room program is actually a client-server application where the server broadcasts messages received from one client to all other clients currently connected to the chat room.
- The application consists of a single server program and up to ten client programs running anywhere on the World Wide Web.
- The chat server creates a server socket connection using the **-server** option to the Tcl **socket** command and accepts up to ten client connections. This is an arbitrary limit based mostly on how many people can have a constructive conversation at one time.
- The chat server maintains a list of the clients currently connected. Whenever a client sends a message to the chat room, the server broadcasts the message to all the connected clients.
- The server port 5020 was arbitrarily selected. Server ports should be selected with the aid of your network administrators.
- The client program also uses the Tcl **socket** command to connect to the server, which must be up and running.
- The Web-based client program is a Tclet (an embedded Tcl application) that runs under the Tcl Web browser plug-in.
- The Tclet takes advantage of the **home** security policy to perform socket communication with the Tclet's home system (the server that it was loaded from).
- The Web browser is just a container for the Tclet. It is only required for the initial connection to get the Tclet loaded from the hosting Web server. After

that all aspects of the user interface and client communications are handled by the Tclet.

- The same client application runs on Netscape and Internet Explorer.

# *Appendix A*

## *HTML Reference Guide*

HTML stands for Hypertext Markup Language and is the underlying structure of most documents on the World Wide Web today. Because CGI, at its essence, is about dynamically generating HTML, it is important that the CGI programmer have a thorough knowledge of this subject.

The purpose of this appendix is to provide a general reference for the most commonly used HTML code. This book assumes that the reader is already familiar with HTML coding. If you are not, there are several HTML books on the market that will describe in detail all HTML and attributes.

In HTML code there is typically a beginning code and an ending code, which can be thought of as a starting attribute and an ending attribute. With a few exceptions, the tag names are pretty logical and the only difference between the beginning and ending is that the ending tag has a slash (/) included in the bracket.

## Basic HTML Page Layout

An HTML document includes certain elements so that the browser knows how to interpret it. The basic elements are described in Table A-1.

**Table A-1** Basic Elements of an HTML Document

| HTML Code | Description |
|---|---|
| <HTML><br></HTML> | This identifies the page as an HTML document, typically with <HTML> being the first thing and </HTML> being the last thing in the source code. |
| <HEAD><br></HEAD> | This identifies the portion of the header of a document that surrounds the TITLE of the document and any META tags. |
| <TITLE><br></TITLE> | Title is used for many purposes behind the scenes by the browser. It can be printed out as a header or footer, returned as a search engine result, and so forth. |
| <BODY><br></BODY> | This identifies the body portion of the HTML document. The <BODY> tag typically follows immediately after the </HEAD> code. The ending </BODY> tag comes immediately before the </HTML> tag toward the bottom of the document. Within the <BODY> tag, colors for the background, links, visited links, and text can be defined. Images for the background can also be included in the <BODY> code. |

Anchors and Images are two other basic elements in an HTML page. Anchors are used to create a hyperlink to another file and are coded in the format of:

```
<A HREF="URL">Name of link</A>
```

Images can be pulled into the HTML document to be displayed in the browser by using the following code:

```
<IMG SRC="URL">
```

Table A-2 lists the attributes that can be added within the Images tag.

**Table A-2** Image Tag Attributes

| Attribute | Description | Values for "n" |
|---|---|---|
| ALIGN="n" | Aligns the text following the graphic as specified by "n." | TOP, MIDDLE, BOTTOM, RIGHT, LEFT |

**Table A-2** Image Tag Attributes (Continued)

| Attribute | Description | Values for "n" |
|---|---|---|
| ALT="n" | Gives an alternate text description of the images used by assistive technology devices or those browsers not supporting graphics. | Text description of graphic |
| BORDER="n" | Puts a border around the graphic. | This value is provided in number of pixels; to turn off border around graphics that include hyperlinks, set BORDER="0" |
| HSPACE="n" | Puts space around the top and bottom of graphic. | This value is provided in number of pixels |
| VSPACE="n" | Puts space around the left and right of the graphic. | This value is provided in number of pixels |

Your source code for the image may appear as

```
<IMG BORDER="0" ALIGN="MIDDLE" VSPACE="3" ALT="maple leaf"
                        SRC="www.mysite.org/images/maple.gif">
```

The following is a sample HTML document and its source code.

# SAMPLE OF AN HTML DOCUMENT

This is an example of the basic HTML page and its related code.

There's really nothing mysterious about HTML code.

```
<HTML>
<HEAD>
<TITLE>SAMPLE HTML DOCUMENT</TITLE>
</HEAD>
<BODY BGCOLOR="#DDF4F1">
<H1>SAMPLE OF AN HTML DOCUMENT</H1>
This is an example of the basic HTML page and its related code.<P>

There's really nothing mysterious about HTML code.<P>
</BODY>
</HTML>
```

# Most Commonly Used HTML Code

The following HTML tags can be used just about anywhere to affect the appearance of text—in sentences, paragraphs, even tables. The codes presented in Table A-3 are provided in their ASCII format with a description and sample for each code.

**Table A-3** Commonly Used Text Tags

| HTML Code | Description | Sample Source Code | Browser Screen |
|---|---|---|---|
| <B> </B> | **B**olds whatever text is between codes. | This is <B>bold</B>. | This is **bold**. |
| <STRONG> </STRONG> | Also bolds whatever text is between codes. | This is <STRONG>bold </STRONG>. | This is **bold**. |
| <U> </U> | **U**nderlines whatever is between codes. | This is <U>underlined </U>. | This is <u>underlined</u>. |
| <I> </I> | **I**talicizes whatever is between codes. | This is <I>italics</I>. | This is *italics*. |
| <EM> </EM> | Also italicizes whatever is between codes. | This is <EM>italics</EM>. | This is *italics*. |
| <P> </P> (the closing </P> is not required) | **P**aragraph designation; inserts a blank line right after <P>. | <P>This is the beginning and end of one paragraph. </P> <P>This is another paragraph.</P> | This is the beginning and end of one paragraph.<br><br>This is another paragraph. |

**Table A-3** Commonly Used Text Tags  (Continued)

| HTML Code | Description | Sample Source Code | Browser Screen |
|---|---|---|---|
| <CENTER> </CENTER> | **Center**s whatever is between codes—text, headings, tables, and so forth. | <P><CENTER>This Is the Title</CENTER> </P><P>This is the intro paragraph.</P> | This Is the Title<br><br>This is the intro paragraph. |
| <PRE> </PRE> | Leaves whatever is between the two codes as **Pre**formatted text, including line breaks and spacing between lines and text. Used for columns, tabs, et cetera, when HTML Tables aren't used. Browser typically interprets preformatted text with a different font. | <PRE><br>This is a list<br>of names and<br>phone numbers.<br><br>NAME      PHONE<br>Bob       555-5555<br>Laura     444-4444<br>Sue       333-3333<br>Tom       222-2222<br></PRE> | ```This is a list of names and phone numbers.  NAME     PHONE Bob      555-5555 Laura    444-4444 Sue      333-3333 Tom      222-2222 ``` |

**Table A-3** Commonly Used Text Tags  (Continued)

| HTML Code | Description | Sample Source Code | Browser Screen |
|---|---|---|---|
| <BLOCKQUOTE> </BLOCKQUOTE> | Indents a whole paragraph or groups of paragraphs. | This is a quote from an unknown source:<P> <BLOCKQUOTE> <I><B>"Life is what you make of it."</B></I> </BLOCKQUOTE> <P> It is a good source of inspiration.<P> | This is a quote from an unknown source: *"Life is what you make of it."* It is a good source of inspiration. |

As mentioned earlier, a few commonly used codes do not have an on/off or start/stop relationship, such as those listed in Table A-4.

**Table A-4** Commonly Used Codes Not Requiring Closing

| HTML Code | Description | Source Code Sample | Browser Screen |
|---|---|---|---|
| <BR> | line **br**eak that starts whatever text follows <BR> onto a new line | <P>The players are:<BR>Mr. Bryce<BR>Ms. Emily<BR>Mr. Scott</P> | The players are: Mr. Bryce Ms. Emily Mr. Scott |
| <HR> | **h**orizontal **r**uler that places a horizontal line across the page (additional attributes are presented later in this appendix) | <P>This is one topic.</P> <HR> <P>This is a separate topic.</P> | This is one topic. _____ This is a separate topic. |

**Table A-4** Commonly Used Codes Not Requiring Closing (Continued)

| HTML Code | Description | Source Code Sample | Browser Screen |
|---|---|---|---|
|   (must be in lowercase) | Special character for a **n**on-**b**reaking **sp**ace to allow manual placement of extra spaces where required | \<P>The times are listed as: \<BR>     1 and 7 pm on Monday\</P> | The times are listed as:<br>   1 and 7 pm on Monday |
| &lt; (must be in lowercase) | Special character for the less than sign (<) | \<P>The following equation is true:\<BR> 5 &lt; 7\</P> | The following equation is true:<br>5 < 7 |
| &gt; (must be in lowercase) | Special character for the greater than sign (>) | \<P>The following equation is true:\<BR> 10 &gt; 7\</P> | The following equation is true:<br>10 > 7 |

The last three codes in Table A-4 belong to a long list of special characters. Some browsers do not recognize the keyboard representative for some characters, such as non-ASCII quotes, percent signs, tildes, et cetera, so an ASCII equivalent that most browsers recognize is used. They can typically be picked out as starting with an ampersand (&) and ending with a semicolon (;).

The characters used within the middle are usually a logical set of characters. For example, the "l" and "t" in the code &lt; represents **l**ess **t**han. These codes are also especially important for foreign languages, where accents appear over some letters. There are special character lists too numerous to include in this appendix; however they are widely available in published HTML books and on the Web.

The previous codes can also be used in conjunction with each other, such as bolding, underlining and italicizing the same text. The source code would look something like:

\<P>This is a sentence in which some \<B>\<I>\<U>general\</U>\</I>\</B> HTML text attribute coding will be combined.\</P> \<P>As you can see, the following codes were used:\<BR>bold\<BR>underline\<BR>italics\<BR>\</P>

The browser would interpret this coding and display the following screen:

This is a sentence in which some ***general*** HTML text attribute coding will be combined.

As you can see, the following codes were used:
bold
underline
italics

## Headings

There are six different headings in HTML. The coding includes a numeric value between 1 and 6, in which 1 is the most prominent and 6 is the least prominent. When you use a heading, you don't need to include any other formatting, such as bolding. Also, headings include blank lines after the text, so paragraph or line breaks are not required. Table A-5 gives you an idea of the difference in levels.

**Table A-5** Text Heading Tags

| HTML Code | Sample Source Code | Browser Appearance |
|---|---|---|
| <H1> </H1> | <H1>TITLE</H1> | TITLE |
| <H2> </H2> | <H2>TITLE</H2> | TITLE |
| <H3> </H3> | <H3>TITLE</H3> | TITLE |
| <H4> </H4> | <H4>TITLE</H4> | TITLE |
| <H5> </H5> | <H5>TITLE</H5> | TITLE |
| <H6> </H6> | <H6>TITLE</H6> | TITLE |

## Lists

There are times that you'll want to list items, either by using dot points (bullets) or other similar characters (unordered) or by using an enumerated scheme (ordered). HTML offers two different formats for lists: unordered lists and ordered lists. They can be used together or nested as fits your needs.

### Dot Points (Unordered Lists)

Dot points can be created in HTML using "Unordered Lists." The type of symbol can be specified, such as the default "disc" or a circle or square.

It may be helpful to remember <UL> stands for **U**nordered **L**ist and that <LI> stands for **L**ist **I**tem. The <LI> code is used at the beginning of each dot point item. A closing </LI> can be used, but is not required. To separate the individual list items with a blank line, simply use a <P> after each item. See Table A-6 and A-7 for examples.

**Table A-6** Dot Point Lists

| HTML Code | Description | Sample Source Code | Browser Appearance |
|---|---|---|---|
| <UL><br>  <LI><br></UL> | dot point using a disc | <UL><br>  <LI>This is a disc.<br>  <LI>And so is this.<br>  <LI>And this.<br></UL> | • This is a disc.<br>• And so is this.<br>• And this. |
| <UL TYPE="CIRCLE"><br>  <LI><br></UL> | dot point using a circle | <UL type="circle"><br>  <LI>This is a circle.<br>  <LI>As well as this.<br>  <LI>And that.<br></UL> | ○ This is a circle.<br>○ As well as this.<br>○ And that. |
| <UL TYPE="SQUARE"><br>  <LI><br></UL> | dot point using a square | <UL type="square"><br>  <LI>This is a square.<br>  <LI>And this also.<br>  <LI>Last one.<br></UL> | ■ This is a square.<br>■ And this also.<br>■ Last one. |

**Table A-7** Dot Point List with Extra Space

| Sample Source Code | Browser Appearance |
| --- | --- |
| <UL TYPE="SQUARE">  <LI>This is a square with space between.<P>  <LI>And this also.<P>  <LI>Last one.<P> </UL> | ■ This is a square with space between.  ■ And this also.  ■ Last one. |

It is important to note that each occurrence of <UL> automatically indents the text that follows and the related closing </UL> removes the indentation. If the ending code is not provided, the text after the list will continue to be indented.

Also, HTML coding does not control the amount of space between the dot point and the text that follows—that is determined by the type and version of browser.

## Enumerated Lists (Ordered Lists)

Lists of items can be enumerated in HTML using "Ordered Lists." The type of enumeration is defaulted to numbers, but can also be specified as upper or lowercase letters or upper or lowercase Roman numerals. In other words the choices are 1, A, a, I, or i. Ordered lists can start at a specified value, the numbering can be interrupted and resumed, and changed to allow parent-child lists. See Table A-8 for examples.

**Table A-8** Ordered Lists

| HTML Code | Description | Sample Source Code | Browser Appearance |
| --- | --- | --- | --- |
| <OL>  <LI>  </OL> | List Item with the default numbering of 1. | <OL>  <LI>This is first.  <LI>This is second.  <LI>And this, third.  </OL> | 1. This is first.  2. This is second.  3. And this, third. |

**Table A-8** Ordered Lists  (Continued)

| HTML Code | Description | Sample Source Code | Browser Appearance |
|---|---|---|---|
| <OL TYPE="A"> <LI> </OL> | List Item using uppercase letters. | <OL TYPE="A"> <LI>This is first. <LI>This is second. <LI>And this, third. </OL> | A. This is first. B. This is second. C. And this, third. |
| <OL TYPE="a"> <LI> </OL> | List Item using lowercase letters. | <OL TYPE="a"> <LI>This is first. <LI>This is second. <LI>And this, third. </OL> | a. This is first. b. This is second. c. And this, third. |
| <OL TYPE="I"> <LI> </OL> | List Item using uppercase Roman numerals. | <OL TYPE="I"> <LI>This is first. <LI>This is second. <LI>And this, third. </OL> | I. This is first. II. This is second. III. And this, third. |
| <OL TYPE="i"> <LI> </OL> | List Item using lowercase Roman numerals. | <OL TYPE="i"> <LI>This is first. <LI>This is second. <LI>And this, third. </OL> | i. This is first. ii. This is second. iii. And this, third. |

**Table A-8** Ordered Lists  (Continued)

| HTML Code | Description | Sample Source Code | Browser Appearance |
|---|---|---|---|
| <OL><br>  <LI><br>    <OL><br>    <LI><br>    </OL><br>  </OL> | List Item using parent-child relation-ships. | <OL><br>  <LI>This is parent.<br>  <OL TYPE="A"><br>    <LI>This is child.<br>    <OL TYPE="a"><br>      <LI>Grandchild.<br>      <LI>Another grandchild.<br>    </OL><br>    <LI>Back to child list, second item.<br>    <LI>Child list, third item.<br>  </OL><br>  <LI>Back to parent, second item.<br>  <LI>Parent, third item.  </OL> | 1. This is parent.<br>  A. This is child.<br>    a. Grandchild.<br>    b. Another grandchild.<br>  B. Back to child list, second item.<br>  C. Child list, third item.<br>2. Back to parent, second item.<br>3. Parent, third item. |
| <OL START="n"><br>  <LI><br>  </OL> | Ordered List starting at "n," where "n" represents the number or letter at which the list is to start. | <OL START="5"><br>  <LI>This is first.<br>  <LI>This is second.<br>  <LI>And this, third.<br>  </OL> | 5. This is first.<br>6. This is second.<br>7. And this, third. |

**Table A-8** Ordered Lists  (Continued)

| HTML Code | Description | Sample Source Code | Browser Appearance |
|---|---|---|---|
| <OL><br><LI VALUE="n"><br></OL> | Ordered List with List Item starting at "n," where "n" represents the number or letter at which the list is to start. | <OL><br>    <LI>This is first.<br>    <LI>This is second.<BR><br><I>(Items 3-86 unassigned)</I><br><BR><br><LI VALUE="87">And this, 87th.<br><LI>This is 88th.<br></OL> | 1. This is first.<br>2. This is second. *(Items 3-86 unassigned)*<br>87. And this, 87th.<br>88. This is 88th. |

It may be helpful to remember <OL> stands for **O**rdered **L**ist and <LI> stands for **L**ist **I**tem. It is important to note that each occurrence of <OL> automatically indents the text that follows and the related closing </OL> removes the indentation. If the ending code is not provided, the text after the list will continue to be indented.

Also, HTML coding does not control the amount of space between the period after enumerated items or, in some cases, even include a period for the <LI> items—that is determined by the type and version of browser.

## Tables

Several pages, if not chapters, can be devoted to just Tables. For the purpose of this appendix, just the basics will be covered.

Tables should be used whenever dealing with two or more columns of text. Table A-9 lists the major components to create Tables. It is helpful to think of this as building a spreadsheet with rows and cells, where the columns fall into place based on the rows and cells defined.

**Table A-9** Basic Table Related Tags

| HTML Code | Description |
|---|---|
| <TABLE><br></TABLE> | Starts/stops a **Table**, and whatever is between the two codes will be displayed in a column/row format. The Table is defaulted to appear as left-justified. Unless specified by pixel or percentage, the browser determines the width of the table based on column content. |
| <TR> </TR> | Starts/stops a **Table R**ow, and whatever is between the two codes will be in the same row of the table. |
| <TH> </TH> | Starts/stops a **Table H**eading, and whatever is between the two codes will be in the same cell. This creates the column names, and the default for the cell content is bolded, centered headings. |
| <TD> </TD> | Starts/stops a **Table D**ata, and whatever is between the two codes will be in the same cell. This creates the content of an individual cell, and the default is for normal, left-justified cell contents. |

Put these codes together, as in the following example, and here's what you get:

```
<TABLE>
<TR><TH>Heading 1</TH>
    <TH>Heading 2</TH></TR>
<TR><TD>Cell 1</TD>
    <TD>Cell 2</TD></TR>
<TR><TD>Cell 3</TD>
    <TD>Cell 4</TD></TR>
</TABLE><P>
```

**Heading 1 Heading 2**

Cell 1      Cell 2

Cell 3      Cell 4

Along with this basic Table coding, there are many different attributes. Table A-10 provides the most commonly used <TABLE> attributes.

**Table A-10** Attributes for Table Tags

| HTML Code | Description of Attribute | Browser Appearance |
|---|---|---|
| <TABLE ALIGN="LEFT"> <TABLE ALIGN="CENTER"> <TABLE ALIGN="RIGHT"> | **TABLE ALIGNMENT** Although the default is left-aligned, you can also center and right-justify the table. | Table is centered, left- or right-justified |
| <TABLE BORDER="n"> | **TABLE BORDER** The default is no border (or 0), "n" represents pixels. The smaller the number, such as 1, the less prominent the lines are. The value of "n" is typically a single-digit number. | BORDER="1"<br><br>| Heading 1 | Heading 2 |<br>| Cell 1 | Cell 2 |<br>| Cell 3 | Cell 4 |<br><br>BORDER="6"<br><br>| Heading 1 | Heading 2 |<br>| Cell 1 | Cell 2 |<br>| Cell 3 | Cell 4 | |
| <TABLE WIDTH="n"> | **TABLE WIDTH** "n" can be expressed in terms of percent or pixels. | Width is set by pixel or % setting <TABLE WIDTH="600"> <TABLE WIDTH="100%"> |

**Table A-10** Attributes for Table Tags  (Continued)

| HTML Code | Description of Attribute | Browser Appearance |
|---|---|---|
| <TABLE CELLPADDING="n"> | **CELL PADDING** This is the space around the text within a cell; "n" represents pixels. The smaller the number, such as 1, the closer the text is to the cell border. The value of "n" is typically a single-digit number. | CELLPADDING="1" <br><br> Heading 1 / Heading 2 <br> Cell 1 / Cell 2 <br> Cell 3 / Cell 4 <br><br> CELLPADDING="8" <br><br> Heading 1 / Heading 2 <br> Cell 1 / Cell 2 <br> Cell 3 / Cell 4 |
| <TABLE CELLSPACING="n"> | **CELL SPACING** This is the space between the cells; "n" represents pixels. The smaller the number, such as 1, the closer cells are to each other. The value of "n" is typically a single-digit number, if used at all. | CELLSPACING="1" <br><br> Heading 1 / Heading 2 <br> Cell 1 / Cell 2 <br> Cell 3 / Cell 4 <br><br> CELLSPACING="8" <br><br> Heading 1 / Heading 2 <br> Cell 1 / Cell 2 <br> Cell 3 / Cell 4 |

Any number of these attributes can be used within the <TABLE> tag as shown in the following example:

```
<TABLE WIDTH="50%" CELLPADDING="4" CELLSPACING="2" BORDER="2">
<TR><TH>Heading 1</TH>
    <TH>Heading 2</TH></TR>
<TR><TD>Cell 1</TD>
    <TD>Cell 2</TD></TR>
<TR><TD>Cell 3</TD>
    <TD>Cell 4</TD></TR>
</TABLE><P>
```

| Heading 1 | Heading 2 |
|-----------|-----------|
| Cell 1    | Cell 2    |
| Cell 3    | Cell 4    |

Along with these <TABLE> attributes, <TD> and <TH> have their own attributes as listed in Table A-11.

**Table A-11** TD and TH Specific Attributes

| HTML Code | Description of Attribute | Browser Appearance |
|-----------|--------------------------|--------------------|
| <TD ALIGN="LEFT"> <TD ALIGN="CENTER"> <TD ALIGN="RIGHT"> | (Also used with <TR> and <TH>) **CELL HORIZONTAL TEXT ALIGNMENT** Although the default is left-aligned, you can also center and right-justify the text within the cell. | ALIGN="LEFT" Cell 1  Cell 2 ALIGN="CENTER" Cell 1  Cell 2 ALIGN="RIGHT" Cell 1  Cell 2 |

**Table A-11** TD and TH Specific Attributes (Continued)

| HTML Code | Description of Attribute | Browser Appearance |
|---|---|---|
| <TD VALIGN="TOP"> <TD VALIGN="MIDDLE"> <TD ALIGN="BOTTOM"> | (Also used with <TR> and <TH>) **CELL VERTICAL TEXT ALIGNMENT** Although the default is middle, you can also align the text to the top or bottom of the cell. If the cell is proportioned all the way around, no noticeable difference will be seen with the VALIGN attribute. In this case a HEIGHT attribute was included, so the source code looks like: <TD HEIGHT="50" VALIGN="BOTTOM"> Cell 2</TD> | VALIGN="TOP" Cell 1 · Cell 2 VALIGN="MIDDLE" Cell 1  Cell 2 VALIGN="BOTTOM" Cell 1  Cell 2 |
| <TD WIDTH="n"> | (Also used with <TH>) **CELL WIDTH** "n" is expressed in terms of pixels. | Width is set by pixel setting <TD WIDTH="90"> |
| <TD HEIGHT="n"> | (Also used with <TH>) **CELL HEIGHT** "n" can be expressed in terms of pixels. | Height is set by pixel setting <TD HEIGHT="45"> |
| <TD COLSPAN="n"> | (Also used with <TH>) **COLUMN SPAN** "n" is a number representing the number of columns the text is to cover. | <TH COLSPAN="2"> **ONE HEADING** Cell 1  Cell 2 |

**Table A-11** TD and TH Specific Attributes (Continued)

| HTML Code | Description of Attribute | Browser Appearance |
|---|---|---|
| <TD ROWSPAN="n"> | (Also used with <TH>)<br><br>**ROW SPAN**<br><br>"n" is a number representing the number of rows the text is to cover. | <TD ROWSPAN="3"><br><br>SMITH   Janice / Sally / Tom |

## Forms

Forms are the way in which HTML pages become a little more interactive. Forms are used to capture data from the user and involve several attributes, as listed in Table A-12.

**Table A-12** Form Tags

| HTML Code | Description |
|---|---|
| <FORM><br></FORM> | Starts/stops a **Form,** and whatever is between the two codes are form components. |
| <FORM ACTION="x"> | ACTION is the URL (location) of the CGI program, represented by "x." |
| <FORM METHOD="x" | METHOD is either GET or POST (described in early chapters in this book), represented by "x." |

For example this code would be put together in the following manner:

```
<FORM METHOD="POST" ACTION="http://www.site.com/cgi-bin/someform.pl">
```

Forms have many components, such as radio buttons, check boxes, text areas, listings of items that can be selected, and so forth. These can be boiled down to three basic types: Input, Textarea, and Select. Tables A-13, A-14, and A-15 present these form element tags.

**Table A-13** Form Element Tags

| HTML Code | Description of Component | Code Example |
|---|---|---|
| <INPUT MAXLENGTH="n"> | **Max**imum **Length** is the number of characters that will be captured, represented by "n." | <INPUT MAXLENGTH="150"> |
| <INPUT SIZE="n"> | **SIZE** is the number of visible characters to be seen in a text area, represented by "n." | <INPUT SIZE="25"> |
| <INPUT NAME="x"> | **NAME** is the unique name of the input—this is critical for the name/value pairing discussed in early chapters of this book. | <INPUT NAME="MONTH"> |
| <INPUT VALUE="x"> | **VALUE** is the specific name of the value offered for the input—this is critical for the name/value pairing discussed in early chapters of this book. | <INPUT VALUE="SEPTEMBER"> |
| <INPUT TYPE="x"> | **TYPE** specifies the use of text, check box, or radio buttons. "x" represents the types of "TEXT," "CHECKBOX," "RADIO," "SUBMIT," and "RESET." | Refer to specific examples in this table. |

**Table A-13** Form Element Tags  (Continued)

| HTML Code | Description of Component | Code Example |
|---|---|---|
| TYPE="TEXT" | **TEXT** provides an area for form users to enter up to a single line of text. | \<FORM\><br>\<B\>City\</B\>:  \<INPUT TYPE="TEXT" SIZE="20" NAME="CITY"\>\<P\><br>\</FORM\><br><br>City: [                    ] |
| TYPE="CHECKBOX" | **CHECKBOX** allows form users to select one or more options. | \<FORM\><br>\<B\>Which products have you used?\</B\>:\<BR\><br>\<INPUT TYPE="CHECKBOX" NAME="PRODUCTS USED" VALUE="ITEM A"\>Item A<br>\<INPUT TYPE="CHECKBOX" NAME="PRODUCTS USED" VALUE="ITEM B"\>Item B<br>\<INPUT TYPE="CHECKBOX" NAME="PRODUCTS USED" VALUE="ITEM C"\>Item C\<P\><br>\</FORM\><br><br>**Which products have you used?**:<br>☐ Item A  ☐ Item B  ☐ Item C |

**Table A-13** Form Element Tags (Continued)

| HTML Code | Description of Component | Code Example |
|---|---|---|
| TYPE="RADIO" | **RADIO** allows form users to select **only** one item from a list of options and not multiple items. | \<FORM> <br> \<B>RESIDENT\</B>: \<INPUT TYPE="RADIO" NAME="RESIDENT" VALUE="YES">\<B>Yes\</B> <br> \<INPUT TYPE="RADIO" NAME="RESIDENT" VALUE="NO">\<B>No\</B> <br> \<P> <br> \</FORM> <br><br> **RESIDENT**: ○ **Yes** ○ **No** |
| TYPE="SUBMIT" | **SUBMIT** is what the form users click on to submit the form data. "VALUE" is what appears in the button that this code generates. | \<FORM> <br> \<INPUT TYPE="SUBMIT" VALUE="Submit"> <br> \</FORM> <br><br> [ Submit ] |
| TYPE="RESET" | **RESET** is what the form users can click on to clear **all** their entries on the HTML form. "VALUE" is what appears in the button that this code generates. | \<FORM> <br> \<INPUT TYPE="RESET" VALUE="Clear"> <br> \</FORM> <br><br> [ Clear ] |

Please note that there is no closing input tag, \</INPUT>, required.

Table A-14 describes the Textarea element (which does require a closing textarea tag). Textarea tags allow the form user to enter free-form text. The column and row definitions are used to define how much text you see on the HTML form—it is not a limit of what can be entered.

**Table A-14** The Text Area Tag

| HTML Code | Description of Component | Code Example |
|---|---|---|
| <TEXTAREA> </TEXTAREA> | **TEXTAREA** allows form users to enter many lines of text. | <FORM> <TEXTAREA></TEXTAREA> </FORM> |
| <TEXTAREA NAME="n"> | **NAME** is the unique name of the textarea, represented by "n"--this is critical for the name/value pairing discussed in early chapters of this book. | <FORM> <B>Describe your experience:</B><BR> <TEXTAREA NAME="EXPERIENCE"> </TEXTAREA> </FORM> Describe your experience: |
| <TEXTAREA COLS="n"> | **COLUMNS** "n" represents the number of columns appearing in the textarea input box. Scroll bars are automatically included—no extra coding required. | <FORM> <B>Describe your experience:</B><BR> <TEXTAREA NAME="EXPERIENCE" COLS="15"></TEXTAREA> </FORM> Describe your experience: |

**Table A-14** The Text Area Tag (Continued)

| HTML Code | Description of Component | Code Example |
|---|---|---|
| <TEXTAREA ROWS="n"> | **ROWS**<br><br>"n" represents the number of rows appearing in the textarea input box. | <FORM><br><br><B>Describe your experience:</B><BR><br><br><TEXTAREA NAME="EXPERIENCE" COLS="20" ROWS="8" ><br><br></TEXTAREA><br><br></FORM> |

Describe your experience:

Select constrains the form user to a limited and defined set of choices. The Select components are described in Table A-15.

**Table A-15** The Select Form Element

| HTML Code | Description of Component | Code Example |
|---|---|---|
| <SELECT><br></SELECT> | **SELECT** is used to give form users a set list of items to choose from and must be used in conjunction with the <OPTION> tag | Must have size and option tags |

**Table A-15** The Select Form Element  (Continued)

| HTML Code | Description of Component | Code Example |
| --- | --- | --- |
| <SELECT NAME="n"> | **NAME** is the unique name of the selection group, represented by "n"—this is critical for the name/value pairing discussed in early chapters of this book. | Must have size and option tags |
| <SELECT SIZE="n"> | **SIZE** is the number of rows appearing in the section area, represented by "n." (The column width is basically determined by the size of the items to choose from.) | Must have option tags, but here's a basic look:<br>&lt;FORM&gt;<br>&lt;B&gt;Which language do you speak?&lt;/B&gt;&lt;BR&gt;<br>&lt;SELECT NAME="LANGUAGE" SIZE="4"&gt;&lt;/SELECT&gt;<br>&lt;/FORM&gt;<br><br>**Which language do you speak?** |

**Table A-15** The Select Form Element  (Continued)

| HTML Code | Description of Component | Code Example |
|-----------|-------------------------|--------------|
| <SELECT MULTIPLE> | **MULTIPLE**<br>This feature allows the form user to select more than one item from the list. | <FORM><br><B>Which language(s) do you speak?</B><BR><br><SELECT MULTIPLE NAME="LANGUAGE" SIZE="4"></SELECT><br></FORM><br><br>**Which language(s) do you speak?** |

Table A-16 describes how the Option tag is used with Select.

**Table A-16** The Option Tag Used with the Select Form Element

| HTML Code | Description of Component | Code Example |
|-----------|-------------------------|--------------|
| <OPTION><br></OPTION> | **OPTION** is used to list each item offered via a <SELECT> tag. | Requires a VALUE definition |

**Table A-16** The Option Tag Used with the Select Form Element  (Continued)

| HTML Code | Description of Component | Code Example |
|---|---|---|
| <OPTION VALUE="n"> | **VALUE** is the specific name of the value to be provided in the selection list. | <FORM><B>Which language do you speak?</B><BR> <SELECT NAME="LANGUAGE" SIZE="4"> <OPTION VALUE="Arabic">Arabic </OPTION> <OPTION VALUE="English">English </OPTION> <OPTION VALUE="French">French </OPTION> <OPTION VALUE="German">German </OPTION> </SELECT></FORM> |

**Which language do you speak?**

```
Arabic
English
French
German
```

**Table A-16** The Option Tag Used with the Select Form Element (Continued)

| HTML Code | Description of Component | Code Example |
|---|---|---|
| <OPTION SELECTED> | **SELECTED** <br> This feature allows a particular item to be the default selection. In this example, we are selecting "English" as the default. | <FORM><B>Which language do you speak?</B><BR> <br> <SELECT NAME="LANGUAGE" SIZE="3"> <br> <OPTION SELECTED VALUE="English">English <br> </OPTION> <br> <OPTION VALUE="Arabic">Arabic <br> </OPTION> <br> <OPTION VALUE="French">French <br> </OPTION> <br> </SELECT></FORM> <br><br> **Which language do you speak?** <br> English <br> Arabic <br> French |

To put the Select form elements all together, we use the example of wanting to capture all the languages spoken by the form user, knowing that English has a 90% probability of being selected. The following is the source code for that example, as well as a screen capture of how it would appear in the browser.

```
<FORM>
<B>Which language(s) do you speak?</B><BR>
<SELECT MULTIPLE NAME="LANGUAGES" SIZE="5">
  <OPTION SELECTED VALUE="English">English</OPTION>
  <OPTION VALUE="Arabic">Arabic</OPTION>
  <OPTION VALUE="Chinese">Chinese</OPTION>
  <OPTION VALUE="French">French</OPTION>
  <OPTION VALUE="German">German</OPTION>
  <OPTION VALUE="Italian">Italian</OPTION>
  <OPTION VALUE="Japanese">Japanese</OPTION>
  <OPTION VALUE="Russian">Russian</OPTION>
  <OPTION VALUE="Spanish">Spanish</OPTION>
  </SELECT>
</FORM><P>
```

**Which language(s) do you speak?**

| English ▲ |
|---|
| Arabic |
| Chinese |
| French |
| German ▼ |

# *Appendix B*

## *Tcl Language Summary*

This appendix contains a summary of the majority of commands available in Tcl 8.0. This material is provided as a reference and not suggested as a tutorial. The goal of this appendix is to provide enough information that programmers with no experience in Tcl could work through all the examples in this book using only this appendix as a reference. However, it is not intended as a substitute for a good book on the language. Tcl is far too rich an environment to cover the entire language in one reference. If you are not already experienced with Tcl, you should consider obtaining one of the many fine books listed in the bibliography.

## Working with Variables

The **set** command is the most basic way to manipulate variables in the Tcl language. The procedure prototype appears as follows:

set *varname ?value?*

The value parameter is optional. If you specify the **set** command with the value option, Tcl will set the *varname* equal to value. If the variable did not exist prior to this call, the variable is created for you.

```
% set temp_var "HELLO WORLD"
```

```
HELLO WORLD
```

If you execute the **set** command without specifying value, Tcl will display the contents of the variable, if it exists, or return an error if the variable does not exist.

```
% set temp_var
HELLO WORLD
```

The **unset** command is provided to remove variables that have been created with the **set** command.

unset *varname*

This command requires only one argument, the name of the variable to delete. Once the command has been executed, subsequent attempts to access *varname* will fail.

```
% unset temp_var
% set temp_var
can't read "temp_var": no such variable
%
```

The *value* arguments to the **set** and **unset** commands are treated as strings. In fact most all arguments in Tcl are dealt with as strings. Once you embrace this concept, you will begin to understand why Tcl is such a powerful language for generating CGI scripts. As an example, if you execute the Tcl command **set temp_var 3**, the variable **temp_var** will contain the string representation of 3. Tcl provides numerous commands to treat these strings as numbers, but the underlying representation is always a string.

# How Tcl Evaluates Commands

Before continuing on with other command descriptions, it is import to understand how Tcl evaluates commands. Every Tcl command can be considered a series of words, or arguments, that are acted upon in the same fashion by the Tcl interpreter.

Note: The terms "word" and "argument" are used interchangeably in this discussion.

The first word is considered to be the name of the command and each additional word is considered to be an argument to the command. Words in a command string are separated by white space (spaces or tabs) unless grouped by quotes or curly braces. Grouping with quotes and curly braces will be discussed in a moment.

Every command is evaluated as a two-step process.

1. The command is sent to the Tcl parser, which performs string substitution based on a defined set of rules.
2. The results of the parser are then sent to a command procedure specified by the first word in the command. It is up to the command procedure to interpret the remaining arguments in any manner it sees fit. The command procedure may be a predefined Tcl command or a user-defined procedure call.

The parser will perform various substitutions of the strings it receives. These substitutions allow for comment lines, line separators, variable substitution, command substitution, and backslash substitution. Each one of these are discussed in the following sections.

## Comment Lines and Line Separators

The Tcl parse will ignore any lines where the first nonwhite space character is the # character. If Tcl encounters the # character in any other position, it is treated as an ordinary character.

```
% # This is a valid comment line.
% set temp_var "HELLO WORLD"
HELLO WORLD
```

The next example attempts to use the comment character at an inappropriate place. The Tcl parser treats the # character and the characters that follow as additional arguments to the set command, which results in an error.

```
% set temp_var "HELLO WORLD"    #This is not a valid comment
wrong # args: should be "set varName ?newValue?"
%
```

In order to place a comment in the middle of the line, you must make it appear as two lines to the Tcl parser. This is done with the line separator character, the semicolon. The Tcl parser will break lines for you whenever it encounters a semicolon outside of quotes or braces.

```
% set temp_var "HELLO WORLD"    ;#This is a valid comment
HELLO WORLD
```

## Variable Substitution

Variable substitution is one of three forms of substitution provided by Tcl. The remaining two are command and backslash substitution and will be discussed next. Variable substitution is triggered by the presence of the dollar sign character anywhere in the command string and causes the variable name prefaced with the dollar sign to be replaced by the value of the variable.

As an example, consider the modification to our earlier example of the **set** command.

```
% set temp_var "HELLO WORLD"
HELLO WORLD
% set greeting "$temp_var from Dave"
HELLO WORLD from Dave
%
```

Notice how the contents of the **temp_var** variable were substituted by the Tcl parse when the second **set** command was executed. This is variable substitution.

## Command Substitution

The next form of substitution is *command substitution*. This form of substitution is used when you would like to evaluate a command as part of an expression. Command substitution is triggered by enclosing a command in square brackets.

```
[command string]
```

Once again, the command string is passed through the Tcl parser before being sent to the command procedure being called. See how the following example achieves the results from the previous example in a single line of code.

```
% set greeting "[set temp_var "HELLO WORLD"] from dave"
HELLO WORLD from dave
%
```

When the Tcl parser sees the square brackets, it evaluates the command contained inside before parsing the rest of the command string. The result of the command substitution is whatever the normal command procedure would have returned after execution. In the case of the **set** command, the return value is always equal to the value contained by the value of the variable being set. After execution of this example, both the greeting and **temp_var** variables contain the same values as they did when executed as separate command lines. To examine the contents of any variable, you may use the **set** command without a value argument.

```
    % set greeting
HELLO WORLD from dave
% set temp_var
HELLO WORLD
%
```

## Backslash Substitution

The final form of substitution handled by the Tcl parser is *backslash substitution*, which allows you to embed special characters in your strings. Many of the backslash substitutions that can be performed in Tcl are identical to their counterparts in the C programming language.

Table B-1 shows the backslash characters understood by the Tcl parser.

**Table B-1** Tcl Backslash Characters

| Backslash Sequence | Substitution Performed |
|---|---|
| \a | Audible Alert (0x7) |
| \b | Backspace (0x8) |
| \f | Form Feed (0xc) |
| \n | Newline (0xa) |
| \r | Carriage Return (0xd) |
| \t | Tab (0x9) |
| \v | Vertical Tab (0xb) |
| \d \dd or \ddd | Octal representation of ddd |
| \xhh | Hex representation of hh (any number of h's allowed) |
| \newline spaces | A single space character |
| \char | For any character not defined above, this sequence represents the literal character char |

Consider the following example.

```
% set dollar_amount 300
300
```

```
% set text "Your charge card balance is \$$dollar_amount\n\
                      Your charge card payment is \$25.00"
Your charge card balance is $300
 Your charge card payment is $25.00
%
```

This example uses several backslash substitutions. The first backslash character is used to prevent the Tcl parser from attempting variable substitution of the first dollar sign. The second dollar sign does cause variable substitution and replaces the **$dollar_amount** variable with its current value. The \n near the end of the first line of the **set text** command forces a new line character to be generated. The backslash character immediately followed by a new line is used to break up long lines. Any number of spaces following the backslash-newline sequence will be replaced by a single space character.

## Grouping with Quotes

In many cases it is desirable to prevent the parser from viewing each word as a command argument. This was already seen in a previous example.

```
% set temp_var "HELLO WORLD"
```

This is so normal to look at that you probably didn't realize the quotes were actually directing the interpreter to not break words at white space boundaries. You can actually execute the same command without quotes, but it will look peculiar.

```
% set temp_var HELLO\ WORLD
HELLO WORLD
```

In this case the backslash character causes the space to be treated as a literal space rather than a word separator. In practice you would never write the code this way, but it serves to illustrate the action that the quotes perform.

## Grouping with Braces

Braces can be used to prevent any interpretation on the enclosed characters. Tcl treats all characters enclosed between curly braces as literals.

```
% set temp_var {You owe the credit card company $25.00}
You owe the credit card company $25.00
%
```

In the preceding example, the {} characters prevented the Tcl parser from attempting variable substitution when it encountered the dollar sign. If the braces were replaced with quotes, the parser would have tried to interpret $25.00 as a variable, which would most likely result in an error.

### Return Values in Tcl

During normal execution, Tcl commands return their result as a string. The **set** command, used in the previous example, is a typical example of this. In some cases the command may return an error that will result in the termination of the interpreter process. Errors and error return values will be covered in more detail later in this section. For now just remember that Tcl commands normally return a string result. This includes commands executed inside square brackets.

```
% set var1 "some text"
some text
% set var2 [set var1]
some text
% set var2
some text
%
```

In this example the return value from the command [**set var1**] is the value of **var1**, which was set to "some text." This return value is returned, in position, by the interpreter as the expression is evaluated. This causes the **var2** variable to be set with the same string.

## String Manipulation

All variables in Tcl are represented as a string. It is the common thread throughout Tcl. A number of commands are provided for manipulating strings. The **set** command, discussed in the last section, is the principal way of assigning string values to simple Tcl variables. The **string** command is provided for manipulating these string values. Like many commands in Tcl, the **string** command is not just one command but a number of commands depending on the command option that follows the basic command.

As an example, the **string match** command takes two arguments, a pattern and a string to match against the pattern. The command returns the value 1 if the *string* matches the *pattern* and 0 if it does not.

```
% string match "this*" "this is a test" .
1
```

In this example the **string match** command returned a 1, indicating the string matches the pattern. Notice the pattern is specified with the * character. The pattern matching in the **string match** command follows the glob-style pattern matching rules, which you may be used to if you use the C shell under UNIX. In this style of pattern matching, several characters have specific meanings. Here, the * character says to match whatever follows the word *this*.

Table B-2 lists all the special characters defined for glob-style pattern matching and what each character means when a match is being performed.

Another useful string command is **string index**. This command returns a specific character from *string* that occupies the position specified by *index*.

```
% set str "abcdefghijklmnop"
abcdefghijklmnop
% string index $str 5
f
%
```

**Table B-2** Glob-Style Pattern Matching Characters

| Character | Meaning |
| --- | --- |
| * | Matches any sequence of 0 or more characters. |
| ? | Matches any single character. |
| [chars] | Matches any single character in chars. You may specify a range of characters to match by using a hyphen between characters. As an example, [f-m] will match any single character between f and m, inclusive. |
| \char | Matches any single character (char). This is the same concept as using the backslash to prevent interpreting special characters such as *? or [ ]. |

Notice that the index is again a zero-based integer, where 0 indicates the first character of the string. This is typical of most Tcl commands. An index is usually zero-based, whereas a length is one-based. The **string length** command is a good example where the result is one-based rather than zero-based.

```
% set str "abcde"
abcde
% string length $str
```

```
5
%
```

The length of the string "abcde" is five characters. The **string length** command returns a result of 5. However, if you wished to reference the last character with the **string index** command, you would use an index of 4, because indexes are zero-based.

```
% string index $str 4
e
%
```

Several other commands deal with setting string variables and manipulating string contents. The **set** command is the principal command used to set a variable equal to a value but is not the only one. Another string-related command is **append**.

This command will append all of the *value* arguments to *varname*. If *varname* does not exist, it is created with its value set to the concatenation of all the *value* arguments. In its simplest form this command emulates the **set** command.

```
% append str "this is a test"
this is a test
```

In the preceding example, the variable **str** did not exist, prior to the **append** command being called, so it was created and assigned the value of the single argument. There is no advantage to using the **append** command over the **set** command in this example. The following example uses the **append** command to build up a string from various pieces.

```
% set str "abcde"
abcde
% append str "fghi"  "jklmn"   "opqrs"  ;# str does not exist, so it
will be created.
abcdefghijklmnopqrs
```

In actual practice you may have numerous variables that you wish to concatenate together into a single string. In such cases the **append** command is more convenient than trying to use multiple **set** commands.

## Tcl Lists

Tcl also provides a robust set of commands for dealing with lists of text. A very important concept in Tcl is that all strings can be represented as a list, and all lists can be represented as a string. As an example, the following string

```
"The quick brown fox jumped over the lazy dog"
```

is interpreted by some commands in Tcl as a single string, or by other commands as a list with nine elements. By default list elements in a Tcl list are delimited by standard white space characters, which in this case are simply space characters.

### Creating Lists: list, lappend, concat

The list command is the basic command for forming lists in Tcl. The list command returns a list comprising the arguments that follow it, or an empty string if no arguments are described.

```
% list The quick brown fox jumped over the lazy dog
The quick brown fox jumped over the lazy dog
```

In this example there appears to be no difference between a list and a string. That is true. The list command concatenated all the arguments that followed into a single list with a space character delimiting each element of the list. In this form there is no difference between the string representation and the list representation.

But what if you would like to group the elements of the list differently? Let's say you want the words "The quick brown fox" to be one element of the list and the remaining words to be the second element of the list. In that case you would simply use quotes to group the words you want in each element.

```
% list "The quick brown fox"  "jumped over the lazy dog"
{The quick brown fox} {jumped over the lazy dog}
```

The list command provides a convenient way to build Tcl lists but is not required to do so. You can build the list just as easily by placing curly braces inside the string yourself.

```
% set lvalue "{The quick brown fox} {jumped over the lazy dog}"
{The quick brown fox} {jumped over the lazy dog}
% llength $lvalue
2
```

The **lappend** command will append its arguments to the specified list name. If the specified variable does not exist, it will be created in the process.

```
% lappend str abc def ghi
abc def ghi
% lappend str jkl mno
abc def ghi jkl mno
```

Notice that this command requires the name of the list, not the actual list itself. This is one of the few list commands that operates directly on the original list!

## Querying Lists: llength, lindex, lsearch

Tcl provides a number of commands for obtaining information about Tcl lists or extracting desired values from lists. The **llength** command provides the ability to count the number of elements in a string. Its only argument is an actual Tcl list.

```
% set text [list The quick brown fox jumped over the lazy dog]
The quick brown fox jumped over the lazy dog
% set text
The quick brown fox jumped over the lazy dog
% llength $text
9
```

It is important to note that the **llength** command takes the actual list as an argument—not the variable name. Some **list** commands, such as **lappend**, require the name of the variable as an argument, and some of the commands, such as **llength**, require the actual list as an argument.

The **lindex** command allows you to extract a particular element from a list. The arguments to this command are a valid Tcl list and the index of the element to extract. It returns the contents of the specified index. The index is a zero-based integer index into the list.

```
% list "The quick brown fox"  "jumped over the lazy dog"
{The quick brown fox} {jumped over the lazy dog}
% lindex $lvalue 0
The quick brown fox
```

The **lsearch** command is used to search lists and return elements that match a particular pattern. This command will return the zero-based index to the first element that matches the pattern. If no match is found, the command will return -1. This command has three modes of operation, **-exact** requires the pattern and element to match exactly, **-glob** uses glob-style pattern matching, and **-regexp** uses regular expression pattern matching. This first example uses the **-exact** mode of pattern matching.

```
% set txt [list "The quick brown fox"  "jumped over the lazy dog"]
{The quick brown fox} {jumped over the lazy dog}
% lsearch -exact $txt "The quick brown fox"
0
```

Now for the same example using glob-style pattern matching. Notice the use of the * character to match any characters after the word "the".

```
% set txt [list "The quick brown fox"  "jumped over the lazy dog"]
{The quick brown fox} {jumped over the lazy dog}
% lsearch -glob $txt "The*"
0
```

To use a regular expression for pattern matching, specify the **-regexp** option and provide a regular expression for the pattern. The following example searches for any element that starts with "fox", followed by one or more characters, followed by the word "dog".

```
% set txt [list "The quick brown"  "fox jumped over the lazy dog"]
{The quick brown} {fox jumped over the lazy dog}
% lsearch -regexp $txt "fox.+dog"
1
```

## Manipulating Lists: linsert, lreplace, lsort

Two other commands are provided for inserting and deleting elements of a Tcl list. They are **linsert** and **lreplace**. The command syntax for these two commands is very similar. The **linsert** command will locate the element, reference by an index, and insert one or more *elements* at that position in the list. The command returns the list that results from inserting the new elements into the original list. This is an important point to remember. Many of the list commands do not operate on the original list but return a newly created list. One of the most common mistakes made by Tcl programmers is forgetting to assign the return value of such a command to some variable—assuming that the command will modify the original list.

```
% set lvalue [list "abc" "def" "jkl" "mno"]
abc def jkl mno
% linsert $lvalue 2 ghi
abc def ghi jkl mno
% set lvalue
abc def jkl mno
```

Here, the characters "ghi" were omitted when the list was initially built and inserted using the linsert command. Notice that the last set command shows the original list was not changed by the linsert command. If you wish to retain the new list, you must assign it to a new variable name.

```
% set lvalue [list "abc" "def" "jkl" "mno"]
abc def jkl mno
% set new_lvalue [linsert $lvalue 2 ghi]
abc def ghi jkl mno
%
```

Now the contents of new_lvalue will contain the updated list. It is not necessary to use a different name for the updated list. The preceding example could have simply reassigned the new list back to the original variable, lvalue, in the following manner.

```
% set lvalue [linsert $lvalue 2 ghi]
```

Because inserting elements at the end of a list is such a common activity, you may use the special identifier *end* for the index argument when appending elements to the end of a list.

```
% set lvalue
abc def ghi jkl mno
%linsert $lvalue end pqr
abc def ghi jkl mno pqr
```

The lreplace command is similar to the linsert command but replaces elements in the list rather than inserting new ones. This command requires a minimum of three arguments. This first argument is the list to operate on. The next two arguments are the first and last index of the elements to be replaced. The remaining arguments specify the elements to use as replacements.

```
% set str "This is a test"
this is a test
% lreplace $str 1 2 was a
this was a test
%
```

Once again, this command returns a newly created list and does not modify the original list. If you do not specify any replacement elements, the elements between first and last are deleted.

```
% set str "This is a test"
This is a test
% lreplace $str 1 2
This test%
```

The lsort command is used to sort the elements of a list. The lsort command has multiple options that control the manner in which the elements are sorted. Tcl 8.x has several new options that were not available in earlier versions.

By default the lsort command sorts the elements alphabetically (-ascii) in ascending (-ascending) order.

```
% set txt [list def ghi abc jkl]
def ghi abc jkl
% lsort $txt
abc def ghi jkl
```

You can reverse the order of the sort by specifying the -decreasing option.

```
% lsort -decreasing $txt
jkl ghi def abc
```

One of the new options to the lsort command in Tcl 8.x is the dictionary sort. The -dictionary option ignores case unless needed for a tie breaker, and embedded integers sort as integers rather than ASCII characters.

```
% set txt "a b c d e f A B C D 1 2 3 4"
a b c d e f A B C D 1 2 3 4
% lsort -dictionary $txt
1 2 3 4 A a B b C c D d e f
```

Notice how this differs from the default -ascii option.

```
% lsort $txt
1 2 3 4 A B C D a b c d e f
```

The -integer option can be used to sort a list of integer numbers.

```
% set txt "76 98 23 1 19 88"
76 98 23 1 19 88
% lsort -integer $txt
1 19 23 76 88 98
```

Likewise, the -real option can be used to sort a list of floating decimal point numbers.

```
% set txt "23.4 15.67 78.98  12.1 1.2"
23.4 15.67 78.98  12.1 1.2
% lsort -real $txt
1.2 12.1 15.67 23.4 78.98
```

The last sort option is -command, which requires the name of an external command procedure to perform the actual sort.

## Tcl Arrays

In addition to strings and lists, Tcl also provides support for arrays. Arrays are a collection of elements, just like lists. The difference is each element of an array has its own name.

Tcl arrays may be used anywhere simple variables may be used. A good example of this is the **set** command. You can create an array variable with the **set** command by appending an element name to the variable name and enclosing it in ( ) characters.

```
set ages(John)   32
set ages(Dave)   42
set ages(Helen)  28
set ages(Betty)  16
```

You can interrogate the value of an array with the **set** command, just as you would for a simple variable.

```
%set ages(John)
32
```

The element names are case sensitive, which means that attempting to reference ages(john) in the preceding example would result in a Tcl error. Element names may be any arbitrary string, including, but not restricted to, integers. Tcl arrays are often referred to as associative arrays because you are not restricted to numeric indexes as you are in languages like C.

### Multidimensional Arrays

Tcl only implements single dimensional arrays. However, you can simulate multidimensional arrays by concatenating multiple indices into a single element name. For example you can simulate a two-dimensional array spreadsheet as shown here.

```
set spreadsheet(1,1) 10
set spreadsheet(1,2) 15
set spreadsheet(2,1) 20
set spreadsheet(2,3) 25

set row 1,
set col 2
set spreadsheet($row,$col)
15
```

Because the element name is always treated as a single string, spaces will change the interpretation of the string so that spreadsheet(1,2) is not the same as spreadsheet(1, 2). It will also cause an error when using the Tcl set command because the space will cause the characters 2) to show up as a third argument.

## The array Command

Tcl provides the **array** command for working with arrays. The **array** command is actually a collection of commands that operate on arrays. As such, it requires an option specifying which operation you wish to perform on the array. This is similar to the list and **string** commands.

All of the following examples will operate on the array used in the previous example.

```
set ages(John)  32
set ages(Dave)  42
set ages(Helen) 28
set ages(Betty) 16
```

### Getting Array Info: array exists, array names, array size

One of the more common array commands is **array exists**, which is used to determine if a specific variable is an array. The command returns 1 if the variable is an array, 0 if it is not.

```
% array exists ages
1
```

The **array names** command can be used to return a list containing all the element names in the array.

```
% array names ages
Betty Helen Dave John
```

You may supply a glob-style *pattern* to the **array names** command, in which case the command will return only those array element names that match the pattern.

```
%  array names ages Da*
Dave
```

The **array size** command returns the number of elements in the array. If the variable is not an array, then 0 is returned.

```
% array size ages
4
```

## Searching Arrays:

The array command provides four options for searching through an array, one element at a time. State information is maintained from one command to the next so that successive operations produce the proper results.

To start the search, execute the array startsearch command. This command returns a search identifier which is used to identify which search subsequent commands will refer to because it is possible to have multiple searches executing at the same time against a single array.

The array nextelement command is used to return the next element in the search. If all elements in the array have been returned, this command will return an empty string. Because some elements of the array may actually contain an empty string, the array anymore command is provided to validate the end of the search. The array donesearch command terminates the search, specified by the search id, against the specified array.

```
%  set search_id [array startsearch ages]
s-1-ages
%  array nextelement ages $search_id
Betty
%  array nextelement ages $search_id
Helen
% array anymore ages $search_id
1
% array nextelement ages $search_id
Dave
% array nextelement ages $search_id
John
% array nextelement ages $search_id
% array anymore ages $search_id
0
% array  donesearch ages $search_id
%
```

## Converting Arrays to Lists: array get

The array get command returns a list of name/value pairs from the specified array. The name contains the element name and the value contains the value held by this array element. The order in which the elements are returned is undefined.

```
% array get ages
Betty 16 Helen 28 Dave 42 John 32
```

You may specify an optional *pattern* to restrict the name/value pairs that are returned by the command. The pattern follows glob-style pattern matching rules.

```
% array get ages Dav*
Dave 42
```

### Converting Lists to Arrays: array set

The **array set** command is provided for converting lists to arrays. The list must have the form returned by the **array get** command. The command takes the elements two at a time and assigns the first element as the array name and the second element as the value for that array element.

```
% array set new_ages "Sam 45 George 34 Sally 29 Ruth 47"
% array names new_ages
Sally George Sam Ruth
```

If the name of an existing array is given to the **array set** command, then the elements specified are added to the existing array.

```
% array set ages "Sam 45 George 34 Sally 29 Ruth 47"
% array names ages
Betty Helen Dave Sally George Sam Ruth John
```

# Pattern Matching

Tcl provides two commands that deal specifically with matching patterns in strings. They are known by the names "glob" and "regular expression." The simplest of these is the glob-style pattern matching. The term is derived from the file name expansion in UNIX, which is called globbing. Glob-style pattern matching is easy to learn but lacks the power of regular expression pattern matching. For a discussion of this topic, see String Manipulation on page 411.

The second form is known as regular expression pattern matching. Tcl's implementation of regular expression pattern matching is based on Henry Spencer's publicly available implementation.

Regular expressions have a different set of characters than glob-style pattern matching as described in the previous section on string handling. Table B-3 shows the special characters that may be used in a regular expression.

**Table B-3** Regular Expression Pattern Matching Characters

| Character(s) | Meaning |
|---|---|
| . | Matches any single character. |
| ^ | When used as the first character in the regular expression, this character signifies the beginning of the input string. |
| $ | When used as the last character in the regular expression, this character signifies the end of the input string. |
| * | Matches 0 or more occurrences of the preceding atom.[a] |
| ? | Matches zero or one instance of the preceding atom. |
| + | Matches 1 or more occurrences of the preceding atom. |
| \x | Matches the literal character x. |
| ( ) | Used to group a subpattern. Subpatterns are treated as an atom. |
| [chars] | Matches any single character in chars. You may specify a range of characters to match by using a hyphen between characters. As an example, [f-m] will match any single character between f and m, inclusive. If the first character is ^, it indicates that the match will be made against any characters not contained in chars. |
| \| | Indicates an OR operation. For example "regexp1 \| regexp2" will check for a match of either regexp1 or regexp2. |

[a]. An atom is the basic building block of regular expressions. The smallest atom is a single character.

The basic building block of a regular expression is called an atom, and most regular expressions will contain one or more atoms. The smallest atom is a single character. The regular expression "Dan" will match any string containing these letters, which includes "Dandelion" or "Jerry and Dan". The ^ character, as the first character of the pattern, will anchor the pattern to the beginning of the string being tested. This will cause the pattern ^Dan to match "Dandelion" but not "Jerry and Dan". The $ character as the last character of the pattern will anchor the pattern to the end of the string being tested. This will cause the pattern Dan$ to match "Jerry and Dan" but not "Dandelion".

Parentheses may be used to group pieces of a pattern together. This is useful when you want to apply characters such as the * to a whole expression. For example the following pattern, (Jerry)(+and+)(Dan), matches the word "Jerry", followed by the word "and" with any number of spaces before or after it, followed by the word "Dan". Many patterns like this can be specified just as easily without the braces, but, as you will see in a moment, the braces allow you to extract sections from the input string.

Ranges of characters are specified with square brackets. The expression [abc] will match any character in the set of a, b, or c. You may use a hyphen between characters to more easily specify ranges of characters. The pattern [a-z] will match any character between the letters a and z.

The Tcl **regexp** command is used to perform regular expression matching. The procedure prototype is as follows:

> regexp *?switches? exp string ?matchVar? ?subMatchVar subMatchVar ...?*

This **regexp** command will match the regular expression *exp* against *string* and return a 1 if a match is found and 0 if no match is found. The following example will test a string to see if it contains a single positive integer.

```
% regexp {^[0-9]+$} 546
1
```

This example will only return a 1 if a single positive integer containing no white space or alphanumeric characters is detected.

You will notice that the regular expression in the preceding example, was placed inside curly braces. This is because certain regular expression characters, such as the dollar sign or the square brackets, have special significance to the Tcl parser. You can escape these characters with a backslash character or you can enclose the pattern in curly braces { } to prevent the Tcl parser from performing substitution on the expression before it is sent to the regular expression parser. Be wary of extra spaces inside the curly braces, because the regular expression parser will treat these as part of the regular expression pattern.

If the *matchVar* and *subMatchVar* arguments are supplied, the **regexp** command will fill in these variables with the matching substrings found in *string*. For example:

```
% set date "January 27 1999"
```

```
January 27 1999
% regexp {^([A-Z][a-z]+) ([0-9]+) ([0-9]+)+$} $date str month day year
1
% set str
January 27 1999
% set month
January
% set day
27
% set year
1999
%
```

This regular expression matches any date of the format "month day year" and updates the variables at the end of the command with the various substrings that are found in the expression. The entire matched string is always placed into the *matchVar* variable, which is always the first variable specified. The remaining substrings are placed in order into the remaining *subMatchVar* variables. In this case the month is placed into the variable *month*, the day into the variable *day* and the year into the variable *year*.

This regular expression is a little harsh for matching date strings because it won't accept extra spaces anywhere in the string and does not tolerate things like a comma between the day and the year. It is easy to adjust as follows.

```
% set date "  January 27,   1999"
   January 27,   1999
%  regexp {^ *([A-Z][a-z]+) +([0-9]+)[, ] *([0-9]+)} $date str month
day year
1
%  set date "  January 27 1999"
   January 27 1999
% regexp {^ *([A-Z][a-z]+) +([0-9]+)[, ] *([0-9]+)} $date str month day
year
1
% set date "  January 27,,1999"
   January 27,,1999
% regexp {^ *([A-Z][a-z]+) +([0-9]+)[, ] *([0-9]+)} $date str month day
year
0
```

The new expression allows for one or more spaces between each word and a comma immediately following the day. The first two date strings match this new pattern. The third string does not match because there are two commas after the day. As you can see, regular expressions can become quite complicated. In fact there are several books devoted to nothing but regular expression pattern matching.

The **regexp** command has two options that can be used to alter its behavior. The -**index** will cause the character position of various matches to be stored away in the *matchVar* and *subMatchVar* arguments rather than the actual characters themselves.

```
% regexp -indices {^([A-Z][a-z]+) ([0-9]+) ([0-9]+)+$} $date str month
day year
1
% set str
0 14
% set month
0 6
% set day
8 9
% set year
11 14
%
```

The -**nocase** option can be used to ignore the case of the characters in the string to be searched.

```
%  regexp {[A-Z]+} hello
0
% regexp -nocase {[A-Z]+} hello
1
%
```

The first attempt to match the string "hello" failed because the pattern is looking for only uppercase characters. The -**nocase** option can be used to force the case to be ignored, resulting in a match.

A close cousin of the **regexp** command is the **regsub** command. This command can be used to perform substitution on a string based on some regular expression.

> regsub *?switches? exp string subSpec varName*

The **regsub** command looks for the regular expression *exp* in *string*. If a match is found, then the characters that match are replaced with the contents of *subSpec*. The resulting string is placed into *varName*.

```
% regsub hot "It is very hot today" cold new_string
1
% set new_string
It is very cold today
%
```

This simple example looks for the word "hot" and replaces it with "cold". The new string that results is placed into the variable new_string. The regsub command returns the number of substitutions that it performed. In this case only a single substitution was performed, so the command returned 1. By default the regsub command substitutes only the first match that is found. The following code only substitutes the first space character with an underscore and returns 1 for the number of substitutions that were made.

```
% regsub " " "It is very hot today" "_" new_string
1
% set new_string
It_is very hot today
```

You can force the regsub command to substitute all matches it finds by using the -all option. The following example substitutes all space characters found with an underscore and returns 4 for the number of substitutions that were made.

```
% regsub -all " " "It is very hot today" "_" new_string
4
% set new_string
It_is_very_hot_today
%
```

The -nocase option is also available for the regsub command and has the same meaning as it did for the regexp command previously described. You can also use the -- option to mark the end of the options. This will force the next argument to be treated as *exp* even if it starts with a dash.

## Control Flow Commands

Tcl provides commands for controlling the execution flow of a program. These commands are very similar to the control flow commands provided in the C programming language.

### Conditional Statements

The if command will conditionally execute code based on the results of an expression evaluation. The Tcl if command understands all the traditional clauses supported by the C programming language. The use of then is implied and seldom used.

if expr1 ?then? body1 elseif expr2 ?then? body2 elseif ... ?else? ?bodyN?

The if command evaluates *expr1* and executes *body1* if the boolean result of *expr1* is true. The expression must evaluate to a boolean result. In Tcl a boolean false value is 0 and any other value is considered true. If *expr1* evaluates to be true, then *body1* is executed and the evaluation of the if command completes. If *expr1* evaluates to be false, then *expr2* is evaluated, if it is present. If *expr2* evaluates to true, then *body2* is executed. Any number of elseif statements are permissible in the if command, but only the body of code associated with the first true expression will be evaluated.

The following code checks to see if a number is positive, negative, or zero, and prints the appropriate finding.

```
if { $x > 0 } {
   puts "positive number found"
} elseif { $x < 0 } {
   puts "negative number found"
} else {
   puts "zero found"
}
```

Many of the Tcl commands return binary values, which allow them to be used directly inside of the if command. The following code uses the strcmp command to test the contents of the variable *username* for valid user names.

```
if { [strcmp $username Mary] } {
   puts "Valid user Mary detected"
} elseif { [strcmp $username John] } {
   puts "Valid user John detected"
} else {
   puts "Invalid user $username detected"
}
```

In the preceding example, command substitution using the square brackets is used to execute the strcmp command inside the if command. It's very common to evaluate a Tcl command inside the expression portion of an if command.

Oftentimes there may be numerous comparisons that have to be made inside a single if statement. The Tcl switch command provides a more abbreviated syntax for these scenarios.

switch ?options? string pattern body ?pattern body ...?
switch ?options? string {pattern body ?pattern body ...?}

The switch command evaluates the *body* of code associated with the *pattern* that matches *string*. The patterns are tested in the order that they appear in the command. An optional default string may be used, which will always be executed if none of the other patterns match *string*.

The switch command accepts four options, three of which determine the type of pattern matching to use. These options are listed in Table B-4.

**Table B-4** Options to switch Command

| Option | Description |
|--------|-------------|
| -exact | Uses literal string comparison to check for an exact match. This is the default for the switch command. |
| -glob | This option specifies the glob-style pattern matching. This is the same type of matching performed on the strcmp command. See Table B-2 on page 412 for a description of the glob-style special characters. |
| -regexp | Use this option if you want to use a regular expression for your patterns. Regular expressions are more powerful than glob-style pattern matching. |
| -- | Marks the end of the options. The argument that follows will be treated as the string to match even if it begins with a leading dash (-) character. |

## Looping: for, foreach, while

Tcl also provides traditional looping control. The for and while commands are very nearly identical to other languages, like C, while the foreach command is unique to Tcl and allows iterating through each element of a Tcl list.

The for command requires four arguments. *Start*, *next*, and *body* are treated as normal Tcl command strings. *Test* is treated as an expression to be evaluated.

    for start test next body

Command execution proceeds as follows. The for command invokes the Tcl interpreter to execute *start*. It then evaluates *test* and if the result is non-zero it invokes the Tcl interpreter on *body*. The command continues by invoking the Tcl interpreter on *next* and then evaluating *test* again. If *test* is still non-zero, then *body* is executed again. This process continues until *test* evaluates to zero.

If a **continue** command is encountered in *body*, then any commands left in *body* are skipped and *test* is evaluated again to decide if the looping should continue. If a **break** command is executed inside of *body*, then the for command terminates and processing continues with the next Tcl command in the script.

The for command returns an empty string upon completion.

```
% for { set i 0 } { $i <= 5 } {incr i} { puts "i is now equal to $i" }
i is now equal to 0
i is now equal to 1
i is now equal to 2
i is now equal to 3
i is now equal to 4
i is now equal to 5
```

The **while** command requires only two arguments:

    while test body

In this command *body* is executed if *test* evaluates to a non-zero value. The evaluation of *test* is performed first so it is possible for the loop to not execute the statements in *body* at all if *test* initially evaluates false (a zero value). In general any loop that can be accomplished with the for command can also be executed with a while loop.

```
% while { $i <= 5 } { puts "i is now equal to $i" ; incr i }
i is now equal to 0
i is now equal to 1
i is now equal to 2
i is now equal to 3
i is now equal to 4
i is now equal to 5
%
```

The **foreach** command accepts three arguments:

    foreach varname list body

This command is unique to Tcl and allows you to iterate through the elements of a list. It is not necessary to know the length of the list up front.

```
% set txt "The quick brown fox jumped over the lazy dog"
The quick brown fox jumped over the lazy dog
% foreach word $txt { puts $word }
The
quick
brown
fox
```

```
jumped
over
the
lazy
dog
%
```

The same results can always be achieved with a for loop or while loop; however, you must then determine the length of the list with the **llength** command and extract the words from the list with the **lindex** command.

```
% for { set i 0 } {$i < [llength $txt] } {incr i } {puts [lindex $txt
$i] }
The
quick
brown
fox
jumped
over
the
lazy
dog
%
```

# File Access Commands

Tcl provides a rich set of commands for dealing with file I/O. The commands are similar to the standard file I/O library provided in the C programming language. Likewise, the file facility may be used to access the same types of devices as it's C language counterpart. These include disk files, serial devices, and running processes. Network access is provided by the **socket** command, discussed later in this appendix.

### Opening and Closing Files: open, close

The **open** command opens a file and returns a file handle. The calling convention is similar to the *fopen* command in C.

open *fileName access permissions*

The first argument, *fileName*, is the name of the file to open, and the second argument is the access mode, which will determine how the file may be accessed after it is opened. If a new file is being created, then permissions may be used to set the permissions for the new file. Permissions is an integer value and defaults to 0666.

There are six choices for the access mode.

| | |
|---|---|
| a | Opens the file for read-only access. If the file does not exist, a new empty file is created. The initial access point is set to the end of the file. |
| a+ | Opens the file for read and write access. If the file does not exist, a new empty file is created. The initial access point is set to the end of the file. |
| r | Opens the file for read-only access. This is the default mode for the **open** command. |
| r+ | Opens the file for reading and writing. The file must already exist. |
| w | Opens the file for write-only access. If the file exists, it is truncated to the beginning of the file, otherwise the file is created. |
| w+ | Opens the file for reading and writing. If the file exists, it is truncated to the beginning of the file, otherwise the file is created. |

The file handles returned by the **open** command comprise a simple string. Here we see the value of the file handle returned by the **open** command is file3. Once a file is open, you may use this string directly when accessing files or assign it to a variable and use the contents of the variable to access the file.

```
% set fptr [open test.txt w+]
file3
```

The **close** command is provided to close a file opened with the **open** command. The only argument required by the **close** command is the file handle returned by the **open** command.

```
% set fptr [open test.txt w+]
file3
close $fptr
%
```

## Command Pipelines

If the first character of the *fileName* argument is the pipe (|) character, the remaining characters are treated as a command pipeline to invoke. For example the following code would open a command pipeline to a telnet session on specified *host_name* and *port*. You could then use the **puts** and **gets** commands to read and write to the telnet connection.

```
%set tnet [open {|telnet host_name port} w+]
file3
%
```

## Connecting to Serial Devices

*Filename* may also reference a serial device. In this case the device is opened and initialized in a platform-dependent manner. On Windows platforms the name of the serial device is typically comX:, where X is the number of the port that you are opening. On UNIX platforms the name of the serial device is /dev/ttyX. The following code would open com port 3 for reading and writing on a Windows-based platform.

```
%set comptr [open :com3 w+]
file3
```

Once the serial device is open, you can use the **fconfigure** command with the **-mode** option to configure the attributes of the serial port.

```
% set comptr [open com1: w+]
file84
% fconfigure file84 -mode 9600,n,8,1
```

This example configures the serial port for 9,600 baud, no parity, 8 data bits, and one stop bit. The parameters to the **-mode** option are comma-separated values in the following order: *baud-rate*, *parity*, *data-size*, *stop-bits*.

You can interrogate the current configuration of a port by executing the **fconfigure** command and specifying just the channel identifier.

```
% set comptr [open com1: w+]
file84
% fconfigure file84 -mode 9600,n,8,1
% fconfigure file84
-blocking 1 -buffering full -buffersize 4096 -eofchar {? {}} -
translation {autocrlf} -mode 9600,n,8,1
%
```

Connections to serial devices are closed with the close command in the same manner as normal files are closed.

## Interfacing to the File System

Tcl provides several other commands for interfacing to the underlying file system. The file command is actually a set of commands where the first argument defines the option to be invoked. The format of the command is

    file options ?arg arg ...?

For example the file tail command can be used to separate the file name from the rest of a pathname.

```
% set pathname /usr/local/bin/tclsh
/usr/local/bin/tclsh
% file tail $pathname
tclsh
%
```

Most of these commands are straightforward and require very little explanation to use. Table B-5 gives a brief description of each of the options to the file command.

**Table B-5** file Command Summary

---

file *atime name*
    This command returns the last time the file *name* was accessed. The number returned is the number of seconds from midnight on January 1, 1970.

file *dirname name*
    This command is used to extract the directory portion of the file name. It returns all characters in *name* up to but not including the final / character, or dot (.) if name contains no slashes, or / if the last slash in *name* is its first character.

file *executable name*
    Returns 1 if *name* is executable by the current user and 0 if it is not.

file *exists name*
    Returns 1 if *name* exists and is accessible by the current user. Otherwise 0 is returned.

Table B-5 file Command Summary (Continued)

`file extension name`

Retrieves the file extension including the dot. An empty string is returned if there is no valid file extension in *name*.

`file isdirectory name`

Returns 1 if *name* is a directory and 0 if it is not.

`file isfile name`

Returns a 1 if *name* is a file and 0 if it is not.

`file lstat name array_name`

Invokes the lstat system call on *name* and constructs an array with associated elements to those returned by lstat and places it into *array_name*. The following elements are set:

atime, ctime, dev, gid, ino, mode, mtime, nlink, size, uid

If *name* refers to a link, then information about the link, not the file, is returned by this command. The file stat command can be used to retrieve information about the file.

`file mtime name`

Returns the time the file was last modified. The time is a string containing the number of seconds from midnight on January 1, 1970.

`file owned name`

Returns a 1 if *name* is owned by the current user, 0 if it is not.

`file readable name`

Returns a 1 if *name* is readable by the current user and 0 if it is not.

`file readlink name`

Returns the name of the file that the symbolic link *name* points to.

`file rootname name`

Returns the valid root name in *name*. This is all the characters up to but not including the last dot character. If no dot character exists in *name* or no dot character exists in *name* after the last slash (/) character, then *name* is returned.

`file size name`

Returns the size of *name*, as a number of bytes, represented as a decimal string.

**Table B-5** file Command Summary (Continued)

---

file *tail name*
> Returns all the characters in *name* after the last / character. If no slash characters are contained in *name*, then *name* is returned.

file *type name*
> Returns the type of *name*, which will be one of the following:
>
> > file, directory, characterSpecial, blockSpecial, fifo, link, or socket

file *writable*
> Returns 1 if the file is writable by the current user.

---

## File I/O: puts, gets

Writing to files is accomplished with the **puts** command. The only required argument to this command is the string to be written. In this case the string is simply written to standard out.

```
%puts "HELLO WORLD"
HELLO WORLD
```

You may specify an optional file id, which causes the string to be written to the designated file. The file must have been opened with the **open** command. The **gets** command is provided to read information from a specified file. Like the **puts** command, if you do not specify a file id, the string is obtained from standard in. This example creates a file, writes two lines of text to the file, and closes it.

```
% set fptr [open test.txt w+]
file3
% puts $fptr "Sending one line to the file"
% puts $fptr "Sending another line to the file"
% close $fptr
```

A file named test.txt will now exist in the current working directory with the following contents:

```
Sending one line to the file
Sending another line to the file
```

# Procedures

Procedures group a commonly executed sequence of commands, allowing them to be executed as a single command. In addition to this, procedures provide a new local scope for variables. That is to say, variables defined inside a procedure are not visible outside the procedure. The proc command is used to define a Tcl procedure.

> proc name parameters body

The procedure will be known by *name*, which will be added to the list of commands understood by the Tcl interpreter. The next argument contains a list of *parameters*. This is the way that information can be passed into (or out of) the procedure from the code that executes it. The last argument is the actual *body* of code to be executed. This body argument may contain any commands currently defined, including standard Tcl commands or user-defined procedures.

You may create and invoke procedures from inside the Tcl shell.

```
%  proc add { num1 num2 } { expr $num1 + $num2 }
% add 4 5
9
```

By default procedures return the results from the last command they execute. Here, the result of the expr command was returned to the console because we were executing under the Tcl shell but could be assigned to a variable just as easily.

```
% set result [add 4 5]
9
% set result
9
```

## The return Command

Now, after the procedure executes, the result variable contains the value 9. The return command may be used to override this default behavior of returning the results of the last command.

> return *?-code code? ?-errorinfo info? ?-errorcode code? ?string?*

The return command causes execution to return immediately from the current procedure with *string* as the return value. If you do not specify a value for the *string* argument, an empty string is returned. All values returned using the return command are returned as strings.

The return command can be used to force the earlier stringMatch procedure to explicitly return a string describing the results of the match.

```
%  proc stringMatch { str1 str2 } {
       if { $str1 == $str2 } {
           return "str1 and str2 are equal"
       } else {
           return "str1 and str2 are not equal"
       }
    }
% stringMatch hello Howdy
str1 and str2 are not equal
%
```

## Forcing Errors with the return Command

The -code, -errorinfo, and -errorcode options to the return command are rarely used but do provide a way to return exceptional conditions (errors) back to the caller. The -code option is used to force the exception. The additional options, -errorcode and -errorinfo, can be used to provide additional information about the exceptional condition.

```
proc divide { num1 num2 } {
    if { $num2 == 0 } {
        return -code error "divide by 0 encountered"
    } else {
        return  [expr $num1/$num2]
    }
}
```

Here the -code option is used to force the divide procedure to return an error if the divisor (num2) is 0.

```
% divide 4 0
divide by 0 encountered
```

When the -code option is used, you may optionally store additional information into a variable named errorInfo by using the -errorinfo option. The -code error option causes the current procedure to terminate execution and return an error to the caller. If the caller does not handle the error (with a catch), then this unwinding process continues until the top level script terminates. At each step along the way, information is added to a global variable named errorInfo, which provides a useful trace of the error as the code unwinds. The -errorinfo option may be used by the procedure that produced the initial error to initialize the errorInfo global with a meaningful value. Additionally the -errorcode options allow the procedure that initiated the exception to store an error code into the global variable errorCode. Some additional values for the -code option are shown in Table B-6.

**Table B-6** Values for Code Option

| | |
|---|---|
| ok | This is a normal return and is the same as if the -code option was omitted. |
| error | Returns a completion code of TCL_ERROR, which causes the current procedure to terminate execution and return an error to the caller. If the caller does not handle the error (with a catch), then this unwinding process continues until the top level script terminates. |
| | The -errorinfo option may be used to initialize the errorInfo global variable. This variable is used to contain stack trace information as the execution unwinds. The -errorcode option can be used to place a value into the global errorCode. |
| return | Returns a completion code of TCL_RETURN, which will cause the calling procedure to return as well. |
| break | Returns a completion code of TCL_BREAK, which terminates the innermost nested loop of the calling code. |
| continue | Returns a completion code of TCL_CONTINUE, which terminates the current iteration of the innermost nested loop in the code that invoked the current procedure. |

Normally when executing from a Tcl script the -code option with a value of *error* will cause the currently executing script to terminate and display the associated error. When we executed the divide procedure from the tclsh, the "divide by 0 encountered" message was displayed, but the tclsh remains running. This is because the Tcl shell *catches* errors for you, displays the associated message, but does not terminate. If you were to call the divide procedure with the divisor set to 0 inside a Tcl script, the script would normally terminate, displaying the error message, unless the caller takes special precautions to handle the potential error.

## Catching Errors with the catch Command

The catch command is used to prevent errors from terminating the Tcl interpreter when errors are encountered. The catch command returns a decimal string value of 0 if no error was encountered during the execution of a script and 1 if an error was encountered. If *varname* is supplied, the string return value of script will be placed there:

> catch *script ?varname?*

In the following code, the divide command is executed inside a catch command. If an error occurs, the catch command returns 1, and result will contain the error string returned from divide.

```
% catch { divide 4 0 } result
1
% set result
divide by 0 encountered
%
```

If an error does not occur, the catch command returns 0, and result will contain the normal return value of the divide command.

```
% catch { divide 4 2 } result
0
% set result
2
```

## Default Argument Values in Procedures

You may also assign default values to procedure parameters by enclosing the parameter name and its default value in curly braces.

```
% proc add { {num1 7} {num2 3} } { expr $num1 + $num2 }
% add 15 3
18
% add 5
8
% add
10
```

In the first execution of the add procedure, both num1 and num2 parameters are supplied so the procedure adds them together to produce a result of 18. In the second execution only the first parameter is provided so the default value of 3 is used for num2, producing the value of 8. In the third execution no parameters are supplied so both default values are used yielding a value of 10.

## Passing Variable Number of Arguments to Procedures

It is sometimes necessary to pass variable lists of parameters to a procedure. This is accomplished by specifying the *args* keyword as the last parameter to the procedure.

```
proc add { args } {
    set count 0
    foreach number $args { set count [expr $count + $number] }
    return $count
}
% add 4 7 9 15
35
```

## Passing by Reference with the upvar Command

The default in Tcl is to pass value to procedures. That is to say, the procedure does not have access to the original variable that may have contained the value that was passed to it as an argument.

```
% proc stringChop { str length } {
    for { set i 0 } { $i < $length } { incr i} {
        append tmp_string [string index $str $i]
    }
    return $tmp_string
}
% stringChop "Here's a long string to chop" 10
Here's a l
%
```

In the preceding code example, the stringChop procedure will return the original string, passed to it in the *str* argument, trimmed to the number of characters specified in *length*. The contents of *str* are a copy of the original passed in by the caller so there is no way for the procedure to operate directly on the caller's original variable.

However, it is often desirable to modify the original variable in the caller's scope rather than to return a copy. This is known as pass by reference because the caller passes a reference to the variable rather than a copy of its value. In C this is typically accomplished with pointers. In Tcl the upvar command is used to resolve the name of a variable into a reference to the original.

```
% proc stringChop { str_name length } {
    upvar $str_name str
    for { set i 0 } { $i < $length } { incr i} {
        append tmp_string [string index $str $i]
    }
    set str $tmp_string
    return 1
}
% set txt "Here's a long string to chop"
% stringChop txt 10
1
% set txt
Here's a l
%
```

Here, the name of the **txt** variable (txt) was passed to the **stringChop** procedure rather than the value ($txt). The **upvar** command was then used to obtain a reference to the variable name contained in its *str_name* argument. The **stringChop** procedure then updates the caller's variable with the contents of the **tmp_string** variable with the chopped string that it builds internally. When the **stringChop** procedure returns, the caller's *txt* variable now contains the modified string.

# Network Communication

Network sockets provide communications between two computers connected to a network. Tcl provides excellent support for network sockets using the TCP protocol. This protocol is very popular in most network environments today and is the basis for other protocols like HTTP, telnet, and ftp. The TCP protocol handles all the issues of routing messages to the appropriate destination and provides automatic error recovery if data is lost or corrupted during transmission.

The type of network programming done with sockets is referred to as the client-server model because one end of the connection is designated as a client and the other end as a server. Generally, multiple client programs typically connect to a single server application. The server normally contains information that is desired by one or more client programs.

Tcl sockets can be used just like open files in your Tcl scripts. However, instead of opening them with the **open** command, you use the **socket** command. The socket command along with the **fconfigure** command provides the ability to build either client or server connections with just a few lines of code.

There are two versions of the command available. The first form is used to create client-side connections while the second form is used to create server connections.

socket *?options? host port*
socket *-server command ?options? port*

We will first consider the second form, which provides a server connection to a network socket. We will then come back and look at the first form that creates a client connection.

When the **socket** command is invoked with the **-server** option, it creates a *server* connection for the specified *port*. This means that Tcl will automatically accept connections to this port number whenever a client sends a message to the port.

Each time a connection is made, *command* will be executed with three additional arguments: the name of the new channel, the address of the client's host, and the client's port number. Command is written as a standard Tcl procedure but is automatically called whenever a socket connection is accepted from a client. This is referred to as a call back procedure, which is just a Tcl procedure that is to be executed when some future event happens.

It's actually possible to test the **socket** command from the Tcl shell although it is easier to write a couple of scripts. The following code was executed from the shell. This code calls the **socket** command and specifies the **accept** procedure as the call back to make when a socket connection is accepted. The **accept** procedure is then defined with the three arguments required for a socket call back procedure. These arguments are the socket id, the host making the connection, and the port being connected to.

```
% socket -server accept 5350
sock3
% proc accept {sock host port} {puts "Accepted socket from $host on
port $port"}
% vwait forever
```

The final command that is executed is the **vwait** command. The **vwait** command accepts a single argument, which is a variable name:

vwait *varname*

When the **vwait** command is executed, it causes the Tcl interpreter to enter what is known as an event loop, processing *events* as they become available and *blocking* (waiting) if no events exist. It continues processing events until some event causes the value of the variable *varName* to change. Once *varName* has been set, the **vwait** command will return. In this program the **vwait** command never returns! The variable *forever* in our example is never intended to be modified. The whole purpose of the **vwait** command is to cause the program to enter the *event loop* and wait for a socket connection.

Once you execute this command, the Tcl interpreter will wait for some event, such as a network socket message to be received. You can then start a second Tcl interpreter running and execute the following line:

```
> tclsh8.0
% socket localhost 5350
sock3
```

Once you execute this command, you will see the first Tcl shell print the line:

```
Accepted socket from 127.0.0.1 on port 2760
```

This indicates that the second Tcl interpreter successfully made a client connection to the first interpreter. There are two things to notice about the response from the server. The first is the 127.0.0.1 address. This will always indicate the local host, which was specified in the socket command from the client. The second item of interest is the port number (2760) that the server accepted the connection on. This number is assigned automatically by the underlying Tcl socket code whenever the server accepts a connection to the client and will change from connection to connection.

```
#!/usr/local/bin/tclsh8.0

proc process { sock } {

    if { [eof $sock] || [catch { gets $sock line}] } {
       puts "closing socket $sock"
       close $sock
    } elseif { $line != "" } {
       puts $line
       puts $sock "server: $line"
    }
    return 0
}
proc accept { sock addr port} {
    puts "Accept $sock from $addr port $port"
    fconfigure $sock -buffering line
```

```
        fileevent $sock readable [ list process $sock ]
        return 0
}

puts "Server started"
socket -server accept 5350
vwait   forever
```

This is all that can be done with this simple example, but it doesn't take many additional lines of code to build client and server script files that allow the client to send messages to the server and receive responses.

This code builds a server that accepts client connections and prints out any messages received from the client on the local console. It also echoes the string back to the client with the letters "server:" prepended to the text. This lets the client know that the server received the message.

This code is similar to the earlier example that was run from the Tcl shell but adds the **process** procedure, which prints out the messages received from the client. The last two lines of the file create the server socket connection, which will monitor port 5350 and enter the Tcl event loop, via the **vwait** command, to wait for messages from the client. The **socket** command has set up the **accept** procedure as the call back to make when a client connects to the server. This is the same as our simple example. The **accept** procedure takes the three standard arguments that define the *socket*, the *host*, and the *port* being connected to. The **accept** procedure sets up another call back, process, to handle all incoming messages from the client.

This is accomplished with the **fileevent** command. This command tells Tcl to call the **process** procedure whenever the socket connection to the client becomes readable. The **fileevent** command has two standard formats:

> fileevent *channelId readable ?script?*
> fileevent *channelId writable ?script?*

The command waits for *channelId* to become *readable* or *writable* and then calls *script*. Waiting is done in the background so other processing may be occurring until the specific file event occurs. In order for this background waiting to occur, the Tcl event loop must be active. Once again, in a standard Tcl script file this is the purpose of the **vwait** command. (The **vwait** command is not necessary in Tk programs because the Tcl event loop is already running to process inputs from the various GUI widgets.)

Notice the expression [list process $sock] where you would expect to find the *script* argument to the fileevent command. This often confuses many Tcl programmers and generally requires some explanation. The fileevent command tucks away the contents of the script argument until the corresponding file event condition occurs and then tries to execute it from the *global* scope. This means that any variables that are passed in the script argument also have to be known in the global scope, which would not be the case for the sock variable declared inside the process procedure. The embedded list command causes the Tcl interpreter to replace the $sock variable with the actual string representation of the socket id, which can be used at a later time by the process procedure. The list command also formats the script argument appropriately to be executed by the Tcl interpreter later.

So, we now have a server program that is ready to accept messages from a client program. All we need now is a client to talk to the server. Building the client program is very straightforward as well.

The following code shows how simple the client program is. This program makes a connection to the server, running on port 5350, and then enters an infinite loop, reading lines from the keyboard and sending them to the server. The fconfigure command sets the client-side socket connection to line buffering. This causes messages to be sent a line at a time.

```
#!/usr/local/bin/tclsh8.0

proc process_socket {sock} {
    gets $sock line
    puts $line
}

proc process_stdin { channel } {
    global sock
    gets $channel line
    puts $sock $line
}

set sock [socket localhost 5350]
fconfigure $sock -buffering line
fileevent $sock readable [list process_socket $sock]
fileevent stdin readable [list process_stdin stdin]

vwait forever
```

This program sets up two call back procedures using the fileevent command. The first fileevent command establishes the process_socket procedure as the call back for handling messages from the server. Remember that the server was designed to echo the messages received from the client, so the client itself has to be able to process incoming messages. The **process_socket** procedure is identified as the call back for incoming socket messages. This procedure reads a line from the socket connection and prints the line to the console.

The second **fileevent** command sets up the **process_stdin** as the call back to make whenever there is a line to be read from the keyboard. The **process_stdin** procedure echoes this input line to the local console as well as sends it to the server. The **vwait** command, once again, causes the script to enter the Tcl event loop to wait for the file events that were just established.

If you have done any Tk programming, the concept of the Tcl event loop is probably second nature to you by now because it is the way input is handled for all Tk programs. If you are not familiar with this concept, it is worth studying because it eliminates the need to poll when you have asynchronous input coming into your program from multiple sources.

## Querying Tcl Internals

The Tcl **info** command is provided to interrogate the state of various internal aspects of the Tcl interpreter. With this command you can check for the existence of specific local and global variables, obtain the code body for user-defined procedures, check the current version of the Tcl interpreter, and much more. Once again, the **info** command is not a single command but a group of commands where the first argument selects the actual operation to be performed. For example you can use the **info exists** command to see if a specified variable name has been defined.

```
% info exists tmpvar
0
% set tmpvar 1
1
% info exists tmpvar
1
%
```

This command accepts the name of a variable and returns 1 if the variable has been defined and 0 if the variable does not exist. Another common use for the **info** command is to return a list of local or global variables defined by using the options locals or globals followed by a pattern. The pattern is a glob-style pattern so wildcard characters are permitted.

```
% info globals arg*
argv argv0 argc
```

In a similar fashion you can list commands that are currently available in the interpreter. The following code lists all the commands that begin with the letter l.

```
% info commands l*
list lrange lsearch lappend llength linsert lreplace load lindex lsort
```

Or you can list defined procedures by using the info procs command. Once again the only argument to this command is a glob-style pattern.

```
% info procs str*
stringWrite
```

The *args* and *body* options are provided for gathering information about defined procedures. The *args* option returns the names of the arguments to a procedure, as a Tcl list, and the *body* command actually returns the code for the specified procedure. The following code defines a procedure and then uses the *args* and *body* options to retrieve information about it.

```
% proc stringWrite { str } { puts $str }
% info args stringWrite
str
% info body stringWrite
 puts $str
%
```

If an argument to a procedure has a default value, the info default command can be used to find out what the default value is. The arguments to the info default command are the name of the procedure, the name of the argument in question, and the name of a user-defined variable where the default value is to be stored. If a default exists, the routine returns 1, otherwise it returns 0.

```
% proc stringWrite { {str {Hello World}} } { puts $str }
% info default stringWrite str buff
1
% set buff
Hello World
%
```

The remaining info commands are summarized in Table B-7.

**Table B-7** info Command Summary

info *cmdcount*
> Returns the number of Tcl commands executed since the interpreter was invoked.

info level ?number?
> If *number* is not specified, this command returns the current stack level as a zero-based integer where zero corresponds to the top level.
>
> If *number* is specified, this command returns the name and arguments of the procedure at the specified level as a Tcl list.

info library
> Returns the full path of the library directory where standard Tcl scripts are stored.

info script
> Returns the name of the script being evaluated. A null string is returned if no script is being evaluated.

info tclversion
> Returns the version number for the current Tcl interpreter in major.minor format. Changes to the minor portion of the version number indicate bug fixes, new features, and other changes that are backward compatible. Changes to the major version number indicate changes have been made that are incompatible with previous major versions.

info vars ?pattern?
> If *pattern* is not specified, this command returns a list of all variables currently accessible. If *pattern* is specified, the list is filtered according to *pattern* before being returned.

## Organizing Your Code

One of the most critical aspects of code design and implementation is structuring your code so that it can be easily reused in future projects. Fortunately, Tcl provides several nice features that make it easy to build reusable pieces of code, thereby reducing your development efforts on future projects.

### The source Command

The most basic command in this category is the **source** command. The **source** command lets you pull other Tcl script files into a currently executing program. Let's say you have a file named hello.tcl that contains the following procedure call.

```
proc hello_world { } {
    puts "HELLO WORLD"
}
```

You can execute **tclsh** from the command line, source in this file, and then call the procedure.

```
> tclsh
% source hello.tcl
% hello_world
HELLO WORLD
%
```

This allows you to split your project into manageable pieces that are segregated along logical boundaries. This makes it easier to have different people supporting different aspects of a project. The advantage of the **source** command is you do not have to put all the code into one file. The disadvantage of the **source** command is that you cannot easily keep track of version numbers. This problem is addressed with the **package** command.

### The package Command

Tcl 7.5 introduced a new package feature that simplifies the organization of your code. The **package** command allows you to easily break your code into reusable modules, also called packages. It also provides a way to associate a version number with each package. In this way different programs may request different versions of a package. Being able to specify a version number gives you the flexibility to update programs when appropriate (and convenient) rather than being forced to update the program each time a new version of the package becomes available.

The **package** command, like many other commands in Tcl, is actually a collection of commands. A required option to the command specifies which command to invoke. There are several options to the **package** command, but you will normally only use two, **package provide** and **package require**. Their calling syntax is shown here:

> package provide *name ?version?*
> package require *?-exact? name ?version?*

The **package provide** command is placed inside your packages, normally as one of the first lines, and specifies the *name* and *version* number of the package. For instance the first noncommented line of code in the cgi.tcl package, used in most of the CGI programs in this book is

```
package provide cgi.tcl 1.1
```

This specifies that the name of the package is cgi.tcl and 1.1 is the current version of the package. When assigning version numbers to your package, you should update the major revision number only when an interface change has occurred, meaning the calling sequence is different for one or more of the procedures in the package. Existing program code that tries to call the new procedures will most likely fail. This is the type of information that you want to know at a glance when you are evaluating the work necessary to upgrade your programs to the latest reusable packages.

Conversely, you should increment the minor revision number for any bug fix. In this way you can instantly determine if you can upgrade to the latest version without risk. Incrementing the minor revision number should never cause a program to break when you update the package with the latest bug fix. Updating to a package that has a major revision change will most likely break the program because the interface has been changed. Of course you would like to design the packages well enough up front that interface changes are rarely done once the package is released.

Once you define a package, you must use the **pkg_mkIndex** command to generate an index of the package. This index is used by the Tcl interpreter to keep track of what procedures are available inside the package.

> pkg_mkIndex *dir pattern ?pattern pattern ...?*

This command searches *dir* for *pattern(s)* and builds an index containing the procedures available inside the files specified by *pattern*. As an example, to build the index for cgi.tcl package, you can execute the **pkg_mkIndex** command directly from the Tcl shell and specify the directory to use and the pattern to search for.

```
> tclsh
% pkg_mkIndex /usr/local/lib/cgi.tcl *.tcl
%
```

When the Tcl interpreter starts up, it searches the paths specified by a variable named **auto_path** and builds a simple internal database of the packages that are available. The **package require** command can then be used for loading packages into an executing program. You can even load packages into the interpreter from the Tcl shell. The following example shows how the cgi.tcl library can be loaded directly from the Tcl shell.

```
% package require cgi.tcl
1.1
%
```

This code causes the Tcl interpreter to search its internal database of packages available to locate the package that has been asked for. This is the way that the cgi.tcl library is loaded into the CGI programs in this book. If the **package require** command is successful, it returns the version number of the package that is loaded. If it is not, it returns an error.

The **package** command maintains a simple database of the packages that are available to be loaded into the current Tcl interpreter. Tcl makes use of a global variable named **auto_path** to determine where to look for packages. In a standard UNIX environment, the **auto_path** variable is set by default to the following values:

```
> tclsh8.0
% set auto_path
/usr/local/lib /usr/local/lib
%
```

If more than one path appears, machine-dependent packages (such as binary shared libraries) should be stored under the first path and machine-independent packages (those containing only Tcl scripts) should be placed under the second path. As you can see in the preceding lines of code, the paths may be the same.

The **auto_path** variable is just a list of pathnames that will be searched when you ask the Tcl interpreter for a particular package. If you need to change the value of the **auto_path** variable, you should use the **lappend** command to append new values to the end of this list rather than simply using the **set** command, which would overwrite the contents of the **auto_path** variable.

```
% lappend auto_path /my/package/directory
```

```
/usr/local/lib/ /usr/local/lib /my/package/directory
%
```

You can also affect the **auto_path** variable when the Tcl interpreter is initializing by setting the TCLLIBPATH environment variable to your desired path. When the Tcl interpreter first starts, it executes a script named init.tcl that performs various initialization tasks. One of these is to update the **auto_path** variable with the contents of the TCLLIBPATH environment variable.

```
>TCLLIBPATH=/my/package/directory
> export TCLLIBPATH
> tclsh
%  set auto_path
/my/package/directory /usr/local/lib/tcl8.0 /usr/local/lib
%
```

It is preferable to place packages in one of the default directories specified by the **auto_path** variable so programs don't have to worry about the details of where the packages live. If this is not an option, then use the **lappend** command or the TCLLIBPATH environment variable to change the **auto_path** settings. For the examples in this book, the packages were placed into the /usr/local/lib sub-directory.

## Namespaces

Prior to Tcl 8.0 all procedures existed at the same level and variables existed at one of two levels. Variables defined outside of procedures were in the global scope and could be seen by all procedures. Variables defined inside procedures were assigned a local scope and were available only to the procedure that contained them. The **namespace** command is new to Tcl 8.0 and allows you to build new scopes referred to as *namespaces*.

The **namespace** command allows you to bind a group of variables and procedures together so they exist in a separate scope from other Tcl procedures.

The concept is similar to objects in C++ where one object may contain many methods (function calls). A method in one object may have the same name as the method in another object without naming collisions. Likewise in Tcl, you may use the **namespace** command to group procedures together in an object-like fashion knowing they will be separate and distinct from other procedures.

The **namespace** command is similar to the other Tcl commands in that it represents a group of commands. The most common of the **namespace** command options are **eval, export,** and **import.** To create a namespace you use the **namespace eval** command. Typically you will use the **namespace export** command inside the namespace you create to identify the procedures that you wish to make available to the outside world. This allows you to hide local procedures that are intended for internal use only.

```
#!/usr/local/bin/tclsh

namespace eval fifo {

    namespace export push pull
    variable buffer

    proc push { value } {
        variable buffer
        # add the new item to the end of the list
        lappend buffer $value
        return 1
    }

    proc pull { } {
        variable buffer
        # return the first item and delete it from the list
        if { $buffer == "" } {
            return ""
        } else {
            set item [lindex $buffer 0]
            set buffer [lreplace $buffer 0 0]
            return $item
        }
    }
}
```

The preceding code creates a new namespace, named **fifo,** containing two procedures named **push** and **pull.** The **namespace export** command is used to make both the **push** and **pull** procedures available for use outside the **fifo** namespace.

Let's assume that this code is in a file named fifo.tcl. You could source the code in from the Tcl shell and execute the fifo commands by using the fully qualified namespace command name.

```
% source fifo
% fifo::push value1
1
% fifo::push value2
```

```
1
% fifo::push value3
1
% fifo::pull
value1
% fifo::pull
value2
% fifo::pull
value3
%
```

If you do not wish to use the fully qualified name to refer to the command, you can use the **namespace import** command to make the commands available in your current namespace.

```
% source fifo.tcl
% namespace import fifo::*
% info commands p*
pwd pid proc pkg_mkIndex package push pull puts
% push value1
1
% push value2
1
% pull
value1
% pull
value2
```

You can use the **namespace children** command to see which namespaces are currently loaded into the current namespace.

```
% namespace children
::fifo ::auto_mkindex_parser ::tcl
```

And you can use the **namespace delete** command to delete a loaded namespace.

```
% namespace delete ::fifo
% namespace children
::auto_mkindex_parser ::tcl
```

The remaining **namespace** commands are summarized in Table B-8.

**Table B-8** The namespace Command

---

`namespace children ?namespace? ?pattern?`

Returns a list of fully qualified child namespaces, matching *pattern*, that belong to namespace *namespace*. If namespace is not specified, children of the current namespace are returned. If the optional glob-style pattern is specified, then only children names that match *pattern* will be returned.

`namespace code script`

Primarily used to build call back commands that deal with commands in another scope.

`namespace current`

Returns the fully qualified name for the current namespace.

`namespace delete ?namespace namespace ...?`

Deletes each *namespace* specified including all variables, procedures, and child namespaces contained in the namespace.

`namespace eval namespace arg ?arg ...?`

Evaluates each *arg* in namespace *namespace*. If *namespace* does not already exist, it is created. This is similar to executing code with the standard **eval** command except that the code is executed in the specified *namespace*.

`namespace export ?-clear? ?pattern pattern ...?`

Allows you to specify which commands are exported from a namespace. Each pattern may contain glob-style pattern matching characters but may not contain namespace qualifiers. The procedures specified by *pattern* do not have to exist when this command is executed.

`namespace forget ?pattern pattern ...?`

Removes commands that were previously imported from another namespace. The pattern arguments must contain qualified namespace names (containing the :: characters) and may also include glob-style pattern matching characters.

`namespace import ?-force? ?pattern pattern ...?`

Used to import commands from another namespace. The commands must be declared as exportable (with the **namespace export** command) by the other namespace before they can be imported. Importing the commands eliminates the need to refer to the command by its fully qualified name (junk::command1) and allows you to refer to it with its abbreviated name (command1).

**Table B-8** The namespace Command (Continued)

---

`namespace inscope` *`namespace arg ?arg ...?`*

Concatenates *args* into a script and executes them in the context of another namespace. This command is not normally called directly. Instead the namespace code command is used to build the namespace inscope command.

`namespace origin` *`command`*

Returns the fully qualified name of *command*. The command must have been imported using the namespace import command.

`namespace parent` *`?namespace?`*

Returns the fully qualified name of the parent namespace of *namespace*.

`namespace qualifiers` *`string`*

Returns the namespace qualifier portion of *string*. For the string ::junk::yard::dog this command would return ::junk::yard.

`namespace tail` *`string`*

Returns the command name at the end of a fully qualified *string*. For the string ::junk::yard::dog this command would return dog.

`namespace which` *`?-command? ?-variable? name`*

Returns the fully qualified name for *name*. If no flag is supplied, then name is treated as a command. If the -variable flag is supplied, then *name* is considered to be a variable and looked up accordingly.

---

# Appendix C

## cgi.tcl Reference

This appendix contains a reference for the cgi.tcl package. The cgi.tcl package contains a number of procedures that make it easier to construct dynamic Web pages from inside your CGI code.

This package should not be confused with one of the same name in the public domain that was written by Don Libes. The cgi.tcl package contained in this book was developed without knowledge of Libes's package and has proved sufficient for all the applications the author has been involved with. If you're interested in a more feature-rich package (at about twice the size) then check out Libes's package at http://expect.nist.gov/cgi.tcl/.

In order to use the cgi.tcl package contained in this book effectively, you should have a good understanding of the Hypertext Markup Language (HTML). If you are not familiar with HTML, there are numerous books available that will help you develop an understanding of this language.

The procedure calls in the cgi.tcl package are written in such a way that dynamically generated HTML code can be returned immediately to the requesting Web browser or written to a disk file for retrieval at future dates.

This package uses a naming convention where all procedures are preceded by the letters tcl_, which should eliminate naming collisions with other packages. The package has been implemented without the use of the namespace facility, and is known to be compatible with Tcl version 7.6 and above.

The routines provided deal with three principal areas.

- Acquisition of CGI data: Two routines are provided for this function. They are cgi_parse and cgi_parse_cookie. These procedures take care of all the issues involved in obtaining the form data that was submitted by the client Web browser.
- Generation of HTML tag data: A large number of procedures are available for the dynamic generation of HTML code from your CGI programs. The bulk of the cgi.tcl library is geared toward this job.
- Generation of complete HTML pages: A number of convenient functions are provided that construct entire Web pages with a single procedure call.

## Procedure Summary

Table C-1 provides an alphabetical listing of the procedures available in the cgi.tcl library, along with a one-line description of each procedure's purpose. The remaining sections will describe these procedure calls in more detail.

**Table C-1** Description of Procedure Names in the cgi-tcl Package

| Procedure Name | Description |
|---|---|
| cgi_anchor | Returns a formatted string for an anchor |
| cgi_br | Generates the <BR> string |
| cgi_build_table | Completely builds an HTML table |
| cgi_checkbox | Writes out the code for a form checkbox |
| cgi_clink | Generates code for a link in color |
| cgi_counter | Reads a counter value from a file |
| cgi_decode | Support function for cgi_parse |
| cgi_dump_fields | Generates an HTML page displaying cgi fields |
| cgi_dump_text_file | Generates an HTML page displaying a text file |
| cgi_end | Closes an HTML page with the </HTML> tag |

**Table C-1** Description of Procedure Names in the cgi-tcl Package (Continued)

| Procedure Name | Description |
| --- | --- |
| cgi_fc | Generates the HTML code for colored font |
| cgi_form | Generates opening HTML code for a form |
| cgi_form_end | Generates ending HTML code for a form |
| cgi_h1 | Produces HTML code for a <H1> tag |
| cgi_h2 | Produces HTML code for a <H2> tag |
| cgi_h3 | Produces HTML code for a <H3> tag |
| cgi_h4 | Produces HTML code for a <H4> tag |
| cgi_h5 | Produces HTML code for a <H5> tag |
| cgi_h6 | Produces HTML code for a <H6> tag |
| cgi_header | Generates the HTML header code for a page |
| cgi_hidden | Generates the HTML code for a hidden field |
| cgi_hr | Generates the HTML code for a horizontal line |
| cgi_html_tag | Can be used to generate any type of generic HTML tag |
| cgi_li | Produces the HTML tag for a list item |
| cgi_link | Returns the HTML tag data for a link |
| cgi_ol | Creates the opening HTML code for an Ordered List |
| cgi_ol_end | Writes the closing tag for an HTML Ordered List |
| cgi_p | Generates HTML code for a paragraph break <P> |
| cgi_parse | Parses the cgi form data, if any |
| cgi_parse_cookies | Parses cookie data |
| cgi_password | Produces the HTML code for the form password element |
| cgi_pre | Beginning of preformatted text section |
| cgi_pre_end | End of preformatted text section |
| cgi_print_error | Generates HTML page with message |
| cgi_print_message | Generates HTML page with error and return link |
| cgi_puts | Writes to cgi_outStream |
| cgi_radio | Writes out the code for a form radio button |
| cgi_redirect | Used to redirect to another HTML form |
| cgi_select | Generates HTML code for a form select element |
| cgi_set_outstream | Used to set the cgi_outStream variable for future output |

**Table C-1** Description of Procedure Names in the cgi-tcl Package (Continued)

| Procedure Name | Description |
| --- | --- |
| cgi_submit | Generates the HTML code for a submit button |
| cgi_table | Opens an HTML table section |
| cgi_table_end | Closes an HTML table section |
| cgi_td | Writes a complete table data <TD> $str </TD> line |
| cgi_td_open | Opens an HTML table data <TD> section |
| cgi_td_end | Closes an HTML table data </TD> section |
| cgi_text | Generates the HTML code for text with size and color |
| cgi_text_field | Generates HTML code for a form text field |
| cgi_text_area | Generates HTML code for a form text area |
| cgi_tr | Opens an HTML table row <TR> section |
| cgi_tr_end | Closes an HTML table row </TR> section |
| cgi_ul | Writes the complete HTML code for an unordered list |
| cgi_validate_fields | Validates cgi data against a list of desired fields |
| cgi_validate_cookies | Validates cookies against a list of desired names |

As you can see, the list of procedure calls is rather lengthy. Most of the procedure names correspond to the HTML code they produce, making it easy to remember. It should not take long to familiarize yourself with the procedure calls if you have a good understanding of HTML syntax.

## Understanding the cgi.tcl Output

This section will familiarize you with the underlying concept of the cgi.tcl package output. The cgi.tcl package defaults to writing its output to standard out, which is the typical method of returning dynamically generated HTML pages to a requesting Web browser. There are cases, however, where you may wish to save the output to a disk file. This makes it easy to dynamically create static HTML pages for later use by your applications.

In a typical CGI program, all of the dynamically created HTML code is written to standard out, which has been redirected to the Web server that executed the CGI program. The Web server then returns this formatted output to the requesting Web browser. This flow is diagramed in Figure C-1.

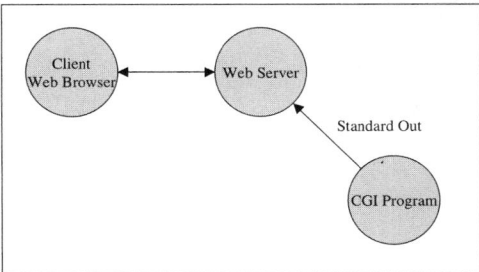

**Figure C-1** Data Flow from the CGI Program

Oftentimes you may want to redirect some dynamically created HTML code to a file, rather than have it immediately return to the browser. The cgi.tcl package is written to easily allow this redirection. All of the cgi.tcl procedures write to a channel named cgi_outstream, which is defaulted to standard out when you first load the package. If you wish to redirect the output to a file, simply open the file and then call the cgi_set_outstream procedure with the name of the channel you just opened. All future procedure calls made to the cgi.tcl package will now be sent to the file you specified with the cgi_set_outstream procedure call.

This flow is shown in Figure C-2.

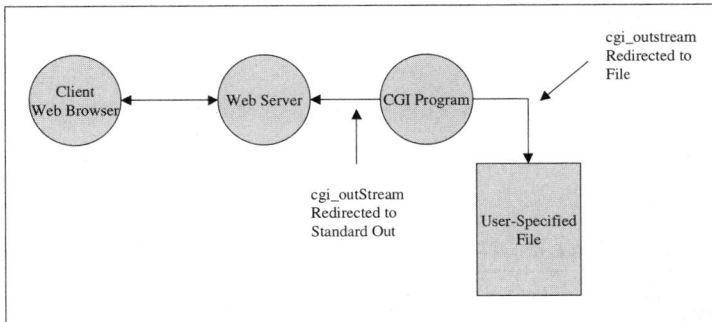

**Figure C-2** Redirecting Dynamically Created HTML Code to a File

You can easily alternate between sending output to a file and returning it to the requesting Web browser by repeatedly calling the cgi_set_outstream procedure with alternating channel names.

The following program will dynamically produce a file named test.html with the necessary code to write HELLO WORLD on any Web browser that points to the file.

```
#!/usr/local/bin/tclsh

package require cgi.tcl

set fptr [open hello.html w+]
cgi_set_outstream $fptr
cgi_header "HELLO WORLD" {bgcolor=white TEXT=black}
cgi_h4 "HELLO WORLD"
cgi_end
```

Executing this program will produce a file named hello.html in the same directory. The hello.html file will contain the following HTML code.

```
Content-Type: text/html

<HTML>
<HEAD>
<TITLE>HELLO WORLD</TITLE>
</HEAD>
<BODY bgcolor=white TEXT=black>
<H4>HELLO WORLD</H4>
</BODY>
</HTML>
```

## Library Call Reference

This section contains the detailed reference for each of the calls in the cgi.tcl library.

### cgi_anchor *link_text address*

**Description:** This procedure generates the HTML code for a hypertext link whose destination is *address* and whose description is *link_text*. This procedure actually calls the cgi_link procedure and then writes the output to the channel defined by cgi_outStream.

**Example:**    % cgi_link "test link" test.cgi

```
<A href="test.cgi">test link</A>
%
```

## cgi_br

**Description:**    Generates the HTML code for a line break.

**Example:**    % cgi_br

```
<BR>
%
```

## cgi_build_table *border width headers rows {params { }}*

**Description:**    This procedure generates the complete HTML output for a table whose border width is specified by the *border* argument and whose table width is specified by the *width* argument. The table width parameter is always interpreted as a percentage of the browser window.

**Example:**    % set headers { {Column A} {Column B} {Column C} }

```
 {Column A} {Column B} {Column C}
% set rows { { 1 2 3 } { 4 5 6 } { 7 8 9 } }
 { 1 2 3 } { 4 5 6 } { 7 8 9 }
%    cgi_build_table 1 50 $headers $rows
<TABLE BORDER="1" WIDTH="50%" >
<TR><TD >Column A</TD>
<TD >Column B</TD>
<TD >Column C</TD>
</TR>
<TR><TD >1</TD>
<TD >2</TD>
<TD >3</TD>
</TR>
<TR><TD >4</TD>
<TD >5</TD>
<TD >6</TD>
</TR>
<TR><TD >7</TD>
<TD >8</TD>
<TD >9</TD>
</TR>
</TABLE>
%
```

## cgi_checkbox *name value*

| | |
|---|---|
| **Description:** | Outputs the HTML code for a checkbox element named *name* with a value of *value*. The code is written to the channel defined by cgi_outStream. This is a form element and therefore must be between the cgi_form and cgi_form_end procedure calls. |
| **Example:** | % cgi_checkbox checkbox1 12345 |

```
<INPUT TYPE="CHECKBOX" NAME="checkbox1" VALUE="12345">
%
```

## cgi_clink *color text href*

| | |
|---|---|
| **Description:** | This call returns the HTML code necessary for a hypertext link. The link appears in the color *color*, with a description defined by *text*, and points to the address specified by *href*. The code is not written to cgi_outStream but returned to the caller. This allows the code to be easily embedded inside other HTML tags. |
| **Example:** | % cgi_clink blue "test link" test.cgi |

```
<A href="test.cgi"><FONT COLOR=blue>test link</FONT></A>
%
```

## cgi_counter *filename*

| | |
|---|---|
| **Description:** | This procedure automatically increments the counter number located in *filename*. |
| **Example:** | In this example, a file named counter.txt contains the number 76 at the top of the file. After executing the cgi_counter procedure, the number in the file will be incremented to 77. |

```
% cgi_counter counter.txt
77
% cat counter.txt
77
%
```

## cgi_decode *str*

**Description:** This procedure is used to decode an HTTP-style encoded message. One common encoded character is the space character, which is represented as %20. The example below shows how these encoded spaces are converted to normal space characters.

**Example:** % set arg1 this%20string%20has%20encoded%20spaces

```
this%20string%20has%20encoded%20spaces
% cgi_decode $arg1
this string has encoded spaces
%
```

## cgi_dump_fields

**Description:** The cgi_dump_fields is intended for debugging purposes during CGI application development. This call will write an HTML-formatted page to cgi_outStream, displaying all the form data, including embedded cookies, received from the requesting Web browser.

**Example:** By placing the following two lines at the top of a file, you can easily determine what data your HTML form sent to your CGI application.

```
cgi_dump_fields
return
```

If you run this command from the command line with no QUERY_STRING or HTTP_COOKIE environment variables defined, the following HTML output will be written to the channel pointed to by cgi_outStream.

```
% cgi_dump_fields
Content-Type: text/html

<HTML>
<HEAD>
<TITLE>CGI FIELD DUMP</TITLE>
</HEAD>
<BODY BGCOLOR=white TEXT=black>
<H3>No query data found</H3>
</BODY>
</HTML>
0
%
```

## cgi_dump_text_file *filename*

**Description:**    This call is intended to display the contents of the text file *filename* as an HTML-formatted page. The < > characters are translated into &lt and &gt to prevent the browser from trying to interpret them as HTML tag delimiters. This allows HTML files to be displayed as text files, as well as display text files with these characters embedded.

The content of the text file is displayed using the HTML tags <PRE> </PRE> to preserve its original formatting. Remember that browsers will still try to interpret text as HTML code, even inside the <PRE> </PRE> tags. This is the reason that < > characters are translated by the cgi_dump_text_file call.

The following example uses this command to dump the contents of the helloworld.html file developed in Chapter 4. Notice how the < > and & characters have been encoded so they will not be interpreted as HTML by the browser.

**Example:**    % cgi_dump_text_file helloworld.html

```
Content-Type: text/html

<HTML>
<HEAD>
<TITLE>Text File Dump</TITLE>
</HEAD>
<BODY BGCOLOR=white TEXT=black>
<H3>CURRENT FILE  = helloworld.html</H3>
<HR>
<PRE>
&amp;lt;!DOCTYPE HTML PUBLIC "-//W3C//DTD HTML
3.2//EN"&amp;gt;
&amp;lt;HTML&amp;gt;
&amp;lt;/HEAD&amp;gt;

&amp;lt;BODY&amp;gt;

&amp;lt;P&amp;gt;&amp;lt;FONT
SIZE="5"&amp;gt;&amp;lt;/FONT&amp;gt;&amp;lt;/P&amp;gt;

&amp;lt;P&amp;gt;&amp;lt;FONT SIZE="5"&amp;gt;Hello
World&amp;lt;/FONT&amp;gt;
&amp;lt;/BODY&amp;gt;

&amp;lt;/HTML&amp;gt;
</PRE>
```

## cgi_encode *args*

**Description:** This command accepts a series of name/value pairs as a Tcl string and encodes them according to the same rules used for the query string portion of an URL. Spaces are converted to + characters, special characters are converted to their %x equivalents, an equal sign (=) is placed between each name and value, and an ampersand (&) character is placed between each name/value pair.

This command calls the HTTP 1.0 package that comes with the Tcl 8.0 distribution.

**Example:**
```
% cgi_encode arg1 "this is arg1" arg2 "this is arg2"
arg1=this+is+arg1&arg2=this+is+arg2
%
```

## cgi_end

**Description:** This call writes the closing </BODY> and </HTML> tags to cgi_outStream. This procuedure, which should always be the last call your CGI application makes before returning, requires no arguments.

**Example:**
```
% cgi_end
</BODY>
</HTML>
%
```

## cgi_form *url ?method?*

**Description:** Writes the HTML code to cgi_outStream for the opening form tag. This call should always be used in conjunction with the cgi_form_end tag in the following format:

```
cgi_form
    .... generate all form code here
cgi_form_end
```

**Example:** If this procedure is called with only an URL argument, it defaults the form action statement to POST.

```
% cgi_form default.cgi
```

```
<FORM action="default.cgi" method=POST>
%
```

If the procedure is called with the *method* argument specified, then *method* specifies the method attribute in the HTML output.

```
% cgi_form default.cgi GET
<FORM action="default.cgi" method=GET>
%
```

## cgi_form_end

**Description:**   Writes the closing HTML form tag to cgi_outStream. This call should always be used to close a form that you opened with the cgi_form call.

**Example:**   % cgi_form_end

```
</FORM>
%
```

## cgi_h1 *str ?params?*

**Description:**   This call writes *str* as the HTML document heading <H1>. If the optional *params* argument is used to specify additional attributes for this tag, it must be formatted appropriately.

Attributes such as font size and color may be specified with the optional params argument as shown in the second call to the procedure in the example below.

**Example:**   % cgi_h1 "This text will be displayed in Heading 1 style"

```
<H1>This text will be displayed in Heading 1 style</H1>
% cgi_h1 "Red Font" "FONT COLOR=RED"
<H1 FONT COLOR=RED>Red Font</H1>
```

## cgi_h2 *str ?params?*

**Description:**   This call writes *str* as the HTML document heading <H2>. If the optional *params* argument is used to specify additional attributes for this tag, it must be formatted appropriately. (See cgi_h1.)

**Example:**    % cgi_h2 "This text will be displayed in Heading 2 style"

```
<H2>This text will be displayed in Heading 2 style</H2>
%
```

## cgi_h3 *str ?params?*

**Description:**    This call writes *str* as the HTML document heading <H3>. If the optional *params* argument is used to specify additional attributes for this tag, it must be formatted appropriately. (See cgi_h1.)

**Example:**    % cgi_h3 "This text will be displayed in Heading 3 style"

```
<H3>This text will be displayed in Heading 3 style</H3>
%
```

## cgi_h4 *str ?params?*

**Description:**    This call writes *str* as the HTML document heading <H4>. If the optional *params* argument is used to specify additional attributes for this tag, it must be formatted appropriately. (See cgi_h1.)

**Example:**    % cgi_h4 "This text will be displayed in Heading 4 style"

```
<H4>This text will be displayed in Heading 4 style</H4>
%
```

## cgi_h5 *str ?params?*

**Description:**    This call writes *str* as the HTML document heading <H5>. If the optional *params* argument is used to specify additional attributes for this tag, it must be formatted appropriately. (See cgi_h1.)

**Example:**    % cgi_h5 "This text will be displayed in Heading 5 style"

```
<H5>This text will be displayed in Heading 5 style</H5>
%
```

## cgi_h6 *str ?params?*

**Description:**   This call writes *str* as the HTML document heading <H6>. If the optional *params* argument is used to specify additional attributes for this tag, it must be formatted appropriately. (See cgi_h1.)

**Example:**   % cgi_h6 "This text will be displayed in Heading 6 style"

```
<H6>This text will be displayed in Heading 6 style</H6>
%
```

## cgi_header *title ?bodyparams? ?headerparams?*

The cgi_header procedure is used to generate the opening code for an HTML document, including the required HTTP headers. You should normally use this as the first call of your dynamically created HTML document. The output of this call is sent to the channel referred to by the cgi_outStream variable.

The optional *bodyparams* argument is used to include additional attributes for the body of the HTML document, such as background color. The optional *headerparams* argument is used for adding additional HTTP headers at the beginning of the HTML document, such as the Set-Cookie header.

Once you call the cgi_header procedure, you must not write anything to the channel pointed to by cgi_outStream other than properly formatted HTML code.

When you are done generating the dynamic HTML output, close the page with a call to cgi_end.

**Example:**   This first example only supplies the title argument:

```
% cgi_header "Test Header"
Content-Type: text/html

<HTML>
<HEAD>
<TITLE>Test Header</TITLE>
</HEAD>
<BODY >
%
```

The next example uses the *bodyparams* argument to set the default text and background colors for the page.

```
% cgi_header "Page Title"  {BGCOLOR=white TEXT=black}
Content-Type: text/html

<HTML>
<HEAD>
<TITLE>Page Title</TITLE>
</HEAD>
<BODY BGCOLOR=white TEXT=black>
%
```

The next example uses the *headerparams* argument to generate a cookie by writing out a Set-Cookie header before the opening <HTML> tag.

```
% cgi_header "Page Title" {} "Set-Cookie: mycookie=12345"
Content-Type: text/html
Set-Cookie: mycookie=12345

<HTML>
<HEAD>
<TITLE>Page Title</TITLE>
</HEAD>
<BODY >
%
```

## cgi_hidden *name value*

**Description:** Writes the HTML code for a hidden form field to the channel pointed to by **cgi_outStream**. This call produces a form element and must only be called after the execution of a **cgi_form** call.

**Example:** % cgi_hidden HIDDEN 12345

```
<INPUT TYPE="HIDDEN" NAME="HIDDEN" VALUE="12345">
%
```

## cgi_hr

**Description:** Writes the HTML code for a hidden field to the channel pointed to by **cgi_outStream**.

Example:          % cgi_hr

                  <HR>
                  %

## cgi_html_tag *tag params str*

**Description:**   This call is for generating HTML tags not specifically dealt
                   with in the rest of the cgi.tcl library. The tag written to
                   **cgi_outStream** will be of the form *<tag params>str</tag>*.

**Example:**       % cgi_html_tag FONT "FACE=Courier" "This font is Courier"

                   <FONT FACE=Courier>This font is Courier</FONT>
                   %

## cgi_li *params*

**Description:**   This call generates the output for the cgi <LI> tag, used for
                   ordered and unordered lists. The *params* argument allows the
                   caller to supply its own attributes to the tag. The following
                   values for *params* are interpreted by the parameter and
                   generate the appropriate HTML code

                           a,   A,   i,   I,   1

                   These values specify the type of list prefix to use and have the
                   same meaning as they do for the HTML TYPE attribute as it is
                   used with lists. Values other than those specified above are
                   inserted as tag attributes. Proper formatting of *params*, other
                   than those defined above, is left up to the caller.

**Example:**       <LI TYPE="a">% cgi_li i

                   <LI TYPE="i">%

## cgi_link *text href*

**Description:**   Generates the HTML code for a hypertext link whose address
                   is *href* and whose description is *text*. Rather than writing the
                   result to **cgi_outStream**, this call returns the formatted string.
                   This allows it to be easily embedded in other functions such as

cgi_td calls, or any other place where a link may be required to be displayed.

**Example:** % cgi_link "Point to default.cgi" default.cgi

```
<A href="default.cgi">Point to default.cgi</A>
%
```

# cgi_ol *?params?*

**Description:** This procedure call is used to generate the opening HTML code for an ordered list. The procedure recognizes the shortcuts a, A, I, i, and 1 for TYPE attributes to the <OL> tag and generates the appropriate string. If any other value is detected, it is used as a literal string in the attributes location of the tag. The proper formatting of any other *params* value is left up to the caller.

**Example:** % cgi_ol a

```
<OL TYPE="a">
% cgi_ol A
<OL TYPE="A">
%
```

# cgi_ol_end

**Description:** This procedure call outputs the closing ordered list tag </OL> to cgi_outStream. This call accepts no arguments.

**Example:** % cgi_ol_end

```
</OL>
%
```

# cgi_p

**Description:** This procedure simply outputs the HTML tag for a paragraph break.

**Example:** % cgi_p

```
<P>
%
```

# cgi_parse

**Description:**    This procedure parses the form data received from the client Web browser. Depending on the type of transaction, the form data is obtained from environment variables, read from standard in, or a combination of the two. The CGI parse routine does all the work of determining how the data was passed and parsing the data. The result is a global array named cgi( ), where each element name and its associated value corresponds to one name/value pair submitted from the client Web browser.

The example below sets the QUERY_STRING environment variable and calls the **cgi_parse** procedure to process it. An array named **cgi** is created with each element of the array equaling one of the name/value pairs in the QUERY_STRING environment variable.

**Example:**    % global env

```
%set env(QUERY_STRING)
   \FUNCTION=Login&USER=dogbert&PASSWORD=woof
% cgi_parse
0
% set cgi(FUNCTION)
Login
% set cgi(USER)
dogbert
% set cgi(PASSWORD)
woof
%
```

# cgi_parse_cookies

**Description:**    Like the **cgi_parse** procedure, this procedure requires no arguments. This call will look for the presence of an environment variable named HTTP_COOKIE and, if found, process the string into an array of name/value pairs that correspond to the cookies sent by the requesting Web browser.

To test this routine from the Tcl shell, you must set the HTTP_COOKIES environment variable, start the Tcl shell, load the cgi.tcl package, and then execute the cgi_parse command. This sets up an environment similar to the one that would exist during the execution of a CGI script.

**Example:**

> HTTP_COOKIE="oatmeal=yummy;peanut+butter=tasty"

```
> export HTTP_COOKIE
> tclsh
% package require cgi.tcl
1.1
% cgi_parse_cookies
0
%  array names cgi_cookies
{peanut butter} oatmeal
% set cgi_cookies(oatmeal)
yummy
%
```

## cgi_password *name ?size?*

**Description:** This procedure call outputs the HTML tag for a form input field with TYPE attribute set to PASSWORD. The form element name is supplied by the *name* argument. The *size* argument specifies the size of the input field in characters and is optional. If *size* is not supplied, the size defaults to 25. Because the output of this procedure is an HTML form element, this call should only be made after the cgi_form procedure has been called.

**Example:** % cgi_password PASS 15

```
<INPUT TYPE="PASSWORD" NAME="PASS" SIZE="15">
%
```

## cgi_pre

**Description:** Outputs the opening HTML tag for a predefined text area. Any text output between this tag and the cgi_pre_end tag will retain its original formatting. The browser will still attempt to interpret the text inside of the <PRE> </PRE> tags as HTML code, so you must substitute characters such as < > with their equivalents, &lt and &gt.

**Example:**    % cgi_pre

```
<PRE>
%
```

## cgi_pre_end

**Description:**    This is the companion to the **cgi_pre** procedure call. It outputs the closing HTML tag for a predefined text area.

**Example:**    % cgi_pre_end

```
</PRE>
%
```

## cgi_print_error *err_msg*

**Description:**    This is a high-level procedure call that generates the complete code for an HTML page containing a user-specified error message, *err_msg*. Because this call generates the complete HTML page, no other HTML code should have been written to **cgi_outStream** prior to using this call.

**Example:**    % cgi_print_error "This could be any user-defined error message"

```
Content-Type: text/html

<HTML>
<HEAD>
<TITLE>ERROR</TITLE>
</HEAD>
<BODY BGCOLOR=white TEXT=red>
This could be any user-defined error message
</BODY>
</HTML>
0
%
```

## cgi_print_message *msg link_text link*

**Description:**    This call generates a complete HTML page containing a message, a link, and the associated link text. This is useful for responding to user input or redirecting users to another site.

**Example:** % cgi_print_message "Entry Accepted" "Return to main screen"
main.cgi

```
Content-Type: text/html

<HTML>
<HEAD>
<TITLE>MESSAGE</TITLE>
</HEAD>
<BODY BGCOLOR=white TEXT=black>
<A href="main.cgi">Return to main screen</A>
<BR>
<BR>
Entry Accepted
</BODY>
</HTML>
0
%
```

## cgi_puts *str*

**Description:** This procedure simply writes *str* to the channel currently defined by **cgi_outStream**. This call may be used to write out your own HTML tags not covered by the cgi.tcl library.

**Example:** In the following example the text is simply written back to standard out. This is due to the fact that the default assignment for **cgi_outStream** is standard out when the **cgi.tcl** package is first loaded.

```
% cgi_puts "HELLO WORLD"
% cgi_puts "HELLO WORLD"
HELLO WORLD
%
```

## cgi_radio *name value*

**Description:** This call outputs the HTML code for a radio button with the NAME attribute equal to *name* and the VALUE attribute equal to *value*. Because the output of this procedure is an HTML form element, this call should only be made after the **cgi_form** procedure has been called.

**Example:** % cgi_radio FUNCTION PANIC

```
<INPUT TYPE="RADIO" NAME="FUNCTION" VALUE="PANIC">
%
```

## cgi_select *name option_list selection ?size?*

**Description:** This call generates the complete HTML code for a selection list. The NAME attribute will be set to *name*. The selection list contents are defined by the *option_list* argument. The *option_list* argument is a normal Tcl list containing a separate string for each individual selection element. The default selection is defined by *selection* and is a numeric index that references one of the strings in option_list. The number of selection items that will be visible in the list is defined by size and defaults to 1.

The following example produces a list with 5 options. The selection box will display 3 elements at a time and the default selection is the third element in the list.

**Example:** % set list { "Option 1" "Option2" "Option3" "Option4" "Option 5" }

```
 "Option 1" "Option2" "Option3" "Option4" "Option 5"
% cgi_select "OPTION LIST" $list 3 5
<SELECT NAME="OPTION LIST" SIZE="5">
<OPTION>Option 1</OPTION>
<OPTION>Option2</OPTION>
<OPTION SELECTED>Option3</OPTION>
<OPTION>Option4</OPTION>
<OPTION>Option 5</OPTION>
</SELECT>
%
```

## cgi_set_outstream *fptr_name*

**Description:** This call reassigns the cgi_outStream global to point to the channel defined by the file pointer *fptr_name*. The file pointer must be a valid channel that was created with open or one of the predefined channels such as stdin. This command does not produce any output so no example will be shown.

## cgi_submit *name value*

**Description:** This call outputs the HTML code for a submit button with the NAME attribute equal to *name* and the VALUE attribute equal to *value*. Because the output of this procedure is an HTML form element, this call should only be made after the cgi_form procedure has been called.

This call is typically used to generate the submit button that will cause the browser to send its form data to the Web server. The destination is defined in the actual cgi_form call.

**Example:**  % cgi_submit FUNCTION submit

```
<INPUT TYPE="SUBMIT" NAME="FUNCTION" VALUE="submit">
%
```

## cgi_table *border width ?params?*

**Description:**  This call creates the opening HTML code for a table. The border width is defined by *border*. The width of the table, as a percentage of the Web browser page, is defined by *width*. The optional *params* argument can be used to supply additional parameters for the table. Any valid HTML attributes may be supplied in the *params* argument.

This call is used in conjunction with several other library calls to manually construct a table. The general form of the calls required to construct a table is shown next. The code between the cgi_table and cgi_table_end is repeated for the numbers of rows and columns:

```
cgi_table
    cgi_tr
      cgi_td_open
            cgi_td
      cgi_td_end
      cgi_td_open
            cgi_td
      cgi_td_end
      ...
    cgi_tr_end
    cgi_table_end
```

**Example:**  % cgi_table 1 50

```
<TABLE BORDER="1" WIDTH="50%" >
%
```

## cgi_table_end

**Description:**   This call generates the closing HTML tag for a table. See cgi_table for a more complete description of table building.

**Example:**   % cgi_table_end

```
</TABLE>
%
```

## cgi_td *?text? ?params?*

**Description:**   This call writes out the HTML code for a table data tag (TD).

**Example:**   % cgi_td "This is a table cell"

```
<TD >This is a table cell</TD>
```

## cgi_td_open *?str? ?params?*

**Description:**   This call writes just the opening HTML tag for a table data element. This is useful for more complex cells that require additional embedded HTML tags, such as you might do when nesting a table inside a cell of another table.

**Example:**   % cgi_td_open "This is a table cell"

<TD >This is a table cell

## cgi_td_end

**Description:**   This call produces the closing tag for a table data element.

**Example:**   % cgi_td_end

</TD>

## cgi_text *str ?size? ?color?*

**Description:**   This procedure call will generate the HTML code necessary to display *str* in the *size* and *color* specified. The default value for *size* is 2 and *color* is black.

**Example:**     % cgi_text "This is size 4 and color red" 4 red

```
<FONT SIZE=4 COLOR=red>This is size 4 and color
red</FONT>
```

## cgi_text_field *name ?size?*

**Description:**     Generates the HTML code for an INPUT form element of type TEXT. This is a single line text input element. The optional *size* argument can be used to specify the length of the displayed element on the resulting form. The size parameter defaults to 25.

**Example:**     % cgi_text_field "this is a 40 character text box" 40

```
<INPUT TYPE="TEXT" NAME="this is a 40 character text box"
SIZE="40">
```

## cgi_text_area *rows columns name text ?params?*

**Description:**     This call generates the HTML code necessary to produce a text area form element. The element contains the specified numbers of rows and columns and is identified by *name*. The *text* argument is used to specify the default text that will appear when the text area element is first displayed on the browser.

**Example:**     % cgi_text_area 5 40 text_box "default text"

```
<TEXTAREA NAME="text_box" ROWS="5" COLS="40">default
text</TEXTAREA>
```

## cgi_tr

**Description:**     This call creates just the opening tag for a table row. This call is meant to be used when constructing more complex tables. For simple tables the **cgi_build_table** command can be used to generate the entire table.

Notice that this call does not generate a carriage return after it prints the <TR> tag. This makes for more compact HTML code.

**Example:**        % cgi_tr

                                                  `<TR>%`

## cgi_tr_end

**Description:**    Writes the HTML closing tag for a table row.

**Example:**        % cgi_tr_end

                                                  `</TR>`

## cgi_ul items *?size? ?color?*

**Description:**    Generates all the code necessary for an ordered list. Each item in the list will be of the *size* and *color* specified. The default *size* is 2 and the default *color* is black.

```
% set items {
"this is item 1"
"this is item 2"
"this is item 3"
}
"this is item 1"
"this is item 2"
"this is item 3"
% package require cgi.tcl
1.1
%  cgi_ul $items
<UL>
    <LI><FONT SIZE="2" COLOR="black">this is item 1</FONT>
    <LI><FONT SIZE="2" COLOR="black">this is item 2</FONT>
    <LI><FONT SIZE="2" COLOR="black">this is item 3</FONT>
</UL>
%
```

## cgi_validate_fields *names error_buffer*

**Description:**    This procedure will validate that the list of field *names* exists in the current global cgi array. You must call the **cgi_parse** routine first to parse the cgi variables passed from the Web browser. If all the fields are not found, then an error message is returned in *error_buffer* that describes the first missing field detected by the routine.

You can test this routine from the Tcl shell by performing the following steps. First, set the QUERY_STRING environment variable. Then start the Tcl shell and load the cgi.tcl package. Finally, execute the cgi_parse command. This sets up an environment similar to the one that would exist during the execution of a CGI script. The cgi_validate_fields procedure may now be called to validate the field names.

**Example:**

```
> QUERY_STRING="FNAME=John&LNAME=Doe&AGE=41"
> export QUERY_STRING
> tclsh
% package require cgi.tcl
1.1
0
%cgi_parse
1
% cgi_validate_fields "FNAME LNAME AGE ADDRESS" error
0
% set error
field name 'ADDRESS' required but not defined
%
```

## cgi_validate_cookies *names error_buffer*

**Description:** This procedure ensures that the list of cookie *names* exists in the current global cookies array. You must first call the cgi_parse_cookies routine to parse the cookies passed from the Web browser. If all the cookies in *names* are not found, an error is returned in *error_buffer* describing the first missing field detected by the routine.

To test this routine from the Tcl shell, you must set the HTTP_COOKIES environment variable, start the Tcl shell, load the cgi.tcl package, execute the cgi_parse command, and then execute the cgi_parse_cookies command. This sets up an environment similar to the one that would exist during the execution of a CGI script.

**Example:**

```
> HTTP_COOKIE="oatmeal=yummy;peanut+butter=tasty"
> export HTTP_COOKIE
> tclsh
% package require cgi.tcl
1.1
% cgi_parse_cookies
```

```
0
% cgi_validate_cookies [list oatmeal "peanut butter"]
err_msg
0
% cgi_validate_cookies ["chocolate chip"] err_msg
1
% set err_msg
cookie 'chocolate chip' required but not defined
%
```

# Appendix D

## The Web Browser Plug-In

---

## Overview

The Web browser plug-in is a browser extension that lets you run Tcl/Tk applications directly inside your browser window. This allows you to build more powerful graphical user interfaces than is possible with HTML or embed entire applications inside your Web pages.

The Web browser plug-in is free, and there are versions that run on multiple operating systems including Solaris, Macintosh, and Windows-based platforms. It is easy to acquire and lets you, as the CGI programmer, provide more powerful applications without having to learn another language, such as Java.

### Obtaining and Installing the Plug-In

There are several sources on the Internet for obtaining the Web browser plug-in, but the easiest place is probably from Scriptics, which can be contacted at the following URL:

http://www.scriptics.com

Installation is easy. For example on a Windows machine you simply download a self-installing executable file and then run it. A directory containing the necessary support files is built and the plug-in is automatically installed on your browser.

In Netscape version 4.*x* you can check to see which plug-ins you have available by clicking on the Help menu and then selecting About Plug-Ins. This will display a list of the currently installed plug-ins. After installing the Tcl Web browser plug-in, you should see an entry similar to the one shown in Figure D-1.

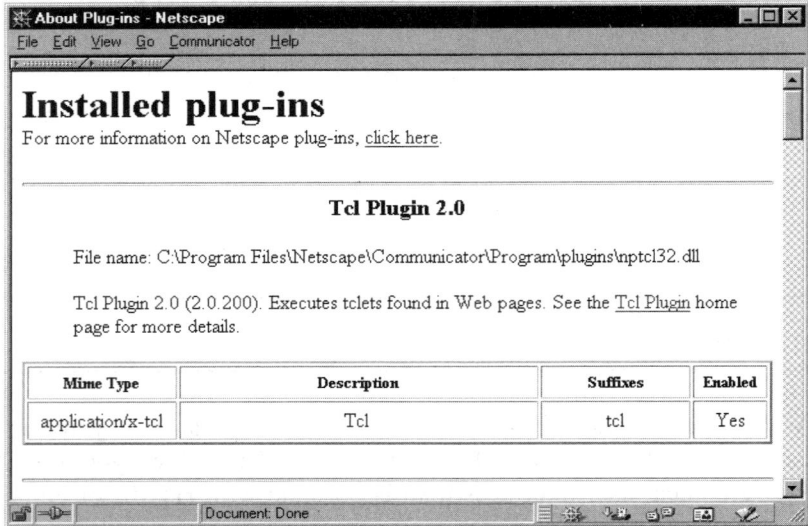

**Figure D-1** Netscape's Plug-In Page

## Plug-In Configuration Files

When you install the Tcl browser plug-in on your machine, several directories are created on your local hard drive as shown in Figure D-2. In this appendix we will only concern ourselves with the *config* directory. The config directory holds a .cfg file for each of the predefined security policies. For example the name of the config policy for the home security policy is home.cfg. In addition to a configuration file for each security policy, this directory also contains a file named plug-in.cfg. The plug-in.cfg file is read by the master interpreter at initialization time to determine which security policies may be requested by a Tclet. The determination is made based on the URL of the executing Tclet.

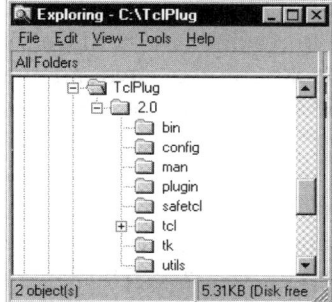

**Figure D-2** Plug-In Directories

## Making It Safe

It is important to understand the implications of loading a plug-in that will dynamically execute downloaded code on your computer. If, for example, the plug-in blindly executed the full Tcl/Tk instruction set, a malicious programmer could embed a very destructive Tcl application inside an otherwise harmless looking Web page. This program could erase all the files on your hard drive, lock out your keyboard, or transmit sensitive data over the Internet to some eager computer voyeur halfway around the world. This is certainly not desirable behavior!

Fortunately, the Tcl Web browser plug-in has more than adequate security measures to prevent all of these things from happening. The plug-in uses *security policies* to limit what actions the embedded Tcl application (Tclet) can perform. This is accomplished by creating a slave interpreter, under which the Tclet operates.

Slave interpreters are created with the Tcl **interp** command and provide a convenient mechanism for imposing security restrictions on untrusted scripts. This is done by either hiding certain Tcl commands from the slave interpreter or redefining them to reduce their functionality. Because even experienced Tcl programmers may have little experience with the **interp** command, a short discussion of its usage is appropriate.

The **interp** command allows for the creation of one or more slave interpreters that co-exist with the interpreter that created them. The creating interpreter is referred to as the master interpreter. The master interpreter has complete control over each slave interpreter that it creates. For example the master interpreter may restrict the types of access the slave has to certain system resources, such as disk files or network sockets. In fact the master may completely eliminate the slave's ability to access certain commands, such as **open** or **socket**, in the slave interpreter. The master interpreter then executes untrusted scripts inside the slave interpreter, where they are prevented from performing malicious activities. The slave interpreter is created with the **create** option.

Once the slave is created, a new command name is automatically created in the master interpreter that corresponds to the name of the slave. This command has several options that allow the master interpreter to control the slave. For example the master interpreter can evaluate scripts or commands inside the slave using the **slave eval**, where *slave* is the name of the slave that was created. The following example creates a slave named child and uses the **slave eval** command to set a global variable named **temp_variable** inside the slave's global variable space. Notice that the variable is not available inside the master interpreter's global variable space.

```
% interp create slave child
child
% child eval { set temp_variable "I am a slave interpreter" }
I am a slave interpreter
% child eval { info globals temp* }
temp_variable
% child eval { set temp_variable }
I am a slave interpreter
% info globals temp*
%
```

Each slave interpreter has its own namespace for commands, procedures, and global variables. By default when a slave interpreter is created, it contains the full set of commands available to its master. In many cases it is desirable to prevent a slave from executing certain commands or at least restrict the functionality of these commands in the slave. This can be accomplished in a couple of ways.

The **interp** command provides two ways of accomplishing this. The first method provides the ability for the master interpreter to redefine commands in the slave interpreter by a mechanism called an *alias*. An alias is the only way to create connections between a master and its slaves. An alias is a command in a slave interpreter that causes a corresponding command to be invoked in its master interpreter. From the standpoint of security, one of the most important aspects of the alias mechanism is the ability to redefine commands in the slave interpreter. For example the following code segment redefines the normal Tcl **puts** command in the slave interpreter to actually call the **slave_puts** procedure that has been created in the master interpreter. In this fashion any standard Tcl command can be redefined in the slave, providing complete control over execution of untrusted scripts inside the slave interpreter.

```
% interp create foo
foo
%  proc slave_puts { str } { puts "slave--$str"}
%  foo alias puts slave_puts
puts
%  foo eval { puts "This is the slave talking" }
slave--This is the slave talking
%
```

The only other connections between a master interpreter and its slaves are through environment variables that are normally shared among all interpreters in the application. Note that the namespace for files (such as the names returned by the **open** command) is no longer shared between interpreters. Explicit commands are provided to share files and to transfer references to open files from one interpreter to another.

The second mechanism provided to restrict a slave interpreter access is through the use of the **hide** option to the **interp** command. This allows the master interpreter to hide selected commands. The slave interpter, as was previously mentioned, is created fully functional by default. This means that the slave interpreter has access to the full command set available to the master interpreter. This is not always desirable, so the master interpreter may hide commands inside the slave, making them unavailable to untrusted code that is executed through the slave interpreter. The following code segment uses the hide option to the **interp** command to hide the **open** command from scripts that are executed inside the slave interpreter.

```
% interp create foo
foo
% foo eval  { info commands o*}
open
% foo hide open
%
% foo eval { info commands o* }
```

## The Safe Interpreter

The **interp** command provides support for the creation of a safe interpreter. A safe interpreter is a slave whose functions have been greatly restricted. This allows for the easy creation of a slave interpreter that may be used to execute untrusted scripts without fear of them damaging other interpreters or the application's environment.

By default, all IO channel creation commands and subprocess creation commands are made inaccessible to safe interpreters. The dangerous commands are not removed from the safe interpreter, they are hidden from it, just as the **open** command was hidden from the slave interpreter in the previous example. The set of commands that are available to the safe interpreter when it is first created are shown in Table D-1.

**Table D-1** Default Safe Interpreter Exposed Commands

| | | | |
|---|---|---|---|
| after | append | array | binary |
| break | case | catch | clock |
| close | concat | continue | eof |
| error | eval | expr | fblocked |
| fcopy | fileevent | flush | for |
| foreach | format | gets | global |
| if | incr | info | interp |
| join | lappend | lindex | linsert |
| list | llength | lrange | lreplace |
| lsearch | lsort | namespace | package |
| pid | proc | puts | read |
| regexp | regsub | rename | return |
| scan | seek | set | split |
| string | subst | switch | tell |
| time | trace | unset | update |
| uplevel | upvar | variable | vwait |
| while | | | |

You can use the **hidden** option to view the list of commands that have been hidden from the safe interpreter.

```
% interp create -safe foo
foo
% foo hidden
glob file fconfigure load source exec socket open exit pwd cd
%
```

The commands that are hidden from the default safe interpreter are shown in Table D-2.

**Table D-2** Commands Hidden from Safe Interpreters

| | | | |
|------|--------|--------|------------|
| cd | exec | exit | fconfigure |
| file | glob | load | open |
| pwd | socket | source | |

You can use the **expose** option to make hidden commands available to the slave interpreter. Only the master interpreter can expose hidden commands to a slave. In the following example the **exit** command has been made available to the slave interpreter by the master interpreter.

```
% foo expose exit
% foo hidden
glob file fconfigure load source exec socket open pwd cd
%
```

Through this process of hiding commands and aliasing them to restrict their functionality, the Web browser plug-in is able to provide adequate protection when executing untrusted scripts. A slave interpreter created with the -**safe** option is most likely safe enough to execute scripts received from your worst enemies. In fact its functionality has been so crippled that it may be nearly useless for typical Web programming tasks. The really hard part about security is determining how safe is safe!

## The Plug-In Security Model

The Tcl browser plug-in provides a robust mechanism for controlling security. This model can be a little difficult to understand at first, so read through this entire appendix before lapsing into despair! The plug-in security model is built upon two abstract concepts, *features* and *security policies*.

Features are named collections of capabilities that the master interpreter may install into an executing Tclet. By default, because the new Tclet is created as a safe interpreter, it is prohibited from accessing critical system resources. In many instances the Tclet must be allowed more functionality in order to complete the task that it was designed for. This can be accomplished by requesting additional functionality, or features, from the master interpreter.

Features provide this extra functionality to the slave interpreter by providing aliases to the executing Tclet that reenables certain commands. In the case of the network feature described in the next section, the master interpreter allows the executing Tclet to perform certain network-related functions by providing aliases for the Tcl network-related commands such as socket and fconfigure. The amount of functionality provided depends on the feature that is enabled.

# Plug-In Features

*Features* provide additional functionality to the Tclet operating under the slave interpreter by exposing commands that are hidden from the slave interpreter under the default safe interpreter implementation. This is generally done by providing aliases to these commands rather than simply exposing the command. The alias normally has restricted access privileges compared with the original Tcl command.

The plug-in version 2.0 installation provides five predefined features. They are

- Network
- Persist
- Stream
- Unsafe
- URL

Each feature provides increased functionality along logical boundaries. For example the network feature returns certain networking functions, such as the use of the Tcl socket command to the executing Tclet.

## Browser Namespaces

In addition to exposing commands that were hidden from the default safe interpreter, the plug-in also provides additional commands through the use of several new namespaces. A brief summary of these namespaces is provided in Table D-3. The procedures available in each namespace will be discussed in detail in the sections that follow.

**Table D-3** Browser Namespaces Provided

| | |
|---|---|
| ::browser | Provides several procedures to interact with the browser application hosting the Tclet. Different aspects of the browser namespace are made available to the Tclet depending on the controlling security policy. |
| ::cfg | Provides procedures to interrogate the current browser configuration. Like the ::browser namespace, different aspects of the ::cfg namespace are made available to the Tclet based on the controlling security policy. |
| ::log | This namespace can be used by executing Tclets to log messages to a file. |

## The Network Feature

The network feature provides the Tclet with network capabilities that are normally denied to the default safe interpreter. It does this by providing the Tclet with aliases for the **socket** and **fconfigure** commands. These commands are limited from the full implementations provided by the standard Tcl interpreter.

**socket** *host port*

> This is a limited version of the standard Tcl **socket** command. It opens a client network connection to a service running on the remote host/port combination defined by the two arguments *host* and *port*. Only client sockets are supported, and no client-side options are supported.

> The host argument may contain a network name, such as www.scriptics.com; a network address, such as 205.149.189.25; or the empty string. The empty string is used if the executing Tclet wishes to connect back to the host it was loaded from. Only numeric ports are supported, and connecting to services by name are not supported.

> The **socket** command returns the name of the new socket channel that may be used for future network communications.

**fconfigure** *sock ?options...?*

> This limited version of the **fconfigure** command disables the **-peername** option of the full command. All other options are fully supported.

## The Persist Feature

The persist feature allows the Tclet to use local persistent storage. It does this by providing the Tclet with aliases to the commands that deal with persistent storage. These commands include open, close, fconfigure, puts, file delete, seek, tell, and glob.

open *fileName ?mode?*

> Opens a local persistent file with the name *fileName* in the requested mode and returns a handle to the file. The file is created if it does not exist.
>
> Local persistent files are maintained in a specific directory; therefore, only the last component of the *fileName* path is used as the file name. All other path information is ignored. This isolates the Tclet from the file system of the local client machine while still providing it with local storage.
>
> The *mode* argument has the same meaning as in the standard Tcl open command. If the limit on the number of open channels or the limit on the number of stored files would be exceeded by the execution of this command, it returns an error.

close *channel*

> This command closes the channel associated with a local persistent file and decrements the number of open channels.

fconfigure *channel ?options...?*

> The fconfigure command allows a Tclet to configure settings for open channels. The channels may have resulted from any command that returns a channel name (that is, the open or socket commands).

file delete *fileName*

> Used to delete local persistent files created with the open command. The *fileName* argument is the name of the file to delete. As with the open command, only the last component of the path is used as the file name to delete.

glob *pattern ?pattern...?*

> Returns the list of the file names from the local persistent storage area that match the given patterns.

**puts** *?-newline? ?channel? string*

Allows the executing Tclet to write to local persistent files, while observing the file size limits defined by the controlling security policy. If execution of this command would cause the local persistent file to grow larger than the file size limit imposed by the controlling security policy, the command will return an error.

**seek** *channel offset ?whence?*

Moves the access point in *channel* to a new location as specified by *offset* and the optional *whence* argument. This procedure prevents the **seek** from increasing the file size beyond the limit specified in the controlling policy's configuration. However, if the file is opened for reading, the Tclet is allowed to seek to all the file, even if its current size exceeds the file size limit.

**tell** *channel*

Computes the offset of the current access point in *channel* from the start of the file.

## The Stream Feature

This feature provides aliases that allow the Tclet to invoke JavaScript functions, which allows the Tclet to open and close streams (communication channels) to frames managed by the hosting application. This in turn allows the executing Tclet to read and write information to frames managed by the Web browser. The stream feature provides the following procedures.

**::browser::openStream** *frame ?mimeType?*

Opens a stream to *frame* managed by the hosting application and returns the name of the new stream. Data sent to the stream is interpreted as having the mime type *mimeType*, which defaults to text/html. The name of the stream is returned. The frame names **_self**, **_current**, and the empty string are disallowed because their use causes data sent on the stream to replace the contents of the frame containing the Tclet, which causes some hosting applications to operate incorrectly.

If *frame* does not exist, it is created with the current default size, toolbar decorations, and location for the hosting application. Otherwise, the current contents of the frame are discarded and the frame is repainted with the current default background color for the hosting application.

### ::browser::writeToStream *stream data*

This procedure writes data to *stream*. The stream must have been previously opened with ::browser::openStream procedure. The data will be interpreted according to the mime type specified in the ::browser::openStream procedure call.

### ::browser::closeStream *stream*

Closes *stream* previously opened with ::browser::openStream procedure.

### ::browser::javascript *javascriptCmd ?callback?*

This procedure is used to request execution of a JavaScript command by the hosting application. Care should be taken when granting the Tclet the ability to use this procedure, because it gives the executing Tclet access to all of JavaScript's capabilities.

The results of the JavaScript command, including any errors that may have resulted, are returned by this procedure. Some JavaScript commands do not produce a result, in which case no results are returned by this procedure. If no *callback* argument is supplied, the operation blocks until the operation completes or until a time-out occurs. If the optional *callback* argument is supplied, the procedure returns immediately and arranges for the procedure named by the *callback* argument to be called when the operation completes or a time-out occurs. The *callback* argument is explained next.

### callback *name stream reason data*

The ::browser::javascript procedure accepts an optional callback that will be called when the result of the JavaScript computation arrives from the hosting application. It is invoked with the same arguments as the *endCallback* explained in the manual page for the URL feature.

### ::browser::email *recipients text*

This procedure is used to send electronic mail to a list of recipients. The list in this case must be comma-separated. Each recipient in the list is sent the content of the *text* argument. Because of limitations in some hosting applications, a subject field or other common header fields cannot be specified.

Care should be taken with this procedure because it allows untrusted Tcl programs to send electronic mail using the user's originating address. This procedure is enabled only by the JavaScript security policy.

## The Unsafe Feature

The unsafe feature restores a safe Tclet to a completely trusted (unsafe) state. All commands that were previously hidden from the Tclet are exposed. A great deal of care should be exercised when granting this feature. The Tclet must be highly trusted because it can perform any function a normal Tcl program can perform. This policy may be acceptable in a very controlled environment, such as your company's intranet, but should rarely be granted to URLs outside your domain.

## The URL Feature

This feature enables a Tclet to utilize the HTTP protocol to fetch the contents of a URL and post data to remote sites.

### ::browser::status *message*

Displays a message in the status bar of the hosting application. *Message* is a standard Tcl string of any length. For browsers, the status bar is normally at the bottom of the browser window. The message may be overwritten at any time because the status bar is shared among all subsystems running within the application.

### ::browser::getURL *URL ?timeOut ?newCallback? ?writeCallback? ?endCallback?*

This procedure fetches the contents of a URL and calls one of the three callback procedures depending on the operation being performed.

*timeOut*—The optional timeOut argument specifies a length of time in milliseconds to wait or block before timing out. If no time-out is specified, a default time-out is used.

*newCallback*—The optional *newCallback* argument specifies a callback to call when the contents of *URL* start to arrive from the network.

*writeCallBack*—The optional *writeCallback* argument specifies a procedure to call each time a part of the contents of *URL* arrives from the network. When data starts to arrive, *newCallback* is called once, then writeCallback is called for each subsequent part of the data received. The *endCallback* procedure is then called once for the last portion of the data that arrives from the URL or for a time-out or abort condition.

*endCallback*—The optional *endCallback* argument gives the name of a procedure to call when the entire contents of *URL* have arrived, or when a time-out occurs. If no *endCallback* was given, the operation blocks until the complete contents of *URL* have been fetched or until the operation is aborted or times out. If no data ever arrives, *endCallback* is guaranteed to be called when the operation times out. If the call is blocking, it returns the data fetched from *URL*. If the call is nonblocking, it returns *endCallback*.

### ::browser::displayURL `URL frame`

Displays the contents of *URL* in a *frame*. This operation may create new top level frames in the hosting application. The operation is asynchronous and the invoking interpreter does not have access to the contents of *URL*.

Several frame names have special meaning as follows:

*_self* and *_current* cause the hosting application to replace the contents of the frame containing the Tclet with the result.

*_blank* creates a new frame to display the result.

*_top* replaces the contents of the top-most frame in the hosting application-specific hierarchy with the results of the procedure.

*_parent* is the parent frame.

### ::browser::getForm `URL data ?raw? ?timeOut? ?newCallback? ?writeCallback? ?endCallback?`

This procedure posts data to the remote service identified by *URL* and receives the result. If the *raw* argument is zero or omitted, the data is encoded to protect special characters, such as spaces, during transmission. In this case the data should be a standard Tcl list containing alternating field names and values. If *raw* is non-zero, no encoding is performed on the data. The rest of the arguments have the same meaning as in the ::browser::getURL procedure. This operation is blocking if no **endCallback** is given, and returns the result of posting the data to the form. If the operation is nonblocking, then *endCallback*.

### ::browser::displayForm `URL frame data ?raw?`

This procedure posts data to the remote service identified by *URL* and displays the result in *frame*. The *raw* argument has the same meaning as for ::browser::getForm. The special frame names have the same meaning as those described in the ::browser::displayURL procedure.

# Security Policies

Tclets don't typically request features directly from the master interpreter; instead, they request a *security policy* that includes the features required to perform their function. Security policies are configuration files that define which features will be allowed to a given Tclet. The plug-in version 2.0 includes five predefined security policies as outlined in Table D-4.

**Table D-4** Policy Overviews

| Policy Name | Policy Overview |
|---|---|
| Home | Allows a Tclet to connect to resources on the host from which it was loaded. The intent of this policy is to restrict access to resources on the home machine from which the Tclet was loaded. The host may be inside or outside of your site's firewall. This is analogous to a CGI script running on the Web server. The CGI script has access to the system resources of the Web server and no access to the resources of the client machine. The main difference, of course, is the Tclet running on the client machine. |
| Inside | The inside policy allows a Tclet to only connect to resources inside a site's intranet. The intent of this policy is to enable access to only those resources that reside inside the intranet and are controlled by trusted system administrators. |
| JavaScript | This policy allows a Tclet to connect to arbitrary resources via HTTP using sockets. It also enables the Tclet to affect frames managed by the hosting application, call JavaScript functions, and send electronic mail. |
| | This policy enables dangerous functionality. If used properly, this policy can allow Tclets to be used as compelling Web applications. If used improperly, this policy could compromise security on the client machine. |
| Outside | The outside policy allows a Tclet to connect to resources outside a site's intranet only. The intent of this policy is to enable access to resources that are only outside the intranet and not under the control of your site's system administrators. |
| Trusted | The trusted security policy installs features that restore the plug-in to its fully trusted, unsafe state. A Tclet running in such an interpreter is able to perform any action a regular, trusted Tcl program could have performed. This policy is by far the most dangerous but provides the most power and flexibility to the embedded Tclet. |

Security policies are, in essence, levels of functionality that may be allowed or disallowed based on the origin of the script to be executed. Under this concept levels of trust are assigned to a given Tclet based on the URL that the script originated from. The level of functionality provided to an executing Tclet is controlled by enabling or disabling certain features.

Security policies are requested from the browser plug-in through the use of the policy command. The policy command is provided by the plug-in environment and is not a part of the standard Tcl interpreter distribution.

Security policies are defined in configuration files installed on your machine when you download the plug-in. Currently, you must edit these configuration files manually to change the default characteristics of a given policy.

In addition to the predefined security policies, the plug-in provides users with the ability to define their own.

### Understanding the Configuration File Format

All the configuration files shipped with the plug-in are organized in a similar fashion. Understanding their format is the key to being able to effectively configure the plug-in. The simplest way to understand these config files is to examine them.

The following sections will look first at the plug-in.cfg file and then at the configuration file for the home security policy, which is the only policy enabled by default in the plug-in distribution. The body of the plug-in.cfg file is reproduced here.

```
# This section defines which policies are available and under
# which conditions.
section policies
    # Home should be safe enough for any Tclet:
    allow     home
    # Javascript requires some Trust:
    allow     javascript ifallowed trustedJavascriptURLs $originURL
    # Those policies aren't safe for everybody:
    disallow outside
    disallow inside
    # The following MUST not be allowed unless high trust is granted:
    disallow trusted

# This part allows the administrator to globally add/remove
```

```
# features sets.
# List of all available/possible features:

variable featuresList {url stream network persist unsafe}

# This part allows the administrator/user to limit the total number
# of frames all the Tclets can access:

variable maxFrames 5

# This section lists the allowed origin URLs for the JavaScript
# policy access: currently includes only Sunscript's Web server
# plug-in/JavaScript subtree for security reasons.

section trustedJavascriptURLs
    allow http://sunscript.sun.com:80/plug-in/javascript/*
# Other User Preferences. If you uncomment these, reload the plug-in
# and the changes will take effect immediately:

# set ::env(TCL_PLUGIN_CONSOLE) 1
# set ::env(TCL_PLUGIN_LOGWINDOW) 1
# set ::env(TCL_PLUGIN_LOGFILE) foo.log
# set ::env(TCL_PLUGIN_WISH) 1
```

The file is broken down into named *sections*. Each section begins with a *section* statement and continues until the end of the file or the next section statement. A section may contain other configuration statements. The most common configuration statements are shown in Table D-5.

**Table D-5** Configuration Statements

| | |
|---|---|
| ALLOW | Used to define allowable conditions inside a given section |
| DISALLOW | Used to define conditions that are not allowed inside a given section |
| CONSTANT | Used to define constants inside the scope of a section |

Lines beginning with the # character are considered comment lines, just as with Tcl scripts, and are ignored.

The first section in the plug-in.cfg file is the policies section. This section describes which security policies are allowed and which ones are disallowed. In this file the home and JavaScript policies are allowed and the outside, inside, and trusted security policies are disallowed. The home policy is the safest policy of the five we will discuss. This is the reason that it is allowed by default. The

JavaScript policy is also allowed, but only conditionally by the following line:

```
allow    javascript ifallowed trustedJavascriptURLs $originURL
```

This line conditionally allows the JavaScript policy for URLs that are specified in the trustedJavascriptURLs section that appears toward the bottom of the configuration file.

```
section trustedJavascriptURLs
    allow http://sunscript.sun.com:80/plug-in/javascript/*
```

The ifallowed statement provides conditional functionality. This statement accepts a section followed by a number of arguments as shown.

```
ifallowed section arg arg...
```

In this case the section referred to is the trustedJavascriptURLs section, and the single argument is originURL. The originURL variable is one of several that are available at runtime when the configuration file is processed by the plug-in. The contents of the Tcl variable originURL will contain the canonical form of the URL from which the Tclet was loaded. This allows you to filter, either broadly or very narrowly, which URLs may load and execute Tclets. Table D-6 shows other variables that are also available and their meaning.

**Table D-6** Plug-In Variables

| Variable Name | Variable Description |
|---|---|
| originUrl | The URL from which the Tclet was loaded. |
| originPageURL | The URL for the page containing the embed statement that caused the Tclet to be loaded. This can be used by policies or Tclets to control copying of the Tclet. For example a Tclet may refuse to execute if it is loaded from an unauthorized page. |
| originHomeDirURL | The URL naming the directory containing the file from which the Tclet was loaded. |
| originProto | The protocol used to load the Tclet. This could be HTTP, file or other protocols supported by the hosting browser. |
| originHost | The host from which the Tclet was loaded. If the Tclet was embedded in a Web page, this variable is set to the URL of the Web page. If the Tclet was loaded from a URL using the file: protocol, the host is set to localhost. |

**Table D-6** Plug-In Variables (Continued)

| Variable Name | Variable Description |
|---|---|
| originSocketHost | The value of this variable is the host name to use when connecting back to the originHost via sockets. In some cases this may be different from originHost variable. |
| originPort | The port used to load the Tclet from the remote Web server. If the Tclet was loaded using the HTTP protocol and no port was specified, the originPort is set to 80, which is the default port used by the HTTP protocol. |
| originPath | The path portion of the originURL attribute. |
| originKey | If the URL from which the Tclet was loaded contains a key (# followed by an alphanumeric string) that identifies a location within the page, the value of this attribute will contain the key. |
| browserArgs | A list of the arguments and values supplied in the embed statement. |
| script | The script evaluated in the Tclet. This consists of the value of the script argument, if present in the embed statement, concatenated with the contents of the URL specified in the *src* argument to the embed statement, if present. |
| windowGeometry | Geometry of the window: the format is width x height. All elements are specified in pixel values. |
| width | The current width in pixels of the window. Not updated if the geometry of the window subsequently changes. |
| height | The current height in pixels of the window. Not updated if the geometry of the window subsequently changes. |
| completeWindowGeometry | A Tcl list specifying the geometry of the Tclet's main window in pixels. The list elements are<br><br>1. The *x* and *y* offsets of the top left corner of the Tclet window, relative to the top left corner of the containing window.<br><br>2. The width and height of the Tclet window.<br><br>3. The left, top, right, and bottom coordinates of the clip rectangle. These values have meaning on Macintosh platforms and are meaningless on UNIX and Win32 platforms. |

**Table D-6** Plug-In Variables  (Continued)

| Variable Name | Variable Description |
| --- | --- |
| apiVersion | The major and minor version numbers of the API provided by the browser to the Tcl plug-in. |
| userAgent | A string identifying the browser in which the Tclet is executing. |
| Tk | The value is 1 if Tk should be loaded into the Tclet interpreter, which is the default. Hidden Tclets do not use Tk, and hence the value will be 0 for them. |

Another important configuration statement in the policies section is one that establishes the variable featuresList and initializes it with a list of feature names:

```
variable featuresList {url stream network persist unsafe}
```

This statement specifies the features that are globally available to security policies. In this case all of the named features that come with the plug-in distribution are available to any security policy that might want to include them. Removing any of the policies from this list will make that feature unavailable to any security policy that might want to use it.

The next variable statement initializes the variable maxFrames to a value of 5. This variable limits the number of frames that may be created by the executing Tclet.

```
variable maxFrames 5
```

The commented lines at the bottom of the plug-in.cfg file may be used to initialize certain environment variables in the master interpreter when the browser plug-in is loaded. These variables enable or disable certain functionality of the plug-in.

```
# set ::env(TCL_PLUGIN_CONSOLE) 1
# set ::env(TCL_PLUGIN_LOGWINDOW) 1
# set ::env(TCL_PLUGIN_LOGFILE) foo.log
# set ::env(TCL_PLUGIN_WISH) 1
```

As an example, one of the features of the plug-in is the ability to display a console window that may be used when debugging Tclets that you create yourself. By uncommenting the line set ::env(TCL_PLUGIN_CONSOLE) 1, you enable the console window to be displayed whenever the plug-in is loaded into your Web browser. The console allows you to execute commands directly inside of the master interpreter's environment.

Additionally, you may define the name of the log file that will be used to capture messages from your application and create a log window to display these messages while you are debugging. The use of the plug-in console and log file will be described in more detail later in this appendix.

### Examining the home Policy

This section will analyze the home security policy, which is designed to allow a Tclet the ability to access resources from its home system. A Tclet's home system is the system it was loaded from. The format of the other security policies is similar to that of the home policy. The body of the home security policy as it exists in the 2.0 distribution installed under Windows NT follows. Notice that the file has several sections presented in the following order.

```
features
urls
frames
hosts ports
persist
aliases
```

This is typical of all the included security policies that come with the standard plug-in distribution. Each of these sections will be discussed in detail next.

```
# home.cfg --
#
#Configuration file for the "home" policy.
#
#    Check the 'config.n' manual page for more details on the format
#    of this and other configuration files.
#
#    This file (home.cfg) is not supposed to be edited. You can copy
#    it under a new name to make another policy to suit your particular
#    needs (if you need a different behavior for the regular 'home'
#    policy), but if you change this file, some Tclets that expect
#    the "standard" 'home' will probably fail and your Tclets that would
#    take advantage of the new 'home' would not work for other people
#    anyway.
#
# CONTACT:sunscript-plugin@sunscript.sun.com
#
# AUTHORS:Jacob Levy,Laurent Demailly
#jyl@eng.sun.comdemailly@eng.sun.com
#jyl@tcl-tk.comL@demailly.com
#
# Please contact us directly for questions, comments, and enhancements.
#
```

```
# Copyright (c) 1995-1997 Sun Microsystems, Inc.
#
# See the file "license.terms" for information on usage ·and
# redistribution of this file, and for a DISCLAIMER OF ALL WARRANTIES.
#
# SCCS: @(#) home.cfg 1.32 97/12/02 13:06:52

# What features are enabled in this policy?
section features
    allow url
    allow network
    allow persist unless {[string match {UNKNOWN *} [getattr
originURL]]}

# What URLs are allowed?
section urls
    # Expected format (by the url feature):
    # allow <urlPattern>
    allow $originHomeDirURL*

# What frames (targets) are allowed for displayURL,...?
# allow all frames (including _blank ,...) but there is the
# variable maxFrames to limit their absolute total number.
section frames
    allow *
    disallow {}

# What addresses can be used in a socket command?
section hosts ports
    # Expected format (by the network feature):
    # allow <hostPattern> <portPattern>
    allow $originSocketHost >1024
    allow $originSocketHost 21

# What are the resources available in the persist feature?
section persist
    # The base name where the storage actually happens
    # (use the same name to share between policies)
    # The default is to use the policy name (to avoid unwanted sharing)
    #constant storage "sharingPrefix"
    # Number of allowed open files
    constant openFilesLimit 4
    # Number of allowed files in the persist storage directory
    constant storedFilesLimit 6
    # Max size of each file (in bytes): here we give 128K per file.
    constant fileSizeLimit [expr 128*1024]

# What aliases are supported by this policy?
# (fine tuning, you should not need to change this)
section aliases
    # Expected format (by all features installing aliases)
    # allow <commandNamePattern>
```

```
allow socket
allow fconfigure
allow open
allow file
allow close
allow puts
allow tell
allow seek
allow glob
allow ::browser::getURL
allow ::browser::displayURL
allow ::browser::getForm
allow ::browser::displayForm
allow ::browser::status
disallow ::browser::sendMail
```

The first section, features, defines which features the policy makes available to the executing Tclet. Once again, features are named collections of capabilities that the master interpreter may install into a executing Tclet to increase its functionality. The features enabled by the **home** security policy are **url**, **network**, and **persist**. Here, the **persist** feature is allowed conditionally using the **unless** keyword.

```
allow persist unless {[string match {UNKNOWN *} [getattr originURL]]}
```

This statement allows the **persist** feature, unless any part of the URL from which the Tclet was loaded contains the word UNKNOWN. The **persist** feature allows access to the local file system of the hosting Web browser. The access is provided in a controlled manner for the purposes of persistent storage.

The URL feature is the one that allows us to send requests to the Web server. This feature requires a frames section and a URL section in the enabling security policy. The URL section defines which URLs may be used in procedures accepting URL arguments.

```
# What URLs are allowed?
section urls
    # Expected format (by the url feature):
    # allow <urlPattern>
    allow $originHomeDirURL*
```

In the **home** security policy, only URLs from the original home directory where the Tclet was loaded from are permitted. This is specified through the use of the **originHomeDirURL** variable. The plug-in security policies allow you to restrict execution of Tclets based on the URL that they originated from.

# Understanding the Risks

It is important to understand what resources and capabilities each policy makes accessible to Tclets before changing the default configuration of your Tcl browser plug-in. It is wise to prevent untrusted scripts from accessing sensitive resources on your machine. As an example, the inside security policy is intended to allow access to resources on your company's intranet. Because this would allow malicious scripts to attack these resources, the default plug-in.cfg file disables this policy. Before enabling the inside policy, be sure you understand the ramifications to your local environment. Always assume a script to be untrusted unless you know for sure that it can be trusted!

The security policies provided with the Tcl Web browser plug-in make a variety of resources available to Tclets. Some of the policies are disabled by default because they provide access to features that would be dangerous in the hands of malicious scripts.

The risks incurred by enabling one of the predefined security policies stem from the combination of features that each policy enables. You should consult the manual pages that come with your plug-in distribution before enabling any of the disabled security policies. The manual page for each feature describes the risks for that feature, and the manual page for each security policy lists which features it enables. Armed with this information, you should be able to evaluate the risks incurred by a specific policy.

The browser plug-in declares that security risks can be divided into four general classes as discussed next.

## Integrity Risks

An integrity risk exists when the executing Tclet is provided with access to sensitive resources on the client machine, such as the file system. As an example, providing the ability for a Tclet to delete files on the local disk would constitute an integrity risk. If used improperly by a malicious Tclet, this level of access could be used to indiscriminately destroy files in the local file system. The safe interpreter is designed to protect the integrity of a computer on which Tclets are executed. Security policies provided in the plug-in distribution relax the restrictions imposed on Tclets. It is important to realize that relaxing these restrictions also lessens the security that is provided by the safe interpreter.

## Privacy Risks

A privacy risk exists when the executing Tclet is provided with the ability to access sensitive information and leak it to other parties. Providing executing Tclets with access to the network is probably the biggest source of privacy risk. With this type of access, a malicious Tclet could transmit sensitive information to computers outside of your domain. The Safe Base is designed to prevent these types of privacy attacks. Using security policies that relax restrictions on a Tclet's ability to send sensitive information across the network exposes the hosting computer to privacy risks.

## Loss of Reputation

Allowing access to resources or capabilities that can be used to compromise the reputation of the human responsible for the hosting computer constitutes a loss of reputation risk. An example of this would be a malicious Tclet sending inflammatory e-mail, or posting articles to news groups in such a way as to make it appear the owner of the computer is the one who actually sent the information rather than the author of the malicious Tclet.

Here again, the Safe Base prevents such attacks, however, certain security policies may expose the computer's owner to this type of risk by relaxing some inherent protection afforded by the Safe Base.

## Annoyance and Resource Attacks

Annoyance or resource attacks are operations that disrupt the work of the person using the hosting computer. Examples of this would be ringing the bell or opening a large number of windows on the computer's display. Another example would be a malicious Tclet that tries to exhaust some resource on the hosting computer, such as storage space or memory space. In its current form the Safe Base does not attempt to prevent all types of annoyance and resource attacks, because they are merely annoying and not generally destructive. As is the case with all security concerns, it is important to evaluate the implications of these types of attacks and take the appropriate measures to prevent them, if necessary.

The principal method of limiting access to any predefined security policy is through the validation of the URL that the Tclet originated from. The browser plug-in version 2.0 has no way to validate the author of the Tclet. This means that all scripts originating from a given URL will be afforded the same level of trust. This is adequate in some situations, like your company's intranet, but may pose risks when allowing Tclets from outside your domain to request security policies that extend its capabilities from those granted to a safe interpreter. It is conceivable to imagine that both malicious and nonmalicious scripts may even exist in the same directory in some machines on the World Wide Web.

If all of this sounds a little ominous, it should! Allowing untrusted scripts to execute on your machine can be a dangerous proposition and should be dealt with accordingly.

## The Plug-In Logging Facility

The Tcl plug-in provides a comprehensive logging facility. The plug-in uses this facility to log important events such as the starting and stopping Tclets. The resulting log file provides an excellent way to diagnose problems when debugging your Tclets.

The logging facility is controlled through the use of two environment variables named TCL_PLUGIN_LOGFILE and TCL_PLUGIN_LOGWINDOW. Default entries are already provided in the plugin.cfg file for both the logging facility and the plug-in console, which is described at the end of this appendix. The lines in the default plugin.cfg file are commented out, so you must uncomment the appropriate lines and restart the plug-in to enable the logging facility.

```
# set ::env(TCL_PLUGIN_CONSOLE) 1
set ::env(TCL_PLUGIN_LOGWINDOW) 1
#set ::env(TCL_PLUGIN_LOGFILE) foo.log
# set ::env(TCL_PLUGIN_WISH) 1
```

Here we have enabled the log window to be displayed. When the plug-in is loaded into your Web browser, you will be presented with a log window with a simple menu bar that allows the following options:

- Save the contents of the window to a file.
- Clear the current contents of the window.
- Suspend logging.
- Resume logging.

It can be quite educational to bring up the log window (see Figure D-3) while you are experimenting with the browser plug-in. The plug-in environment logs frequent messages during execution.

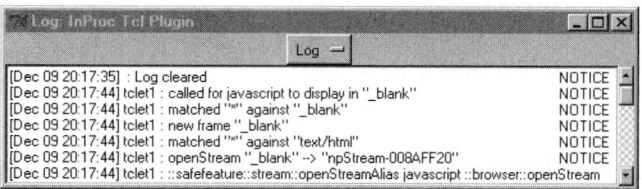

**Figure D-3** The Web Browser Log Window

The log:log procedure is provided for writing messages to the log window. The calling sequence for the procedure is discussed next.

```
log::log id message ?class?
```
All arguments are included in the log message. The *id* argument is an identifier that will be used to tag the message. By convention, *id* is the name of the Tclet or feature for which this log entry was generated, but it can be anything because its only use is to make the log entry more readable. The message argument is the informational content of the message.

The class argument is provided to identify different classes of messages. The plug-in has five predefined class arguments. They are NOTICE, WARNING, SECURITY, ERROR, and SLAVE. The default class, if no value is supplied for the class argument, is NOTICE. The SLAVE class is used for all log entries generated by Tclets. Each class may have a set of associated attributes that change its display characteristics.

For example the WARNING class will be highlighted in yellow while the ERROR class will be highlighted in red. This makes it easy to distinguish the different classes of messages from each other. Of course, overuse of this feature can make the log file annoying to read. See the log::attributes description for a description of class attributes and how to create your own classes.

In order to take advantage of these class attributes, your class name must exist in the log::attributes list, along with the associated attributes. If you call log::log with a class name that does not exist in the log::attributes list, the entry will be recorded with that class but no attributes will be applied to alter its display.

In addition to the log::log procedure, the following procedures are also provided by the log package.

`log::refreshAttributes`
Refreshes the list of classes known to the logging facility. Use this after modifying the value of log::attributes.

`log::setup` *flag*
This procedure is used to configure the logging facility. The following values are valid for the *flag* argument.

window—Logging will be done to a window.
suspend—Suspends logging. Use the resume command to continue.
stop—Stops logging.
clear—Clears the current log.

If the *flag* argument starts with a period (.), it is assumed to be a window name and log entries will be directed to that window. If *flag* is a string not matching any of the above values, the logging facility will attempt to locate a channel with that name. If no such channel is found, it is assumed to be a file name and log entries will be appended to the named file. You can call log::setup in the console window to modify the behavior of logging interactively.

The following variables are provided by the log package.

`log::attributes`
A list of log classes and their attributes: These attributes affect the manner in which the log entry is displayed in the log window and also serve to group message types in the log file. The browser plug-in contains five predefined classes labeled NOTICE, WARNING, SECURITY, ERROR, and SLAVE. The SLAVE class is used for all log entries generated by Tclets. The remaining classes are used by the master interpreter.

You can lappend new classes and their attributes to this list and then call log::refreshAttributes to make the logging facility aware of the changes.

You can view the current list of attributes using the plug-in console, which will be discussed in the next section.

```
(Program) 1 % tclet1 eval {set log::attributes }

DEBUG     {}
NOTICE    {}
```

```
ERROR     {-background orange -foreground black}
WARNING   {-background yellow -foreground black}
SECURITY  {-background red -foreground blue}
all {-lmargin2 24p -tabs {{expr {{winfo width $Dest.f.msg]-10}] right}}
```

### log::max

The maximum number of entries that are kept in the log window.

### log::strTruncLen

The maximum length of a log entry: Log entries that exceed this length are truncated.

## The Plug-In Console

In addition to the logging facility, the plug-in also has the ability to create a console that is connected to the master interpreter. Commands that you type in the console window will be executed in the master interpreter and the result will be displayed in the console.

The plug-in console is enabled if the TCL_PLUGIN_CONSOLE environment variable is set. The plugin.cfg file that is shipped with the browser plug-in has the following lines commented out at the bottom of the file. To enable the console window, remove the comment (#) and reload the plug-in.

```
# set ::env(TCL_PLUGIN_CONSOLE) 1
# set ::env(TCL_PLUGIN_LOGWINDOW) 1
# set ::env(TCL_PLUGIN_LOGFILE) foo.log
# set ::env(TCL_PLUGIN_WISH) 1
```

If the value of **TCL_PLUGIN_CONSOLE** is set to 1, the console will be created by using the TkCon application written by Jeff Hobbs. For more information, see the TkCon documentation on the Web at

http://www.hobbs.wservice.com/tcl/tclet

If the environment variable is set to 0, no console window will be created. If the environment variable is set to any other value than 0 or 1, it is taken to be the name of the application file to source containing the console to be created.

The plug-in is unloaded when the last instance is destroyed, and the console is destroyed when the last Tclet is destroyed. If you leave one page containing a

Tclet to visit another page that also contains a Tclet, the console window will be destroyed if the page you left contained the last active Tclet.

When Tclets are hosted in an external process, two console windows will be provided. The title of each window identifies which process it is connected to: One is connected to the plug-in executing within the browser address space, and the other is connected to the main interpreter in the external process as shown in Figure D-4. This arrangement allows you to debug communication problems between the two processes. Setting the ::env(TCL_PLUGIN_CONSOLE) variable to 1 will produce the following display when running Netscape on an NT machine.

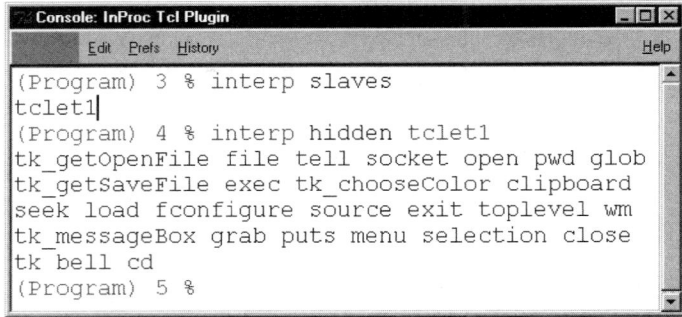

**Figure D-4** Plug-In Console Window

You can see here that the interp command was used to determine what slave interpreters were running. In this example there was only one slave running, and its name was tclet1. Whenever a slave interpreter is created, a new command with the same name is created to allow the master interpreter to communicate with the slave. Here we see that the tclet1 command was used to determine which commands were hidden from the slave. Remember, the plug-in console provides console communications with the master interpreter. This can be quite a powerful debugging aid when trying to get your Tclets up and running.

The menu bar provides a number of options, including a history list that allows you to execute previously executed commands with a simple mouse click.

# Bibliography

## RFCs

RFC1601: Huitema, C., "Charter of the Internet Architecture Board (IAB)," March 1994.

RFC1700: Reynolds, J., and Postel, J. "Assigned Numbers," October 1994.

RFC1739: Kessler, G., and Shepard, S. "A Primer on Internet and TCP/IP Tools," December 1994.

RFC1945: Berners-Lee, T., Fielding, R., and Frystyk, H. "Hypertext Transfer Protocol—HTTP/1.0," May 1996.

RFC2026: Bradner, S., "The Internet Standards Process—Revision 3," October 1996.

RFC2068: Fielding, R., Gettys, J., Mogul, J., Frystyk, H., and Berners-Lee, T. "Hypertext Transfer Protocol—HTTP/1.1," January 1997.

RFC2109: Kristol, D., and Montulli, L. "HTTP State Management Mechanism," February 1997.

RFC2616: Fielding, R., Gettys, J., Mogul, J., Frystyk, H., Masinter, L., Leach, P., and Berners-Lee, T. "Hypertext Transfer Protocol—HTTP/1.1," June 1999.

## Books

Comer, D. E. *The Internet Book*. Englewood Cliffs, New Jersey:  Prentice Hall, 1995.

Gundavavum, S. *CGI Programming on the World Wide Web*. Sebastopol, California: O'Reilly and Associates, 1996.

Harrington, J. *SQL Clearly Explained*. Chestnut Hill, Massachusetts: Academic Press, 1998.

Harrison, M. *Tcl/Tk Tools*. Boston, Massachusetts: O'Reilly and Associates, 1997.

Laurie, B., and Laurie, P. *Apache: The Definitive Guide*. second edition. Sebastopol, California:  O'Reilly and Associates, 1999.

Libes, D. *Exploring Expect*. Sebastopol, California: O'Reilly and Associates, 1995.

Miller, P. *TCP/IP Explained*. Newton, Massachusetts: Digital Press, 1997.

Ousterhout, J. *Tcl and the Tk Toolkit*. Reading, Massachusetts: Addison-Wesley, 1994.

Powell, T. A., and Whitworth, D. *HTML Programmer's Reference*. Berkeley, California:  Osborne/McGraw-Hill, 1998.

Welch, B. *Practical Programming in Tcl and Tk*. second edition. Upper Saddle River, New Jersey: Prentice Hall, 1997.

# *Index*